THE ANNOTATED She

VISIONS

Harry M. Geduld,
General Editor

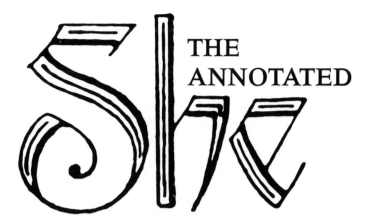

THE ANNOTATED She

A Critical Edition of
H. Rider Haggard's Victorian Romance
with Introduction and Notes
by Norman Etherington

Indiana
University
Press

BLOOMINGTON AND INDIANAPOLIS

The paper used in this publication meets the minimum requirements of American
National Standard for Information Sciences—Permanence of Paper for Printed
Library Materials, ANSI Z39.48-1984.
⊗™
Manufactured in the United States of America

Library of Congress Cataloging-in-Publication Data

Haggard, H. Rider (Henry Rider), 1856–1925.
The annotated She: a critical edition of H. Rider Haggard's
Victorian romance with introduction and notes / by Norman
Etherington.
p.   cm. — (Visions)
Includes bibliographical references.
ISBN 0-253-32072-0 (alk. paper)
I. Etherington, Norman.   II. Title.   III. Series: Visions
(Bloomington, Ind.)
PR4731.S6   1991
823'.8—dc20   90-43751
CIP
1 2 3 4 5 95 94 93 92 91

THIS EDITION IS DEDICATED

To my father, Robert, who encouraged my
childhood interest in science fiction and fantasy
by voraciously reading at the breakfast table the
wonders I brought home from the library.

"Lend me something to read," she said. I offered her Rider Haggard's *She*. "A *strange* book, but full of hidden meaning."
—Sigmund Freud, *The Interpretation of Dreams*

The mythical status of *She* is indisputable.
—C. S. Lewis, *Of This and Other Worlds*

There is a duality in Rider Haggard which intrigues me enormously. An earth-bound individual, conventional in his ways, orthodox in his beliefs, though full of curiosity and tolerance, endowed with great vitality and practical wisdom, this man who is reticent and reserved, English to the core, one might say, reveals through his "romances" a hidden nature, a hidden being, a hidden lore which is amazing.
—Henry Miller, *The Books in My Life*

Contents

ACKNOWLEDGMENTS

I would like especially to acknowledge financial support from the University of Adelaide, which made it possible to compile this text from the manuscript at the Norwich Library and the first five printed editions. The initial work of checking editions against the manuscript was done with infinite care and patience by Irene Cassidy of the Institute of Historical Research, University of London. Expert advice on specific questions was unstintingly given by former colleagues in the Departments of History, English, and Classics at the University of Adelaide. The General Editor of this series, Harry M. Geduld of Indiana University, gave my initial typescript a thorough reading and contributed many useful suggestions.

I would also like to thank Dr. Helen Winefield of the Department of Psychiatry, University of Adelaide, and Pen Hetherington of the Department of History, University of Western Australia, for the insights they contributed in relation to psychological theory and history.

A BRIEF CHRONOLOGY

THROUGH 1887

1856 June 22: Henry Rider Haggard (d. May 14, 1925), sixth son of William Meybohm Rider Haggard and Ella (Doveton) Haggard, born in West Bradenham Hall, Norfolk, England.

In this year, the same in which Sigmund Freud is born in Vienna, Charles Darwin (1809–1882) is 47; his *Origin of Species* will be published three years later. The Zulu kingdom in South Africa, which will inspire Haggard's first novels of African adventure, is rent by civil war between the sons of the king, Mpande.

1862–72 Haggard is educated at home by private tutors and for a short time at Ipswich Grammar School.

1875 Goes to South Africa as private secretary to Sir Henry Bulwer, governor of the colony of Natal.

1877 Joins the staff of Sir Theophilus Shepstone on a special mission to the Transvaal that results in annexation of the territory by the British government. Haggard personally helps to hoist the Union Jack at Pretoria.

1878 Haggard serves as Master and Registrar of the High Court of the Transvaal, although he has no previous legal training.

1879 Returns to England on leave.

1880 Haggard marries Mariana Louisa Margitson, a Norfolk heiress and daughter of Major John Margitson, and returns to South Africa to begin farming in northern Natal.

1881 The successful rebellion against British rule mounted by Transvaal Afrikaners causes Haggard to give up his farm and return to England in October.

1882 Haggard publishes *Cetywayo and His White Neighbours*, a defense of British imperial policies in the Transvaal and the Zulu kingdom.

1884 After studying for the bar, Haggard is called to Lincoln's Inn and commences the practice of law. Publishes at his own expense his first work of fiction, *Dawn*, in April. At the end of December a second novel, *The Witch's Head*, appears.

1885 Haggard "read in one of the weekly papers a notice of Stevenson's *Treasure Island* so laudatory" that he "procured and studied that work, and . . . was impelled by its perusal to try to write a book for boys." The result, *King Solomon's Mines*, is a runaway success and catapults Haggard instantly into the front rank of popular novelists.

1886 February: Begins the manuscript of *She*.
 March 18: Finishes the manuscript.
 October 2: Serial publication of *She* begins in the *Graphic* weekly magazine, continuing until January 8, 1887.

1887 January 1: First edition of *She* released by Longmans, Green and Co.

CRITICAL

INTRODUCTION

Early in February 1886, Rider Haggard sat down to write *She*. By the eighteenth of March he had finished the draft of his manuscript. It was a remarkable performance in a remarkable period of the author's life. Within the space of little more than a year he turned out *King Solomon's Mines*, *She*, *Jess*, and *Allan Quatermain*, four books that were to prove among the most popular of all his voluminous outpouring of fiction in a literary career that spanned more than four decades. Two of those four books, *King Solomon's Mines* and *She*, have never been out of print and have captivated the imaginations of authors as diverse as C. S. Lewis, Edgar Rice Burroughs, Sigmund Freud, Graham Greene, C. G. Jung, Henry Miller, and Frederick Forsyth. The very speed with which Haggard wrote his most celebrated works has become part of the legend, zealously propagated by the author, that they gushed forth unconsciously from mysterious inner springs of creativity. In reality, a great deal of thought and experience contributed to the making of *She*.

THE MAKING OF A NOVELIST

Rider Haggard belonged by birth to the minor country gentry of Victorian England. His was the sort of family that expected eldest sons to inherit the estate and younger sons to go into the army, the church, or the civil service. In important ways, however, the family deviated from the norm. On one side the Haggards could and did lay a shadowy claim to descent from the ancient Norse invaders of eastern Britain, while one of Rider's grandparents had come from Russia and was thought by some to have Jewish ancestry. His father played the bluff, overbearing squire convincingly enough, but his mother, whose father had been in the East India Company service, nourished literary ambitions.[1] The family pretended to a social position it could not quite keep up. Haggard's older brothers went to Cambridge, but there was not enough money to give Rider a university education. Apart from a few years at Ipswich Grammar School, he was educated by private tutors. After he tried and failed to enter the public service by "cramming" in London for the annual examinations, his family used Norfolk social connections to find the teenager a position as private secretary to the newly appointed lieutenant governor of Natal, Sir Henry Bulwer.

South Africa was the making of the boy. He found a surrogate father in the fascinating Theophilus Shepstone, who had acquired a fund of strange and riveting stories during his long tenure as Natal's secretary for native affairs. When Shepstone annexed the Transvaal Republic to the British Empire, Haggard was at his side and rose rapidly in the fledgling civil service of the new colony. During a trip back to England Haggard married, then took his bride back to South Africa. There he engaged in a brief fling at ostrich farming, which was brought to an abrupt halt by the successful Boer rebellion of 1881. Haggard then returned to England for good. While preparing for a career in the law, he wrote his first important work, a defense of Shepstone's policy in South Africa and, by extension, of the colonial policy of Disraeli's Conservative government, which had been successfully assaulted by William Gladstone's "anti-imperialist" Liberals in the general election of 1880.[2] The book nailed Haggard's political colors to the mast of the Tory party, which he never deserted and which led him in the 1890s to campaign for election to Parliament.

Haggard's first book was respectfully received as a thoughtful and strongly argued contribution to political debate. This success may have encouraged him to try his hand at fiction. His first novel, *Dawn*, was published in April 1884, and *The Witch's Head* followed a few months later. Both revolved around the romantic dilemmas of young men torn by the competing attractions of rival young women. In the first the hero seeks escape from his problems by fleeing to the Canary Islands. In the second he plunges into South African wars. Despite occasional hints of the uncanny, both works stick close to the conventions of the Victorian novel. Both initially failed to recoup the money Haggard spent getting them published, but they gave him the confidence to make an impetuous bet with one of his brothers. When the brother marveled at the sensation created by Robert Louis Stevenson's *Treasure Island* in 1885, Rider wagered that he could do better. The result was *King Solomon's Mines*, whose instant success freed Haggard from travail at the bar.

The underpinning of that success and the feature that most strikingly differentiated *King Solomon's Mines* from Haggard's first attempts at fiction was the unifying theme of a quest into unknown territory. Following Stevenson's lead, the author produced a treasure map that led his heroes into desperate conflicts with ruthless people in an undiscovered land. *She*, written a few months later, also knits disparate elements together using the device of a quest. But it is much more elaborately worked out and boldly executed. *King Solomon's Mines* was conceived as a boys' book (though it won an enthusiastic adult audience) and was punctuated by a series of spectacular contests against big game and hostile Africans. *She* returned to the adult themes Haggard had explored in *Dawn* and *The Witch's Head:* love triangles, the contest between conventional morality and sexual attraction, the interaction between young men and powerful older women.

STRUCTURE

The quest in *King Solomon's Mines* is linear; its prime symbol is the treasure map. The protagonists of *She* quest for an inner truth whose central symbol is the ruined Temple of Truth in the lost city of Kôr. The temple is "arranged in a series of courts, each one enclosing another of smaller size, on the principle of a Chinese nest of boxes."[3] The central court contains a statue of Truth portrayed as a veiled goddess. An inscription on the base proclaims that *"By death only can thy veil be drawn, oh Truth!"*

The Chinese nest of boxes appears in many guises throughout the book. It is present first of all in the layers of authorial voices with which Haggard distances himself from the central subject. An unnamed "Editor" introduces the story. Although "Editor" is said to have written a book "describing a Central African adventure," he cannot be precisely identified with Haggard, for he claims actually to have met the fictional heroes of the tale. The principal narrator, L. Horace Holly, does not directly address readers; his voice reaches them through the manuscript sent by post to "Editor." And the relationship between She and Leo Vincey, which is central to the story—the innermost of the Chinese nest of boxes—is recounted not by the predestined lovers themselves but by Holly, whose voice is in turn mediated through the manuscript.

The artifact which leads Holly, Leo, and their servant, Job, from Cambridge University to the heart of Africa is the Sherd of Amenartas, an inscribed fragment of ancient Greek pottery. At the opening of the third chapter it is described as wrapped in yellow linen, under an old parchment, under "some brown shredded material," in a locked silver casket decorated with sphinxes, which is contained in a locked ebony box inside a rusty iron chest inside the vault of a bank. The route to the lost city of Kôr lies across a storm-tossed sea, then up a river that becomes a canal where the adventurers encounter Africans who carry them asleep across grassy plains, then through a "rocky defile of lava" and into the crater of an extinct volcano from which they are later carried across yet another plain to yet another dead volcano whose crater is reached via a tunnel through which the blindfolded heroes are conducted until the ruined city is revealed on the crater's floor. And at the center of the ruined city lies the Temple of Truth with its further series of enclosing courts. The catacombs that wind endlessly beneath the crater walls are lined with countless sepulchers containing the perfectly preserved dead bodies of the inhabitants of vanished Kôr, each wrapped in fine linen. Some of them crumble at the touch, however, to reveal a macabre inner reality hidden by the embalmer's art.

One further quest must be accomplished before the adventurers arrive at the final truth about She. They must climb up a cliff of the inner wall of the crater, along a ledge into a fold of rock leading to a cave that winds tortuously for a quarter of a mile until a dark and bottomless chasm is reached. This chasm must be crossed via a jutting spur of rock and a plank leading to a small chamber in the rock, from which steps lead down the sides of an "inverted cone" at the apex of which a narrow passage is found leading to a series of three consecutive natural caverns. The final drama unfolds in the innermost cavern, where the mysterious Fire of Life endlessly ebbs and flows.

When, in that climactic moment, She steps naked into the fire, another unwrapping is completed. Ayesha is first seen in the novel wrapped from head to foot in a "gauze-like" material, which Holly calls her "winding-sheet like wrappings." The servant, Job, mistakes her for a ghost or mummy. Even without the gauze, She wears a veil to conceal the irresistible beauty of her gaze. Holly speculates in chapter XXIV that "she originally got the idea of covering up her beauty from that statue" of veiled Truth, which in turn suggests that her real veil, like the statue's, can only be drawn by death.

These sequences have a fourth dimension that is also vital to Haggard's tale. Progress toward the core of each sequence involves movement through time. The Sherd of Amenartas is inscribed with ancient Greek characters, a text which the novel unveils in a series of translations: first into medieval Latin, then into Old English, finally into modern English. The sherd is also engraved with a series of names tracing the lineage of a single family, whose members successively resided in Egypt, Greece, Rome, France, and England. This engraving thus presents the essence of world history as it was commonly and complacently believed by Haggard's contemporaries. The torch of civilization had been progressively passed from Egypt to Greece and Rome and on to western Europe.[4]

The adventurers invert this evolutionary sequence, stripping away layers of history as they travel from Cambridge, the epitome of high civilization, back through Islamic East Africa to a "semi-savage" people living among the ruins of Kôr, a civilization said to have flourished thousands of years before the rise of Pharaonic Egypt. There in a cave Leo Vincey encounters the embalmed body of his own ancestor, Kallikrates the Greek. In the final sequence the travelers move backward in geological time, through caves blasted eons ago by volcanic action and toward the Fire of Life, which is asserted to be as old as Earth itself. When Ayesha enters that fire she undergoes a personal evolution in reverse, losing her youthful beauty and shriveling first into a time-ravished hag, then into the shape of a monkey, our Darwinian ancestor. Like the mummified denizens of the catacombs of Kôr, her fair skin proves to be wrapped round an inner reality of death and putrefaction.

Taken as a whole, the structure of Haggard's novel achieves a rare combination of economy and complexity. The paradigm of the Chinese nest of boxes is one that can be expanded to a journey as vast as the distance from Cambridge to the heart of Africa or reduced to the dimensions of Ayesha's dazzling body. Every nest of boxes is also a sequence in time, which at its greatest extent encompasses all human and natural history.

POLISHING THE TEXT

How seriously, then, should readers take Haggard's claim to have produced the whole text in six weeks with no forethought and very little subsequent rewriting? The issue is clouded by a controversy that arose a few weeks after the book appeared on New Year's Day, 1887. Haggard, buoyed by the apparently unanimous acclaim that surrounded him, rashly wrote an article for the *Contemporary Review,* "About Fiction," that was both immodest and provocative.[5] Many established writers perceived the article as a call for all previous schools of literature to be displaced by Haggard's genre of "romance." The critics responded by minutely raking over his productions. Some questioned the quality of his writing. Others, more cutting, attacked what he considered to be his greatest strength: the originality of his imagination. He was charged, often on flimsy grounds, with having plagiarized a whole range of works.[6] Although Haggard's friends and admirers successfully upheld his honor, the wounds never healed.[7] His subsequent claims to have produced all his fiction at a breakneck pace, inspired by a frenzied muse who would brook no delay, was one way of defending himself against the charge of plagiarism. Another was to leave the text of *She* unaltered in subsequent editions, lest changes be misinterpreted by his literary enemies.

Haggard had in fact worried much over his text between March 18, 1886, when he completed the draft, and his final correction of proofs at the end of the year for the first edition. His first alterations aimed to underpin the credibility of his incredible tale with a material base of scholarship. He commissioned a scholar of classical Greek, H. A. Holden, who had been headmaster of Ipswich Grammar School when Haggard was a pupil there, to provide a more suitable version of the Greek text for the Sherd of Amenartas. Medieval Latin and Old English translations of this version were done by a Dr. Raven. Haggard and his sister-in-law also set to work to fake a sherd that would on first glance pass muster with the experts.[8] A photograph of the finished product appeared in full color in the front plates of the first edition (see the frontispiece in this volume). A second set of changes was made to repair the deficiencies of Haggard's description of college life at Cambridge, a place he knew only at second hand through his older brothers. Not only did the proper slang and jargon have to be added; unthinkable phenomena, such as the bachelor Holly's being permitted to raise a five-year-old boy in his college rooms, also had to be excised: Holly takes an apartment near the college.

Corrections were also made with the intention of improving the authenticity of Haggard's treatment of navigation, geography, and ancient history, especially in chapters IV, XIII, and XVII. One set of such changes was of questionable utility. Even before Haggard finished the manuscript he had second thoughts about the fictional people over whom She rules as queen. He first called them the Askati and gave the names Ukase and Dompté to the characters who eventually became respectively Ustane and Billali. *Askati* vaguely suggests a connection with Astarte, or Astoroth, the goddess of the ancient Phoenicians, and that would have appealed to Haggard because of the belief he shared with many African experts of his time that the builders of the remarkable stone structures of southeastern Zimbabwe were of Phoenician origin. On the other hand, he wanted to locate his people ethnologically among the "savages." For this purpose a more identifiably African name would be preferable. By changing *Askati* to *Amahagger* he suggested that his people belonged to a Bantu-speaking group that forms plurals by adding prefixes, such as *ama*, rather than suffixes to the singular form. Thus *Amazulu* was the word used by the Zulu to refer to themselves as a people. The Swahili language, which developed in East Africa as a lingua franca, is also grounded in a Bantu grammar and therefore was highly suitable for Haggard's purposes. What is more, it contains many words of Arabic origin, though it would have been quite impossible for an Arabic speaker to be understood among Swahili speakers. So from that point of view Haggard's invention of the Amahagger makes linguistic nonsense and detracts from rather than adding to the "authenticity" of his tale.

Other changes were made at the prompting of Andrew Lang, the influential classical scholar, critic, and authority on fairy tales, who first read the manuscript after it had already been accepted for serialization in the *Graphic*.⁹ In the manuscript's chapter VIII the Amahagger people kill the Arab seaman Mohamed by "hot-potting," that is, by clamping a red-hot pot over his head. (Haggard, not surprisingly, was often in trouble with critics for writing too much gratuitous violence into his fiction; a writer for the *Church Quarterly Review* once accused him of propagating "the culture of the horrible."¹⁰) In the revised version of the execution Mohamed is fatally shot while his companions attempt to prevent his hot-potting. Sexual allusions were also toned down in the serialized version and subsequent editions. The manuscript version of chapter VII, for example, strongly implies that Leo slept with the Amahagger girl, Ustane.

Politics was an equally touchy subject. In the manuscript Haggard let his Conservative sympathies run away with him. Leo Vincey is described as "a red hot conservative" who regards William Gladstone as a tyrant and a demagogue. The Liberal party is blamed for "plundering one class of a community to enrich the others." Ayesha delights Leo by proposing to resolve "the Irish problem" (once Holly has explained it to her) by killing all the Irish. Holly dreams that She, dressed in a ball gown, disposes of Gladstone by hot-potting. This sort of thing was doubtless fun for Haggard, but as Lang observed, it risked alienating that large body of readers who supported "the People's William" and his Liberal party. Furthermore, the book was produced during a year of high drama in British political life. Gladstone's government had fallen in June 1885 on a defeat in Parliament, but by February 1886 Gladstone was back as prime minister. A week after Haggard finished the manuscript Joseph Chamberlain resigned from the Cabinet because of Gladstone's plan to give Home Rule to Ireland, an event that destabilized the government and led to the dissolution of Parliament on June 25, 1886, about the time Haggard was correcting galley proofs of the serialized version of the novel. The general election of July brought the Conservatives to power in partnership with Chamberlain's Liberal Unionists, who had split off from the Liberal party. Dropping the political comedy from the text was simple common sense under the circumstances and spared future generations the problem of sorting through obscure references to forgotten quarrels.

The residues of political speculation that remain after the references to current controversies had been cut enhance Ayesha's awesome character. As originally written, the character She was positioned rather comically on the extreme right wing of the Conservative party. She might, Holly speculates, develop into "a kind of glorified Bismarck" in the European environment. After judicious cuts, She emerges as a ruthless tyrant who would, given half a chance, ride to glory over the dead bodies of millions.

Another problem that troubled the author enough to require significant changes before publication of the first edition was the supposedly sublime and poetical language in which Ayesha expressed herself. Haggard was no poet in prose. His standard technique for suggesting antique eloquence was to make his characters speak in the language of the King James Bible. Even here he faltered in the manuscript, frequently writing "ye" when he should have written "you" and committing other grammatical faults needing editorial attention before publication. Practical considerations dictated that Ayesha speak classical Arabic. Having been holed up in central Africa for about twenty-three hundred years, She could not know English, and of all the ancient languages of the Mediterranean only classical Arabic, Latin, and Greek could be plausibly known to and spoken by Leo or Holly. Of those three only Arabic was of any utility to explorers in East Africa. But Haggard knew nothing of Arabic. He did, however, have a model at hand for rendering Arabic into English in Edward Fitzgerald's immensely influential Victorian translation *The Rubiyat of Omar Khayyam*. He may also have seen the translation produced by the African explorer Richard Burton of the *Arabian Nights*, which appeared the year before he sat down to write *She*. But such high-flown eloquence did not come easily to Haggard. Ayesha's songs and speeches were laboriously corrected in the manuscript, altered in the *Graphic* serialization, and changed again before publication of the first edition.

If Haggard had to struggle to make Ayesha sublime, he had to work equally hard to prevent Leo Vincey from seeming ridiculous. Although Lang, as Haggard wrote in his autobiography, praised the manuscript as "the most extraordinary romance I ever read," he noted "a difficulty about Leo. He is not a very interesting person."[11] Why should a person of Ayesha's intelligence fall in love with him? Lang's suggested solution to the problem was that Leo was "probably only a fine animal" and that his look-alike ancestor Kallikrates "was no better." Still, Lang worried that "some of the chaff in awful situations [the pedestrian slang in which Leo expresses himself] lets one down too suddenly." The modern reader of the manuscript can only concur when he finds Leo saying, after the crossing of the bottomless chasm, "Hulloa, old fellow. . . . We're having a pretty parroty time ain't we. It's really getting quite interesting." Improving this passage and others that Lang marked for attention did not raise Leo's intelligence quotient but went a long way toward rescuing him from absurdity. Haggard decided in the end to write Lang's doubts into the introduction by the "Editor" and to provide two further possible reasons for Ayesha's fascination. One is that "extremes meet, and that the very excess and splendour of her mind led her by means of some strange physical reaction to worship at the shrine of matter." The other, "the true explanation," is that "Ayesha, seeing further than we can see, perceived the germ and smouldering spark of greatness which lay hid within her lover's soul, and well knew that under the influence of her gift of life, watered by her wisdom, and shone upon with the sunshine of her presence, it would bloom like a flower."

Andrew Lang concluded his advice to Haggard by saying he should "be very careful with the proofs before it goes out in a volume." The very small number of spelling and typographical errors in the first edition, as well as the numerous changes that differentiate it from the serial version, show how seriously Haggard took that advice. The text remained unaltered in the first seven editions of the novel, which all appeared in 1887. Approximately four hundred minor corrections and emendations were made to orthography, punctuation, and individual words in the "New Edition" of 1888.

Longmans brought out another "New Edition" in 1891 with approximately five hundred more very small changes, many of which appear to have been personally made by Haggard. Some of them concern individual words, apparently on the principle of "elegant variation." Many of the passages that purport to render putative Arabic into English are also changed. For example, the 1891 text renders the forms of address "Oh Holly" and "Oh Queen" as "O Holly" and "O Queen." Inverted forms give way to more straightforward ones, so that "have I fairly warned thee" becomes "I have warned thee fairly." Verbs that were previously separated by interpolations are reconstituted. Only one sentence that was added in the 1891 edition merits attention. In the penultimate paragraph of the last chapter Haggard asks, "And, another question: In this play of reincarnations had Ustane anything to do with the Amenartas of long ago?" This represents a sharpening of the eternal love triangle that looks forward to the sequel to *She* which appeared a decade later.

The chapters in which Ayesha speaks are by far the most worked over in the 1891 edition, which suggests an explanation for the alterations. The previous year Haggard and Lang had published their jointly authored romance, *The World's Desire*, in which Helen of Troy and other beautiful ancient women appear, women who are in some ways alternative versions of Ayesha. It is highly likely that the collaboration with a far more accomplished linguist and scholar made Haggard more conscious of his stylistic shortcomings than he had previously been.

Nonetheless there are many reasons to prefer the 1888 version. It includes more of the flavor of the decade in which it was written. References to contemporary brand names and politics are deleted in the later edition. "Gladstone bag" becomes "hand-bag," "Paysandu potted-tongue" becomes "an excellent potted tongue," and so forth. A reference in chap. X to Keats's poem "On First Looking into Chapman's Homer" is likewise deleted. An entire paragraph of Ayesha's presentation of the original Kallikrates in chap. XXI is struck out. Some of Haggard's original language verging on the colloquial is "elevated" in the 1891 version in ways that make it speak less directly to twentieth-century readers. "Climbed" is rendered as "clomb," "the confusion of senility" as "the dull edge of eld." In many of the altered passages, the effort to avoid repeating a word destroys the original rhythm of Haggard's prose. Another reason for preferring the 1888 version is that purgation of its stylistic infelicities makes it difficult to understand why so many of the first reviewers criticized it for being badly written. Although it is not an entirely easy or straightforward choice, I have chosen the 1888 edition as the best representation of Haggard's early literary art.

The method used to produce the text of the present edition was chosen so as to highlight the changes made between the manuscript finished on March 18, 1886, and the first edition of New Year's Day, 1887. First the text of the *Graphic* serialization was typed into a computer. The text of the first edition was then correlated with the manuscript, and the results were used to change the *Graphic* text. Finally, the changes of 1888 were interpolated, excluding only mistakes in punctuation and orthography. This procedure has required more reading and rereading than would ordinarily be the case, but working backward from the text of 1888 might not have brought to light the most significant of the author's emendations.

PRECURSORS AND SOURCES

Haggard's detractors searched the classics of poetry and prose in their efforts to convict him of plagiarism, ranging as far afield as Bacon's *New Atlantis* and Prescott's *Conquest of Mexico*. In so doing they credited him with a much wider literary knowledge than he possessed. It is much easier to find sources for his ideas among his own experiences and the reading matter that would have been commonly available to mid-Victorian boys of his limited educational attainments.

Haggard's service in South Africa provided a number of useful elements.[12] The language and rituals of the Amahagger owe a great deal to the time Haggard spent among the Zulu people. The quest for unknown peoples living among the ruins of vanished civilizations was suggested by expeditions such as the one mounted from Natal to southern Zimbabwe by the London and Limpopo Gold Mining Company in 1870. Reports of the splendid stone structures of that region were already circulating in South Africa when Haggard arrived in 1875. His biographer Morton Cohen has suggested in addition that Haggard might have heard stories of female rulers among the Lovedu people of the northern Transvaal.[13] But Haggard himself never traveled beyond the borders of the modern South African state and did not succeed in inventing a very convincing locality for his story. The adventurers strike inland from the northern coast of Mozambique. On their return they travel "about a hundred and seventy miles south" of the land of Kôr before they hit the Zambezi River. As they never encounter Lake Malawi (Nyasa), it can be assumed that they did not penetrate that far west. The area in which Haggard's Kôr is situated would therefore have fallen right in the midst of territory that had been disastrously overtaken by warfare and slave trading since the early decades of the nineteenth century. Haggard could easily have written some of this history into his tale if he had wanted to. For his purposes, however, the vaguer he was about African geography the better.

Egypt was another source of inspiration. Although Haggard first visited that country the year *after* he wrote *She*, he had been fascinated by the pharaohs since childhood and had read everything concerning them "on which I could lay my hands."[14] His description of Kôr's ruined capital strongly suggests Karnak and Luxor, even to such details as the resemblance of the stone columns to palm trees. Cleopatra, about whom Haggard later wrote a novel, provided him with a historical exemplar of the absolute ruler as absolute beauty. Most of the similarities which critics noted between Thomas Moore's narrative poem *The Epicurean* and Haggard's *She* can be put down to their common pillage of the nineteenth century's burgeoning storehouse of Egyptian archaeology. Both works concern the individual's quest for immortality, which is stupendously exemplified by the funeral rites and monuments of ancient Egypt. Both make use of the famous temple inscription "I am all that has been, that is, and that will be, and no man hath ever lifted my veil." Both concern a veiled priestess as well, but there the similarity ends, for Moore's vision of loveliness turns out to be a secret Christian who sets about converting the disciple of Epicurus to her faith. In *She* it is Ayesha who spouts Epicurean ideas.[15]

A handier fictional source of ideas for *She* was strangely passed over by the hostile camp: the writings of Edward Bulwer-Lytton, a close relative of Sir Henry Bulwer, the man who took Haggard as his private secretary to Natal in 1875.[16] Bulwer-Lytton was among Haggard's favorite authors. Two of his books contributed much to *She*. *A Strange Story* (1862) concerns a quest for an elixir of life. Its grotesque conclusion is a ritual fire scene presided over by a veiled woman named Ayesha.[17] In *The Coming Race* (1871), a book that itself seems to have been inspired by Jules Verne's *Journey to the Center of the Earth* of 1864, Bulwer-Lytton takes his protagonist down a mine shaft into a vast underground world where a section of the human race has evolved along divergent lines. Empowered by their discovery of a mysterious life force known as "vril," the underground people have exceptionally long life spans and a fund of arcane knowledge. One of them combines great beauty with great wisdom and scientific expertise, and of course it is she who becomes enamored of the simple-minded American who drops unexpectedly into her world.

She deserves to be classed alongside, if not among, the "underground" novels because so much of its action is subterranean.[18] Haggard's Amahagger, like Bulwer-Lytton's Gy-ei people, live in caverns and assign to women the role of seducer in courtship. The walls of the Gy-ei's caverns are decorated with scenes from "the history of the race," just as the catacombs of Kôr are lined with bas reliefs illustrating the lives of the rulers and their religious beliefs. The chasm by which the hero of *The Coming Race* enters the lower world is "shaped like the lower end of a vast funnel," a description that recalls both the chasm that "hath no bottom" and the "inverted cone" which Holly and Leo must traverse en route to the Fire of Life. And that life force itself bears more than a passing resemblance to Bulwer-Lytton's vril. Ayesha resembles Bulwer-Lytton's heroine Zee—even the sound suggests She—in her scientific knowledge, her vegetarianism, and her antidemocratic doctrines. The invisible force She uses to "blast" her enemies is the direct counterpart of the destructive power of vril employed in similar fashion by the Gy-ei. Haggard describes the ancient columns in the Temple of Truth as inspired by local palm trees. In Bulwer-Lytton's underground temples "the capitals of these columns imitated the foliage of the vegetation neighbouring them, some aloe-like, some fern-like."[19]

It is also possible that Haggard, like Bulwer-Lytton, borrowed directly from Verne's *Journey to the Center of the Earth*. The chasm which the adventurers must cross to reach the eternal fire is said by Ayesha to run "down to the very womb of the world." The action of Verne's novel, like Haggard's, is triggered by the decipherment of an ancient text. Verne in his turn was influenced by Edgar Allan Poe's tales of cryptic texts, such as "The Gold Bug" and *The Narrative of Arthur Gordon Pym* (1838), which features in its finale a mysterious figure with some of Ayesha's awe-inspiring characteristics.

There is little point in searching for specific precursors of Haggard's vision of rising and falling empires, for it saturated nineteenth-century politics, philosophy, and literature. Haggard's imperialism sprang as much from fear as from pride. Other civilizations had flourished and died. The most powerful of monarchs would eventually join Shelley's Ozymandias in obscurity. Britain too must sooner or later go under, but the evil day might be staved off by policies of expansion. The lesson taught by the ruins of dead Kôr is that even an unchallenged dominion may be catastrophically cut down by natural disaster. The plague that wipes out Kôr at the height of its greatness has a forerunner in Mary Shelley's novel *The Last Man* (1826) and an analogue in Bulwer-Lytton's *Last Days of Pompeii* (1834). But Haggard reached much further back than either writer when he strove to convey the horror of the fall of Kôr. He turned to the world's greatest compendium of holocaust stories: the Bible. The deluge, the incineration of Sodom and Gomorrah, the fall of the Tower of Babel all contribute something to the tale of Kôr. The very words used by the last surviving priest in chapter XVI to describe the fall of his city paraphrase the fate of Rome as foreshadowed in Revelation.

Notwithstanding all its gaudy trappings of pseudo-Eastern mysticism, *She* owes fewer debts to Buddhism, Hinduism, or any other kind of Orientalism than to the commonplace literature fed to English children in Haggard's youth. References to the Bible and Shakespeare outnumber those to all other literary sources. Walter Scott strongly influenced the language Haggard uses to convey foreignness and antiquity. The influence of Tennyson's *In Memoriam* (1850) and *Idylls of the King (1859)* is also apparent. The quest for the Fire of Life parallels in many respects the Arthurian quest for the Holy Grail. After overcoming many trials and combats in the wilderness, the adventurers come at last to Ayesha's dwelling place in an extinct volcano, which rises from the plain like a "great natural castle." Ayesha attends the Fire of Life as the Grail within the Castle of Carbonek was tended by the fair Grail Maidens. The mysterious hermit Noot who preceded Ayesha in this role corresponds to the hermit of the Grail legend. Like Lancelot, Leo Vincey's ancestor Kallikrates was a great warrior who became a priest in penance for his sins. The Fire of Life, like the lost Grail of Avalon, is to be found beneath the earth. When the adventurers stand in the presence of the fire they shine resplendently before each other's eyes, as Arthur's knights do when the Grail appears at the Round Table. The prose Haggard uses to describe that glory before the fall bears a striking similarity to the poetry used by Tennyson to describe the advent of the Grail.[20]

Nonliterary influences from Haggard's boyhood also contributed to the making of the novel. The original of "She-who-must-be-obeyed" was a rag doll used by the family nurserymaid to frighten the children into obedience. The "little foot" of chapter IX, the tooth of Noot, and the withered limbs of the disintegrating Ayesha all suggest the chilling moment when Haggard first contemplated his own hand as an object doomed to die.[21] An essential ingredient of Haggard's literary achievement was his ability to recapture such primordial horrors of infancy and explode them to Miltonic dimensions.

THEMES AND INTERPRETATIONS

The earliest significant observations on Haggard's novel were made by Sigmund Freud about the time he was developing the key ideas of his theory of psychoanalysis. Asked by a patient in 1895 to recommend something to read, Freud suggested *She*: "A *strange* book, but full of hidden meaning."[22] It is not difficult to see why it appealed to him. Freud had a consuming interest in archeology and antiquities—he once claimed to have read more archaeology than psychology in his lifetime. He looked upon himself as a kind of archaeologist of the mind who labored to strip away the layers of consciousness and repression that concealed the essential truths of the human id. How natural that he should be transfixed by Haggard's tale, which takes two polished English gentlemen on an expedition through savage Africa to colossal ruins and catacombs left by a vanished race. The expedition's object is nothing less than that which Freud himself sought: ultimate truth about life and personal identity.

During the nineteenth century, received opinion on both subjects had been profoundly shaken by discoveries of science. Close upon the heels of Charles Lyell's new geology, which proved the earth to be billions of years old, came Darwin's theory of evolution, which traced the "descent of man" to the operations of blind chance in a universe where only change was constant. Freud and Haggard, both born in 1856, belonged to the first generation to confront these shattering ideas with the clear, fresh eyes of youth. In their different careers they devoted their lives to working out the implications of evolution.

Variations on the theme of evolution. In *She* the "monkey theory" crops up on the second page of chapter I and in one form or another keeps cropping up throughout the book.

The transfer of the sherd in its progress through the centuries from ancient Egypt through Greece and Rome to modern England sums up the evolution of civilization. The adventurers seek the solution to a crime committed more than two thousand years earlier in Africa, the continent where Darwin surmised the human race had first split off from the higher apes. In combat against African animals and the "savage" Amahagger, Leo and Holly move backward from the Industrial Revolution to an earlier "stage" of social development when sexual and cannibalistic urges are openly expressed—and acted upon. Holly suggests that the Amahagger are the degenerate descendants of the ancient people of Kôr, a hypothesis which, if true, raises the nightmare of humanity regressing instead of progressing in the course of a long evolution. Indeed, Haggard claims, on behalf of his imaginary Kôr, engineering achievements more than six thousand years old that rival the Suez Canal and tunnels under the Alps.[23]

Ayesha boasts that she has personally demonstrated the mutability of the human race by experiments in selective breeding—what the Edwardians would call eugenics—by breeding "a race of giants" as well as the deaf mutes who serve her. But she is quick to point out that the scale of these changes is dwarfed by the larger cosmological drama: "What is a span of ten thousand years, or ten times ten thousand years, in the history of time . . . through periods, spaces, and times, from æon unto æon, till the world is dead, and the worlds beyond the world are dead" (chapter XVI).

This certainty that "the worlds beyond the world" will die derives from the Second Law of Thermodynamics. Victorian physicists drew a momentous conclusion from the simple observation that energy cannot pass from cold matter to warm: that the sun and all the galaxies of the universe would eventually arrive at a state of absolute dead coldness. The idea that not all evolution is progressive runs like a thread of arsenic through Haggard's tale, spreading gradually through the fabric until all unravels at the moment of Ayesha's sudden backward evolution from goddess to monkey.

Philosophical and religious speculation. The moral implications of life in a godless Darwinian universe ruled by chance and natural selection are spelled out by Ayesha in chapter XVIII. When Holly asks for what sin Ustane is to be executed, Ayesha replies, "Where is her sin? Her sin is that she stands between me and my desire." She goes on to explain that all human motives can be reduced to sex, wealth, and power. Looking at life as a Social Darwinian, Ayesha considers that this is not a bad thing, for progress comes through the survival of the fittest.

> Is it, then, a crime, oh foolish man, to put away that which stands between us and our ends? Then is our life one long crime, my Holly; for day by day we destroy that we may live, since in this world none, save the strongest, can endure. Those who are weak must perish; the earth is to the strong, and the fruits thereof. For every tree that grows a score shall wither, that the strong ones may take their share. We run to place and power over the dead bodies of those who fail and fall; ay, we win the food we eat from out of the mouths of starving babes. It is the scheme of things. Thou sayest, too, that a crime breeds evil, but therein thou dost lack experience; for out of crimes come many good things, and out of good grows much evil. The cruel rage of the tyrant may prove a blessing to thousands who come after him, and the sweet-heartedness of a holy man may make a nation slaves.

Haggard's ambivalent feelings about evolution stemmed not only from these apparent implications for public morality but also from the analogy he perceived between it and the unstoppable progression of the individual human being from infancy to the grave. Death haunted him nearly as much as it obsessed Poe, that earlier master of the macabre. *She* contains numerous references to Hamlet's reflections on death. Haggard constructs a counterpoise to the laws of change and dissolution by postulating the attainment of immortality through contact with the Fire of Life. The idea is no sooner stated, however, than it begins to be undercut. Ayesha explains to Leo that the fire acts to delay rather than to eliminate the hour of death. After a few more thousand years even she will die. The skilled embalmers of ancient Kôr appeared to halt the ravages of time and change by preserving the body's appearance at the moment of death. But the corpses that litter the catacombs are no less dead for all that. When Ayesha enters the fire a second time, Haggard shows his readers that her dazzling exterior, like that of Oscar Wilde's Dorian Gray, merely concealed the ravages of an internal process of aging and corruption.

In a halfhearted way Haggard offers the Christian doctrine of the resurrection as a second line of defense against the tide of disintegrative change that rolls us on to death. Holly professes to "hope for an immortality . . . which my faith doth promise to me" (chapter XXII). But he shrinks from defending it in argument against Ayesha's challenging assertion that man "himself must work out his own salvation . . . and not cast himself before the image of some unknown God, modelled like his poor self." Holly, "feeling that she would be more likely to convert me than I should to convert her," thinks "it best to leave the matter alone." Later he rejects Ayesha's offer of immortality for the ostensible reason that he looks forward to the Christian heaven, but his real motive is to avoid the unceasing pain of seeing her unattainably and eternally wrapped in Leo's arms. This allows Ayesha a further opportunity to taunt him for seeking hope "through the painted glass of . . . imagination."

It is not Christianity but a hash of Eastern mysticism that Haggard offers most earnestly as a way of escape from a godless universe ruled by chance and change. In this he resembles many of his contemporaries who perceived that Buddhism and Hinduism were far more compatible with the idea of evolution than any form of the Christian faith. The concept of souls being reincarnated in new forms as they advance by stages toward perfection is a kind of spiritual analogue to Darwinian development achieved through natural selection. Leo Vincey's dying father gasps in chapter I that "there is no such thing as death, Holly, only a change, and as you may perhaps learn in time to come." The theme is reiterated throughout the book. It is given as one possible explanation for Ayesha's choice of the boring Leo as her lover. He may be a bonehead now, but he is destined to "bloom like a flower" in subsequent lives. No sooner have Holly and Vincey returned from Kôr than they are off again on an expedition to central Asia to look for She in some new incarnation. Tibet no doubt suggested itself to Haggard because of its variant of Buddhism which holds that the Dalai Lama never dies but is reincarnated as a child through succeeding generations.

From the earliest reviews readers have complained that *She* serves up shallow and confused philosophy.[24] It is difficult to refute the charge. The interest of the book for historians of ideas lies not in the consistency of Haggard's thinking but in its contradictions. Intellectually Haggard accepted the shattering scientific discoveries of Lyell, Darwin, and Kelvin but could not help being deeply troubled by them He lacked the bravado of his more advanced contemporaries Nietzsche and Herbert Spencer, who could confront nothingness with a steady nerve and find solace in the belief that the human race was evolving toward higher forms. His heroes confront the mysteries of life as fallible everymen who will clutch at any hope as they strive in vain to see some personal persistence beyond the veil of death.

She-who-must-be-obeyed: immortal queen, irresistible beauty. Whatever his limitations as a literary stylist and religious philosopher, there can be no disputing that in Ayesha Haggard created a towering fictional character, one fit to stand alongside the monsters of Mary Shelley's *Frankenstein* (1818) and Bram Stoker's *Dracula* (1897). Many of Haggard's readers have chosen to regard *She* and most of his other fiction as beyond analysis—a judgment that the author would enthusiastically have seconded. For P. B. Ellis, Haggard is "a voice from the infinite."[25]

Haggard himself gave no convincing account of Ayesha's origins or meaning. He claimed that when he sat down to write, his "ideas were of the vaguest," the only clear notion in his head being "that of an immortal woman inspired by an immortal love."[26] Hints of She occur in each of his three previous novels. *Dawn* contains three female characters who suggest aspects of Ayesha's character: a beautiful young lady of great learning. another who looks like "an Egyptian sorceress" possessing the "spirit of power," and a wiser, older woman whose favorite retreat is her private museum of Egyptian antiquities. Florence of *The Witch's Head* combines Ayesha's iron will and capacity for patient vengeance. But more important than any of these forerunners is Gagool, the witch of *King Solomon's Mines*. At first glance no creatures could be more unlike than Ayesha the divinely beautiful and Gagool the hideous crone. But they nevertheless have much in common. Both possess vast stores of wisdom and magic. Both know the way to secrets hidden in caverns under the earth. Both are centuries old. Their closest resemblance is revealed at the end of *She* when Ayesha is momentarily transmuted by the fire into the very image of Gagool: a monkeylike being who speaks in a dry, spine-tingling cackle. Under the skin Ayesha was Gagool all along.

It is much easier to itemize anticipations of She in Haggard's writing than it is to fathom her meaning for the author and successive generations of readers. Interpretation may be conducted at several levels. For example, the book may be read as a Victorian gentleman's dialogue with himself on the subject of sexual politics. Holly, the inner narrator of the story, sees himself more or less as others see him—scorned by women and uncomfortable in their company. He pretends indifference to the quest for She, but once embarked upon the journey he is drawn into a world where the normal character of male-female relations undergoes a series of metamorphoses that rivet his attention. First he encounters the Amahagger people, who invert the normal rituals of courtship and marriage. Leo is charmed by the unembarrassed advances of Ustane, while Job shrinks from the woman who claims him as a husband. Holly records as his own opinion that "it was in its way the most delightful thing (putting its impropriety aside for a moment)" that he had ever seen. Thus he appears to endorse simultaneously the feminist proposition that women should be given more choice in romance and the conventional man's desire for women who will fulfill his sexual fantasies without prompting. Haggard's narrative proceeds in similar fashion to undercut each apparent mark of women's power among the Amahagger. They conform to the Victorian idea that exemption from work enhances women's status. Although women are supposed to be in charge of men, their local tribal leader, Billali, is a male. Haggard's final word on Amahagger sexual ethnography verges on farce when Billali confesses that their men only worship women "up to a certain point, till at last they get unbearable. . . . Then . . . we rise, and kill the old ones as an example to the young ones, and to show them that we are the strongest" (chapter X). The murder of the Amahagger woman who organizes the cannibal sacrifice of Mohamed suggests an unconscious fear of women who may eat, i.e., emasculate, men.[27]

The only academic study of Haggard written by a woman steers strangely clear of the sexual politics of *She*, preferring instead to see Ayesha as the embodiment of an imperialist's fantasy of untrammeled power.[28] Ayesha's relationship with Leo and Holly is not, however, one of straightforward dominion. Haggard's treatment of Ayesha reinforces sexual stereotypes even as it seems to challenge them. She, who is all powerful and irresistible, nevertheless claims that being flattered by men is a "dear pleasure which is our sex's only right." In chapter XVII She flutters and coquettes before Holly like a girl, and her analysis of male and female motivation in the following chapter conforms to the worst caricatures of Haggard's time. "Man," she says, can always "be bought with woman's beauty, if it be but beautiful enough; and woman's beauty can be ever bought with gold, if only there be gold enough." When she has at last captured Leo's heart, she pledges to love, honor, and obey him just like any other maiden bride. In all these contradictory messages Haggard responded in the same way many of his contemporaries did to the challenge of "the new woman" who demanded votes, education, and the right to control her own property. Although he was both fascinated and repelled, he did not capitulate.

Writers attracted to the psychoanalytic school of psychology have been the most fertile sources of suggestions for the deeper meaning of *She*. Carl Jung, an early colleague of Freud's, believed that Haggard had dredged Ayesha up from his unconscious, that she was a clear manifestation of what Jung called the anima.[29] She represented the ideal of woman which men constantly seek but never attain because all women, once obtained, fall short of the paragon. That analysis is not far from what Haggard thought he had achieved. When he collaborated with Andrew Lang a few years later to write a parallel romance about Helen of Troy, he expressed the objective in the title: *The World's Desire* (1890).

Another member of Freud's founding circle of psychoanalysts, Wilhelm Reich, expanded Freud's idea of the eternal psychic struggle between love and death, eros and thanatos, in a way that can be readily applied to the story of Ayesha.[30] Nandor Fodor, who won international attention with his work on the psychic implications of birth, pointed the way toward another reading of the novel when he claimed that *She* is "a beautiful allegory of the penalty attendant on our yearning to return to the womb."[31] Although Freud never followed up his interest in *She* by undertaking a detailed analysis, this line of thought can be readily extended through his concept of the Oedipus complex.

A reference to the original Oedipus legend is, after all, met as early as chapter III, when Holly finds the Sherd of Amenartas inside a silver box decorated with the figure of the Sphinx. The colossal head of the Ethiopian, which greets the travelers on the African coast, is also likened to the Sphinx. In the myth Oedipus must answer the riddle posed by the Sphinx before he can advance toward his destiny. The answer to the question "What goes on four legs in the morning, two at noon, and three in the evening?" is

"Man." For Freud the riddle of man's psychological destiny is embodied in what happened to Oedipus after he answered the Sphinx: he unwittingly murdered his father and displaced him in the matrimonial bed of his mother. An essential element in individual development of the male child is, according to Freud, repression of the infantile wish to displace the father in the mother's affections. In a number of ways that primordial family drama is played out again and again in *She*.

Leo Vincey is an orphan whose father, while he lived, could not bear to look upon the boy's face because his appearance had caused his wife to be taken from him (she died in childbirth). What Leo and Holly find inscribed on the Sherd of Amenartas is a message from another woman who died in childbirth. It exhorts her son to grow up and compensate for his father Kallikrates' death by taking revenge on his murderer, Ayesha. After Leo does grow up and find the woman, however, he does not murder her. Instead he replaces his ancestor in her affections. Haggard makes the identification between Kallikrates, the ancestral father, and Leo concrete by having Vincey confront his own image in mummified form in chapter XXI, "The Dead and Living Meet." No sooner does Leo appear on the scene than Ayesha incinerates the corpse of Kallikrates. Then Ayesha escorts Leo to the magical fire, which will enable him to be her spouse forever. When she kisses him just before stepping naked into the fire, she presses her lips to his forehead "like a mother's kiss."[32] Finally, the impossible incestuous mating is halted by Ayesha's disintegration.

Freudians hold that the Oedipal wishes of normal individuals are deeply repressed in the unconscious portions of their psyches. If they are expressed at all in dreams or discourse they appear in a veiled or allegorical form. This insight can be used to explain all the devices Haggard uses to distance himself from the relationship between Leo and Ayesha—and from its mirror, the relationship between Kallikrates and Ayesha. Leo's story is told in the manuscript of Holly, which in turn has been communicated by the unnamed "Editor." Kallikrates' story is told by the sherd in the box within the box within the box, and the meaning is encoded in several languages.

The reader who goes looking for other veiled references to the Oedipal drama does not have far to seek. Consider the figure of L. Horace Holly. The initial *L* suggests that Holly is a variation on Leo. The full name suggests a variation on H. Rider Haggard. When Ayesha enquires about the meaning of the name, she is told that "'Holly' is a prickly tree." She goes on to discern a key to his character in the name. "Well," she observes, "thou hast a prickly and yet a tree-like look" (chapter XIII). Similar word plays could be made on the name Haggard. The hero of *King Solomon's Mines*, Allan Quatermain, is a haggard and grizzled African hunter. Holly is gnarled and misshapen. He is said to resemble a monkey or a baboon: an ancient symbol of animal lust. Like Rider Haggard, he was jilted by a woman he had hoped to marry. It could be argued that Holly's ugly and simian body represents a punishment for some guilty secret. He considers himself "branded" by his ugliness "like Cain." Has he too committed some crime against the family? Is that crime the wish to displace the father? We are told nothing whatever about Holly's parentage; he tells us he had "neither father nor brother nor mother." Nonetheless, in the very midst of these denials and reflections on his ugliness in chapter I, a father appears at his door. It is the dying Vincey, whose visage bears "the remains of great personal beauty." This once attractive father confides to Holly the son he "could not bear to look upon." Before he leaves the room he also gives Holly a kiss on the forehead, similar to the one Ustane will give Leo in chapter VII and Ayesha will give Leo at the climax of the story. The father having been killed off, Holly then replaces him by undertaking to raise the boy.

In Africa Holly finds a substitute father in the patriarchal figure of Billali, chief of the Amahagger. Billali calls Holly both his son and "the baboon." He saves Holly from death in chapter VIII. Holly returns the favor in chapter X, plunging into a pool to save the old man from drowning while his own people look on with a strange indifference, almost as if they willed Billali's death. In chapter IX, the two men are involved in one of the strangest colloquies in the book. Billali tells Holly that as a boy he fell in love with the mummified corpse of one of the ladies of ancient Kôr and used to creep to her side until one day his mother caught him and burned the mummy. D. S. Higgins has argued strongly that this memory represents an adolescent's fear of being surprised in the midst of a masturbatory sexual fantasy.[33] It is Billali, the adopted father, who first brings Holly into the presence of She-who-must-be-obeyed. Although Holly initially feigns indifference to the quest, pretending that he is only going along to humor Leo, he in fact deliberately shadows Leo throughout the story. He too falls victim to Ayesha's irresistible spell and against his will becomes Leo Vincey's jealous rival. When he crawls secretly to Ayesha's bedchamber and spies on her in the company of the corpse of Kallikrates, it is as if a boy were spying on the matrimonial bed of his parents.

The pseudo-family ties between Leo and Holly generate still more opportunities for exploring the complexities of father-son relationships. They take turns saving each other from death. The parental kiss on the forehead that Vincey, Sr., bestows on Holly in chapter I is transferred by Holly to Leo in chapter XXVII when he fears that he is about to die. The multiplication of father-son links represented by Leo-Holly, Billali-Holly, the sequence of names on the sherd, the collapsing of them in the identification of Kallikrates-Leo: all afford Haggard opportunities to ring endless changes on the theme.

A closely related theme is Ayesha's rivalry with Amenartas and Ustane for the love of Kallikrates and Leo. Rivalries of this sort occur throughout Haggard's fiction. Two women compete for the love of a single man; neither is able to triumph decisively, and it is frequently suggested that the triangle is truly eternal, i.e., reincarnations of the central figures play out the drama again and again. Haggard all but advertised that this was a projection of his own emotional relationship to two women: his wife, Louisa, and Lilly, the lost love of his youth.[34] Read in this way, Ustane replicates Amenartas.[35] There is, however, another way of viewing the triangle. If, at the unconscious level, Ayesha represents the desired but unattainable mother, then she is the rival of *all* other women. The effort to break free of her spell is involved in every love encounter. By the same token the image of the mother is reflected in the eyes of all lovers. So Amenartas is not only the rival of Ayesha; she is herself the founding mother of a dynasty of lovers. Though Haggard's prose is not always sure-footed, it must be acknowledged that the Chinese box structure of the novel is superbly suited to the complexity of his themes. It allows the triangular rivalries to be presented over and over without ever being precisely duplicated. Otherwise the identical figures of father, son, mother, and lover would be endlessly bounced back and forth like images cast in facing mirrors, on and on to infinity.

   The dream landscape of the quest. Haggard's landscapes and the way people move through them are subjects worthy of study in their own right. Some writers of fantasy choose islands as settings for unlikely tales; others send their adventurers to distant planets or galaxies. Haggard's favorite setting is a hidden valley or crater surrounded by high mountains. In *She* it appears twice, first in the initial encounter with the Amahagger, second in the advance to the lost capital of Kôr. In each case the approach is difficult and circuitous. The first is "a great cup," formerly a lake that is reached by traveling up a canal and then through a rocky defile lined with "beautiful trees and shrubs." The second was also once a crater lake, which was drained by the builders of Kôr thousands of years before. To reach the crater floor the adventurers must pass along the underground channel that was cut to drain the ancient lake. Holly likens his passage through this channel to a journey into the "bowels of the mountain."

   In *King Solomon's Mines* Haggard gave an explicitly female configuration to the landscape. The treasure hunters must penetrate a hidden valley by traveling between two mountains known as "Sheba's Breasts." It does not require much imagination to see the female body also dominating the topography of *She*. The narrow passes between the beautiful shrubbery suggest the loins of a woman. The two extinct volcanic mountains where most of the action occurs suggest breasts standing up from the broad African plains. The ancient channel cut to drain the crater lake is most strongly reminiscent of the birth canal from which the waters burst at the moment of parturition. That same imagery is repeated more dramatically in the final descent toward the Fire of Life. Guided by Ayesha the adventurers crawl "into a kind of rut or fold of rock," which becomes a tunnel at whose end is the chasm that She tells them "goeth down to the very womb of the world." At this point the imagery becomes suddenly and dramatically male. To reach the entrance to the funnel that leads to the inner cavern of the fire, the party must first crawl out along a narrow rock that juts from the wall of the chasm like a "cock's spur." The rock seems to be actually alive as it "vibrates," "throbs," and "jumps" beneath them. Then they extend a long wooden plank they have carried with them across the void and thus attain their goal: the source of life.

It is impossible to say how aware Haggard was of all the anatomical connotations of the imaginary landscape he created. In chapter XXIII Holly notes that the architects of antiquity often took their inspiration from the female form and recalled its outlines in the columns of their temples. On the other hand, it may be argued that the efforts Haggard takes to distance himself from the story indicate psychological mechanisms of repression at work.

Much of the book is presented in dreamlike visions. Leo Vincey advances toward the goal of his quest in a series of stages punctuated by extended periods of unconsciousness. Fellow students at Cambridge call him "the Greek God" and Holly, "Charon," after the boatman of classical mythology who ferries dead souls across the river Styx. A boat takes Leo to Africa, and in the midst of a storm he is momentarily thought to be drowned but is brought to safety by Holly/Charon. He is knocked out during a fight with the Amahagger and is unconscious again (from malaria) when he is carried into the underworld of Kôr toward his encounter with She. The way in which key landscapes are revealed in the tale recall the dream visions of sleep. The figure of the Negro's head on the African coast is revealed at the first glimmer of dawn. The plain of Kôr spreads itself before the travelers as if in the bird's-eye view of a sleeper.[36] Leo's encounter with his own image when he sees the corpse of Kallikrates also resembles the out-of-body fantasies that sometimes appear in dreams. Aside from the Temple of Truth, Holly's description of the ruined city of Kôr bears little resemblance to any known archaeological site. It has individual houses, parks, and gardens that recall London or other late-Victorian British cities, as if it too were a dream version of reality.

SEQUELS TO *SHE*

She has acquired a seemingly permanent niche among the best-selling novels written in the nineteenth century. Haggard's most recent bibliographer, Denys Whatmore, does not even attempt to list all the editions that have appeared since the author's final corrections of 1888. He merely notes that "there are certainly dozens if not hundreds of editions."[37] *She* has been translated into a large number of the world's written languages, including Esperanto. Hervé Dumont, after counting forty-four translations and fourteen film versions from several countries, concluded that *She* has left its mark upon "the collective unconscious of several generations."[38] Mention has already been made of well-known writers who have recorded their debts to Haggard as a stimulus to their own careers. There are, in addition, many others, less famous, who have flattered Haggard by reproducing or imitating his creation, beginning with the author himself.

Subsequent lives and loves of Haggard's Ayesha. Rider Haggard's imagination continued to flower in romances for about a decade after his initial triumph and then seemed to dry up. None of his twentieth-century fiction achieved the success of his first productions. He came under increasing pressure from his publishers to find new adventures for his most popular characters, Allan Quatermain, Umslopogaas, and Ayesha—pressure to which he eventually succumbed.

In 1905 Haggard brought out *Ayesha, the Return of She.* The story takes up where the other left off. Leo and Holly go as planned to Tibet, where they spend some time soaking up Eastern wisdom in a Buddhist monastery. They then trek off into the snow and arrive via an avalanche at a hidden valley peopled by one of those lost civilizations on which, to borrow Brian Aldiss's word, Haggard held a "patent."[39] There Leo is virtually held captive by the local queen, who turns out to be a reincarnation of Amenartas. Eventually he finds Ayesha, in more or less the same repulsive form that she assumed just before her last disappearance, appropriately serving as the veiled priestess of a shrine to universal motherhood. Leo suppresses his physical disgust and through his kiss restores Ayesha to her original beauty.[40] For a while she reverts to her old boundlessly ambitious self, plotting to rule the earth with Leo by transmuting iron into gold in her laboratory and using it to buy a Chinese mercenary army of millions in Peking. This version of the popular Yellow Peril theme is averted when Leo, unable any longer to control his physical desire, embraces her and drops dead on the spot. Ayesha and Holly follow him soon after into the great unknown.

Having killed off Ayesha for a second time, Haggard needed some ingenuity to resuscitate her for further adventures, even when fresh royalties beckoned. He managed the feat first in 1921 by inventing a tale of *She and Allan,* which is set some years before the first coming of Leo and Holly. She repays the great white hunter for leading an army against an evil rival set up by the wicked giant Rezu by giving Allan a potion that sends him off in a dream to the world of the dead to check up on some of his lost loves.

Two years later Haggard brought Ayesha back for a final appearance in *Wisdom's Daughter.* This novel purports to tell the original story of Kallikrates and his love triangle. In a manuscript left by Ayesha for Horace Holly's edification and found among his papers after his death, She explains that she told some white lies in her earlier account of Kallikrates' death. The real story is that after growing up as the smartest pretty girl in all Arabia, she meets the Egyptian priest Noot, who finds her a place as a priestess of Isis at the court of Pharaoh Nectanebes. There she meets Kallikrates, a Greek mercenary soldier who seeks to atone for the murder of his brother by becoming a priest of Isis. It turns out that it was Pharaoh's beautiful but evil daughter Amenartas who got him into this difficulty and who later tempts him into betraying his priestly vows. When the Persian army drives the Egyptians into exile, Amenartas and Kallikrates flee to the land of Kôr. Ayesha follows them later at the invitation of Noot, who bids her take his place as keeper of the sacred fire. She is only tempted to enter the fire after she is taunted by Amenartas for having lost some of her good looks. The fire not only restores her beauty but imbues her with sensual desires, which were previously foreign to her nature. Her triumph over Amenartas seems assured, but the wily Egyptian adjures her husband in the name of their dead son to resist the temptation.[41] It is then that Ayesha strikes the fatal blow.

All three of Haggard's sequels are weak fare compared with the original novel. Their principal interest lies in the way the author seemed compelled to transform Ayesha's original character. In *She* Ayesha is the wicked slayer of Kallikrates and Ustane; Amenartas is an innocent young mother. Ayesha's irresistible beauty draws men to her despite her repellent Darwinian commitment to power and self-gratification. In *The Return of She*, Ayesha is nobler and less sensual than her rival. The sweeter she becomes, the more she bores us. By the time Haggard penned *Wisdom's Daughter* he had shorn Ayesha of practically all her unworthy motives. Was this perhaps because he had become gradually and uncomfortably aware of the perilous psychological ground he had trod in the original novel? In any case, the sanitized later versions of Ayesha held little interest for the reading public.

Haggard and the movies. Although a stage adaptation of *She* opened in London as early as May 1888, Haggard's concept did not lend itself readily to live theater.[42] The opulence of its visual demands made it too expensive, and the climax was difficult to render convincingly.

Cinema, with its extended capacity for illusion and special effects, was a far more suitable medium, though it was always impossible to portray superhuman beauty with flesh and blood actresses.[43] It is probably for this reason that many of the films attribute Ayesha's hold on Leo to her magic rather than her physique. The celebrated pioneer of film, Georges Méliès, produced *La Danse du Feu* (also called *Pillar of Fire*) in 1899; it may have been based on the spectacle of Ayesha in the fire. Six adaptations of *She* followed in the silent era, of which only the last appears to have survived.[44] A lavish 1925 production, it was reasonably faithful to Haggard's text (he was paid the princely sum of £2,500 for the film rights). Featured as Ayesha was the American actress Betty Blythe, one of many rivals to Theda Bara's "vamp," and as Horace Holly, the German actor Heinrich George, who played some notable roles in films by the director Fritz Lang. The film makes no attempt to render the splendors of fictional Kôr, relying instead on the Egyptian props that formed part of the standard equipment of filmmakers in that era.[45] The Amahagger are played by German extras made up to look darkly tanned. The servant, Job, survives the adventure, and the Fire of Life shoots up like a pyrotechnic Old Faithful geyser, but otherwise the scenario adheres closely to Haggard's last chapters. Blythe makes a very convincing Ayesha: imperious, totally faithful to Leo/Kallikrates, yet also very sensual, showing plenty of flesh in a backless outfit with a split skirt. Had the film been made a few years later it would almost certainly have fallen victim—in America, at least—to the notorious Hays Code, which aimed to curb eroticism in the movies.

The *She* of 1925 was to be the last film version for more than sixty years that paid much attention to Haggard's original text. Several factors seem to have been responsible for later travesties. Whereas the linguistic mélange of Haggard's original (English, Greek, Latin, Arabic) was no problem for silent films with multinational casts, talking pictures were a different matter. When American stars were cast in leading roles, the plot was changed to fit their accents. The excitement and mystery of exploration in Africa had by the 1920s given way to the humdrum routine of colonialist exploitation; new venues needed to be found for Ayesha's kingdom. Another complication was that a great many other white queens were elbowing their way onto celluloid. Some of them came out of the Bible—Sheba, Jezebel, Salome. Some were creations of Haggard's imitators. Still others were the mortal heroines of his own books.[46]

A parallel race of African queens was spawned in 1919 by Pierre Benoit's novel *L'Atlantide*.[47] In Benoit's fantasy some of the inhabitants of ancient Atlantis manage to escape the engulfing deluge and continue their civilization in the middle of the Sahara. Their twentieth-century queen, Antinéa, is descended on one side of her family from Neptune and on the other from Cleopatra. She rules over the mysterious Blue Tuareg in and around the Hoggar massif of Saharan mountains. Her life is devoted to the pleasure she derives from seducing and then killing gentlemen from the outside world who have the misfortune to wander into her kingdom from time to time. Their preserved corpses rest in stone niches around the inner rotunda of her subterranean desert retreat. When an officer of the expanding French West African empire stumbles upon her domain and falls victim to her spell, many complications ensue. The plot sounded enough like *She* to provoke legal proceedings.[48] But in her most important features Benoit's promiscuous heroine is quite unlike Ayesha, who is saving all her love for one man. Antinéa employs her passionless sexuality for sadistic purposes, not unlike the heroine of Puccini's *Turandot*.

The distinction did not trouble film producers dedicated to satisfying the public appetite for more love goddesses of the silver screen. Since Haggard's death, the characters of various queens have often been hashed together under his title. In 1935 Helen Gahagan's Ayesha was transported, in an RKO version directed by Irving Pichel, along with her kingdom of cannibals to crystal caves beneath the icy wastes of northern Russia. Randolph Scott played an American Vincey who seeks out the secret of immortal life in the company of a gold miner's daughter, Tania, played by Helen Mack, who had most recently acted as consort to the *Son of Kong* for the same studio. Tania and Leo survive Ayesha's immolation and go off together. With its art deco sets and Egypto-Incan-Mongol-Hellenic costumes, the movie provoked one reviewer to name it the silliest film of the year.[49] It lost RKO hundreds of thousands of dollars. Aside from a bizarre musical version of the story made in Bombay in 1953 (*Malika Solomi*), no studio risked Haggard's story again until 1964, when Hammer Studios in Britain struck box-office gold with Ursula Andress in the title role. This version was directed by Robert Day. Elements of another Haggard novel, *Queen Sheba's Ring* (1910), were borrowed for the plot, and Kôr was re-sited to Benoit's Sahara. Hammer's production crews had already developed a pat formula for generating frissons of horror in their vampire films, a formula they translated into some stunning effects. But Andress's smoldering décolletage smacks far more of Antinéa than Ayesha. And rather than commanding love with imperial force, she seems simply to offer Leo the fulfillment of any secret desires he might harbor.[50]

Two more recent versions, both South African, deserve comment because of their implicit political content. Dirk de Villiers's *The Virgin Goddess* (1973) was made on location in the ruins of Great Zimbabwe and casts black Africans as Ayesha's subjects. In this version her immortality depends on the preservation of her virginity. With this story De Villiers was able to cash in on the sexual anxieties of white South Africans while reinforcing the hoary and politically convenient belief that a lost white civilization rather than black men raised the walls of the spectacular buildings at Zimbabwe. A television adaptation made in Johannesburg in 1979 came closer to Haggard's original, but it also cast Ayesha as an absolute ruler of black Africans in a South African setting.[51] Through all the vicissitudes of Ayesha's screen career only one feature of Haggard's original survives more or less intact: Ayesha's instant aging in her second encounter with the Fire of Life.

The influence of She *on twentieth-century science fiction and fantasy.* Haggard called his novel a "romance," a label applied in the nineteenth century to works in a literary line of descent from Walter Scott and the "Gothic" novels of late eighteenth-century romanticism.[52] The label will not do today because in the course of the twentieth century the genre has bifurcated. Some list makers include Haggard among the practitioners of science fiction. Others leave him out.[53] Brian Aldiss states flatly that "Haggard himself never wrote science fiction."[54] Robert Scholes and Eric Rabkin would exclude Haggard from science fiction proper because he does not use fantasy incidentally, like Jules Verne, but "centrally, exhaustively." They would consign him instead to the "sword and sorcery" subfamily of their category "space opera." Certainly Haggard made little use of the technology that is so important to most writers of science fiction. There is no need, however, to enter into this taxonomic discussion here. What is important is that certain themes of *She* have been widely acknowledged to have exerted a pervasive influence on the literary genres commonly called science fiction and fantasy. In particular, Haggard's ideas permeate that literature whose central theme is, in Aldiss's words, "descent from a 'natural world' to inferno or incarceration, where a protagonist goes, willingly or otherwise, in search of a secret, an identity, or a relationship."[55]

Haggard's technique for inducing belief in the unbelievable is a variation on a trick used by many writers of fantasy and science fiction. H. G. Wells held that any writer of fantastic stories must help the reader "in every possible unobtrusive way to *domesticate* the impossible hypothesis." Whereas Wells employed "an ingenious use of scientific patter" about time and physics to undermine disbelief in his time machine, Haggard used archaeological and linguistic artifacts.[56] Once the reader has plowed through the minute description of the Sherd of Amenartas and all its translations into other languages, he is prepared to have the impossible hypothesis confirmed by the appearance of the deathless queen. Horace Holly's long-winded accounts of geographical, zoological, and ethnographical particulars serve the same purpose by imitating the productions of late-Victorian scientific expeditions.

The secret valley where time stands still for savage peoples and ancient civilizations has been taken up and developed in works as diverse as Arthur Conan Doyle's *Lost World*, James Hilton's *Lost Horizon*, Edgar Wallace's concept for the motion picture *King Kong*,[57] and Edgar Rice Burroughs's John Carter series of Martian adventures. In 1895 Wells introduced the world to time travel by machine, but many other writers of science fiction have stuck to Haggard's method, which is to move spatially into zones where creatures live as our ancestors did, or as our descendants may live in times to come.[58] His invention of the lost civilization of Kôr—where, thousands of years before the rise of Pharaonic Egypt, awe-inspiring feats of science and engineering were accomplished—prefigures many a tale that ascribes to extraterrestrial beings of long ago superiority over the technical achievements of modern times.[59]

Most of Haggard's striking fictional characters—Allan Quatermain, Umslopogaas, Henry Curtis—belong specifically to a colonial Africa that is fast slipping away from contemporary consciousness.[60] How appropriate that Ayesha alone appears destined to exercise a deathless influence on writers of fantastic tales. Under various names she can be found, enthroned amid archaic architecture, exercising absolute dominion over barbarous kingdoms and adventurous hearts from one end of the fictional universe to the other. Buck Rogers met her in the caverns of other planets. So did Flash Gordon. And so have innumerable other intergalactic travelers. It is difficult to dissent from Henri Gougaud's prediction that she will always be there, waiting "at the edge of the farthest frontiers, femme fatale, the woman whose encounters direct destinies to life eternal or death, according to the stature of the heroes. She has a legion of sisters in Outer Space. . . . For the seeker of the absolute, She exists as a sort of Holy Grail on the highest tower of desire."[61]

NOTES

1. Ella Haggard's narrative poem *Myra, or the Rose of the East, a Tale of the Afghan War* was published in London in 1857, the year after her son's birth, by Longmans, which later published most of Rider's works as well.

2. Haggard's first book, *Cetywayo and His White Neighbours*, was published in London in 1882.

3. Chap. XXIII.

4. This concept was expressed most cogently in Haggard's lifetime by Lord Acton; see William H. McNeill, ed., *Essays in the Liberal Interpretation of History* (Chicago, 1967), xviii.

5. "About Fiction," *Contemporary Review*, February 1887, 172–80.

6. Contributions to the controversy are listed in D. E. Whatmore, *H. Rider Haggard: A Bibliography* (London, 1987), 144.

7. George Nathaniel Curzon, who later became a powerful force in British imperial politics, wrote in Haggard's defense. So did Andrew Lang, in a clever article ("Literary Plagiarism," *Contemporary Review*, June 1887, 831–40) that disputed the idea that *She* was based on Thomas Moore's *Epicurean* (1827). Lang pointed out that Moore himself had borrowed from many sources. The plagiarism controversy is reviewed by D. S. Higgins, *Rider Haggard: The Great Storyteller* (London, 1981), 111–14. Other works from which it was suggested Haggard had borrowed were Bacon's *New Atlantis*, Prescott's *Conquest of Mexico*, and Bishop Hall's *Mundus Alter et Item*.

8. H. R. Haggard, *The Days of My Life* (London, 1926), vol. 1, 245, 251.

9. Higgins, *Rider Haggard*, 109–11, discusses Lang's influence on the development of the first edition.

10. "The Culture of the Horrible: Mr. Rider Haggard's Stories," *Church Quarterly Review*, January 1888, 389–411.

11. *Days of My Life*, 1:247.

12. See Norman Etherington, "South African Origins of Rider Haggard's Early African Romances," *Notes and Queries* N.S. 24 (October 1977): 436–38.

13. Morton Cohen, *Rider Haggard—His Life and Works* (London, 1960), 109.

14. *Days of My Life*, 1:254.

15. Thomas Moore, *The Epicurean* (London, 1827): the inscription is quoted on 35–36. Moore did not invent the veiled priestess. Such beings presided at the oracles of ancient Greece. The *Winged Victory of Samothrace*, now in the Louvre in Paris, is another ancient veiled figure likely to have inspired Haggard.

16. Brian Aldiss misses this connection in *Trillion Year Spree: The History of Science Fiction* (London, 1986), 139, by confusing Sir Henry Bulwer with Sir Redvers Buller, who served in South Africa with the British army. Bulwer-Lytton, who began life as Edward Bulwer, was raised to the peerage as Lord Lytton.

17. Cited by Higgins, *Rider Haggard*, 100.

18. For an analysis of the "underground" genre, see L. Thomas Williams, "Journeys to the Center of the Earth: Descent and Initiation in Selected Science Fiction," Ph.D. thesis, Indiana University, 1983.

19. Edward Bulwer-Lytton, *The Coming Race and The Haunted and the Haunters* (Oxford, 1928), 9.

20. See chap. XXV, note 21. Cohen, *Rider Haggard*, 220, notices other ways in which Haggard "helped to Victorianize the medieval romance."

21. *Days of My Life*, 1:28–29.

22. Sigmund Freud, *The Interpretation of Dreams*, ed. James Strachey (London, 1954), 452–55.

23. For comparisons with real ancient works, see L. Sprague de Camp, *The Ancient Engineers* (Cambridge, Mass., 1970), especially chaps. 2 and 3.

24. *Pall Mall Gazette* 45 (January 4, 1887): 5; C. S. Lewis, *Rehabilitations and Other Essays* (London, 1939), 100–102.

25. Peter Berresford Ellis, *H. Rider Haggard: A Voice from the Infinite* (London, 1978).

26. *Days of My Life*, 1:245.

27. Gender reversals occur throughout imaginative literature. Haggard's contemporary Charlotte Perkins Gilman used the lost valley formula he popularized as the vehicle for a feminist treatment of the theme in *Herland*. Later examples of alternative roles in alternative worlds are explored by Joana Russ, "Amor Vincit Foeminam: The Battle of the Sexes in Science Fiction," *Science Fiction Studies* 7 (1980):2–15.

28. Wendy Katz, *Rider Haggard and the Fiction of Empire* (Cambridge, 1987), 125–30.

29. These and other thoughts on Haggard may be found in C. G. Jung, *Collected Works* (London, 1966), vol. 13, 82–93.

30. The skeleton of this line of analysis is sketched by Hervé Dumont, "Ayesha et Antinéa: Le mythe de la reine immortelle au cinema," *L'Ecran Fantastique*, no. 57 (June 1985), 56.

31. Nandor Fodor, *The Search for the Beloved* (New York, 1949), 231.

32. The phrase also appears in chap. XX when Ayesha tells Leo that before entering the fire he ought to "dream upon thy mother's kiss."

33. Higgins, *Rider Haggard*, p. 8. See also Norman Etherington, "Rider Haggard, Imperialism and the Layered Personality," *Victorian Studies* 22, no.1 (1978): 71–88.

34. Higgins, *Rider Haggard*, 13–15, 60, reveals the lost lover's name, Mary Elizabeth Jackson, and other previously unknown details of the relationship.

35. In Haggard's sequel *Ayesha, the Return of She*, a rival queen vies for Leo's attention and is pronounced by Ayesha to be the reincarnation of Amenartas. It is more difficult to cast Ustane in this role because of her racial ambiguity.

36. The bird's-eye landscapes that recur in Haggard's novels are treated by Peter F. Pierce, "Rider Haggard," B.Litt thesis, Oxford University, 1975, 13–21.

37. Whatmore, *H. Rider Haggard*, xiii.

38. Dumont, "Ayesha et Antinéa," *L'Ecran Fantastique*, no. 57 (June 1985), 56.

39. Aldiss, *Trillion Year Spree*, 139. The story also bears some striking similarities to "The Man Who Would Be King," a story by Haggard's friend Rudyard Kipling.

40. It is interesting, in view of Haggard's early use of the Grail Quest theme, that Leo here replays another Arthurian legend, the story of Sir Gawain and the Lady Ragnell.

41. No son previous to Tisisthenes of the sherd is mentioned in *She*. This alteration may have been a cruel if veiled taunt aimed at Haggard's wife, Louisa: their only son died in 1891, and the suggestion is that Haggard only stayed with Louisa for the sake of his son's memory.

42. Written by Edward Rose, W. Sidney, and C. Graves, the stage play opened at the Novelty Theatre on May 10, 1888. Haggard attended the first night and addressed the audience. It received mixed reviews, the most unfavorable of which was "She-That-Ought-Not-to-Be-Played," *Punch*, Sept. 22, 1888, 132.

43. The filmographies included in Whatmore, *H. Rider Haggard*, 132–35, and Dumont, "Ayesha et Antinéa," complement rather than replicate each other. Taken together they provide the most comprehensive listing yet available.

44. The six adaptations are *She*, 1908 (USA, Edison), 17 minutes; *She*, 1911 (USA, Thanhouser), 30 minutes; *His Egyptian Affair*, 1915 (USA, Universal), 15 minutes (a parody); *She, A Strange Adventure*, 1916 (U.K., W. G. Barker), 5,400 feet; *She*, 1917 (USA, Fox), 75 minutes; and *She*, 1925 (English titles), *Mirakel der Liebe* (German titles) (U.K. and Germany, G. B. Samuelson and EFA joint production), 104 minutes.

45. These comments are based on my viewing of a copy of the film held by the British National Film Archive, 21 Stephen Street, London.

46. Most notable of the Haggard adaptations were Fox's *Cleopatra* (1917) and Stoll Pictures' British release of the Austrian production of *Moon of Israel* (1924).

47. The genesis and subsequent filmography of *L'Atlantide* are reviewed by Dumont in "Ayesha et Antinéa," *L'Ecran Fantastique*, no. 58 (July 1985), 56–69.

48. Benoit claimed ignorance of both Haggard and his language. The case did not come to court; Benoit compensated for any damage he might have inflicted by writing an elegant introduction to the first French translation of *She*.

49. Clipping collection, British National Film Institute Library, London.

50. A sequel, *Vengeance of She*, was made by Hammer in 1967 under the direction of Cliff Owen. Starring Olinka Berova as a girl possessed by the spirit of Ayesha, it was presented as "based on characters created by Rider Haggard." In fact the film was grounded on two little-known American imitations of Haggard's general idea: John Morgan's *Companion to She* (New York, 1887) and Sidney Marshall's *The King of Kôr* (Washington, D.C., 1908).

51. Paul Raleigh/Thys Heyns Film & Television, Ltd., Johannesburg; filmed in eight one-hour episodes.

52. Similarly, H. G. Wells called the works of his we now recognize as science fiction "scientific romances."

53. For example, Frank N. Magill, ed., *Survey of Science Fiction*, vol. 4:1908–1911 (Englewood Cliffs, N.J., 1979), rates Haggard as a "profound influence." Brian Ash's *Who's Who in Science Fiction* (London, 1976) ignores Haggard (while letting in the equally unscientific William Golding's *Lord of the Flies)*, but the *Visual Encyclopedia of Science Fiction* by the same author (London, 1977) acknowledges his influence.

54. Aldiss, *Trillion Year Spree*, 138–39.

55. Ibid., 16–17.

56. H. G. Wells, *Seven Famous Novels* (London, 1933), viii; quoted in Harry Geduld, ed., *The Definitive Time Machine* (Bloomington, Ind., 1987), 15.

57. Wallace developed the idea for the 1933 RKO film in collaboration with the co-director, M. C. Cooper.

58. Mark Rose perceptively notices that Jules Verne, who is often placed at the technological end of the spectrum among writers of science fiction, takes Professor Lidenbrook on a journey toward the center of the earth that is also a journey backward in time; see Rose, *Alien Encounters: Anatomy of Science Fiction* (Cambridge, Mass., 1981), 199.

59. The most salient examples are the stories of H. P. Lovecraft.

60. John Dean, "The Uses of Wilderness in American Science Fiction," *Science Fiction Studies* 9 (1982): 68–81, looks at the way outer space has given an extended life to fictional themes of confrontation with the wilderness.

61. Henri Gougaud, *Demons et merveilles de la science fiction* (Paris, 1974), 139; my translation.

HANHART LITH.

FACSIMILE OF THE SHERD OF AMENARTAS.

ONE ½ SIZE.

Greatest length of the original 10 ½ inches.
Greatest breadth   7   inches
Weight   1 lb 5½ oz.

A HISTORY
OF
ADVENTURE

By
H. Rider Haggard

author of
"King Solomon's Mines"
"Dawn"
"The Witch's Head"
etc.

IN EARTH AND SKIE AND SEA
STRANGE THYNGES THER BE
Doggerel couplet from the Sherd of Amenartas

I INSCRIBE THIS HISTORY

TO

ANDREW LANG

IN TOKEN OF PERSONAL REGARD

AND OF

MY SINCERE ADMIRATION FOR HIS LEARNING AND HIS WORKS[1]

INTRODUCTION.

In giving to the world the record of what, looked at as an adventure only, is I suppose one of the most wonderful and mysterious experiences ever undergone by mortal men, I feel it incumbent on me to explain what my exact connection with it is. And so I may as well say at once that I am not the narrator[2] but only the editor of this extraordinary history, and then go on to tell how it found its way into my hands.

Some years ago I, the editor, was stopping with a friend, *"vir doctissimus et amicus meus,"* at a certain University, which for the purposes of this history we will call Cambridge, and was one day much struck with the appearance of two people whom I saw going arm-in-arm down the street.[3] One of these gentlemen was I think, without exception, the handsomest young fellow I have ever seen. He was very tall, very broad, and had a look of power and a grace of bearing that seemed as native to him as it is to a wild stag. In addition his face was almost without flaw—a good face as well as a beautiful one, and when he lifted his hat, which he did just then to a passing lady, I saw that his head was covered with little golden curls growing close to the scalp.

"Good gracious!" I said to my friend, with whom I was walking, "why, that fellow looks like a statue of Apollo come to life. What a splendid man he is!"

"Yes," he answered, "he is the handsomest man in the University, and one of the nicest too. They call him 'the Greek god;' but look at the other one, he's Vincey's (that's the god's name) guardian, and supposed to be full of every kind of information. They call him 'Charon.' "[4] I looked, and found the older man quite as interesting in his way as the glorified specimen of humanity at his side. He appeared to be about forty years of age, and was I think as ugly as his companion was handsome. To begin with, he was shortish, rather bow-legged, very deep chested, and with unusually long arms. He had dark hair and small eyes, and the hair grew right down on his forehead, and his whiskers grew right up to his hair, so that there was uncommonly little of his countenance to be seen. Altogether he reminded me forcibly of a gorilla, and yet there was something very pleasing and genial about the man's eye. I remember saying that I should like to know him.

"All right," answered my friend, "nothing easier. I know Vincey; I'll introduce you," and he did, and for some minutes we stood chatting—about the Zulu people, I think, for I had just returned from the Cape at the time. Presently, however, a stoutish lady, whose name I do not remember, came along the pavement, accompanied by a pretty fair-haired girl, and these two

Mr. Vincey, who clearly knew them well, at once joined, walking off in their company. I remember being rather amused because of the change in the expression of the elder man, whose name I discovered was Holly, when he saw the ladies advancing. He suddenly stopped short in his talk, cast a reproachful look at his companion, and, with an abrupt nod to myself, turned and marched off alone across the street. I heard afterwards that he was popularly supposed to be as much afraid of a woman as most people are of a mad dog, which accounted for his precipitate retreat. I cannot say, however, that young Vincey showed much aversion to feminine society on this occasion. Indeed I remember laughing, and remarking to my friend at the time that he was not the sort of man whom it would be desirable to introduce to the lady one was going to marry, since it was exceedingly probable that the acquaintance would end in a transfer of her affections.[5] He was altogether too good-looking, and, what is more, he had none of that consciousness and conceit about him which usually afflicts handsome men, and makes them deservedly disliked by their fellows.

That evening my visit came to an end, and this was the last I saw or heard of "Charon" and "the Greek god" for many a long day. Indeed, I have never seen either of them from that hour to this, and do not think it probable that I shall. But a month ago I received a letter and two packets, one of manuscript, and on opening the first found that it was signed by "Horace Holly," a name that at the moment was not familiar to me. It ran as follows:—

"——— College, Cambridge, May 1st, 18—.[6]
"MY DEAR SIR,— You will be surprised, considering the very slight nature of our acquaintance, to get a letter from me. Indeed, I think I had better begin by reminding you that we once met, now some five years ago, when I and my ward Leo Vincey were introduced to you in the street at Cambridge.[7] To be brief and come to my business. I have recently read with much interest a book of yours describing a Central African adventure.[8] I take it that this book is partly true, and partly an effort of the imagination. However this may be, it has given me an idea. It happens, how you will see in the accompanying manuscript (which together with the Scarab, the 'Royal Son of the Sun,' and the original sherd, I am sending to you by hand), that my ward, or rather my adopted son, Leo Vincey and myself have recently passed through a real African adventure, of a nature so much more marvellous than the one which you describe, that to tell the truth I am almost ashamed to submit it to you lest you should disbelieve my tale. You will see it stated in this manuscript that I, or rather we, had made up our minds not to make this history public during our joint lives. Nor should we alter our determination were it not for a circumstance which has recently arisen. We are, for reasons that, after perusal of this manuscript, you may be able to guess, going away again this time to Central Asia where, if anywhere upon this earth, wisdom is to be found, and we anticipate that our sojourn

there will be a long one.[9] Possibly we shall not return. Under these altered conditions it has become a question whether we are justified in withholding from the world an account of a phenomenon which we believe to be of unparalleled interest, merely because our private life is involved, or because we are afraid of ridicule and doubt being cast upon our statements. I hold one view about this matter, and Leo holds another, and finally, after much discussion, we have come to a compromise, namely, to send the history to you, giving you full leave to publish it if you think fit, the only stipulation being that you shall disguise our real names, and as much concerning our personal identity as is consistent with the maintenance of the *bona fides* of the narrative.[10]

"And now what am I to say further? I really do not know beyond once more repeating that everything is described in the accompanying manuscript exactly as it happened. As regards *She* herself I have nothing to add. Day by day we have greater occasion to regret that we did not better avail ourselves of our opportunities to obtain more information from that marvellous woman.[11] Who was she? How did she first come to the Caves of Kôr, and what was her real religion? We never ascertained, and now, alas! we never shall, at least not yet. These and many other questions arise in my mind, but what is the good of asking them now?

"Will you undertake the task? We give you complete freedom, and as a reward you will, we believe, have the credit of presenting to the world the most wonderful history, as distinguished from romance, that its records can show. Read the manuscript (which I have copied out fairly for your benefit), and let me know.

"Believe me, very truly yours,
L. Horace Holly"*[12]

"P.S.—Of course, if any profit results from the sale of the writing should you care to undertake its publication, you can do what you like with it, but if there is a loss I will leave instructions with my lawyers, Messrs. Geoffrey and Jordan, to meet it. We entrust the sherd, the scarab, and the parchments to your keeping till such time as we demand them back again."[13]—L.H.H.

This letter, as may be imagined, astonished me considerably, but when I came to look at the MS., which the pressure of other work prevented me from doing for a fortnight, I was still more astonished, as I think the reader will be also, and at once made up my mind to press on with the matter. I wrote to this effect to Mr. Holly, but a week afterwards received a letter from that gentleman's lawyers, returning my own, with the information that their client and Mr. Leo Vincey had already left this country for Thibet,[14] and they did not at present know their address.

Well, that is all I have to say. Of the history itself the reader must judge. I give it him, with the exception of a very few alterations, made with the

---

*This name is varied throughout in accordance with the writer's request—EDITOR.

object of concealing the identity of the actors from the general public, exactly as it has come to me. Personally I have made up my mind to refrain from comments.[15] At first I was inclined to believe that this history of a woman on whom, clothed in the majesty of her almost endless years, the shadow of Eternity itself lay like the dark wing of Night, was some gigantic allegory of which I could not catch the meaning. Then I thought that it might be a bold attempt to portray the possible results of practical immortality, informing the substance of a mortal who yet drew her strength from Earth, and in whose human bosom passions yet rose and fell and beat as in the undying world around her the winds and the tides rise and fall and beat unceasingly. But as I went on I abandoned that idea also. To me the story seems to bear the stamp of truth upon its face. Its explanation I must leave to others, and with this slight preface, which circumstances make necessary, I introduce the world to Ayesha and the Caves of Kôr.—THE EDITOR.

P.S.—There is on consideration one circumstance that, after a reperusal of this history, struck me with so much force that I cannot resist calling the attention of the reader to it. He will observe that so far as we are made acquainted with him there appears to be nothing in the character of Leo Vincey which in the opinion of most people would have been likely to attract an intellect so powerful as that of Ayesha. He is not even, at any rate to my view, particularly interesting. Indeed, one might have imagined that Mr. Holly would under ordinary circumstances have easily outstripped him in the favour of *She*. Can it be that extremes meet, and that the very excess and splendour of her mind led her by means of some strange physical reaction to worship at the shrine of matter? Was that ancient Kallikrates nothing but a splendid animal beloved for his hereditary Greek beauty? Or is the true explanation what I believe it to be, namely,—that Ayesha, seeing further than we can see, perceived the germ and smouldering spark of greatness which lay hid within her lover's soul, and well knew that under the influence of her gift of life, watered by her wisdom, and shone upon with the sunshine of her presence, it would bloom like a flower and flash out like a star, filling the world with light and fragrance?

Here also I am not able to answer, but must leave the reader to form his own judgment on the facts before him, as detailed by Mr. Holly in the following pages.

I.

My Visitor.

There are some events of which each circumstance and surrounding detail seems to be graven on the memory in such fashion that we cannot forget it, and so it is with the scene that I am about to describe. It rises as clearly before my mind at this moment as though it had happened yesterday.[1]

It was in this very month something over twenty years ago that I, Ludwig Horace Holly, was sitting one night in my rooms at Cambridge, grinding away at some mathematical work, I forget what. I was to go up for my fellowship[2] within a week, and was expected by my tutor and my College generally to distinguish myself. At last, wearied out, I flung my book down, and, going to the mantelpiece, took down a pipe and filled it. There was a candle burning on the mantelpiece, and a long, narrow glass at the back of it; and as I was in the act of lighting the pipe I caught sight of my own countenance in the glass, and paused to reflect. The lighted match burnt away till it scorched my fingers, forcing me to drop it; but still I stood and stared at myself in the glass, and reflected.[3]

"Well," I said aloud, at last, "it is to be hoped that I shall be able to do something with the inside of my head, for I shall certainly never do anything by the help of the outside."

This remark will doubtless strike anybody who reads it as being slightly obscure, but I was in reality alluding to my physical deficiencies. Most men of twenty-two are endowed, at any rate with some share of the comeliness of youth, but to me even this was denied. Short,[4] thick-set, and deep-chested almost to deformity, with long, sinewy arms, heavy features, deep-set grey eyes, a low brow half overgrown with a mop of thick black hair, like a deserted clearing on which the forest had once more begun to encroach; such was my appearance nearly a quarter of a century ago, and such, with some modification, is it to this day. Like Cain, I was branded—branded by Nature with the stamp of abnormal ugliness, as I was gifted by Nature with iron and abnormal strength and considerable intellectual powers.[5] So ugly was I that the spruce young men of my College, though they were proud enough of my feats of endurance and physical prowess, did not even care to be seen walking with me. Was it wonderful that I was misanthropic and sullen? Was it wonderful that I brooded and worked alone, and had no friends—at least, only one? I was set apart by Nature to live alone, and draw comfort from her breast, and hers only. Women hated the sight of me. Only a week before I had heard one call me a "monster" when she thought I was out of hearing, and say that I converted her to the monkey theory.[6] Once, indeed, a woman pretended to care for me, and I lavished all the pent-up affection of my nature upon her. Then money that was to have come to me went elsewhere, and she discarded me. I pleaded with her as I have never pleaded with any living creature before or since, for I was caught by her sweet face, and loved her; and in the end by way of answer she took me to the glass, and stood side by side with me, and looked into it.

"Now," she said, "if I am Beauty, who are you?"[7] That was when I was only twenty.

And so I stood and stared, and felt a sort of grim satisfaction in the sense of my own loneliness; for I had neither father, nor mother, nor brother; and as I did so there came a knock at my door.

I listened before I went to open it, for it was nearly twelve o'clock at night, and I was in no mood to admit any stranger. I had but one friend in the College, or, indeed, in the world—perhaps it was he.

Just then the person outside the door coughed, and I hastened to open it, for I knew the cough.

A tall man of about thirty, with the remains of great personal beauty, came hurrying in, staggering beneath the weight of a massive iron box which he carried by a handle with his right hand. He placed the box upon the table, and then fell into an awful fit of coughing. He coughed and coughed till his face became quite purple, and at last he sank into a chair and began to spit up blood. I poured out some whisky into a tumbler, and gave it to him. He drank it, and seemed better; though his better was very bad indeed.

"Why did you keep me standing there in the cold?" he asked pettishly. "You know the draughts are death to me."

"I did not know who it was," I answered. "You are a late visitor."

"Yes; and I verily believe it is my last visit," he answered, with a ghastly attempt at a smile. "I am done for, Holly. I am done for. I do not believe that I shall see to-morrow!"

"Nonsense!" I said. "Let me go for a doctor."

He waved me back imperiously with his hand. "It is sober sense; but I want no doctors. I have studied medicine and I know all about it. No doctors can help me. My last hour has come! For a year past I have only lived by a miracle. Now listen to me as you never listened to anybody before; for you will not have the opportunity of getting me to repeat my words. We have been friends for two years; now tell me how much do you know about me?"

"I know that you are rich, and have had a fancy to come to College long after the age that most men leave it. I know that you have been married, and that your wife died; and that you have been the best, indeed almost the only, friend I ever had."

"Did you know that I have a son?"

"No."

"I have. He is five years old. He cost me his mother's life, and I have never been able to bear to look upon his face in consequence. Holly, if you will accept the trust, I am going to leave you that boy's sole guardian."

I sprang almost out of my chair. "*Me!*" I said.

"Yes, you. I have not studied you for two years for nothing. I have known for some time that I could not last, and since I realised the fact, I have been searching for some one to whom I could confide the boy and this," and he tapped the iron box. "You are the man, Holly; for, like a rugged tree, you are hard and sound at core. Listen; the boy will be the only representative of one of the most ancient families in the world, that is, so far as families can be traced. You will laugh at me when I say it, but one day it will be proved to you beyond a doubt, that my sixty-fifth or sixty-sixth lineal ancestor, was an Egyptian priest of Isis, though he was himself of Grecian extraction, and was called Kallikrates.* His father was one of the Greek mercenaries raised by Hak-Hor, a Mendesian Prince of the twenty-ninth dynasty, and his grandfather or great-grandfather, I believe, was that very Kallikrates mentioned by Herodotus.** In or about the year 339 before Christ, just at the time of the final fall of the Pharaohs, this Kallikrates (the priest) broke his vows of celibacy and fled from Egypt with a Princess of Royal blood who had fallen in love with him, and was finally wrecked upon the coast of Africa, somewhere, as I believe, in the neighbourhood of where Delagoa Bay now is, or rather to the north of it, he and his wife being saved, and all the remainder of their company destroyed in one way or another. Here they endured great hardships, but were at last entertained by the mighty Queen of a savage people, a white woman of peculiar loveliness, who, under circumstances which I cannot enter into, but which you will one day learn, if you live, from the contents of the box, finally murdered my ancestor Kallikrates. His wife, however, escaped, how, I know not, to Athens, bearing a child with her, whom she named Tisisthenes, or the Mighty Avenger. Five hundred years or more afterwards the family migrated to Rome under circumstances of which no trace remains, and here, probably with the idea of preserving the idea of vengeance which we find set out in the name of Tisisthenes, they appear to have pretty regularly assumed the cognomen of Vindex, or Avenger. Here, too, they remained for another five centuries or more, till

*The Strong and Beautiful, or, more accurately, the Beautiful in Strength!

**The Kallikrates here referred to by my friend was a Spartan, spoken of by Herodotus (Herod. ix. 72) as being remarkable for his beauty. He fell at the glorious battle of Platæa (September 22, B.C. 479), when the Lacedæmonians and Athenians under Pausanias routed the Persians, putting nearly 300,000 of them to the sword. The following is a translation of the passage, "For Kallikrates died out of the battle, he came to the army the most beautiful man of the Greeks of that day—not only of the Lacedæmonians themselves, but of the other Greeks also. He when Pausanias was sacrificing was wounded in the side by an arrow; and then they fought, but on being carried off he regretted his death, and said to Arimnestus, a Platæan, that he did not grieve at dying for Greece, but at not having struck a blow, or, although he desired so to do, performed any deed worthy of himself." This Kallikrates, who appears to have been as brave as he was beautiful, is subsequently mentioned by Herodotus as having been buried among the ἰρέϑεσ (young commanders), apart from the other Spartans and the Helots.—L.H.H.[8]

about 770 A.D., when Charlemagne invaded Lombardy, where they were then settled, whereon the head of the family seems to have attached himself to the great Emperor, and to have returned with him across the Alps, and finally to have settled in Brittany. Eight generations later his lineal representative crossed to England in the reign of Edward the Confessor, and in the time of William the Conqueror was advanced to great honour and power.[9] From that time till the present day I can trace my descent without a break. Not that the Vinceys—for that was the final corruption of the name after its bearers took root in English soil—have been particularly distinguished —they never came much to the fore. Sometimes they were soldiers, sometimes merchants, but on the whole they have preserved a dead level of respectability, and a still deader level of mediocrity. From the time of Charles II. till the beginning of the present century they were merchants. About 1790 my grandfather made a considerable fortune out of brewing, and retired. In 1821 he died, and my father succeeded him, and dissipated most of the money. Ten years ago he died also, leaving me a net income of about two thousand a year. Then it was that I undertook an expedition in connection with *that*," and he pointed to the iron chest, "which ended disastrously enough. On my way back I travelled in the South of Europe, and finally reached Athens. There I met my beloved wife, who might well also have been called the 'Beautiful,' like my old Greek ancestor. There I married her, and there, a year afterwards, when my boy was born, she died."

He paused a while, his head sunk upon his hand, and then continued—

"My marriage had diverted me from a project which I cannot enter into now. I have no time, Holly—I have no time! One day, if you accept my trust, you will learn all about it. After my wife's death I turned my mind to it again. But first it was necessary, or, at least, I conceived that it was necessary, that I should attain to a perfect knowledge of Eastern dialects, especially Arabic. It was to facilitate my studies that I came here. Very soon, however, my disease developed itself, and now there is an end of me." And as though to emphasise his words he burst into another terrible fit of coughing.

I gave him some more whisky, and after resting he went on—

"I have never seen my boy, Leo, since he was a tiny baby. I never could bear to see him, but they tell me that he is a quick and handsome child. In this envelope," and he produced a letter from his pocket addressed to myself, "I have jotted down the course I wish followed in the boy's education. It is a somewhat peculiar one. At any rate, I could not entrust it to a stranger. Once more, will you undertake it?"

"I must first know what I am to undertake," I answered.

"You are to undertake to have the boy, Leo, to live with you till he is twenty-five years of age—not to send him to school, remember. On his twenty-fifth birthday your guardianship will end, and you will then, with the keys that I give you now" (and he placed them on the table) "open the iron box, and let him see and read the contents, and say whether or no he is willing to undertake the quest. There is no obligation on him to do so. Now, as regards terms. My present income is two thousand two hundred a year. Half of that income I have secured to you by will for life, contingently on your undertaking the guardianship—that is, one thousand a year remuneration to yourself, for you will have to give up your life to it, and one hundred a year to pay for the board of the boy. The rest is to accumulate till Leo is twenty-five, so that there may be a sum in hand should he wish to undertake the quest of which I spoke."

"And suppose I were to die?" I asked.

"Then the boy must become a ward of Chancery and take his chance. Only be careful that the iron chest is passed on to him by your will. Listen, Holly, don't refuse me. Believe me, this is to your advantage. You are not fit to mix with the world—it would only embitter you. In a few weeks you will become a Fellow of your College, and the income that you will derive from that combined with what I have left you will enable you to live a life of learned leisure, alternated with the sport of which you are so fond, such as will exactly suit you."

He paused, and looked at me anxiously, but I still hesitated. The charge seemed so very strange.

"For my sake, Holly. We have been good friends, and I have no time to make other arrangements."

"Very well," I said, "I will do it, provided there is nothing in this paper to make me change my mind," and I touched the envelope he had put upon the table by the keys.

"Thank you, Holly, thank you. There is nothing at all. Swear to me by God that you will be a father to the boy, and follow my directions to the letter."

"I swear it," I answered solemnly.

"Very well, remember that perhaps one day I shall ask for the account of your oath, for though I am dead and forgotten, yet shall I live. There is no such thing as death, Holly, only a change, and, as you may perhaps learn in time to come, I believe that even here that change could under certain circumstances be indefinitely postponed," and here again he broke into one of his dreadful fits of coughing.

"There," he said, "I must go. You have the chest, and my will will be found among my papers, under the authority of which the child will be handed over to you. You will be well paid, Holly, and I know that you are honest, but if you betray my trust, by Heaven, I will haunt you."

I said nothing, being, indeed, too bewildered to speak.

He held up the candle, and looked at his own face in the glass. It had been a beautiful face, but disease had wrecked it. "Food for the worms," he said. "Curious to think that in a few hours I shall be stiff and cold— the journey done, the little game played out. Ah me, Holly! life is not worth the trouble of life, except when one is in love—at least, mine has not been; but the boy Leo's may be if he has the courage and the faith. Good-bye, my friend!" and with a sudden access of tenderness he flung his arm about me and kissed me on the forehead, and then turned to go.

"Look here, Vincey," I said, "if you are as ill as you think, you had better let me fetch a doctor."

"No, no," he said, earnestly. "Promise me that you won't. I am going to die, and, like a poisoned rat, I wish to die alone."

"I don't believe that you are going to do anything of the sort," I answered. He smiled, and with the word "Remember" on his lips, was gone. As for myself, I sat down and rubbed my eyes, wondering if I had been asleep. As this supposition would not bear investigation I gave it up, and began to think that Vincey must have been drinking. I knew that he was, and had been, very ill, but still it seemed impossible that he could be in such a condition as to be able to know for certain that he would not outlive the night. Had he been so near dissolution surely he would scarcely have been able to walk, and carry a heavy iron box with him. The whole story, on reflection, seemed to me utterly incredible, for I was not then old enough to be aware how many things happen in this world that the common sense of the average man would set down as so improbable as to be absolutely impossible. This is a fact that I have only recently mastered. Was it likely that a man would have a son five years of age whom he had never seen since he was a tiny infant? No. Was it likely that he could foretell his own death so accurately? No. Was it likely that he could trace his pedigree for more than three centuries before Christ, or that he would suddenly confide the absolute guardianship of his child, and leave half his fortune, to a college friend? Most certainly not. Clearly Vincey was either drunk or mad. That being so, what did it mean? and what was in the sealed iron chest?

The whole thing baffled and puzzled me to such an extent that at last I could stand it no longer, and determined to sleep over it. So I jumped up, and having put the keys and the letter that Vincey had left away into my despatch-box and stowed the iron chest in a large portmanteau, I turned in, and was soon fast asleep.

As it seemed to me, I had only been asleep for a few minutes when I was awakened by somebody calling me. I sat up and rubbed my eyes; it was broad daylight—eight o'clock in fact.

"Why, what is the matter with you, John?" I asked of the gyp[10] who waited on Vincey and myself. "You look as though you had seen a ghost!"

"Yes, sir, and so I have," he answered; "leastways I've seen a corpse, which is worse. I've been in to call Mr. Vincey, as usual, and there he lies stark and dead!"

II.

The Years Roll By.

As might be expected, poor Vincey's sudden death created a great stir in the College; but, as he was known to be very ill, and a satisfactory doctor's certificate was forthcoming, there was no inquest. They were not so particular about inquests in those days as they are now; indeed, they were generally disliked, because of the scandal.[1] Under all these circumstances, being asked no questions, I did not feel called upon to volunteer any information about our interview on the night of Vincey's decease, beyond saying that he had come into my rooms to see me, as he often did. On the day of the funeral a lawyer came down from London and followed my poor friend's remains to the grave, and then went back with his papers and effects, except, of course, the iron chest which had been left in my keeping. For a week after this I heard no more of the matter, and, indeed, my attention was amply occupied in other ways, for I was up for my Fellowship, a fact that had prevented me from attending the funeral or seeing the lawyer. At last, however, the examination was over, and I came back to my rooms and sank into an easy chair with a happy consciousness that I had got through it very fairly.

Soon, however, my thoughts, relieved of the pressure that had crushed them into a single groove during the last few days, turned to the events of the night of poor Vincey's death, and again I asked myself what it all meant, and wondered if I should hear anything more of the matter, and if I did not, what it would be my duty to do with the curious iron chest. I sat there and thought and thought till I began to grow quite disturbed over the whole occurrence: the mysterious midnight visit, the prophecy of death so shortly to be fulfilled, the solemn oath that I had taken, and which Vincey had called on me to answer to in another world than this. Had the man committed suicide? It looked like it. And what was the quest of which he spoke? The circumstances were uncanny, so much so that, though I am by no means nervous, or apt to be alarmed at anything that may seem to cross the bounds of the natural, I grew afraid, and began to wish I had had nothing to do with them. How much more do I wish it now, over twenty years afterwards!

As I sat and thought, there came a knock at the door, and a letter, in a big blue envelope, was brought in to me. I saw at a glance that it was a lawyer's letter, and an instinct told me that it was connected with my trust. The letter, which I still have, runs thus:—

"SIR,—Our client, the late M. L. Vincey, Esq.,[2] who died on the 9th instant in———College, Cambridge, has left behind him a Will of which you will please find copy enclosed, and of which we are the executors. Under this Will you will perceive that you take a life-interest in about half of the late Mr. Vincey's property, now invested in Consols,[3] subject to your acceptance of the guardianship of his only son, Leo Vincey, at present an infant, aged five. Had we not ourselves drawn up the document in question in obedience to Mr. Vincey's clear and precise instructions, both personal and written, and had he not then assured us that he had very good reasons for what he was doing, we are bound to tell you that its provisions seem to us of so unusual a nature, that we should have felt bound to call the attention of the Court of Chancery to them, in order that such steps might be taken as seemed desirable to it, either by contesting the capacity of the testator or otherwise, to safeguard the interests of the infant.[4] As it is, knowing that the testator was a gentleman of the highest intelligence and acumen, and that he has absolutely no relations living to whom he could have confided the guardianship of the child, we do not feel justified in taking this course.

"Awaiting such instructions as you please to send us as regards the delivery of the infant and the payment of the proportion of the dividends due to you,

"We remain, Sir, faithfully yours,
"Geoffrey and Jordan.

"Horace L. Holly, Esq."[5]

I put down the letter, and ran my eye through the Will, which appeared, from its utter unintelligibility, to have been drawn on the strictest legal principles. So far as I could discover, however, it exactly bore out what my friend Vincey had told me on the night of his death. So it was true after all. I must take the boy. Suddenly I remembered the letter which Vincey had left with the chest. I fetched and opened it. It only contained such directions as he had already given to me as to opening the chest on Leo's twenty-fifth birthday, and laid down the outlines of the boy's education, which was to include Greek, the higher Mathematics, and *Arabic*. At the end there was a postscript to the effect that if the boy died under the age of twenty-five, which, however, he did not believe would be the case, I was to open the chest, and act on the information I obtained if I saw fit. If I did not see fit, I was to destroy all the contents. On no account was I to pass them on to a stranger.

As this letter added nothing material to my knowledge, and certainly raised no further objection in my mind to entering on the task I had promised my dead friend to undertake, there was only one course open to me—namely, to write to Messrs. Geoffrey and Jordan, and express my acceptance of the trust, stating that I should be willing to commence my guardianship of Leo in ten days' time. This done I went to the authorities of my college, and, having told them as much of the story as I considered desirable, which was not very much, after considerable difficulty succeeded in persuading them to stretch a point, and, in the event of my having obtained a fellowship, which I was pretty certain I had done, allow me to have the child to live with me. Their consent, however, was only granted on the condition that I vacated my rooms in college and took lodgings. This I did, and with some difficulty succeeded in obtaining very good apartments quite close to the college gates. The next thing was to find a nurse. And on this point I came to a determination. I would have no woman to lord it over me about the child, and steal his affections from me. The boy was old enough to do without female assistance, so I set to work to hunt up a suitable male attendant.[6] With some difficulty I succeeded in hiring a most respectable round-faced young man, who had been a helper in a hunting-stable, but who said that he was one of a family of seventeen and well-accustomed to the ways of children, and professed himself quite willing to undertake the charge of Master Leo when he arrived. Then, having taken the iron box to town, and with my own hands deposited it at my banker's, I bought some books upon the health and management of children, and read them, first to myself, and then aloud to Job—that was the young man's name—and waited.

At length the child arrived in the charge of an elderly person, who wept bitterly at parting with him, and a beautiful boy he was. Indeed, I do not think that I ever saw such a perfect child before or since. His eyes were grey, his forehead was broad, and his face, even at that early age, clean cut as a cameo, without being pinched or thin. But perhaps his most attractive point was his hair, which was pure gold in colour and tightly curled over his shapely head. He cried a little when his nurse finally tore herself away and left him with us. Never shall I forget the scene. There he stood, with the sunlight from the window playing upon his golden curls, his fist screwed over one eye, whilst he took us in with the other. I was seated in a chair, and stretched out my hand to him to induce him to come to me, while Job, in the corner, was making a sort of clucking noise, which, arguing from his previous experience, or from the analogy of the hen, he judged would have a soothing effect, and inspire confidence in the youthful mind, and running a wooden horse of peculiar hideousness backwards and forwards in a way that was little short of inane. This went on for some minutes, and then all of a sudden the lad stretched out both his little arms and ran to me.

"I like you," he said: "you is ugly, but you is good."

Ten minutes afterwards he was eating large slices of bread and butter, with every sign of satisfaction; Job wanted to put jam on to them, but I sternly reminded him of the excellent works we had read, and forbade it.

In a very little while (for, as I expected, I got my fellowship) the boy became the favourite of the whole College—where, all orders and regulations to the contrary notwithstanding, he was continually in and out—a sort of chartered libertine, in whose favour all rules were relaxed. The offerings made at his shrine were simply without number, and I had a serious difference of opinion with one old resident Fellow, now long dead, who was usually supposed to be the crustiest man in the University, and to abhor the sight of a child. And yet I discovered, when a frequently recurring fit of sickness had forced Job to keep a strict look-out, that this unprincipled old man was in the habit of enticing the boy to his rooms, and there feeding him upon unlimited quantities of brandy-balls, and making him promise to say nothing about it. Job told him that he ought to be ashamed of himself, "at his age, too, when he might have been a grandfather if he had done what was right," by which Job understood had got married, and thence arose the row.

But I have no space to dwell upon those delightful years, around which memory still fondly hovers. One by one they went by, and as they passed we two grew dearer and yet more dear to each other. Few sons have been loved as I love Leo, and few fathers know the deep and continuous affection that Leo bears to me.

The child grew into the boy, and the boy into the young man, while one by one the remorseless years flew by, and as he grew and increased so did his beauty and the beauty of his mind grow with him. When he was about fifteen they used to call him Beauty at the College, and me they nicknamed the Beast. Beauty and the Beast was what they called us when we went out walking together, as we used to every day. Once Leo attacked a great strapping butcher's man, twice his size, because he sang it out after us, and thrashed him, too—thrashed him fairly. I walked on and pretended not to see, till the combat got too exciting, when I turned round and cheered him on to victory. It was the chaff[7] of the College at the time, but I could not help it. Then when he was a little older the undergraduates found fresh names for us. They called me Charon, and Leo the Greek god! I will pass over my own appellation with the humble remark that I was never hand-some, and did not grow more so as I grew older. As for his, there was no doubt about its fitness. Leo at twenty-one might have stood for a statue of the youthful Apollo. I never saw anybody to touch him in looks, or any-body so absolutely unconscious of them. As for his mind, he was brilliant and keen-witted, but not a scholar. He had not the dulness necessary for that result. We followed out his father's instructions as regards his education strictly enough, and on the whole the results, especially in the matters of Greek and Arabic, were satisfactory. I learnt the latter language in order to help to teach it to him, but after five years of it he knew it as well as I did—almost as well as the professor who instructed us both. I always was a great sportsman—it is my one passion—and every autumn we went away somewhere shooting or fishing, sometimes to Scotland, sometimes to Nor-way, once even to Russia. I am a good shot, but even in this he learnt to excel me.

When Leo was eighteen I moved back into my rooms, and entered him at my own College, and at twenty-one he took his degree—a respectable degree, but not a very high one.[8] Then it was that I, for the first time, told him something of his own story, and of the mystery that loomed ahead. Of course he was very curious about it, and of course I explained to him that his curiosity could not be gratified at present. After that, to pass the time away, I suggested that he should get himself called to the Bar; and this he did, reading at Cambridge, and only going up to London to eat his dinners.[9]

I had only one trouble about him, and that was that every young woman who came across him, or, if not every one, nearly so, would insist on falling in love with him. Hence arose difficulties which I need not enter into here, though they were troublesome enough at the time. On the whole, he behaved fairly well; I cannot say more than that.

And so the time went by till at last he reached his twenty-fifth birthday, at which date this strange and, in some ways, awful history really begins.

III.
The Sherd of Amenartas.[1]

On the day preceding Leo's twenty-fifth birthday we both journeyed to London, and extracted the mysterious chest from the bank where I had deposited it twenty years before. It was, I remember, brought up by the same clerk who had taken it down. He perfectly remembered having hidden it away. Had he not done so, he said, he should have had difficulty in finding it, it was so covered up with cobwebs.

In the evening we returned with our precious burden to Cambridge, and I think that we might both of us have given away all the sleep we got that night and not have been much the poorer. At daybreak Leo arrived in my room in a dressing-gown, and suggested that we should at once proceed to business. I scouted the idea as showing an unworthy curiosity. The chest had waited twenty years, I said, so it could very well continue to wait until after breakfast. Accordingly at nine—an unusually sharp nine—we breakfasted; and so occupied was I with my own thoughts that I regret to state that I put a piece of bacon into Leo's tea in mistake for a lump of sugar. Job, too, to whom the contagion of excitement had, of course, spread, managed to break the handle off my Sèvres china tea-cup, the identical one I believe that Marat had been drinking from just before he was stabbed in his bath.[2]

At last, however, breakfast was cleared away, and Job, at my request, fetched the chest, and placed it upon the table in a somewhat gingerly fashion, as though he mistrusted it. Then he prepared to leave the room.

"Stop a moment, Job," I said; "if Mr. Leo has no objection, I should prefer to have an independent witness to this business, who can be relied upon to hold his tongue unless he is asked to speak."

"Certainly, Uncle Horace," answered Leo; for I had brought him up to call me uncle—though he varied the appellation somewhat disrespectfully by calling me "old fellow," or even "my avuncular relative."

Job touched his head, not having a hat on.

"Lock the door, Job," I said, "and bring me my despatch-box."

He obeyed, and from the box I took the keys that poor Vincey, Leo's father, had given me on the night of his death. There were three of them; the largest a comparatively modern key, the second an exceedingly ancient one, and the third entirely unlike anything of the sort that we had ever seen before, being fashioned apparently from a strip of solid silver, with a bar placed across to serve as a handle, and leaving some nicks cut in the edge of the bar. It was more like a model of an antediluvian railway key than anything else.

"Now are you both ready?" I said, as people do when they are going to fire a mine.[3] There was no answer, so I took the big key, rubbed some salad oil into the wards, and after one or two bad shots, for my hands were shaking, managed to fit it, and shoot the lock.[4] Leo bent over and caught the massive lid in both his hands, and with an effort, for the hinges had rusted, forced it back. Its removal revealed another case covered with dust. This we extracted from the iron chest without any difficulty, and removed the accumulated filth of years from it with a clothes-brush.

It was, or appeared to be, of ebony, or some such close-grained black wood, and was bound in every direction with flat bands of iron. Its antiquity must have been extreme, for the dense heavy wood was in parts actually commencing to crumble from age.

"Now for it," I said, inserting the second key.

Job and Leo bent forward in breathless silence. The key turned, and I flung back the lid, and uttered an exclamation, and no wonder, for inside the ebony case was a magnificent silver casket, about twelve inches square by eight high.[5] It appeared to be of Egyptian workmanship, for the four legs were formed of Sphinxes, and the dome-shaped cover was also surmounted by a Sphinx. The casket was of course much tarnished and dinted with age, but otherwise in fairly sound condition.

I drew it out and set it on the table, and then, in the midst of the most perfect silence, I inserted the strange-looking silver key, and pressed this way and that until at last the lock yielded, and the casket stood open before us. It was filled to the brim with some brown shredded material, more like vegetable fibre than paper, the nature of which I have never been able to discover. This I carefully removed to the depth of some three inches, when I came to a letter enclosed in an ordinary modern-looking envelope, and addressed in the handwriting of my dead friend Vincey.

"To my son Leo, should he live to open this casket."

I handed the letter to Leo, who glanced at the envelope, and then put it down upon the table, making a motion to me to go on emptying the casket.

The next thing that I found was a parchment carefully rolled up. I unrolled it, and seeing that it was also in Vincey's handwriting, and headed, "Translation of the Uncial Greek Writing on the Potsherd," put it down by the letter.[6] Then followed another ancient roll of parchment, that had become yellow and crinkled with the passage of years. This I also unrolled. It was likewise a translation of the same Greek original, but into blackletter Latin, which at the first glance from the style and character appeared to me to date from somewhere about the beginning of the sixteenth century.[7] Immediately beneath this roll was something hard and heavy, wrapped up in yellow linen, and reposing upon another layer of the fibrous material. Slowly and carefully we unrolled the linen, exposing to view a very large but undoubtedly ancient potsherd of a dirty yellow colour!*[8] This potsherd had in my judgment, once been a part of an ordinary amphora[9] of medium size. For the rest, it measured ten and a half inches in length by seven in width, was about a quarter of an inch thick, and densely covered on the convex side that lay towards the bottom of the box with writing in the later uncial Greek character, faded here and there, but for the most part perfectly legible, the inscription having evidently been executed with the greatest care, and by means of a reed pen, such as the ancients often used. I must not forget to mention that in some remote age this wonderful fragment had been broken in two, and rejoined by means of cement and eight long rivets. Also there were numerous inscriptions on the inner side, but these were of the most erratic character, and had clearly been made by different hands and in many different ages, and of them, together with the writings on the parchments, I shall have to speak presently.

"Is there anything more?" asked Leo, in a kind of excited whisper.

I groped about, and produced something hard, done up in a little linen bag. Out of the bag we took first a very beautiful miniature done upon ivory, and, secondly, a small chocolate-coloured composition *scarabæus,*[10] marked thus:

symbols which, we have since ascertained, mean "Suten se Rā," which is being translated the "Royal Son of Rā or the Sun."[11] The miniature was a picture of Leo's Greek mother—a lovely, dark-eyed creature. On the back of it was written, in poor Vincey's handwriting, "My beloved wife."[12]

"That is all," I said.

_____
*_See_ Frontispiece.—EDITOR.

"Very well," answered Leo, putting down the miniature, at which he had been gazing affectionately; "and now let us read the letter," and without further ado he broke the seal, and read aloud as follows:

"MY SON LEO,—When you open this, if you ever live to do so, you will have attained to manhood, and I shall have been long enough dead to be absolutely forgotten by nearly all who knew me. Yet in reading it remember that I have been, and for anything you know may still be, and that in it, through this link of pen and paper, I stretch out my hand to you across the gulf of death, and my voice speaks to you from the silence of the grave. Though I am dead, and no memory of me remains in your mind, yet am I with you in this hour that you read. Since your birth to this day I have scarcely seen your face. Forgive me this. Your life supplanted the life of one whom I loved better than women are often loved, and the bitterness of it endureth yet. Had I lived I should in time have conquered this foolish feeling, but I am not destined to live. My sufferings, physical and mental, are more than I can bear, and when such small arrangements as I have to make for your future well-being are completed it is my intention to put a period to them. May God forgive me if I do wrong. At the best I could not live more than another year."

"So he killed himself," I exclaimed. "I thought so."

"And now," Leo went on, without replying, "enough of myself. What has to be said belongs to you who live, not to me, who am dead, and almost as much forgotten as though I had never been. Holly, my friend (to whom, if he will accept the trust, it is my intention to confide you), will have told you something of the extraordinary antiquity of your race. In the contents of this casket you will find sufficient to prove it. The strange legend that you will find inscribed by your remote ancestress upon the potsherd was communicated to me by my father on his deathbed, and took a strong hold in my imagination. When I was only nineteen years of age I determined, as, to his misfortune, did one of our ancestors about the time of Elizabeth, to investigate its truth. Into all that befell me I cannot enter now. But this I saw with my own eyes. On the coast of Africa, in a hitherto unexplored region, some distance to the north of where the Zambesi falls into the sea, there is a headland, at the extremity of which a peak towers up, shaped like the head of a negro, similar to that of which the writing speaks. I landed there, and learnt from a wandering native who had been cast out by his people because of some crime which he had committed, that far inland are great mountains, shaped like cups, and caves surrounded by measureless swamps. I learnt also that the people there speak a dialect of Arabic, and are ruled over by a *beautiful white woman* who is seldom seen by them, but who is reported to have power over all things living and dead. Two days after I had ascertained this the man died of fever contracted in crossing the swamps, and I was forced by want of provisions and by symptoms of an illness which afterwards prostrated me to take to my dhow again.

"Of the adventures that befell me after this I need not now speak. I was wrecked upon the coast of Madagascar, and rescued some months afterwards by an English ship that brought me to Aden, whence I started for England, intending to prosecute my search as soon as I had made sufficient preparations. On my way I stopped in Greece, and there, for 'Omnia vincit amor,'[13] I met your beloved mother, and married her, and there you were born and she died. Then it was that my last illness seized me, and I returned hither to die. But still I hoped against hope, and set myself to work to learn Arabic, with the intention, should I ever get better, of returning to the coast of Africa, and solving the mystery of which the tradition has lived so many centuries in our family. But I have not got better, and, so far as I am concerned, the story is at an end.

"For you, however, my son, it is not at an end, and to you I hand on these the results of my labour, together with the hereditary proofs of its origin. It is my intention to provide that they shall not be put into your hands until you have reached an age when you will be able to judge for yourself whether or no you will choose to investigate what, if it is true, must be the greatest mystery in the world, or to put it by as an idle fable, originating in the first place in a woman's disordered brain.

"I do not believe that it is a fable; I believe that if it can only be rediscovered there is a spot where the vital forces of the world visibly exist. Life exists; why therefore should not the means of preserving it indefinitely exist also? But I have no wish to prejudice your mind about the matter. Read and judge for yourself. If you are inclined to undertake the search, I have so provided that you will not lack for means. If, on the other hand, you are satisfied that the whole thing is a chimera, then, I adjure you, destroy the potsherd and the writings, and let a cause of troubling be removed from our race for ever. Perhaps that will be wisest. The unknown is generally taken to be terrible, not as the proverb would infer, from the inherent superstition of man, but because it so often *is* terrible. He who would tamper with the vast and secret forces that animate the world may well fall a victim to them. And if the end were attained, if at last you emerged from the trial ever beautiful and ever young, defying time and evil, and lifted above the natural decay of flesh and intellect, who shall say that the awesome change would prove a happy one? Choose, my son, and may the Power who rules all things, and who says 'thus far shalt thou go, and thus much shalt thou learn,' direct the choice to your own happiness and the happiness of the world, which, in the event of your success, you would one day certainly rule by the pure force of accumulated experience.—Farewell!"

Thus the letter, which was unsigned and undated, abruptly ended.

"What do you make of that, Uncle Holly?" said Leo, with a sort of gasp, as he replaced it on the table. "We have been looking for a mystery, and we certainly seem to have found one."

"What do I make of it? Why, that your poor dear father was off his head, of course," I answered, testily. "I guessed as much that night, twenty years ago, when he came into my room. You see he evidently hurried his own end, poor man. It is absolute balderdash."

"That's it, sir!" said Job solemnly. Job was a most matter-of-fact specimen of a matter-of-fact class.

"Well, let's see what the potsherd has to say, at any rate," said Leo, taking up the translation in his father's writing, and commencing to read:—

"*I, Amenartas, of the Royal House of the Pharaohs of Egypt, wife of Kallikrates* (the Beautiful in Strength),[14] *a Priest of Isis whom the gods cherish and the demons obey, being about to die, to my little son Tisisthenes* (the Mighty Avenger). *I fled with thy father from Egypt in the days of Nectanebes,** causing him through love to break the vows that he had vowed. We fled southward, across the waters, and we wandered for twice twelve moons on the coast of Libya* (Africa) *that looks towards the rising sun, where by a river is a great rock carven like the head of an Ethiopian. Four days on the water from the mouth of a mighty river were we cast away, and some were drowned and some died of sickness. But us wild men took through wastes and marshes, where the sea fowl hid the sky, bearing us ten days' journey till we came to a hollow mountain, where a great city had been and fallen, and where there are caves of which no man hath seen the end; and they brought us to the Queen of the people who place pots upon the heads of strangers, who is a magician having a knowledge of all things, and life and loveliness that does not die. And she cast eyes of love upon thy father, Kallikrates, and would have slain me, and taken him to husband, but he loved me and feared her, and would not. Then did she take us, and lead us by terrible ways, by means of dark magic, to where the great pit is, in the mouth of which the old philosopher lay dead, and showed to us the rolling Pillar of Life that dies not, whereof the voice is as the voice of thunder; and she did stand in the flames, and come forth unharmed, and yet more beautiful. Then did she swear to make thy father undying even as she is, if he would but slay me, and give himself to her, for me she could not slay because of the magic of my own people that I have, and that prevailed thus far against her. And he held his hand before his eyes to hide her beauty, and would not. Then in her rage did she smite him by her magic, and he died; but she wept over him, and bore him thence with lamentations: and being afraid, me she sent to the mouth of the great river where the ships come, and I was carried far away on the ships where I gave thee birth, and hither to Athens I came at last after many wanderings. Now I say to thee, my son, Tisisthenes, seek out the woman, and learn the secret of Life, and if thou mayest find a way slay her, because of thy father Kallikrates; and if thou dost fear or fail, this I say to all of thy seed who come after thee, till at last a brave man be found among them who shall bathe in the fire and sit in the place of the Pharaohs. I speak of those things, that though they be past belief, yet I have known, and I lie not.*"

**Nekht-nebf, or Nectanebe II., the last native Pharaoh of Egypt fled from Ochus to Ethiopia, B.C. 339.—EDITOR.

"May the Lord forgive her for that," groaned Job, who had been listening to this marvellous composition with his mouth open.

As for myself, I said nothing: my first idea being that my poor friend, being demented, had composed the whole thing, though it scarcely seemed likely that such a story could have been invented by anybody. It was too original. To solve my doubts I took up the potsherd and began to read the close uncial[15] Greek writing on it; and very good Greek of the period it is, considering that it came from the pen of an Egyptian born.[16] Here is an exact transcript of it.—

```
ΑΜΕΝΑΡΤΑΣΤΟΥΒΑΣΙΛΙΚΟΥΓΕΝΟΥΣΤΟΥΑ
ΙΓΥΓΤΙΟΥΗΤΟΥΚΑΛΛΙΚΡΑΤΟΥΣΙΣΙΔΟΣΙΕΡ
ΕΩΣΗΝΟΙΜΕΝΘΕΟΙΤΡΕΦΟΥΣΙΤΑΔΕΔΑΙΜΟ
ΝΙΑΥΓΟΤΑΣΣΕΤΑΙΗΔΗΤΕΛΕΥΤΩΣΑΤΙΣΙΣ
ΘΕΝΕΙΤΩΓΑΙΔΙΕΓΙΣΤΕΛΛΕΙΤΑΔΕΣΥΝΕΦΥΓΟ
ΝΓΑΡΓΟΤΕΕΚΤΗΣΑΙΓΥΓΤΙΑΣΕΓΙΝΕΚΤΑΝΕΒ
ΟΥΜΕΤΑΤΟΥΣΟΥΓΑΤΡΟΣΔΙΑΤΟΝΕΡΩΤΑΤΟ
ΝΕΜΟΝΕΓΙΟΡΚΗΣΑΝΤΟΣΦΥΓΟΝΤΕΣΔΕΓΡΟ
ΣΝΟΤΟΝΔΙΑΓΟΝΤΙΟΙΚΑΙΚΔΜΗΝΑΣΚΑΤΑΤΑ
ΓΑΡΑΘΑΛΑΣΣΙΑΤΗΣΛΙΒΥΗΣΤΑΓΡΟΣΗΛΙΟΥ
ΑΝΑΤΟΛΑΣΓΛΑΝΗΘΕΝΤΕΣΕΝΘΑΓΕΡΓΕΤΡΑ
ΤΙΣΜΕΓΑΛΗΓΛΥΓΤΟΝΟΜΟΙΩΜΑΑΙΘΙΟΓΟΣ
ΚΕΦΑΛΗΣΕΙΤΑΗΜΕΡΑΣΔΑΓΟΣΤΟΜΑΤΟΣΓΟ
ΤΑΜΟΥΜΕΓΑΛΟΥΕΚΓΕΣΟΝΤΕΣΟΙΜΕΝΚΑΤΕ
ΓΟΝΤΙΣΘΗΜΕΝΟΙΔΕΝΟΣΩΙΑΓΕΘΑΝΟΜΕΝΤ
ΕΛΟΣΔΕΥΓΑΓΡΙΩΝΑΝΘΡΩΓΩΝΕΦΕΡΟΜΕΘΑ
ΔΙΑΕΛΕΩΝΤΕΚΑΙΤΕΝΑΓΕΩΝΕΝΘΑΓΕΡΓΤΗΝ
ΩΝΓΛΗΘΟΣΑΓΟΚΡΥΓΤΕΙΤΟΝΟΥΡΑΝΟΝΗΜ
ΕΡΑΣΙΕΩΣΗΛΘΟΜΕΝΕΙΣΚΟΙΛΟΝΤΙΟΡΟΣΕΝ
ΘΑΓΟΤΕΜΕΓΑΛΗΜΕΝΓΟΛΙΣΗΝΑΝΤΡΑΔΕΑΓ
ΕΙΡΟΝΑΗΓΑΓΟΝΔΕΩΣΒΑΣΙΛΕΙΑΝΤΗΝΤΩΝΞ
ΕΝΟΥΣΧΥΤΡΑΙΣΣΤΕΦΑΝΟΥΝΤΩΝΗΤΙΣΜΑΓΕ
ΙΑΜΕΝΕΧΡΗΤΟΕΓΙΣΤΗΜΗΔΕΓΑΝΤΩΝΚΑΙΔ
ΗΚΑΙΚΑΛΛΟΣΚΑΙΡΩΜΗΝΑΓΗΡΩΣΗΝΗΔΕΚΑ
ΛΛΙΚΡΑΤΟΥΣΤΟΥΣΟΥΓΑΤΡΟΣΕΡΑΣΘΕΙΣΑΤ
ΟΜΕΝΓΡΩΤΟΝΣΥΝΟΙΚΕΙΝΕΒΟΥΛΕΤΟΕΜΕΔ
ΕΑΝΕΛΕΙΝΕΓΕΙΤΑΩΣΟΥΚΑΝΕΓΕΙΘΕΝΕΜΕΓΑ
ΡΥΓΕΡΕΦΙΛΕΙΚΑΙΤΗΝΞΕΝΗΝΕΦΟΒΕΙΤΟΑΓΗ
ΓΑΓΕΝΗΜΑΣΥΓΟΜΑΓΕΙΑΣΚΑΘΟΔΟΥΣΣΦΑΛ
ΕΡΑΣΕΝΘΑΤΟΒΑΡΑΘΡΟΝΤΟΜΕΓΑΟΥΚΑΤΑΣ
ΤΟΜΑΕΚΕΙΤΟΟΓΕΡΩΝΟΦΙΛΟΣΟΦΟΣΤΕΘΝΕ
ΩΣΑΦΙΚΟΜΕΝΟΙΣΔΕΔΕΙΞΕΦΩΣΤΟΥΒΙΟΥΕΥ
ΘΥΟΙΟΝΚΙΟΝΑΕΛΙΣΣΟΜΕΝΟΝΦΩΝΗΝΙΕΝΤ
ΑΚΑΘΑΓΕΡΒΡΟΝΤΗΣΕΙΤΑΔΙΑΓΥΡΟΣΒΕΒΗΚ
ΥΙΑΑΒΛΑΒΗΣΚΑΙΕΤΙΚΑΛΛΙΩΝΑΥΤΗΕΑΥΤΗΣ
ΕΞΕΦΑΝΗΕΚΔΕΤΟΥΤΩΝΩΜΟΣΕΚΑΙΤΟΝΣΟ
ΝΓΑΤΕΡΑΑΘΑΝΑΤΟΝΑΓΟΔΕΙΞΕΙΝΕΙΣΥΝΟΙΚ
```

ΕΙΝΟΙΒΟΥΛΟΙΤΟΕΜΕΔΕΑΝΕΛΕΙΝΟΥΓΑΡΟΥ
ΝΑΥΤΗΑΝΕΛΕΙΝΙΣΧΥΕΝΥΓΟΤΩΝΗΜΕΔΑΓΩ
ΝΗΝΚΑΙΑΥΤΗΕΧΩΜΑΓΕΙΑΣΟΔΟΥΔΕΝΤΙΜΑ
ΛΛΟΝΗΘΕΛΕΤΩΧΕΙΡΕΤΩΝΟΜΜΑΤΩΝΓΡΟΙ
ΣΧΩΝΙΝΑΔΗΤΟΤΗΣΓΥΝΑΙΚΟΣΚΑΛΛΟΣΜΗ
ΟΡΩΗΕΓΕΙΤΑΟΡΓΙΣΘΕΙΣΑΚΑΤΕΓΟΗΤΕΥΣΕΜ
ΕΝΑΥΤΟΝΑΓΟΛΟΜΕΝΟΝΜΕΝΤΟΙΚΛΑΟΥΣΑ
ΚΑΙΟΔΥΡΟΜΕΝΗΕΚΕΙΘΕΝΑΓΗΝΕΓΚΕΝΕΜΕΔ
ΕΦΟΒΩΙΑΦΗΚΕΝΕΙΣΣΤΟΜΑΤΟΥΜΕΓΑΛΟΥΓ
ΟΤΑΜΟΥΤΟΥΝΑΥΣΙΓΟΡΟΥΓΟΡΡΩΔΕΝΑΥΣΙ
ΝΕΦΩΝΓΕΡΓΛΕΟΥΣΑΕΤΕΚΟΝΣΕΑΓΟΓΛΕΥΣ
ΑΣΑΜΟΛΙΣΓΟΤΕΔΕΥΡΟΑΘΗΝΑΖΕΚΑΤΗΓΑΓ
ΟΜΗΝΣΥΔΕΩΤΙΣΙΣΘΕΝΕΣΩΝΕΓΙΣΤΕΛΛΩΜ
ΗΟΛΙΓΩΡΕΙΔΕΙΓΑΡΤΗΝΓΥΝΑΙΚΑΑΝΑΖΗΤΕΙ
ΝΗΝΓΩΣΤΟΤΟΥΒΙΟΥΜΥΣΤΗΡΙΟΝΑΝΕΥΡΗ
ΣΚΑΙΑΝΑΙΡΕΙΝΗΝΓΟΥΓΑΡΑΣΧΗΔΙΑΤΟΝΣΟ
ΝΓΑΤΕΡΑΚΑΛΛΙΚΡΑΤΗΝΕΙΔΕΦΟΒΟΥΜΕΝΟ
ΣΗΔΙΑΑΛΛΟΤΙΑΥΤΟΣΛΕΙΓΕΙΤΟΥΕΡΓΟΥΓΑ
ΣΙΤΟΙΣΥΣΤΕΡΟΝΑΥΤΟΤΟΥΤΟΕΓΙΣΤΕΛΛΩΕ
ΩΣΓΟΤΕΑΓΑΘΟΣΤΙΣΓΕΝΟΜΕΝΟΣΤΩΓΥΡΙΛ
ΟΥΣΑΣΘΑΙΤΟΛΜΗΣΕΙΚΑΙΤΑΑΡΙΣΤΕΙΑΕΧΩΝ
ΒΑΣΙΛΕΥΣΑΙΤΩΝΑΝΘΡΩΓΩΝΑΓΙΣΤΑΜΕΝΔ
ΗΤΑΤΟΙΑΥΤΑΛΕΓΩΟΜΩΣΔΕΑΑΥΤΗΕΓΝΩΚ
ΑΟΥΚΕΨΕΥΣΑΜΗΝ

For general convenience in reading, I have here accurately transcribed this inscription into the cursive character.

Ἀμενάρτας, τοῦ βασιλικοῦ γένους τοῦ Αἰγυπτίου, ἡ τοῦ Καλλικράτους Ἴσιδος ἱερέως, ἣν οἱ μὲν θεοὶ τρέφουσι τὰ δὲ δαιμόνια ὑποτάσσεται, ἤδη τελευτῶσα Τισισθένει τῷ παιδὶ ἐπιστέλλει τάδε· συνέφυγον γάρ ποτε ἐκ τῆς Αἰγυπτίας ἐπὶ Νεκτανέβου μετὰ τοῦ σοῦ πατρός, διὰ τὸν ἔρωτα τὸν ἐμὸν ἐπιορκήσαντος. φυγόντες δὲ πρὸς νότον διαπόντιοι καὶ κ'δ' μῆνας κατὰ τὰ παραθαλάσσια τῆς Λιβύης τὰ πρὸς ἡλίου ἀνατολὰς πλανηθέντες, ἔνθαπερ πέτρα τις μεγάλη, γλυπτὸν ὁμοίωμα Αἰθίοπος κεφαλῆς, εἶτα ἡμέρας δ' ἀπὸ στόματος ποταμοῦ μεγάλου ἐκπεσόντες, οἱ μὲν κατεποντίσθημεν, οἱ δὲ νόσῳ ἀπεθάνομεν· τέλος δὲ ὑπ' ἀγρίων ἀνθρώπων ἐφερόμεθα διὰ ἑλέων τε καὶ

τεναγέων ἔνθαπερ πτηνῶν πλῆθος ἀποκρύπτει τὸν
οὐρανόν, ἡμέρας ἱ, ἕως ἤλθομεν εἰς κοῖλόν τι ὄρος, ἔνθα
ποτὲ μεγάλη μὲν πόλις ἦν, ἄντρα δὲ ἀπείρονα· ἤγαγον
δὲ ὡς βασίλειαν τὴν τῶν ξένους χύτραις στεφανούντων,
ἥτις μαγείᾳ μὲν ἐχρῆτο ἐπιστήμῃ δὲ πάντων καὶ δὴ καὶ
κάλλος καὶ ῥώμην ἀγήρως ἦν· ἡ δὲ Καλλικράτους
τοῦ σοῦ πατρὸς ἐρασθεῖσα τὸ μὲν πρῶτον συνοικεῖν
ἐβούλετο ἐμὲ δὲ ἀνελεῖν· ἔπειτα, ὡς οὐκ ἀνέπειθεν,
ἐμὲ γὰρ ὑπερεφίλει καὶ τὴν ξένην ἐφοβεῖτο, ἀπήγαγεν
ἡμᾶς ὑπὸ μαγείας καθ’ ὁδοὺς σφαλερὰς ἔνθα τὸ βά-
ραθρον τὸ μέγα, οὗ κατὰ στόμα ἔκειτο ὁ γέρων ὁ
φιλόσοφος τεθνεώς, ἀφικομένοις δ’ ἔδειξε φῶς τοῦ
βίου εὐθύ, οἷον κίονα ἐλισσόμενον φώνην ἱέντα καθάπερ
βροντῆς, εἶτα διὰ πυρὸς βεβηκυῖα ἀβλαβὴς καὶ ἔτι
καλλίων αὐτὴ ἑαυτῆς ἐξεφάνη. ἐκ δὲ τούτων ὤμοσε
καὶ τὸν σὸν πατέρα ἀθάνατον ἀποδείξειν, εἰ συνοικεῖν
οἱ βούλοιτο ἐμὲ δε ἀνελεῖν, οὐ γὰρ οὖν αὐτὴ ἀνελεῖν
ἴσχυεν ὑπὸ τῶν ἡμεδαπῶν ἦν καὶ αὐτὴ ἔχω μαγείας.
ὁ δ’ οὐδέν τι μᾶλλον ἤθελε, τὼ χεῖρε τῶν ὀμμάτων
προΐσχων ἵνα δὴ τὸ τῆς γυναικὸς κάλλος μὴ ὁρῴη·
ἔπειτα ὀργισθεῖσα κατεγοήτευσε μὲν αὐτόν, ἀπολόμενον
μέντοι κλάουσα καὶ ὀδυρομένη ἐκεῖθεν ἀπήνεγκεν, ἐμὲ
δὲ φόβῳ ἀφῆκεν εἰς στόμα τοῦ μεγάλου ποταμοῦ
τοῦ ναυσιπόρου, πόρρω δὲ ναυσίν, ἐφ’ ὦνπερ πλέουσα
ἔτεκόν σε, ἀποπλεύσασα μόλις ποτὲ δεῦρο Ἀθηνάζε
κατηγαγόμην. σὺ δέ, ὦ Τισίσθενες, ὦν ἐπιστέλλω μὴ
ὀλιγώρει· δεῖ γὰρ τὴν γυναῖκα ἀναζητεῖν ἥν πως τὸ τοῦ
βίου μυστήριον ἀνεύρῃς, καὶ ἀναιρεῖν, ἥν που παρασχῇ,
διὰ τὸν σὸν πατέρα Καλλικράτην. εἰ δὲ φοβούμενος
ἢ διὰ ἄλλο τι αὐτὸς λείπει τοῦ ἔργου, πᾶσι τοῖς
ὕστερον αὐτὸ τοῦτο ἐπιστέλλω, ἕως ποτὲ ἀγαθός τις
γενόμενος τῷ πυρὶ λούσασθαι τολμήσει καὶ τὰ ἀριστεῖα
ἔχων βασιλεῦσαι τῶν ἀνθρώπων· ἄπιστα μὲν δὴ τὰ
τοιαῦτα λέγω, ὅμως δὲ ἃ αὐτὴ ἔγνωκα οὐκ ἐψευσάμην.

The English translation was, as I discovered on further investigation, and as the reader may easily see by comparison, both accurate and elegant. Besides the uncial writing on the convex side of the sherd at the top, painted in dull red, on what had once been the lip of the amphora, was the cartouche already mentioned[17] as being on the *scarabæus*, which we had also found in the casket. The hieroglyphics or symbols, however, were reversed, just as though they had been pressed on wax. Whether this was a cartouche of the original Kallikrates,*** or of some Prince or Pharaoh from whom his wife Amenartas was descended, I am not sure, nor can I tell if it was drawn upon the sherd at the same time that the uncial Greek was inscribed, or copied on more recently from the Scarab by some other member of the family. Nor was this all. At the foot of the writing, painted in the same dull red, was the faint outline of a somewhat rude drawing of the head and shoulders of a Sphinx wearing two feathers, symbols of majesty, which, though common enough upon the effigies of sacred bulls and gods, I have never before met with on a Sphinx.

Also on the right-hand side of this surface of the sherd, painted obliquely in red on the space not covered by the uncial characters, and signed in blue paint, was the following quaint inscription:—

> IN EARTH AND SKIE AND SEA
> STRANGE THYNGES THER BE.
> HOC FECIT
> DOROTHEA VINCEY.

Perfectly bewildered, I turned the relic over. It was covered from top to bottom with notes and signatures in Greek, Latin, and English. The first in uncial Greek was by Tisisthenes, the son to whom the writing was addressed. It was, "I could not go. Tisisthenes to his son Kallikrates." Here it is in fac-simile with its cursive equivalent:—

ΟΥΚΑΝΔΥΝΑΙΜΗΝΓΟΡΕΥΕCΘΑΙΤΙCΙCΘΕΝΗ
CΚΑΛΛΙΚΡΑΤΕΙΤΩΙΓΑΙΔΙ

οὐκ ἂν δυναίμην πορεύεσθαι.
Τισισθένης Καλλικράτει τῷ παιδί.

This Kallikrates (probably, in the Greek fashion, so named after his grandfather) evidently made some attempt to start on the quest, for his entry written in very faint and almost illegible uncial is, "I ceased from my going, the gods being against me. Kallikrates to his son." Here it is also:—

***The cartouche, if it be a true cartouche, cannot have been that of Kallikrates, as Mr. Holly suggests. Kallikrates was a priest and not entitled to a cartouche, which was the prerogative of Egyptian royalty, though he might have inscribed his name or title upon an *oval*.—EDITOR

ΤΩΝΘΕΩΝΑΝΤΙΣΤΑΝΤΩΝΕΓΑΥΣΑΜΗΝΤΗΣ
ΓΟΡΕΙΑΣΚΑΛΛΙΚΡΑΤΗΣΤΩΙΓΑΙΔΙ

τῶν θεῶν ἀντιστάντων ἐπαυσάμην τῆς πορείας.
Καλλικράτης τῷ παιδί.

Between[18] these two ancient writings, the second of which was inscribed upside down and was so faint and worn that, had it not been for the transcript of it executed by Vincey, I should scarcely have been able to read it, since, owing to its having been written on that portion of the tile which had, in the course of ages, undergone the most handling, it was nearly rubbed out— was the bold, modern-looking signature of one Lionel Vincey, "Ætate sua 17," which was written thereon, I think, by Leo's grandfather. To the right of this were the initials "J. B. V.," and below came a variety of Greek signatures, in uncial and cursive character, and what appeared to be some carelessly executed repetitions of the sentence "τῷ παιδι" (to my son), showing that the relic was religiously passed on from generation to generation.

The next legible thing after the Greek signatures was the word "ROMAE, A.U.C.," showing that the family had now migrated to Rome. Unfortunately, however, with the exception of its termination (cvi) the date of their settlement there is for ever lost, for just where it had been placed a piece of the potsherd is broken away.

Then followed twelve Latin signatures, jotted about here and there, wherever there was a space upon the tile suitable to their inscription. These signatures, with three exceptions only, ended with the name "Vindex" or "the Avenger," which seems to have been adopted by the family after its migration to Rome as a kind of equivalent to the Grecian "Tisisthenes," which also means an avenger. Ultimately, as might be expected, this Latin cognomen of Vindex was transformed first into De Vincey and then into the plain modern Vincey.[19] It is very curious to observe how the idea of revenge, inspired by an Egyptian who lived before the time of Christ, is thus, as it were, embalmed in an English family name.

A few of the Roman names inscribed upon the sherd I have actually since found mentioned in history and other records. They were, if I remember right,

MVSSIVS. VINDEX
SEX. VARIS. MARVLLVS.
C. FVFIDIVS. C.F. VINDEX.

and

LABERIA POMPEIANA. CONIVX. MACRINI. VINDICIS.

the last being, of course, the name of a Roman lady.

The following list, however, comprises all the Latin names upon the sherd:—

C. CAECILIVS VINDEX
M. AIMILIVS VINDEX
SEX. VARIVS. MARVLLVS
Q. SOSIVS PRISCVS SENECIO VINDEX
L VALERIVS COMINIVS VINDEX
SEX. OTACILIVS. M.F.
L. ATTIVS VINDEX
MVSSIVS VINDEX
C. FVFIDIVS. C.F. VINDEX
LICINIVS FAVSTVS
LABERIA POMPEIANA CONIVX MACRINI VINDICIS
MANILIA LVCILLA CONIVX MARVLLI VINDICIS

After the Roman names there is evidently a gap of very many centuries. Nobody will ever know now what was the history of the relic during those dark ages, or how it came to have been preserved in the family. My poor friend Vincey had, it will be remembered, told me that his Roman ancestors finally settled in Lombardy, and when Charlemagne invaded it, returned with him across the Alps, and made their home in Brittany, whence they crossed to England in the reign of Edward the Confessor. How he knew this I am not aware, for there is no reference to Lombardy or Charlemagne upon the tile, though, as will presently be seen, there is a reference to Brittany. To continue: the next entries on the sherd, if I may except a long splash either of blood or red colouring matter of some sort, consist of two crosses drawn in red pigment, and probably representing Crusaders' swords, and a rather neat monogram ("D.V.") in scarlet and blue, perhaps executed by that same Dorothea Vincey who wrote, or rather painted, the doggerel couplet. To the left of this, inscribed in faint blue, were the initials A. V., and after them a date, 1800.

Then came what was perhaps as curious an entry as anything upon this extraordinary relic of the past. It is executed in black letter, written over the crosses or Crusaders' swords, and dated fourteen hundred and forty-five. As the best plan will be to allow it to speak for itself, I here give the black letter facsimile, together with the original Latin without the contractions, from which it will be seen that the writer was a fair mediæval Latinist. Also we discovered what is still more curious, an English version of the black-letter Latin. This, also written in black-letter, we found inscribed on a second parchment that was in the coffer, apparently somewhat older in date than that on which was inscribed the mediæval Latin translation of the uncial Greek of which I shall speak presently. This I also give in full.

Fac-simile of Black-Letter Inscription on the Sherd of Amenartas.

Ista reliqia est valde misticū et myrificū
opꝰ ꝙd maiores mei ex Armorica ſſ
Brittania mīore secū cōvehebāt et ꝙdm scs
clericꝰ sꝑer ꝓri meo in manu ferebat ꝙd
ꝓritus illud destrueret affirmās ꝙd esset ab
ipso sathana cōſſatū prestigiosa et dyabolica
arte ꝗre ꝓter mevs cōfregit illud ī dvas ꝓtes
ꝗs ꝙdm ego Johēs de Vīceto salvas servavi et
adaptavi sicut apparet die lūe ꝓx post fest beate
Marie virg anni gͬe mccccxlv

Expanded Version of the above Black-Letter Inscription.

"ISTA reliquia est valde misticum et myrificum opus, quod majores mei ex
Armorica, scilicet Britannia Minore, secum convehebant; et quidam sanctus
clericus semper patri meo in manu ferebat quod penitus illud destrueret,
affirmans quod esset ab ipso Sathana conflatum prestigiosa et dyabolica arte,
quare pater meus confregit illud in duas partes, quas quidem ego Johannes
de Vinceto salvas servavi et adaptavi sicut apparet die lune proximo post
festum beate Marie Virginis anni gratie MCCCCXLV."

*Fac-simile of the Old English Black-Letter Translation of the above Latin Inscription
from the Sherd of Amenartas found inscribed upon a parchment.*

Thys rellike ys a ryghte mistycall worke
& a marveylous ye whyche myne aun=
ceteres afore tyme dyd conveighe hider wt ym
ffrom Armoryke whe ys to seien Britayne ye
lesse & a certayne holye clerke shoulde allweyes
beare my ffadir on honde yt he owghte vttirly
ffor to ffrusshe ye same affirmynge yt yt was
ffourmyd & confflatyd off sathanas hym selffe
by arte magike & dyvellysshe wherefore my

ffaðir ðyð take yᵉ ſame & to braſt yt yn tweyne
but J Joħn ðe Uincey ðyð ſave wħool yᵉ tweye
ꝑtes tħerof & topeecyð yᵐ togyðer agayne ſoe
as yee ſe on yˢ ðeye monðaye nert ffolowynge
after yᵉ ffeeſte of ſeynte Ɱarye yᵉ bleſſeð
vyrgyne yn yᵉ yeere of ſalvacioun ffowertene
ħunðretħ & ffyve & ffowrti.

Modernised Version of the above Black Letter Translation.

"Thys rellike ys a ryghte mistycall worke and a marvaylous, ye whyche
myne aunceteres aforetyme dyd conveigh hider with them from Armoryke
which ys to seien Britaine ye Lesse and a certayne holye clerke should
allweyes beare my fadir on honde that he owghte uttirly for to frusshe ye
same, affyrmynge that yt was fourmed and conflatyd of Sathanas hym selfe
by arte magike and dyvellysshe wherefore my fadir dyd take the same and
tobrast yt yn tweyne, but I, John de Vincey, dyd save whool ye tweye partes
thereof and topeecyd them togydder agayne soe as yee se, on this daye
mondaye next followynge after ye feeste of Seynte Marye ye Blessed Vyrgyne
yn ye yeere of Salvacioun fowertene hundreth and fyve and fowerti."

The next and, save one, last entry was Elizabethan, and dated 1564,
"A most strange historie, and one that did cost my father his life; for in
seekynge for the place upon the east coast of Africa, his pinnance was sunk
by a Portuguese galleon off Lorenzo Marquez, and he himself perished.—
JOHN VINCEY."

Then came the last entry, apparently, to judge by the style of writing,
made by some representative of the family in the middle of the eighteenth
century. It was a misquotation of the well-known lines in Hamlet, and ran
thus: "There are more things in Heaven and earth than are dreamt of in
your philosophy, Horatio."****

And now there remained but one more document to be examined—
namely, the ancient black-letter translation into mediæval Latin of the uncial
inscription on the sherd.[20] As will be seen, this translation was executed
and subscribed in the year 1495, by a certain "learned man," Edmundus
de Prato (Edmund Pratt) by name, licæntiate in Canon Law, of Exeter Col-

---

****Another thing that makes me fix the date of this entry at the middle of the eighteenth
century is that, curiously enough, I have an acting copy of "Hamlet," written about 1740,
in which these two lines are misquoted almost exactly in the same way, and I have little doubt
but that the Vincey who wrote them on the potsherd heard them so misquoted at that date.
Of course, the lines really run:—
> There are more things in heaven and earth, Horatio,
> Than are dreamt of in your philosophy—L.H.H.

lege, Oxford, who had actually been a pupil of Grocyn, the first scholar who taught Greek in England.***** No doubt on the fame of this new learning reaching his ears, the Vincey of the day, perhaps that same John de Vincey who years before had saved the relic from destruction and made the black-letter entry on the sherd in 1445, hurried off to Oxford to see if perchance it might avail to dissolve the secret of the mysterious inscription. Nor was he disappointed, for the learned Edmundus was equal to the task. Indeed his rendering is so excellent an example of mediæval learning and latinity that, even at the risk of sating the learned reader with too many antiquities, I have made up my mind to give it in fac-simile, together with an expanded version for the benefit of those who find the contractions troublesome. The translation has several peculiarities on which this is not the place to dwell, but I would in passing call the attention of scholars to the passage "duxerunt autem nos ad reginam *advenaslasaniscoronantium*," which strikes me as a delightful rendering of the original,

'ἤγαγον δὲ ὡς βασίλειαν τὴν τῶν ξένους χύτραις στεφανούντων.'

Mediæval Black Letter Latin Translation of the Uncial Inscription on the Sherd of Amenartas.[21]

Amenartas e gen. reg. Egyptii vror Cal-licratis facerdot Jfidis qua dei fovet demonia attedvt filiol' fvo Tififtheni ia mori-būda ita mādat: Effugi quōdā er Egypto regnāte Nectanebo cū patre tvo, ꝓpter mei amorē pejerato. Fvgiētes autē v'fus Notū trans mare et rriiij mēfes p'r litora Libye v'fus Oriētē erranī vbi eft petra quedā ñgna fcvlpta inftar Ethioꝑ capif, deinde dies iiij ab oft fluñ ñgni ciecti p'tim fubmerfi fumus p'tim morbo mortui fuñ: in fine autē a fer hōībs portabamur ꝓr palvō et vada. vbi aviū m'titvdo celū obūbrat dies r. donec adveniñ ad

*****Grocyn, the instructor of Erasmus, studied Greek under Chalcondylas the Byzantine at Florence, and first lectured in the Hall of Exeter College, Oxford, in 1491.—EDITOR.

cavū quēdā montē, ubi olim m̄gna vrbs erat, caverne quoq̄ im̄ēse : dvxerūt autē nos ad reginā Aduenaꝛlasaniscoronātiū que magicē vtebatr et peritia omniū reꝝ et saltē pvlcriē et vigore īsēescibil' erat. Hec m̄gno patr̄ tui amore p̄cvlsa p'mū q'dē ei conubiū michi mortē parabat. postea v'ro recvsāte Callicrate amore mei et timore regine affecto nos p̄r magicā abduxit p'r vias horribil' vbi est puteus ille p̄fūdus, cuius iuxta aditū iacebat senioꝛ philo-sophi cadauer, et advēiētib mōstravit flamā Vite erectā, īstar columne volutātis, voces emittētē q̄si tonitrvs : tūc p̄r ignē īpetu nociuo expers trāsiit et iā ipa sese formosior visa est.

Quib fact̄ iuravit se patrē tuū quoq̄ im̄or-talē ostēsurā esse, si me prius occisa regine cōtvberniū mallet ; neq̄ enī ipsa me occidere valuit, p̄pter nostratū m̄gicā cuius egomet p̄tem habeo. Ille vero nichil huius gen̄ maluit, manib ante ocul̄ passis ne mulieꝛ formositatē adspiceret : postea eū m̄gica p̄cussit arte, at mortuū efferebat īde cū fletib et vagitib, me p̄r timorē expulit ad ostiū m̄gni flumiñ velimoli porro in nave in qua te peperi, uix post dies hvc Athenas invecta sū. At tu, O Tisisthen̄, ne q'd quorū mādo nauci fac : necesse enī est mulierē exqvirere si qva Vite mysteriū īpetres et vīdicare, quātū in te est, patrē tuū Callicrat̄ in regine morte. Sin timore seu aliq̄ cavsa rē reliquis īfectā, hoc ipsū oīb posteꝛ mādo dū bonvs q̄s inveniatur qvi ignis lauacrū nō p̄rhorrescet et p̄tentia dign̄ dōiabit hōiū.

Talia dico incredibilia q̄dē at mīīe ficta de reb michi cognitis.

Hec Grece scripta Latine reddidit vir doctus Edm̄ds de Prato, in Decretis Licenciatus e Coll. Exon: Oxon: doctissimi Grocyni quondam e pupillis, Id. Apr. A°. Dñi. MCCCCLXXXIU°.

Expanded Version of the above Mediæval Latin Translation

AMENARTAS, e genere regio Egyptii, uxor Callicratis, sacerdotis Isidis, quam dei fovent demonia attendunt, filiolo suo Tisistheni jam moribunda ita mandat: Effugi quondam ex Egypto, regnante Nectanebo, cum patre tuo, propter mei amorem pejerato. Fugientes autem versus Notum trans mare, et viginti quatuor menses per litora Libye versus Orientem errantes, ubi est petra quedam magna sculpta instar Ethiopis capitis, deinde dies quatuor ab ostio fluminis magni ejecti partim submersi sumus partim morbo mortui sumus: in fine autem a feris hominibus portabamur per paludes et vada, ubi avium multitudo celum obumbrat, dies decem, donec advenimus ad cavum quendam montem, ubi olim magna urbs erat, caverne quoque immense; duxerunt autem nos ad reginam Advenaslasaniscoronantium, que magicâ utebatur et peritiâ omnium rerum, et saltem pulcritudine et vigore insenescibilis erat. Hec magno patris tui amore perculsa, primum quidem ei connubium michi mortem parabat; postea vero, recusante Callicrate, amore mei et timore regine affecto, nos per magicam abduxit per vias horribiles ubi est puteus ille profundus, cujus juxta aditum jacebat senioris philosophi cadaver, et advenientibus monstravit flamman Vite erectam, instar columne volutantis, voces emittentem quasi tonitrus: tunc per ignem impetu nocivo expers transiit et jam ipsa sese formosior visa est.

Quibus factis juravit se patrem tuum quoque immortalem ostensuram ese, si me prius occisa regine contubernium mallet; neque enim ipsa me occidere valuit, propter nostratum magicam cujus egomet partem habeo. Ille vero nichil hujus generis malebat, manibus ante oculos passis, ne mulieris formositatem adspiceret: postea illum magica percussit arte, at mortuum efferebat inde cum fletibus et vagitibus, et me per timorem expulit ad ostium magni fluminis, velivoli, porro in nave, in qua te peperi, vix post dies huc Athenas vecta sum. At tu, O Tisisthenes, ne quid quorurm mando nauci fac: necesse enim est mulierem exquirere si qua Vite mysterium impetres et vindicare, quantum in te est, patrem tuum Callicratem in regine morte. Sin timore seu aliqua causa rem relinquis infectam, hoc ipsum omnibus posteris mando, dum bonus quis inveniatur qui ignis lavacrum non perhorrescet, et potentia dignus dominabitur hominum.

Talia dico incredibilia quidem at minime ficta de rebus michi cognitis.

Hoc Grece scripta Latine reddidit vir doctus Edmundus de Prato, in

Decretis Licenciatus, e Collegio Exoniensi Oxoniensi doctissimi Grocyni quondam e pupillis, Idibus Aprilis Anno Domini MCCCCLXXXXV°.

"Well," I said, when at length I had read out and carefully examined these writings and paragraphs, at least those of them that were still easily legible, "that is the conclusion of the whole matter, Leo, and now you can form your own opinion on it. I have already formed mine."

"And what is it?" he asked in his quick way.

"It is this. I believe that potsherd to be perfectly genuine, and that, wonderful as it may seem, it has come down in your family from since the fourth century before Christ. The entries absolutely prove it, and therefore, however improbable it may seem, it must be accepted. But there I stop. That your remote ancestress, the Egyptian Princess, or some scribe under her direction, wrote that which we see on the sherd I have no doubt, nor have I the slightest doubt but that her sufferings and the loss of her husband had turned her head, and that she was not right in her mind when she did write it."

"How do you account for what my father saw and heard there?" asked Leo.

"Coincidence. No doubt there are bluffs on the coast of Africa that look something like a man's head, and plenty of people who speak bastard Arabic. Also, I believe that there are lots of swamps. Another thing is, Leo, and I am sorry to say it, but I do not believe that your poor father was quite right when he wrote that letter. He had met with a great trouble, and also he had allowed this story to prey on his imagination, and he was a very imaginative man. Anyway, I believe that the whole thing is the most unmitigated rubbish. I know that there are curious things and forces in nature which we rarely meet with, and, when we do meet them, cannot understand. But until I see it with my own eyes, which I am not likely to, I never will believe that there is any means of avoiding death, even for a time, or that there is or was a white sorceress living in the heart of an African swamp. It is bosh, my boy, all bosh!—What do you say, Job?"

"I say, sir, that it is a lie, and, if it is true, I hope Mr. Leo won't meddle with no such things, for no good can't come of it."

"Perhaps you are both right," said Leo, very quietly. "I express no opinion. But I say this. I am going to set the matter at rest once and for all, and if you won't come with me I will go by myself."

I looked at the young man, and saw that he meant what he said. When Leo means what he says he always puts on a curious look about the mouth. It has been a trick of his from a child. Now, as a matter of fact, I had no intention of allowing Leo to go anywhere by himself, for my own sake, if not for his. I was far too much attached to him for that. I am not a man of many ties or affections. Circumstances have been against me in this respect, and men and women shrink from me, or at least, I fancy that they do, which comes to the same thing, thinking, perhaps, that my somewhat forbidding exterior is a key to my character. Rather than endure this, I have, to a great extent, secluded myself from the world, and cut myself off from those opportunities which with most men result in the formation of relations more or less intimate. Therefore Leo was all the world to me—brother, child and friend—and until he wearied of me, where he went there I should go too. But, of course, it would not do to let him see how great a hold he had over me; so I cast about for some means whereby I might let myself down easy.

"Yes, I shall go, Uncle; and if I don't find the 'rolling Pillar of Life,' at any rate I shall get some first-class shooting."

Here was my opportunity, and I took it.

"Shooting?" I said, "Ah! yes; I never thought of that. It must be a very wild stretch of country, and full of big game. I have always wanted to kill a buffalo before I die. Do you know, my boy, I don't believe in the quest, but I do believe in big game, and really on the whole, if, after thinking it over, you make up your mind to go, I will take a holiday and come with you."

"Ah," said Leo, "I thought that you would not lose such a chance. But how about money? We shall want a good lot."

"You need not trouble about that," I answered. "There is all your income that has been accumulating for years, and besides that I have saved two-thirds of what your father left to me, as I consider, in trust for you. There is plenty of cash."

"Very well, then, we may as well stow these things away and go up to town to see about our guns. By the way, Job, are you coming too? It's time you began to see the world."

"Well, sir," answered Job stolidly, "I don't hold much with foreign parts, but if both you gentlemen are going you will want somebody to look after you, and I am not the man to stop behind after serving you for twenty years."

"That's right, Job," said I. "You won't find out anything wonderful, but you will get some good shooting. And now look here, both of you. I won't have a word said to a living soul about this nonsense," and I pointed to the potsherd. "If it got out, and anything happened to me, my next of kin would dispute my will on the ground of insanity, and I should become the laughing stock of Cambridge."

That day three months we were on the ocean, bound for Zanzibar.

IV.

The Squall.

How different is the scene that I have now to tell from that which has just been told! Gone are the quiet college rooms, gone the wind-swayed English elms, the cawing rooks, and the familiar volumes on the shelves, and in their place there rises a vision of the great calm ocean gleaming in shaded silver lights beneath the beams of the full African moon. A gentle breeze fills the huge sail of our dhow,[1] and draws us through the water that ripples musically against her sides. Most of the men are sleeping forward, for it is near midnight, but a stout swarthy Arab,[2] Mahomed by name, stands at the tiller, lazily steering by the stars. Three miles or more to our starboard is a low dim line. It is the Eastern shore of Central Africa. We are running to the southward, before the North East Monsoon, between the mainland and the reef that for hundreds of miles fringes this perilous coast.[3] The night is quiet, so quiet that a whisper can be heard fore and aft the dhow; so quiet that a faint booming sound rolls across the water to us from the distant land.

The Arab at the tiller holds up his hand, and says one word:—"*Simba* (lion)!"

We all sit up and listen. Then it comes again, a slow, majestic sound, that thrills us to the marrow.

"To-morrow by ten o'clock," I say, "we ought, if the Captain is not out in his reckoning, which I think very probable, to make this mysterious rock with a man's head and begin our shooting."

"And begin our search for the ruined city and the Fire of Life," corrected Leo, taking his pipe from his mouth, and laughing a little.

"Nonsense!" I answered. "You were airing your Arabic with that man at the tiller this afternoon. What did he tell you? He has been trading (slave-trading probably) up and down these latitudes for half of his iniquitous life, and once landed on this very 'man' rock. Did he ever hear anything of the ruined city or the caves?"

"No," answered Leo. "He says that the country is all swamp behind, and full of snakes, especially pythons, and game, and that no man lives there. But then there is a belt of swamp all along the East African coast, so that does not go for much."

"Yes," I said, "it does—it goes for malaria. You see what sort of an opinion these gentry have of the country. Not one of them will go with us. They think that we are mad, and upon my word I believe that they are right. If ever we see Old England again I shall be astonished. However, it does not greatly matter to me at my age, but I am anxious for you, Leo and for Job. It's a Tom Fool's business, my boy."

"All right, Uncle Horace. So far as I am concerned, I am willing to take my chance. Look! What is that cloud?" and he pointed to a dark blotch upon the starry sky, some miles astern of us.

"Go and ask the man at the tiller," I said.

He rose, stretched his arms, and went. Presently he returned.

"He says it is a squall, but it will pass far on one side of us."

Just then Job came up, looking very stout and English in his shooting-suit of brown flannel, and with a sort of perplexed appearance upon his honest round face that had been very common with him since he got into these strange waters.

"Please, sir," he said, touching his sun hat, which was stuck on to the back of his head in a somewhat ludicrous fashion, "as we have got all those guns and things in the whale-boat astern, to say nothing of the provisions in the lockers, I think it would be best if I got down and slept in her. I don't like the looks" (here he dropped his voice to a portentous whisper) "of these black gentry;[4] they have such a wonderful thievish way about them. Supposing now that some of them were to slip into the boat at night and cut the cable, and make off with her? That would be a pretty go, that would."

The whale-boat, I may explain, was one specially built for us at Dundee, in Scotland.[5] We had brought it with us, as we knew that this coast was a network of creeks, and that we might require something to navigate them with. She was a beautiful boat, thirty feet in length, with a centre-board for sailing, copper-bottomed to keep the worm out of her,[6] and full of water-tight compartments. The Captain of the dhow had told us that when we reached the rock, which he knew, and which appeared to be identical with the one described upon the sherd and by Leo's father, he would probably not be able to run up to it on account of the shallows and breakers. Therefore we had employed three hours that very morning, whilst we were totally becalmed, the wind having dropped at sunrise, in transferring most of our goods and chattels to the whale-boat, and placing the guns, ammunition, and preserved provisions in the water-tight lockers specially prepared for them, so that when we did sight the fabled rock we should have nothing to do but step into the boat, and run her ashore. Another reason that induced us to take this precautionary step was that Arab captains are apt to run past the point that they are making, either from carelessness or owing to a mistake in its identity. Now, as sailors will know, it is quite impossible for a dhow which is only rigged to run before the monsoon to beat back against it. Therefore we got our boat ready to row for the rock at any moment.[7]

"Well, Job," I said, "perhaps it would be as well. There are lots of blankets there, only be careful to keep out of the moon, or it may turn your head or blind you."[8]

"Lord, sir! I don't think it would much matter if it did; it is that turned already with the sight of these blackamoors and their filthy, thieving ways. They are only fit for muck,[9] they are; and they smell bad enough for it already."

Job, it will be perceived, was no admirer of the manners and customs of our dark-skinned brothers.

Accordingly we hauled up the boat by the tow-rope till it was right under the stern of the dhow, and Job bundled into her with all the grace of a falling sack of potatoes. Then we returned and sat down on the deck again, and smoked and talked in little gusts and jerks. The night was so lovely, and our brains were so full of suppressed excitement of one sort and another, that we did not feel inclined to turn in. For nearly an hour we sat thus, and then, I think, we both dozed off. At least I have a faint recollection of Leo sleepily explaining that the head was not a bad place to hit a buffalo, if you could catch him exactly between the horns, or send your bullet down his throat, or some nonsense of the sort.

Then I remember no more; till suddenly—a frightful roar of wind, a shriek of terror from the awakening crew, and a whip-like sting of water in our faces. Some of the men ran to let go the haulyards[10] and lower the sail, but the parrel jammed and the yard would not come down. I sprang to my feet and hung on to a rope. The sky aft was dark as pitch, but the moon still shone brightly ahead of us and lit up the blackness. Beneath its sheen a huge white-topped breaker, twenty feet high or more, was rushing on to us. It was on the break—the moon shone on its crest and tipped its foam with light. On it rushed beneath the inky sky, driven by the awful squall behind it. Suddenly, in the twinkling of an eye, I saw the black shape of the whale-boat cast high into the air on the crest of the breaking wave. Then—a shock of water, a wild rush of boiling foam, and I was clinging for my life to the shroud, ay, swept straight out from it like a flag in a gale.

We were pooped.[11]

The wave passed. It seemed to me that I was under water for minutes —really it was seconds. I looked forward. The blast had torn out the great sail, and high in the air it was fluttering away to leeward like a huge wounded bird. Then for a moment there was comparative calm, and in it I heard Job's voice yelling wildly, "Come here to the boat."

Bewildered and half drowned as I was, I had the sense to rush aft. I felt the dhow sinking under me—she was full of water. Under her counter the whale-boat was tossing furiously, and I saw the Arab Mahomed, who had been steering, leap into her. I gave one desperate pull at the tow-rope to bring the boat alongside. Wildly I sprang also, and Job caught me by one arm and I rolled into the bottom of the boat. Down went the dhow bodily, and as she did so Mahomed drew his curved knife[12] and severed the fibre-rope by which we were fast to her, and in another second we were driving before the storm over the place where the dhow had been.

"Great God!" I shrieked, "where is Leo? *Leo! Leo!*"

"He's gone, sir, God help him!" roared Job into my ear, and such was the fury of the squall that his voice sounded like a whisper.

I wrung my hands in agony. Leo was drowned, and I was left alive to mourn him.

"Look out," yelled Job; "here comes another."

I turned; a second huge wave was overtaking us. I half hoped that it would drown me. With a curious fascination I watched its awful advent. The moon was nearly hidden now by the wreaths of the rushing storm, but a little light still caught the crest of the devouring breaker. There was something dark on it—a piece of wreckage. It was on us now, and the boat was nearly full of water. But she was built in airtight compartments —Heaven bless the man who invented them!—and lifted up through it like a swan. Through the foam and turmoil I saw the black thing on the wave hurrying right at me. I put out my right arm to ward it from me, and my hand closed on another arm, the wrist of which my fingers gripped like a vice. I am a very strong man, and had something to hold to, but my arm was nearly torn from its socket by the strain and weight of the floating body. Had the rush lasted another two seconds I must either have let go or gone with it. But it passed, leaving us up to our knees in water.

"Bail out! bail out!" shouted Job, suiting the action to the word.

But I could not bail just then, for as the moon went out and left us in total darkness, one faint, flying ray of light lit upon the face of the man I had gripped, who was now half lying, half floating in the bottom of the boat.

It was Leo. Leo brought back by the wave—back, dead or alive, from the very jaws of Death.

"Bail out! bail out!" yelled Job, "or we shall founder."

I seized a large tin bowl with a handle to it, which was fixed under one of the seats, and the three of us bailed away for dear life. The furious tempest drove over and round us, flinging the boat this way and that, the wind and the storm wreaths and the sheets of stinging spray blinded and bewildered us, but through it all we worked like demons with the wild exhilaration of despair, for even despair can exhilarate. One minute! three minutes! six minutes! The boat began to lighten, and no fresh wave swamped us. Five minutes more, and she was fairly clear. Then, suddenly, above the awful shriekings of the hurricane came a duller, deeper roar. Great Heavens! It was the voice of breakers!

At that moment the moon began to shine forth again—this time behind the path of the squall. Out far across the torn bosom of the ocean shot the ragged arrows of her light, and there, half a mile ahead of us, was a white line of foam, then a little space of open-mouthed blackness, and then another line of white. It was the breakers, and their roar grew clearer and yet more clear as we sped down upon them like a swallow. There they were, boiling up in snowy spouts of spray, smiting and gnashing together like the gleaming teeth of hell.

"Take the tiller, Mahomed!" I roared in Arabic. "We must try and shoot them." At the same moment I seized an oar, and got it out, motioning to Job to do likewise.

Mahomed clambered aft, and got hold of the tiller, and with some difficulty Job, who had sometimes pulled a tub upon the homely Cam,[13] got out his oar. In another minute the boat's head was straight on to the ever nearing foam, towards which she plunged and tore with the speed of a race-horse. Just in front of us the first line of breakers seemed a little thinner than to the right or left—there was a gap of rather deeper water. I turned and pointed to it.

"Steer for your life, Mahomed!" I yelled. He was a skilful steersman, and well acquainted with the dangers of this most perilous coast, and I saw him grip the tiller, bend his heavy frame forward, and stare at the foaming terror till his big round eyes looked as though they would start out of his head. The send of the sea[14] was driving the boat's head round to starboard. If we struck the line of breakers fifty yards to starboard of the gap we must sink. It was a great field of twisting, spouting waves. Mahomed planted his foot against the seat before him, and, glancing at him, I saw his brown toes spread out like a hand with the weight he put upon them as he took the strain of the tiller. She came round a bit, but not enough. I roared to Job to back water, whilst I dragged and laboured at my oar. She answered now, and none too soon. Heavens, we were in them! And then followed a couple of minutes of heart-breaking excitement such as I cannot hope to describe. All that I remember is a shrieking sea of foam, out of which the billows rose here, there, and everywhere like avenging ghosts from their ocean grave. Once we were turned right round, but either by chance, or through Mahomed's skilful steering, the boat's head came straight again before a breaker filled us. One more—a monster. We were through it or over it— more through than over—and then, with a wild yell of exultation from the Arab, we shot out into the comparative smooth water of the mouth of sea between the teeth-like lines of gnashing waves.

But we were nearly full of water again, and not more than half a mile ahead was the second line of breakers. Again we set to and bailed furiously. Fortunately the storm had now quite gone by, and the moon shone brightly, revealing a rocky headland running half a mile·or more out into the sea, of which this second line of breakers appeared to be a continuation. At any rate, they boiled around its foot. Probably the ridge that formed the headland ran out into the ocean, only at a lower level, and made the reef also. This headland was terminated by a curious peak that seemed not to be more than a mile away from us. Just as we got the boat pretty clear for the second time, Leo, to my immense relief, opened his eyes and remarked that the clothes had tumbled off the bed, and that he supposed it was time to get up for chapel. I told him to shut his eyes and keep quiet, which he did without in the slightest degree realizing the position. As for myself, his reference to chapel made me reflect, with a sort of sick longing, on my comfortable rooms at Cambridge. Why had I been such a fool as to leave them? This is a reflection that has several times recurred to me since, and with ever-increasing force.

But now again we were drifting down on the breakers, though with lessened speed, for the wind had fallen, and only the current or the tide (it afterwards turned out to be the tide) was driving us.

Another minute, and with a sort of howl to Allah from the Arab, a pious ejaculation from myself, and something that was not pious from Job, we were in them.[15] And then the whole scene, down to our final escape, repeated itself, only not quite so violently. Mahomed's skilful steering and the air-tight compartments saved our lives. In five minutes we were through, and drifting—for we were too exhausted to do anything to help ourselves except keep her head straight—with the most startling rapidity round the headland which I have described.

Round we went with the tide, until we got well under the lee of the point, and then suddenly the speed slackened, we ceased to make way, and finally appeared to be in dead water. The storm had entirely passed, leaving a clean-washed sky behind it; the headland intercepted the heavy sea that had been occasioned by the squall, and the tide, which had been running so fiercely up the river (for we were now in the mouth of a river), was sluggish before it turned, so we floated quietly, and before the moon went down managed to bail out the boat thoroughly and get her a little ship-shape. Leo was sleeping profoundly, and on the whole I thought it wise not to wake him. It was true he was sleeping in wet clothes, but the night was now so warm that I thought (and so did Job) that they were not likely to injure a man of his unusually vigorous constitution. Besides, we had no dry ones at hand.

Presently the moon went down, and left us floating on the waters, now only heaving like some troubled woman's breast, with leisure to reflect upon all that we had gone through and all that we had escaped. Job stationed himself at the bow, Mahomed kept his post at the tiller, and I sat on a seat in the middle of the boat close to where Leo was lying.

The moon went slowly down in chastened loveliness; she departed like some sweet bride into her chamber, and long veil-like shadows crept up the sky through which the stars peeped shyly out. Soon, however, they too began to pale before a splendour in the east, and then the quivering footsteps of the dawn came rushing across the new-born blue, and shook the high stars from their places. Quieter and yet more quiet grew the sea, quiet as the soft mists that brooded on her bosom, and covered up her troubling, as the illusive wreaths of sleep brood upon a pain-racked mind, causing it to forget its sorrow. From the east to the west sped the angels of the Dawn, from sea to sea, from mountain-top to mountain-top, scattering light with both their hands. On they sped out of the darkness, perfect, glorious, like spirits of the just breaking from the tomb; on, over the quiet sea, over the low coast-line, and the swamps beyond, and the mountains above them; over those who slept in peace and those who woke in sorrow; over the evil and the good; over the living and dead; over the wide world and all that breathes or has breathed thereon.[16]

It was a wonderfully beautiful sight, and yet sad, perhaps, from the very excess of its beauty. The arising sun; the setting sun! There we have the symbol and the type of humanity, and all things with which humanity has to do. The symbol and the type, yes, and the earthly beginning, and the end also. And on that morning this came home to me with a peculiar force. The sun that arose to-day for us had set last night for eighteen of our fellow-voyagers!—had set everlastingly for eighteen whom we knew!

The dhow had gone down with them, they were tossing about among the rocks and seaweed, so much human drift on the great ocean of Death! And we four were saved. But one day a sunrise will come when we shall be among those who are lost, and then others will watch those glorious rays, and grow sad in the midst of beauty, and dream of Death in the full glow of arising Life!

For this is the lot of man.

V.

The Head of the Ethiopian.

At length the heralds and forerunners of the royal sun had done their work, and, searching out the shadows, had caused them to flee away. Then up he came in glory from his ocean-bed, and flooded the earth with warmth and light. I sat there in the boat listening to the gentle lapping of the water and watched him rise, till presently the slight drift of the boat brought the odd-shaped rock, or peak, at the end of the promontory which we had weathered with so much peril, between me and the majestic sight, and blotted it from my view. I still continued, however, to stare at the rock, absently enough, till presently it became edged with the fire of the growing light behind it, and then I started, as well I might, for I perceived that the top of the peak, which was about eighty feet high by one hundred and fifty thick at its base, was shaped like a negro's head and face, whereon was stamped a most fiendish and terrifying expression. There was no doubt about it; there were the thick lips, the fat cheeks, and the squat nose standing out with startling clearness against the flaming background. There, too, was the round skull, washed into shape perhaps by thousands of years of wind and weather, and, to complete the resemblance, there was a scrubby growth of weeds or lichen upon it, which against the sun looked for all the world like the wool on a colossal negro's head. It certainly was very odd; so odd that now I believe that it is not a mere freak of nature but a gigantic monument fashioned, like the well-known Egyptian Sphinx, by a forgotten people out of a pile of rock that lent itself to their design, perhaps as an emblem of warning and defiance to any enemies who approached the harbour. Unfortunately we were never able to ascertain whether or not this was the case, inasmuch as the rock was difficult of access both from the land and the water-side, and we had other things to attend to. Myself, considering the matter by the light of what we afterwards saw, I believe that it was fashioned by man, but whether or not this is so, there it stands, and sullenly stares from age to age out across the changing sea—there it stood two thousand years and more ago, when Amenartas, the Egyptian princess, and the wife of Leo's remote ancestor Kallikrates, gazed upon its devilish face—and there I have no doubt it will stand when as many centuries as are numbered between her day and our own are added to the year that bore us to oblivion.

"What do you think of that, Job?" I asked of our retainer, who was sitting on the edge of the boat, trying to get as much sunshine as possible, and generally looking uncommonly wretched, and I pointed to the fiery and demoniacal head.

"Oh Lord, sir," answered Job, who now perceived the object for the first time, "I think that the Old Genelman[1] must have been sitting for his portrait on them rocks."

I laughed and the laugh woke up Leo.

"Hullo," he said, "what's the matter with me? I am all stiff—where is the dhow? Give me some brandy please."

"You may be thankful that you are not stiffer, my boy," I answered. "The dhow is sunk, everybody on board her is drowned with the exception of us four, and your own life was only saved by a miracle;" and whilst Job, now that it was light enough, searched about in a locker for the brandy for which Leo asked, I told him the history of our night's adventure.

"Great Heavens!" he said, faintly; "and to think that we should have been chosen to live through it!"

By this time the brandy was forthcoming, and we all had a good pull at it, and thankful enough we were for it. Also the sun was beginning to get strength, and warm our chilled bones, for we had been wet through for five hours or more.

"Why," said Leo, with a gasp as he put down the brandy bottle, "there is the head the writing talks of, the 'rock carven like the head of an Ethiopian.'"

"Yes," I said, "there it is."

"Well, then," he answered, "the whole thing is true."

"I don't at all see that that follows," I answered. "We knew this head was here: your father saw it. Very likely it is not the same head that the writing talks of; or if it is, it proves nothing."

Leo smiled at me in a superior way. "You are an unbelieving Jew, Uncle Horace," he said. "Those who live will see."[2]

"Exactly so," I answered, "and now perhaps you will observe that we are drifting across a sandbank into the mouth of the river. Get hold of your oar, Job, and we will row in and see if we can find a place to land."

The river mouth which we were entering did not appear to be a very wide one, though as yet the long banks of steaming mist that clung about its shores had not lifted sufficiently to enable us to see its exact measure. There was, as is the case with nearly every East African river, a considerable bar at the mouth, which, no doubt, when the wind was on shore and the tide running out, was absolutely impassable even for a boat drawing only a few inches. But as things were it was manageable enough, and we did not ship a cupful of water. In twenty minutes we were well across it, with but slight assistance from ourselves, and being carried by a strong though somewhat variable breeze, well up the harbour. By this time the mist was being sucked up by the sun, which was getting uncomfortably hot, and we saw that the mouth of the little estuary was here about half a mile across, and that the banks were very marshy, and crowded with crocodiles lying about on the mud like logs. About a mile ahead of us, however, was what appeared to be a strip of firm land, and for this we steered. In another quarter of an hour we were there, and making the boat fast to a beautiful tree with broad shining leaves, and flowers of the magnolia species, only they were rose-coloured and not white,* which hung over the water, we disembarked. This done we undressed, washed ourselves, and spread our clothes, together with the contents of the boat, in the sun to dry, which they very quickly did. Then, taking shelter from the sun under some trees, we made a hearty breakfast off a "Paysandu" potted tongue, of which we had brought a good quantity with us,[3] congratulating ourselves loudly on our good fortune in having loaded and provisioned the boat on the previous day before the hurricane destroyed the dhow. By the time that we had finished our meal our clothes were quite dry, and we hastened to get into them, feeling not a little refreshed. Indeed, with the exception of weariness and a few bruises, none of us were the worse for the terrifying adventure which had been fatal to all our companions. Leo, it is true, had been half-drowned, but that is no great matter to a vigorous young athlete of five-and-twenty.

After breakfast we started to look about us. We were on a strip of dry land about two hundred yards broad by five hundred long, bordered on one side by the river, and on the other three by endless desolate swamps, that stretched as far as the eye could reach. This strip of land was raised about twenty-five feet above the plain of the surrounding swamps and the river level: indeed it had every appearance of having been made by the hand of man.

"This place has been a wharf," said Leo, dogmatically.

"Nonsense," I answered. "Who would be stupid enough to build a wharf in the middle of these dreadful marshes in a country inhabited by savages —that is, if it is inhabited at all?"

"Perhaps it was not always marsh, and perhaps the people were not

---

*There is a known species of magnolia with pink flowers. It is indigenous in Sikkim, and known as *Magnolia Campbellii.*—EDITOR.

always savage," he said drily, looking down the steep bank, for we were standing by the river. "Look there," he went on, pointing to a spot where the hurricane of the previous night had torn up one of the magnolia trees by the roots, which had grown on the extreme edge of the bank just where it sloped down to the water, and lifted a large cake of earth with them. "Is not that stone work? If not, it is very like it."

"Nonsense," I said again, and we clambered down to the spot and got between the upturned roots and the bank.

"Well?" he said.

But I did not answer this time. I only whistled. For there, laid bare by the removal of the earth, was an undoubted facing of solid stone laid in large blocks and bound together with brown cement, so hard that I could make no impression on it with the file in my shooting-knife. Nor was this all; seeing something projecting through the soil at the bottom of the bared patch of walling, I removed the loose earth with my hands, and revealed a huge stone ring, a foot or more in diameter, and about three inches thick. This fairly staggered me.

"Looks rather like a wharf where good-sized vessels have been moored, does it not, Uncle Horace?" said Leo, with an excited grin.

I tried to say "Nonsense" again, but the word stuck in my throat—the ring spoke for itself. In some past age vessels *had* been moored there, and this stone wall was undoubtedly the remnant of a solidly-constructed wharf. Probably the city to which it had belonged lay buried beneath the swamp behind it.

"Begins to look as though there were something in the story after all, Uncle Horace," said the exultant Leo; and reflecting on the mysterious negro's head and the equally mysterious stonework, I made no direct reply.

"A country like Africa," I said, "is sure to be full of the relics of long dead and forgotten civilisations. Nobody knows the age of the Egyptian civilisation, and very likely it had offshoots. Then there were the Babylonians and the Phœnicians, and the Persians, and all manner of people, all more or less civilised, to say nothing of the Jews whom everybody 'wants' nowadays. It is possible that they, or any one of them, may have had colonies or trading stations about here. Remember those buried Persian cities that the consul showed us at Kilwa."**[4]

"Quite so," said Leo, "but that is not what you said before."

**Near Kilwa, on the East Coast of Africa, about 400 miles south of Zanzibar, is a cliff which has been recently washed by the waves. On the top of this cliff are Persian tombs known to be at least seven centuries old by the dates still legible on them. Beneath these tombs is a layer of *débris* representing a city. Farther down the cliff is a second layer representing an older city, and farther down still a third layer, the remains of yet another city of vast and unknown antiquity. Beneath the bottom city were found some specimens of glazed earthenware, such as are occasionally to be met with on that coast to this day. I believe that they are now in the possession of Sir John Kirk.—EDITOR

"Well, what is to be done now?" I asked, turning the conversation.

As no answer was forthcoming we walked to the edge of the swamp, and looked over it. It was apparently boundless, and vast flocks of every sort of waterfowl flew from its recesses, till it was sometimes difficult to see the sky. Now that the sun was getting high it drew thin sickly looking clouds of poisonous vapour from the surface of the marsh and from the scummy pools of stagnant water.

"Two things are clear to me," I said, addressing my three companions, who stared at this spectacle in dismay, "first, that we can't go across there" (I pointed to the swamp), "and, secondly, that if we stop here we shall certainly die of fever."⁵

"That's as clear as a haystack," said Job.

"Very well, then; there are two alternatives before us. One is to 'bout ship, and try and run for some port in the whale-boat, which would be a sufficiently risky proceeding, and the other to sail or row on up the river, and see where we come to."

"I don't know what you are going to do," said Leo, setting his mouth, "but I am going up that river."

Job turned up the whites of his eyes and groaned, and the Arab murmured "Allah," and groaned also. As for me, I remarked sweetly that as we seemed to be between the devil and the deep sea, it did not much matter where we went. But in reality I was as anxious to proceed as Leo. The colossal negro's head and the stone wharf had excited my curiosity to an extent of which I was secretly ashamed, and I was prepared to gratify it at any cost. Accordingly, having carefully fitted the mast, restowed the boat, and got out our rifles, we embarked. Fortunately the wind was blowing on shore from the ocean, so we were able to hoist the sail. Indeed, we afterwards found out that as a general rule the wind set on shore from daybreak for some hours, and off shore again at sun-set, and the explanation that I offer of this is, that when the earth is cooled by the dew and the night the hot air rises, and the draught rushes in from the sea till the sun has once more heated it through. At least that appeared to be the rule here.

Taking advantage of this favouring wind, we sailed merrily up the river for three or four hours. Once we came across a school of hippopotami, which rose, and bellowed dreadfully at us within ten or a dozen fathoms of the boat, much to Job's alarm, and I will confess, to my own. These were the first hippopotami that we had ever seen, and, to judge by their insatiable curiosity, I should judge that we were the first white men that they had ever seen. Upon my word, I once or twice thought that they were coming into the boat to gratify it. Leo wanted to fire at them, but I dissuaded him, fearing the consequences. Also, we saw hundreds of crocodiles basking on the muddy banks, and thousands upon thousands of waterfowl. Some of these we shot, and among them was a wild goose, which, in addition to the sharp-curved spurs on its wings, had a spur about three-quarters of an

inch long growing from the skull just between the eyes. We never shot an-
other like it, so I do not know if it was a "sport"[6] or a distinct species.
In the latter case this incident may interest naturalists. Job named it the
Unicorn Goose.

About midday the sun grew intensely hot, and the stench drawn up
by it from the marshes which the river drains was something too awful,
and caused us instantly to swallow precautionary doses of quinine.[7] Shortly
afterwards the breeze died away altogether, and as rowing our heavy boat
against stream in the heat was out of the question, we were thankful enough
to get under the shade of a group of trees—a species of willow—that grew
by the edge of the river, and lie there and gasp till at length the approach
of sunset put a period to our miseries. Seeing what appeared to be an open
space of water straight ahead of us, we determined to row there before set-
tling what to do for the night. Just as we were about to loosen the boat,
however, a beautiful waterbuck, with great horns curving forward, and a
white strip across the rump, came down to the river to drink, without perceiving us hidden away within fifty yards under the willows. Leo was the first
to catch sight of it, and, being an ardent sportsman, thirsting for the blood
of big game, about which he had been dreaming for months, he instantly
stiffened all over, and pointed like a setter dog.[8] Seeing what was the matter,
I handed him his express rifle, at the same time taking my own.[9]

"Now then," I whispered, "mind you don't miss."

"Miss!" he whispered back contemptuously; "I could not miss it if I
tried."

He lifted the rifle, and the roan-coloured buck, having drunk his fill,
raised his head and looked out across the river. He was standing right against
the sunset sky on a little eminence, or ridge of ground, which ran across
the swamp, evidently a favourite path for game, and there was something
very beautiful about him. Indeed, I do not think that if I live to a hundred
I shall ever forget that desolate and yet most fascinating scene; it is stamped
upon my memory. To the right and left were wide stretches of lonely death-
breeding swamp, unbroken and unrelieved so far as the eye could reach,
except here and there by ponds of black and peaty water that, mirror-like,
flashed up the red rays of the setting sun. Behind us and before stretched
the vista of the sluggish river, ending in glimpses of a reed-fringed lagoon,
on the surface of which the long lights of the evening played as the faint
breeze stirred the shadows. To the west loomed the huge red ball of the
sinking sun, now vanishing down the vapoury horizon, and filling the great
heaven, high across whose arch the cranes and wildfowl streamed in line,
square, and triangle, with flashes of flying gold and the lurid stain of blood.
And then ourselves—three modern Englishmen in a modern English boat
—seeming to jar upon and look out of tone with that measureless desolation;
and in front of us the noble buck limned out upon a background of ruddy
sky.[10]

Bang! Away he goes with a mighty bound. Leo has missed him. *Bang!* right under him again. Now for a shot. I must have one, though he is going like an arrow, and a hundred yards away and more. By Jove! over and over and over! "Well, I think I've wiped your eye there, Master Leo," I say, struggling against the ungenerous exultation that in such a supreme moment of one's existence will rise in the best-mannered sportsman's breast.

"Confound you, yes," growled Leo; and then, with that quick smile that is one of his charms lighting up his handsome face like a ray of light, "I beg your pardon, old fellow. I congratulate you; it was a lovely shot, and mine were vile."

We got out of the boat and ran to the buck, which was shot through the spine and stone dead. It took us a quarter of an hour or more to clean it and cut off as much of the best meat as we could carry, and, having packed this away, we had barely light enough to row up into the lagoon-like space, into which, there being a hollow in the swamp, the river here expanded. Just as the light vanished we cast anchor about thirty fathoms[11] from the edge of the lake. We did not dare to go ashore, not knowing if we should find dry ground to camp on, and greatly fearing the poisonous exhalations from the marsh from which we thought we should be freer on the water. So we lighted a lantern, and made our evening meal off another potted tongue in the best fashion that we could, and then prepared to go to sleep, only, however, to find that sleep was impossible. For, whether they were attracted by the lantern, or by the unaccustomed smell of a white man for which they had been waiting for the last thousand years or so, I know not; but certainly we were presently attacked by tens of thousands of the most bloodthirsty, pertinacious, and huge mosquitoes that I ever saw or read of. In clouds they came, and pinged and buzzed and bit till we were nearly mad.[12] Tobacco smoke only seemed to stir them into a merrier and more active life, till at length we were driven to covering ourselves with blankets, head and all, and sitting to slowly stew and continually scratch and swear beneath them. And as we sat, suddenly rolling out like thunder through the silence came the deep roar of a lion, and then of a second lion, moving among the reeds within sixty yards of us.

"I say," said Leo, sticking his head out from under his blanket, "lucky we ain't on the bank, eh Avuncular?"[13] (Leo sometimes addressed me in this disrespectful way.) "Curse it! a mosquito has bitten me on the nose," and the head vanished again.

Shortly after this the moon came up, and notwithstanding every variety of roar that echoed over the water to us from the lions on the banks, we began, thinking ourselves perfectly secure, to gradually doze off.

I do not quite know what it was that made me poke my head out of the friendly shelter of the blanket, perhaps because I found that the mosquitoes were biting right through it. Anyhow, as I did so I heard Job whisper, in a frightened voice—

"Oh, my stars, look there!"

Instantly we all of us looked, and this was what we saw in the moon-light. Near the shore were two wide and ever-widening circles of concentric rings rippling away across the surface of the water, and in the heart and centre of the circles were two dark moving objects.

"What is it?" asked I.

"It is those damned lions, sir," answered Job, in a tone which was an odd mixture of a sense of personal injury, habitual respect, and acknowledged fear, "and they are swimming here to *h*eat us," he added, nervously picking up an "h" in his agitation.[14]

I looked again: there was no doubt about it; I could catch the glare of their ferocious eyes. Attracted either by the smell of the newly killed water-buck meat or of ourselves, the hungry beasts were actually storming our position.

Leo already had his rifle in his hand. I called to him to wait till they were nearer, and meanwhile grabbed my own. Some fifteen feet from us the water shallowed on a bank to the depth of about fifteen inches, and presently the first of them—it was the lioness—got on to it, shook herself, and roared. At that moment Leo fired, the bullet went right down her open mouth and out at the back of her neck, and down she dropped, with a splash, dead. The other lion—a full-grown male—was some two paces be-hind her. At this second he got his forepaws on to the bank, when a strange thing happened. There was a rush and disturbance of the water, such as one sees in a pond in England when a pike takes a little fish, only a thousand times fiercer and larger, and suddenly the lion gave a most terrific snarling roar and sprang forward on to the bank, dragging something black with him.

"Allah!" shouted Mahomed, "a crocodile has got him by the leg!" and sure enough he had. We could see the long snout with its gleaming lines of teeth and the reptile body behind it.

And then followed an extraordinary scene indeed. The lion managed to get well on to the bank, the crocodile half standing and half swimming, still nipping his hind leg. He roared till the air quivered with the sound, and then, with a savage, shrieking snarl, turned round and clawed hold of the crocodile's head. The crocodile shifted his grip, having, as we after-wards discovered, had one of his eyes torn out, and slightly turned over; instantly the lion got him by the throat and held on, and then over and over they rolled upon the bank struggling hideously. It was impossible to follow their movements, but when next we got a clear view the tables had turned, for the crocodile, whose head seemed to be a mass of gore, had got the lion's body in his iron jaws just above the hips, and was squeezing him and shaking him to and fro. For his part, the tortured brute, roaring in agony, was clawing and biting madly at his enemy's scaly head, and fixing his great hind claws in the crocodile's, comparatively speaking, soft throat, ripping it open as one would rip a glove.

Then, all of a sudden, the end came. The lion's head fell forward on the crocodile's back, and with an awful groan he died, and the crocodile, after standing for a minute motionless, slowly rolled over on to his side, his jaws still fixed across the carcase of the lion, which, we afterwards found, he had bitten almost in halves.

This duel to the death was a wonderful and a shocking sight, and one that I suppose few men have seen—and thus it ended.

When it was all over, leaving Mahomed to keep a look out, we managed to spend the rest of the night as quietly as the mosquitoes would allow.

VI.
An Early Christian Ceremony.[1]

Next morning, at the earliest light of dawn, we rose, performed such ablutions as circumstances would allow, and generally made ready to start. I am bound to say that when there was sufficient light to enable us to see each other's faces I, for one, burst out into a roar of laughter. Job's fat and comfortable countenance was swollen out to nearly twice its natural size from mosquito bites, and Leo's condition was not much better. Indeed, of the three I had come off much the best, probably owing to the toughness of my dark skin, and to the fact that a good deal of it was covered by hair, for since we started from England I had allowed my naturally luxuriant beard to grow at its own sweet will. But the other two were, comparatively speaking, clean shaved, which of course gave the enemy a larger extent of open country to operate on, though in Mahomed's case the mosquitoes, recognising the taste of a true believer, would not touch him at any price. How often, I wonder, during the next week or so did we wish that we were flavoured like an Arab!

By the time that we had done laughing as heartily as our swollen lips would allow, it was daylight, and the morning breeze was coming up from the sea, cutting lanes through the dense marsh mists, and here and there rolling them before it in great balls of fleecy vapour. So we set our sail, and having first taken a look at the two dead lions and the alligator, which we were of course unable to skin, being destitute of means of curing the pelts,[2] we started, and, sailing through the lagoon, followed the course of the river on the further side. At midday, when the breeze dropped, we were fortunate enough to find a convenient piece of dry land on which to camp and light a fire, and here we cooked two water-ducks and some of the water-buck's flesh—not in a very appetizing way, it is true, but still sufficiently. The rest of the buck's flesh we cut into strips and hung in the sun to dry into "biltong", as, I believe, the South African Dutch call flesh thus prepared.[3] On this welcome patch of dry land we stopped till the following dawn, and, as before, spent the night in warfare with the mosquitoes, but without other troubles. The next day or two passed in similar fashion, and without notice-able adventures, except that we shot a specimen of a peculiarly graceful horn-less buck, and saw many varieties of water-lilies in full bloom, some of them blue and of exquisite beauty, though few of the flowers were perfect, owing to the prevalence of a white water-maggot with a green head that fed upon them.

It was on the fifth day of our journey, when we had travelled, so far as we could reckon, about one hundred and thirty-five to a hundred and forty miles westwards from the coast, that the first event of any real impor-tance occurred. On that morning the usual wind failed us about eleven o'clock, and after pulling a little way we were forced to halt, more or less exhausted, at what appeared to be the junction of our stream with another of a uniform width of about fifty feet. Some trees grew near at hand—the only trees in all this country were along the banks of the river, and under these we rested, and then, the land being fairly dry just here, walked a little way along the edge of the river to prospect, and shoot a few waterfowl for food. Before we had gone fifty yards we perceived that all hopes of getting further up the stream in the whale-boat were at an end, for not two hundred yards above where we had stopped were a succession of shallows and mudbanks, with not six inches of water over them. It was a watery *cul-de-sac*.

Turning back, we walked some way along the banks of the other river, and soon came to the conclusion, from various indications, that it was not a river at all, but an ancient canal, like the one which is to be seen above Mombasa, on the Zanzibar coast, connecting the Tana River with the Ozy, in such a way as to enable the shipping coming down to Tana to cross to the Ozy, and reach the sea by it, and thus avoid the very dangerous bar that blocks the mouth of the Tana.[4] The canal before us had evidently been dug out by man at some remote period of the world's history, and the results of his digging still remained in the shape of the raised banks that had no doubt once formed towing-paths. Except here and there, where they had been hollowed out by the water or fallen in, these banks of stiff, binding clay were at a uniform distance from each other, and the depth of the stream also appeared to be uniform. Current there was little or none, and, as a consequence, the surface of the canal was choked with vegetable growth, intersected by little paths of clear water, made, I suppose, by the constant passage of waterfowl, iguanas, and other vermin.[5] Now, as it was evident that we could not proceed up the river, it became equally evident that we must either try the canal, or else return to the sea. We could not stop where we were, to be baked by the sun and eaten up by the mosquitoes, till we died of fever in that dreary marsh.

"Well, I suppose that we must try it," I said; and the others assented in their various ways—Leo, as though it were the best joke in the world;

Job, in respectful disgust; and Mahomed, with an invocation to the Prophet, and a comprehensive curse upon all unbelievers and their ways of thought and travel.

Accordingly, as soon as the sun got low, having little or nothing more to hope for from our friendly wind, we started. For the first hour or so we managed to row the boat, though with great labour; but after that the weeds got too thick to allow of it, and we were obliged to resort to the primitive and most exhausting resource of towing her. For two hours we laboured, Mahomed, Job, and I, who was supposed to be strong enough to pull against the two of them, on the bank, while Leo sat in the bow of the boat, and brushed away the weeds which collected round the cutwater[6] with Ma-homed's sword. At dark we halted for some hours to rest and enjoy the mosquitoes, but about midnight we went on again, taking advantage of the comparative cool of the night. At dawn we rested for three hours, and then started once more, and laboured on till about ten o'clock, when a thunder-storm, accompanied by a deluge of rain, overtook us, and we spent the next six hours practically under water.

I do not know that there is any necessity for me to describe the next four days of our voyage in detail, further than to say that they were, on the whole, the most miserable that I ever spent in my life, forming one mo-notonous record of heavy labour, heat, misery, and mosquitoes. All that dreary way we passed through a region of almost endless swamp, and I can only attribute our escape from fever and death to the constant doses of quinine and purgatives which we took,[7] and the unceasing toil which we were forced to undergo. On the third day of our journey up the canal we had sighted a round hill that loomed dimly through the vapours of the marsh, and on the evening of the fourth night, when we camped, this hill seemed to be within five-and-twenty or thirty miles of us. We were by now utterly exhausted, and felt as though our blistered hands could not pull the boat a yard farther and that the best thing that we could do would be to lie down and die in that dreadful wilderness of swamp. It was an awful position, and one in which I trust no other white man will ever be placed; and as I threw myself down in the boat to sleep the sleep of utter exhaustion, I bitterly cursed my folly in ever having been a party to such a mad undertak-ing, which could, I saw, only end in our death in this ghastly land. I thought, I remember, as I slowly sank into a doze, of what the appearance of the boat and her unhappy crew would be in two or three months' time from that night. There she would lie, with gaping seams and half filled with fœtid water, which, when the mist-laden wind stirred her, would wash backwards and forwards through our mouldering bones, and that would be the end of her, and of those in her who would follow after myths and seek out the secrets of Nature.

Already I seemed to hear the water rippling against the desiccated bones and rattling them together, rolling my skull against Mahomed's and his against mine, till at last Mahomed's stood straight up upon its vertebrae, and glared at me through its empty eyeholes, and cursed me with its grinning jaws, because I, a dog of a Christian, disturbed the last sleep of a true believer. I opened my eyes, and shuddered at the horrid dream, and then shuddered again at something that was not a dream, for two great eyes were gleaming down at me through the misty darkness. I struggled up, and in my terror and confusion shrieked, and shrieked again, so that the others sprang up too, reeling, and drunken with sleep and fear. And then all of a sudden there was a flash of cold steel, and a great spear was held against my throat, and behind it other spears gleamed cruelly.

"Peace," said a voice, speaking in Arabic, or rather in some dialect into which Arabic entered very largely; "who are ye who come hither swimming on the water? Speak, or ye die," and the steel pressed sharply against my throat, sending a cold chill through me.[8]

"We are travellers, and have come hither by chance," I answered in my best Arabic, which appeared to be understood, for the man turned his head, and, addressing a tall form that towered up in the background, said, "Father, shall we slay?"

"What is the colour of the men?" said a deep voice in answer.

"White is their colour."

"Slay not," was the reply. "Four suns since was the word brought to me from '*She-who-must-be-obeyed*,'[9] 'White men come; if white men come, slay them not.' Let them be brought to the house of '*She-who-must-be-obeyed*.' Bring forth the men, and let that which they have with them be brought forth also."

"Come," said the man, half leading and half dragging me from the boat, and as he did so I perceived other men doing the same kind office to my companions.

On the bank were gathered a company of some fifty men. In that light all I could make out was that they were armed with huge spears, were very tall, and strongly built, comparatively light in colour, and nude, save for a leopard-skin tied round the middle.[10]

Presently Leo and Job were bundled out and placed beside me.

"What on earth is up?" said Leo, rubbing his eyes.

"Oh, Lord! sir, here's a rum go,"[11] ejaculated Job; and just at that moment a disturbance ensued, and Mahomed came tumbling between us, followed by a shadowy form with an uplifted spear.

"Allah! Allah!" howled Mahomed, feeling that he had little to hope from man, "protect me! protect me!"

"Father, it is a black one," said a voice. "What said '*She-who-must-be-obeyed*' about the black one?"

"She said naught, but slay him not. Come hither, my son."

The man advanced, and the tall shadowy form bent forward and whispered something.

"Yes, yes," said the other, and chuckled in a rather blood-curdling tone.[12]

"Are the three white men there?" asked the form.

"Yes, they are there."

"Then bring up that which is made ready for them, and let the men take all that can be brought from the thing which floats."

Hardly had he spoken when men came running up carrying on their shoulders neither more nor less than palanquins—four bearers and two spare men to a palanquin[13]—and in these it was promptly indicated we were expected to stow ourselves.

"Well!" said Leo, "it is a blessing to find anybody to carry us after having to carry ourselves so long."

Leo always takes a cheerful view of things.

There being no help for it, after seeing the others into theirs I tumbled into my own litter, and very comfortable I found it. It appeared to be manufactured of cloth woven from grass-fibre, which stretched and yielded to every motion of the body, and, being bound top and bottom to the bearing-pole, gave a grateful support to the head and neck.

Scarcely had I settled myself when, accompanying their steps with a monotonous song, the bearers started at a swinging trot. For half an hour or so I lay still, reflecting on the very remarkable experiences that we were going through, and wondering if any of my eminently respectable fossil friends down at Cambridge would believe me if I were to be miraculously set at the familiar dinner-table for the purpose of relating them. I do not want to convey any disrespectful notion or slight when I call those good and learned men fossils, but my experience is that people are apt to fossilise even at a University if they follow the same paths too persistently. I was getting fossilised myself, but of late my stock of ideas has been very much enlarged. Well, I lay and reflected, and wondered what on earth would be the end of it all, till at last I ceased to wonder, and went to sleep.

I suppose I must have slept for seven or eight hours, getting the first real rest that I had had since the night before the loss of the dhow, for when I woke the sun was high in the heavens. We were still journeying on at a pace of about four miles an hour. Peeping out through the mist-like curtains of the litter, which were ingeniously fixed to the bearing pole, I perceived to my infinite relief that we had passed out of the region of eternal swamp, and were now travelling over swelling grassy plains towards a cup-shaped hill. Whether or not it was the same hill that we had seen from the canal I do not know, and have never since been able to discover, for, as we afterwards found out, these people will give little information upon such points. Next I glanced at the men who were bearing me. They were of a magnificent build, few of them being under six feet in height, and yellowish in colour. Generally their appearance had a good deal in common with that of the East African Somali,[14] only their hair was not frizzed up, but hung in thick black locks upon their shoulders. Their features were aquiline, and in many cases exceedingly handsome, the teeth being especially regular and beautiful. But notwithstanding their beauty, it struck me that, on the whole, I had never seen a more evil-looking set of faces. There was an aspect of cold and sullen cruelty stamped upon them that revolted me, and which in some cases was almost uncanny in its intensity.

Another thing that struck me about them was that they never seemed to smile. Sometimes they sang the monotonous song of which I have spoken, but when they were not singing they remained almost perfectly silent, and the light of a laugh never came to brighten their sombre and evil countenances. Of what race could these people be? Their language was a bastard Arabic, and yet they were not Arabs; I was quite sure of that. For one thing they were too dark,[15] or rather yellow. I could not say why, but I know that their appearance filled me with a sick fear of which I felt ashamed. While I was still wondering another litter came up alongside of mine. In it—for the curtains were drawn—sat an old man, clothed in a whitish robe, made apparently from coarse linen, that hung loosely about him, who, I at once jumped to the conclusion, was the shadowy figure that had stood on the bank and been addressed as "Father." He was a wonderful-looking old man, with a snowy beard, so long that the ends of it hung over the sides of the litter, and he had a hooked nose, above which flashed out a pair of eyes as keen as a snake's, while his whole countenance was instinct with[16] a look of wise and sardonic humour impossible to describe on paper.

"Art thou awake, stranger?" he said, in a deep and low voice.

"Surely, my father," I answered, courteously, feeling certain that I should do well to conciliate this ancient Mammon of Unrighteousness.[17]

He stroked his beautiful white beard, and smiled faintly.

"From whatever country thou camest," he said, "and by the way it must be from one where somewhat of our language is known, they teach their children courtesy there, my stranger son. And now wherefore comest thou unto this land, which scarce an alien foot has pressed from the time that man knoweth? Art thou and those with thee weary of life?"

"We came to find new things," I answered boldly. "We are tired of the old things; we have come up out of the sea to know that which is unknown. We are of a brave race who fear not death, my very much respected father —that is, if we can get a little fresh information before we die."

"Humph!" said the old gentleman; "that may be true; it is rash to contradict, otherwise I should say that thou wast lying, my son. However, I daresay that 'She-who-must-be-obeyed' will meet thy wishes in the matter."

"Who is 'She-who-must-be-obeyed?'" I asked, curiously.

The old man glanced at the bearers, and then answered, with a little smile that somehow sent my blood to my heart—

"Surely, my stranger son, thou wilt learn soon enough, if it be her pleasure to see thee at all in the flesh."

"In the flesh?" I answered. "What may my father wish to convey?"

But the old man only laughed a dreadful laugh, and made no reply.

"What is the name of my father's people?" I asked.

"The name of my people is Amahagger" (the People of the Rocks).[18]

"And if a son might ask, what is the name of my father?"

"My name is Billali."[19]

"And whither go we, my father?"

"That shalt thou see," and at a sign from him his bearers started forward at a run till they reached the litter in which Job was reposing (with one leg hanging over the side). Apparently, however, he could not make much out of Job, for presently I saw his bearers trot forward to Leo's litter.

And after that, as nothing fresh occurred, I yielded to the pleasant swaying motion of the litter, and went to sleep again. I was dreadfully tired. When I woke I found that we were passing through a rocky defile of a lava formation with precipitous sides, in which grew many beautiful trees and flowering shrubs.[20]

Presently this defile took a turn, and a lovely sight unfolded itself to my eyes. Before us was a vast cup of green from four to six miles in extent, in the shape of a Roman amphitheatre. The sides of this great cup were rocky, and clothed with bush, but the centre was of the richest meadow land, studded with single trees of magnificent growth, and watered by meandering brooks. On this rich plain grazed herds of goats and cattle, but I saw no sheep. At first I could not imagine what this strange spot could be, but presently it flashed upon me that it must represent the crater of some long-extinct volcano which had afterwards been a lake, and was ultimately drained in some unexplained way. And here I may state that from my subsequent experience of this and a much larger, but otherwise similar spot, which I shall have occasion to describe by-and-by, I have every reason to believe that this conclusion was correct. What puzzled me, however, was, that although there were people moving about herding the goats and cattle, I saw no signs of any human habitation. Where did they all live? I wondered. My curiosity was soon destined to be gratified. Turning to the left the string of litters followed the cliffy sides of the crater for a distance of about half a mile, or perhaps a little less, and then halted. Seeing the old gentleman, my adopted "father," Billali, emerge from his litter, I did the same, and so did Leo and Job. The first thing I saw was our wretched Arab companion, Mahomed, lying exhausted on the ground. It appeared that he had not been provided with a litter, but had been forced to run the entire distance, and, as he was already quite worn out when we started, his condition now was one of great prostration.[21]

On looking round we discovered that the place where we had halted was a platform in front of the mouth of a great cave, and piled upon this platform were the entire contents of the whale-boat, even down to the oars and sail. Round the cave stood groups of the men who had escorted us, and other men of a similar stamp. They were all tall and all handsome, though they varied in their degree of darkness of skin, some being as dark as Mahomed, and some as yellow as a Chinese.[22] They were naked, except for the leopard-skin round the waist, and each of them carried a huge spear.

There were also some women among them, who, instead of the leopard skin, wore a tanned hide of a small red buck, something like the oribé, only rather darker in colour. These women were, as a class, exceedingly good-looking, with large, dark eyes, well-cut features, and a thick bush of curling hair—not crisped like a negro's—and ranging from black to chestnut in hue, with all shades of intermediate colour. Some, but very few of them, wore a yellowish linen garment, such as I have described as worn by Billali, but this, as we afterwards discovered, was a mark of rank, rather than an attempt at clothing. For the rest, their appearance was not quite so terrifying as that of the men, and they sometimes, though rarely, smiled. As soon as we had alighted, they gathered round us and examined us with curiosity, but without excitement. Leo's tall, athletic form and clear-cut Grecian face, however, evidently excited their attention, and when he politely lifted his hat to them, and showed his curling yellow hair, there was a slight murmur of admiration. Nor did it stop there; for, after regarding him critically from head to foot, the handsomest of the young women—one wearing a robe, and with hair of a shade between brown and chestnut—deliberately advanced to him, and, in a way that would have been winning had it not been so determined, quietly put her arm round his neck, bent forward, and kissed him on the lips.

I gave a gasp, expecting to see Leo instantly speared; and Job ejaculated, "The hussy—well, I never!" As for Leo, he looked slightly astonished; and then, remarking that we had clearly got into a country where they followed the customs of the early Christians, deliberately returned the embrace.

Again I gasped, thinking that something would happen; but, to my surprise, though some of the young women showed traces of vexation, the older ones and the men only smiled slightly. When we came to understand the customs of this extraordinary people the mystery was explained. It then appeared that, in direct opposition to the habits of almost every other savage race in the world, women among the Amahagger are not only upon terms of perfect equality with the men, but are not held to them by any binding ties. Descent is traced only through the line of the mother, and while individuals are as proud of a long and superior female ancestry as we are of our families in Europe, they never pay attention to, or even acknowledge, any man as their father, even when their male parentage is perfectly well known. There is but one titular male parent of each tribe, or, as they call it, "Household," and he is its elected and immediate ruler, with the title of "Father." For instance, the man Billali was the father of this "household," which consisted of about seven thousand individuals all told, and no other man was ever called by that name. When a woman took a fancy to a man she signified her preference by advancing and embracing him publicly, in the same way that this handsome and exceedingly prompt young lady, who was called Ustane,[23] had embraced Leo. If he kissed her back it was a token that he accepted her, and the arrangement continued till one of them wearied of it. I am bound, however, to say that the change of husbands was not nearly so frequent as might have been expected. Nor did quarrels arise out of it, at least among the men, who, when their wives deserted them in favour of a rival, accepted the whole thing much as we accept the income-tax or our marriage laws, as something not to be disputed, and as tending to the good of the community, however disagreeable they may in particular instances prove to the individual.

It is very curious to observe how the customs of mankind on this matter vary in different countries, making morality an affair of latitude, and what is right and proper in one place wrong and improper in another. It must, however, be understood that, since all civilised nations appear to accept it as an axiom that ceremony is the touchstone of morality, there is, even according to our canons, nothing immoral about this custom, seeing that the interchange of the embrace answers to our ceremony of marriage, which, as we know, justifies most things.[24]

VII.
Ustane Sings.

When the kissing operation was finished—by the way none of the young ladies offered to pet me in this fashion, though I saw one hovering round Job, to that respectable individual's evident alarm—the old man Billali advanced, and graciously waved us into the cave, whither we went, followed by Ustane,[1] who did not seem inclined to take the hints I gave her that we liked privacy.

Before we had gone five paces it struck me that the cave that we were entering was none of Nature's handiwork, but, on the contrary, had been hollowed by the hand of man.[2] So far as we could judge it appeared to be about one hundred feet in length by fifty wide, and very lofty, resembling a cathedral aisle more than anything else. From this main aisle opened passages at a distance of every twelve or fifteen feet, leading, I supposed, to smaller chambers. About fifty feet from the entrance of the cave, just where the light began to get dim, a fire was burning, which threw huge shadows upon the gloomy walls around. Here Billali halted, and asked us to be seated, saying that the people would bring us food, and accordingly we squatted ourselves down upon the rugs of skins which were spread for us, and waited. Presently the food, consisting of goat's flesh boiled, fresh milk in an earthenware pot, and boiled cobs of Indian corn, was brought by young girls.[3] We were almost starving, and I do not think that I ever in my life before ate with such satisfaction. Indeed, before we had finished we literally ate up everything that was set before us.

When we had done, our somewhat saturnine host, Billali, who had been watching us in perfect silence, rose, and addressed us. He said that it was a wonderful thing that had happened. No man had ever known or heard of white strangers arriving in the country of the People of the Rocks. Sometimes, though rarely, black men had come here, and from them they had heard of the existence of men much whiter than themselves, who sailed on the sea in ships, but for the arrival of such there was no precedent. We had, however, been seen dragging the boat up the canal, and he told us frankly that he had at once given orders for our destruction, seeing that it was unlawful for any stranger to enter here, when a message had come from "*She-who-must-be-obeyed*," saying that our lives were to be spared, and that we were to be brought hither.

"Pardon me, my father," I interrupted at this point; "but if, as I understand, '*She-who-must-be-obeyed*' lives yet farther off, how could she have known of our approach?"

Billali turned, and seeing that we were alone—for the young lady, Ustane, had withdrawn when he had begun to speak—said, with a curious little laugh—

"Are there none in your land who can see without eyes and hear without ears? Ask no questions; *She* knew."

I shrugged my shoulders at this, and he proceeded to say that no further instructions had been received on the subject of our disposal, and this being so he was about to start to interview "*She-who-must-be-obeyed*," generally spoken of, for the sake of brevity, as "Hiya" or *She* simply, who he gave us to understand was the Queen of the Amahagger, and learn her wishes.[4]

I asked him how long he proposed to be away, and he said that by travelling hard he might be back on the fifth day, but there were many miles of marsh to cross before he came to where *She* was. He then said that every arrangement would be made for our comfort during his absence, and that, as he personally had taken a fancy to us, he sincerely trusted that the answer he should bring from *She* would be one favourable to the continuation of our existence, but at the same time he did not wish to conceal from us that he thought this doubtful, as every stranger who had ever come into the country during his grandmother's life, his mother's life, and his own life, had been put to death without mercy, and in a way that he would not harrow our feelings by describing; and this had been done by the order of *She* herself, at least he supposed it was by her order. At any rate, she never interfered to save them.

"Why," I said, "but how can that be? You are an old man, and the time you talk of must reach back three men's lives. How therefore could *She* have ordered the death of anybody at the beginning of the life of your grandmother, seeing that herself she would not have been born?"

Again he smiled—that same faint, peculiar smile, and with a deep bow departed, without making any answer; nor did we see him again for five days.

When he had gone we discussed the situation, which filled me with alarm. I did not at all like the accounts of this mysterious Queen, *"She-who-must-be-obeyed,"* or more shortly *She*, who apparently ordered the execution of any unfortunate stranger in a fashion so unmerciful. Leo, too, was depressed about it, but consoled himself by triumphantly pointing out that this *She* was undoubtedly the person referred to in the writing on the potsherd and in his father's letter, in proof of which he advanced Billali's allusions to her age and power. I was by this time so overwhelmed with the whole course of events that I had not even the heart left to dispute a proposition so absurd, so I suggested that we should try to go out and get a bath, of which we all stood sadly in need.

Accordingly, having indicated our wish to a middle-aged individual of an unusually saturnine cast of countenance, even among this saturnine people who appeared to be deputed to look after us now that the Father of the hamlet had departed, we started in a body—having first lit our pipes. Outside the cave we found quite a crowd of people evidently watching for our appearance, but when they saw us come out smoking they vanished this way and that, calling out that we were great magicians. Indeed, nothing about us created so great a sensation as our tobacco smoke—not even our firearms.* After this we succeeded in reaching a stream that had its source in a strong ground spring, and taking our bath in peace, though some of the women, not excepting Ustane, showed a decided inclination to follow us even there.

By the time that we had finished this most refreshing bath the sun was setting; indeed, when we got back to the big cave it had already set. The cave itself was full of people gathered round fires—for several more had now been lighted—and eating their evening meal by their lurid light, and by that of various lamps which were set about or hung upon the walls. These lamps were of a rude manufacture of baked earthenware, and of all shapes, some of them graceful enough. The larger ones were formed of big red earthenware pots, filled with clarified melted fat, and having a reed wick stuck through a wooden disk which filled the top of the pot. This sort of lamp required the most constant attention to prevent its going out whenever the wick burnt down, as there were no means of turning it up. The smaller hand lamps, however, which were also made of baked clay, were fitted with wicks manufactured from the pith of a palm-tree, or sometimes from the stem of a very handsome variety of fern.[6] This kind of wick was passed through a round hole at the end of the lamp, to which a sharp piece of hard wood was attached wherewith to pierce and draw it up whenever it showed signs of burning low.

For a while we sat down and watched this grim people eating their evening meal in silence as grim as themselves, till at length, getting tired

---

*We found tobacco growing in this country as it does in every other part of Africa, and although they are so absolutely ignorant of its other blessed qualities, the Amahagger use it habitually in the form of snuff, and also for medicinal purposes. L.H.H.[5]

of contemplating them and the huge moving shadows on the rocky walls, I suggested to our new keeper that we should like to go to bed.

Without a word he rose, and, taking me politely by the hand, advanced with a lamp to one of the small passages that I had noticed opening out of the central cave. This we followed for about five paces, when it suddenly widened out into a small chamber, about eight feet square, and hewn out of the living rock. On one side of this chamber was a stone slab, about three feet from the ground, and running its entire length like a bunk in a cabin, and on this slab he intimated that I was to sleep.[7] There was no window or air-hole to the chamber, and no furniture; and, on looking at it more closely, I came to the disturbing conclusion (in which, as I afterwards discovered, I was quite right) that it had originally served for a sepulchre for the dead rather than a sleeping-place for the living, the slab being designed to receive the corpse of the departed.[8] The thought made me shudder in spite of myself; but, seeing that I must sleep somewhere, I got over the feeling as best I might, and returned to the cavern to get my blanket, which had been brought up from the boat with the other things. There I met Job, who, having been inducted to a similar apartment, had flatly declined to stop in it, saying that the look of the place gave him the horrors, and that he might as well be dead and buried in his grandfather's brick grave at once, and expressed his determination of sleeping with me if I would allow him. This, of course, I was only too glad to do.[9]

The night passed very comfortably on the whole. I say on the whole, for personally I went through a most horrible nightmare of being buried alive, induced, no doubt, by the sepulchral nature of my surroundings. At dawn we were aroused by a loud trumpeting sound, produced, as we afterwards discovered, by a young Amahagger blowing through a hole bored in its side into a hollowed elephant tusk, which was kept for the purpose.

Taking the hint, we got up and went down to the stream to wash, after which the morning meal was served. At breakfast one of the women, no longer quite young, advanced, and publicly kissed Job.[10] I think it was in its way the most delightful thing (putting its impropriety aside for a moment) that I ever saw. Never shall I forget the respectable Job's abject terror and disgust. Job, like myself, is a bit of a misogynist—I fancy chiefly owing to the fact of his having been one of a family of seventeen—and the feelings expressed upon his countenance when he realised that he was not only being embraced publicly, and without authorisation on his own part, but also in the presence of his masters, were too mixed and painful to admit of accurate description. He sprang to his feet, and pushed the woman, a buxom person of about thirty, from him.

"Well, I never!" he gasped, whereupon probably thinking that he was only coy, she embraced him again.

"Be off with you! Get away, you minx!" he shouted, waving the wooden spoon, with which he was eating his breakfast, up and down before the lady's face. "Beg your pardon, gentlemen, I am sure I haven't encouraged her. Oh, Lord! she's coming for me again. Hold her, Mr. Holly! please, hold her! I can't stand it; I can't, indeed. This has never happened to me before, gentlemen, never!¹¹ There's nothing against my character," and here he broke off, and ran as hard as he could go down the cave, and for once I saw the Amahagger laugh. As for the woman, however, she did not laugh. On the contrary, she seemed to bristle with fury, which the mockery of the other women about only served to intensify. She stood there literally snarling and shaking with indignation, and, seeing her, I wished Job's scruples had been at Jericho,¹² forming a shrewd guess that his admirable behaviour had endangered our throats. Nor, as the sequel shows, was I wrong.

The lady having retreated, Job returned in a great state of nervousness, and keeping his weather eye¹³ fixed upon every woman who came near him. I took an opportunity to explain to our hosts that Job was a married man, and had had very unhappy experiences in his domestic relations, which accounted for his presence here and his terror at the sight of women, but my remarks were received in grim silence, it being evident that our retainer's behaviour was considered as a slight to the "household" at large, although the women, after the manner of some of their more civilised sisters, made merry at the rebuff of their companion.

After breakfast we took a walk and inspected the Amahagger herds, and also their cultivated lands. They have two breeds of cattle, one large and angular, with no horns, but yielding beautiful milk; and the other, a red breed, very small and fat, excellent for meat, but of no value for milking purposes. This last breed closely resembles the Norfolk red-poll strain, only it has horns which generally curve forward over the head, sometimes to such an extent that they have to be cut to prevent them from growing into the bones of the skull.¹⁴ The goats are long-haired, and are used for eating only, at least I never saw them milked. As for the Amahagger cultivation, it is primitive in the extreme, being all done by means of a spade made of iron, for these people smelt and work iron. This spade is shaped more like a big spear-head than anything else, and has no shoulder to it on which the foot can be set. As a consequence, the labour of digging is very great. It is, however, all done by the men, the women, contrary to the habits of most savage races, being entirely exempt from manual toil. But then, as I think I have said elsewhere, among the Amahagger the weaker sex has established its rights.¹⁵

At first we were much puzzled as to the origin and constitution of this extraordinary race, points upon which they were singularly uncommunicative. As the time went on—for the next four days passed without any striking event—we learnt something from Leo's lady friend Ustane, who, by the way, stuck to that young gentleman like his own shadow. As to origin, they had none, at least, so far as she was aware. There were, however, she informed us, mounds of masonry and many pillars near the place where *She* lived, which was called Kôr,¹⁶ and which the wise said had once been houses wherein men lived, and it was suggested that they were descended from these men. No one, however, dared go near these great ruins, because they were haunted: they only looked on them from a distance. Other similar ruins were to be seen, she had heard, in various parts of the country, that is, wherever one of the mountains rose above the level of the swamp. Also the caves in which they lived had been hollowed out of the rocks by men, perhaps the same who built the cities. They themselves had no written laws, only custom, which was, however, quite as binding as law. If any man offended against the custom, he was put to death by order of the Father of the "Household." I asked how he was put to death, and she only smiled, and said that I might see one day soon.

They had a Queen, however. *She* was their Queen, but she was very rarely seen, perhaps once in two or three years, when she came forth to pass sentence on some offenders, and when seen was muffled up in a big cloak, so that nobody could look upon her face. Those who waited upon her were deaf and dumb, and therefore could tell no tales, but it was reported that she was lovely as no other woman was lovely, or ever had been. It was rumoured also that she was immortal, and had power over all things, but she, Ustane, could say nothing of all that. What she believed was that the Queen chose a husband from time to time and as soon as a female child was born, this husband, who was never again seen, was put to death. Then the female child grew up and took the place of the Queen when its mother died, and had been buried in the great caves. But of these matters none could speak with certainty. Only *She* was obeyed throughout the length and breadth of the land, and to question her command was instant death. She kept a guard, but had no regular army, and to disobey her was to die.

I asked what size the land was, and how many people lived in it. She answered that there were ten "Households" like this that she knew of, including the big "Household," where the Queen was, that all the "Households" lived in caves, in places resembling this stretch of raised country, dotted about in a vast extent of swamp, which was only to be threaded by secret paths. Often the "Households" made war on each other until *She* sent word that it was to stop, and then they instantly ceased. That and the fever which they caught in crossing the swamps prevented their numbers from increasing too much. They had no connection with any other race, indeed none lived near them, or were able to thread the vast swamps. Once an army from the direction of the great river (presumably the Zambesi) had attempted to attack them, but they got lost in the marshes, and at night, seeing the great balls of fire[17] that move about there, tried to come to them, thinking that they marked the enemy's camp, and half of them were drowned. As for the rest, they soon died of fever and starvation, not a blow being struck at them. The marshes, she told us, were absolutely impassable except to those who knew the paths, adding, what I could well believe, that we should never have reached this place where we then were had we not been brought thither.

These and many other things we learnt from Ustane during the four days' pause before our real adventures began, and, as may be imagined, they gave us considerable cause for thought. The whole thing was exceedingly remarkable, almost incredibly so, indeed, and the oddest part of it was that so far it did more or less correspond to the ancient writing on the sherd. And now it appeared that there was a mysterious Queen clothed by rumour with dread and wonderful attributes, and commonly known by the impersonal, but, to my mind, rather awesome title of *She*. Altogether, I could not make it out, nor could Leo, though of course he was exceedingly triumphant over me because I had persistently mocked at the whole thing. As for Job, he had long since abandoned any attempt to call his reason his own, and left it to drift upon the sea of circumstance. Mahomed, the Arab, who was, by the way, treated civilly indeed, but with chilling contempt, by the Amahagger, was, I discovered, in a great fright, though I could not quite make out what he was frightened about.[18] He would sit crouched up in a corner of the cave all day long, calling upon Allah and the Prophet to protect him. When I pressed him about it, he said that he was afraid because these people were not men and women at all, but devils, and that this was an enchanted land; and, upon my word, once or twice since then I have been inclined to agree with him. And so the time went on, till the night of the fourth day after Billali had left, when something happened.

We three and Ustane were sitting round a fire in the cave just before bedtime, when suddenly the woman, who had been brooding in silence, rose, and laid her hand upon Leo's golden curls, and addressed him. Even now, when I shut my eyes, I can see her proud, imperial form, clothed alternately in dense shadow and the red flickering of the fire, as she stood, the wild centre of as weird a scene as I ever witnessed, and delivered herself of the burden of her thoughts and forebodings in a kind of rhythmical speech that ran something as follows:—

Thou art my chosen—I have waited for thee from the beginning!
Thou art very beautiful. Who hath hair like unto thee, or skin so white?
Who hath so strong an arm, who is so much a man?
Thine eyes are the sky, and the light in them is the stars.
Thou art perfect and of a happy face, and my heart turned itself towards thee.
Ay, when mine eyes fell on thee, I did desire thee,—
Then did I take thee to me—oh thou Beloved,
And hold thee fast, lest harm should come unto thee.
Ay, I did cover thine head with mine hair, lest the sun should strike it;
And altogether was I thine, and thou wast altogether mine.
And so it went for a little space, till Time was in labour with an evil Day;
And then what befell on that day? Alas! my Beloved, I know not!
But I, I saw thee no more—I, I was lost in the blackness.
And she who is stronger did take thee; ay, she who is fairer than Ustane.
Yet didst thou turn and call upon me, and let thine eyes wander in the darkness.
But, nevertheless, she prevailed by Beauty, and led thee down horrible places,
And then, ah! then, my Beloved—[19]

Here this extraordinary woman broke off her speech, or chant, which was so much musical gibberish to us, for all that we understood of what she was talking about, and seemed to fix her flashing eyes upon the deep shadow before her. Then in a moment they acquired a vacant, terrified stare, as though they were trying to realise some half-seen horror. She lifted her hand from Leo's head, and pointed into the darkness. We all looked, and could see nothing; but she saw something, or thought she did, and something evidently that affected even her iron nerves, for, without another sound, down she fell senseless between us.

Leo, who was growing really attached to this remarkable young person, was in a great state of alarm and distress, and I, to be perfectly candid, was in a condition not far removed from superstitious fear. The whole scene was an uncanny one.

Presently, however, she recovered, and sat up with an extraordinary convulsive shudder.

"What didst thou mean, Ustane?" asked Leo, who, thanks to years of tuition, spoke Arabic very prettily.

"Nay, my chosen," she answered, with a little forced laugh. "I did but sing unto thee after the fashion of my people. Surely, I meant nothing. How could I speak of that which is not yet?"

"And what didst thou see, Ustane?" I asked, looking her sharply in the face.

"Nay," she answered again, "I saw naught. Ask me not what I saw. Why should I fright ye?" And then, turning to Leo with a look of the most utter tenderness that I ever saw upon the face of a woman, civilised or savage, she took his head between her hands, and kissed him on the forehead as a mother might.

"When I am gone from thee, my chosen," she said; "when at night thou stretchest out thine hand and canst not find me, then shouldst thou think at times of me, for of a truth I love thee well, though I be not fit to wash thy feet. And now let us love and take that which is given us, and be happy; for in the grave there is no love and no warmth, nor any touching of the lips. Nothing perchance, or perchance but bitter memories of what might have been. To-night the hours are our own, how know we to whom they shall belong to-morrow?"

VIII.
The Feast, and After!

On the day following this remarkable scene—a scene calculated to make a deep impression upon anybody who beheld it, more because of what it suggested and seemed to foreshadow than of what it revealed—it was announced to us that a feast would be held that evening in our honour. I did my best to get out of it, saying that we were modest people, and cared little for feasts, but my remarks being received with the silence of displeasure, I thought it wisest to hold my tongue.

Accordingly, just before sundown, I was informed that everything was ready, and, accompanied by Job, went into the cave, where I met Leo, who was, as usual, followed by Ustane. These two had been out walking somewhere, and knew nothing of the projected festivity till that moment. When Ustane heard of it I saw an expression of horror spring up upon her handsome features. Turning she caught a man who was passing up the cave by the arm, and asked him something in an imperious tone. His answer seemed to reassure her a little, for she looked relieved, though far from satisfied. Next she appeared to attempt some remonstrance with the man, who was a person in authority, but he spoke angrily to her, and shook her off, and then, changing his mind, led her by the arm, and sat her down between himself and another man in the circle round the fire, and I perceived that for some reason of her own she thought it best to submit.

The fire in the cave was an unusually big one that night, and in a large circle round it were gathered about thirty-five men and two women, Ustane and the woman to avoid whom Job had played the *rôle* of another Scriptural character.[1] The men were sitting in perfect silence, as was their custom, each with his great spear stuck upright behind him, in a socket cut in the rock for that purpose. Only one or two wore the yellowish linen garment of which I have spoken, the rest had nothing on except the leopard's skin about the middle.

"What's up now, sir?" said Job, doubtfully. "Bless us and save us, there's that woman again. Now, surely, she can't be after me, seeing that I have given her no encouragement. They give me the creeps, the whole lot of them, and that's a fact. Why look, they have asked Mahomed to dine, too. There, that lady of mine is talking to him in as nice and civil a way as possible. Well, I'm glad it isn't me, that's all."

We looked up, and sure enough the woman in question had risen, and was escorting the wretched Mahomed from his corner, where, overcome by some acute prescience of horror, he had been seated, shivering, and calling on Allah. He appeared unwilling enough to come, if for no other reason perhaps because it was an unaccustomed honour, for hitherto his food had been given to him apart. Anyway I could see that he was in a state of great terror, for his tottering legs would scarcely support his stout, bulky form, and I think it was rather owing to the resources of barbarism[2] behind him, in the shape of a huge Amahagger with a proportionately huge spear, than to the seductions of the lady who led him by the hand, that he consented to come at all.

"Well," I said to the others, "I don't at all like the look of things, but I suppose we must face it out. Have you fellows got your revolvers on? because, if so, you had better see that they are loaded."

"I have, sir," said Job, tapping his Colt,[3] "but Mr. Leo has only got his hunting-knife, though that is big enough, surely."

Feeling that it would not do to wait while the missing weapon was fetched, we advanced boldly, and seated ourselves in a line, with our backs against the side of the cave.

As soon as we were seated, an earthenware jar was passed round containing a fermented fluid, of by no means unpleasant taste, though apt to turn upon the stomach, made from crushed grain—not Indian corn, but a small brown grain that grows upon its stem in clusters, not unlike that which in the southern part of Africa is known by the name of Kafir corn.[4] The vase which contained this liquor was very curious, and as it more or less resembled many hundreds of others in use among the Amahagger I may as well describe it. These vases are of a very ancient manufacture, and of all sizes. None such can have been made in the country for hundreds, or rather thousands, of years. They are found in the rock tombs, of which I shall give a description in their proper place, and my own belief is that, after the fashion of the Egyptians, with whom the former inhabitants of this country may have had some connection, they were used to receive the viscera of the dead.[5] Leo, however, is of opinion that, as in the case of Etruscan amphora,[6] they were placed there for the spiritual use of the deceased. They are mostly two-handled, and of all sizes, some being nearly three feet in height, and running from that down to as many inches. In shape they vary, but are all exceedingly beautiful and graceful, being made of a very fine black ware, not lustrous, but slightly rough. On this groundwork are inlaid figures much more graceful and lifelike than any others that I have seen on antique vases. Some of these inlaid pictures represent love-scenes with a child-like simplicity and freedom of manner which would not commend itself to the taste of the present day. Others again give pictures of maidens dancing, and yet others of hunting-scenes. For instance, the very vase from which we were then drinking had on one side a most spirited drawing of men, apparently white in colour,[7] attacking a bull-elephant with spears, while on the reverse was a picture, not quite so well done, of a hunter shooting an arrow at a running antelope, I should say from the look of it either an eland or a koodoo.[8]

This is a digression at a critical moment, but it is not too long for the occasion, for the occasion itself was very long. With the exception of the periodical passing of the vase, and the movement necessary to throw fuel on to the fire, nothing happened for the best part of a whole hour. Nobody spoke a word. There we all sat in perfect silence, staring at the glare and glow of the large fire, and at the shadows thrown by the flickering earthenware lamps (which, by the way, were not ancient). On the open space between us and the fire lay a large wooden tray, with four short handles to it, exactly like a butcher's tray, only not hollowed out. By the side of the tray was a great pair of long-handled iron pincers, and on the other side of the fire was a similar pair. Somehow I did not at all like the appearance of this tray and the accompanying pincers. There I sat and stared at them and at the silent circle of the fierce moody faces of the men, and reflected that it was all very awful, and that we were absolutely in the power of this alarming people, who, to me at any rate, were all the more formidable because their true character was still very much of a mystery to us. They might be better than I thought them, or they might be worse. I feared that they were worse, and I was not wrong. It was a curious sort of a feast, I reflected, in appearance indeed, an entertainment of the Barmecide[9] stamp, for there was absolutely nothing to eat.

At last, just as I was beginning to feel as though I were being mesmerised,[10] a move was made. Without the slightest warning, a man from the other side of the circle called out in a loud voice—

"Where is the flesh that we shall eat?"

Thereon everybody in the circle answered in a deep measured tone, and stretching out the right arm towards the fire as he spoke—

"The flesh will come."[11]

"Is it a goat?" said the same man.

"It is a goat without horns, and more than a goat, and we shall slay it," they answered with one voice, and turning half round, they one and all grasped the handles of their spears with the right hand, and then simultaneously let them go.

"Is it an ox?" said the man, again.

"It is an ox without horns, and more than an ox, and we shall slay it," was the answer, and again the spears were grasped, and again let go.

Then came a pause, and I noticed, with horror and a rising of the hair, that the woman next to Mahomed began to fondle him, patting his cheeks, and calling him by names of endearment while her fierce eyes played up and down his trembling form. I do not know why the sight frightened me so, but it did frighten us all dreadfully, especially Leo. The caressing was so snake-like, and so evidently a part of some ghastly formula that had to be gone through.* I saw Mahomed turn white under his brown skin, sickly white with fear.

---

*We afterwards learnt that its object was to pretend to the victim that he was the object of love and admiration, and so to soothe his injured feelings, and cause him to expire in a happy and contented frame of mind.—L.H.H.

"Is the meat ready to be cooked?" asked the voice, more rapidly.

"*It is ready; it is ready.*"

"Is the pot hot to cook it?" it continued, in a sort of scream that echoed painfully down the great recesses of the cave.

"*It is hot; it is hot.*"

"Great heavens!" roared Leo, "remember the writing, '*The people who place pots upon the heads of strangers.*'"

As he said the words, before we could stir, or even take the matter in, two great ruffians jumped up, and, seizing the long pincers, plunged them into the heart of the fire, and the woman who had been caressing Mahomed suddenly produced a fibre noose from under her girdle or moocha,[12] and, slipping it over his shoulders, ran it tight, while the men next him seized him by the legs. The two men with the pincers gave a heave, and, scattering the fire this way and that upon the rocky floor, lifted from it a large earthenware pot, heated to a white heat. In an instant, almost with a single movement, they had reached the spot where Mahomed was struggling.[13] He fought like a fiend, shrieking in the abandonment of his despair, and notwithstanding the noose round him, and the efforts of the men who held his legs, the advancing wretches were for the moment unable to accomplish their purpose, which, horrible and incredible as it seems, was *to put the red-hot pot upon his head.*[14]

I sprang to my feet with a yell of horror, and drawing my revolver fired it by a sort of instinct straight at the diabolical woman who had been caressing Mahomed, and was now gripping him in her arms. The bullet struck her in the back and killed her, and to this day I am glad that it did, for, as it afterwards transpired, she had availed herself of the anthropophagous customs[15] of the Amahagger to organise the whole thing in revenge of the slight put upon her by Job. She sank down dead, and as she did so, to my terror and dismay, Mohamed, by a superhuman effort, burst from his tormentors, and, springing high into the air, fell dying upon her corpse. The heavy bullet from my pistol had driven through the bodies of both, at once striking down the murderess, and saving her victim from a death a hundred times more horrible. It was an awful and yet a most merciful accident.

For a moment there was a silence of astonishment. The Amahagger had never heard the report of a firearm before, and its effects dismayed them. But the next a man close to us recovered himself, and seized his spear preparatory to making a lunge with it at Leo, who was the nearest to him.

"Run for it!" I shouted, setting the example by starting up the cave as hard as my legs would carry me. I would have made for the open air if it had been possible, but there were men in the way, and, besides, I had caught sight of the forms of a crowd of people standing out clear against the skyline beyond the entrance to the cave. Up the cave I went, and after me came the others, and after them thundered the whole crowd of cannibals, mad with fury at the death of the woman. With a bound I cleared the prostrate form of Mahomed. As I flew over him I felt the heat from the red hot pot, which was lying close by, strike upon my legs, and by its glow saw his hands—for he was not quite dead—still feebly moving.[16] At the top of the cave was a little platform of rock three feet or so high by about eight deep, on which two large lamps were placed at night. Whether this platform had been left as a seat, or as a raised point afterwards to be cut away when it had served its purpose as a standing place from which to carry on the excavations, I do not know—at least, I did not then.[17] At any rate, we all three reached it, and, jumping on it, prepared to sell our lives as dearly as we could. For a few seconds the crowd that was pressing on our heels hung back when they saw us face round upon them. Job was on one side of the rock to the left, Leo in the centre, and I to the right. Behind us were the lamps. Leo bent forward, and looked down the long lane of shadows, terminating in the fire and lighted lamps, through which the quiet forms of our would-be murderers flitted to and fro with the faint light glinting on their spears, for even their fury was silent as a bulldog's. The only other thing visible was the red-hot pot still glowing angrily in the gloom. There was a curious light in Leo's eyes, and his handsome face was set like a stone. In his right hand was his heavy hunting-knife. He shifted its thong a little up his wrist, and then put his arm round me and gave me a good hug.

"Good-bye, old fellow," he said, "my dear friend—my more than father. We have no chance against those scoundrels; they will finish us in a few minutes, and eat us afterwards, I suppose. Good-bye. I led you into this. I hope you will forgive me. Good-bye, Job."

"God's will be done," I said, setting my teeth, as I prepared for the end. At that moment, with an exclamation, Job lifted his revolver and fired, and hit a man—not the man he had aimed at by the way: anything that Job shot *at* was perfectly safe.

On they came with a rush, and I fired too as fast as I could, and checked them—between us, Job and I, besides the woman, killed or mortally wounded five men with our pistols before they were emptied. But we had no time to reload, and they still came on in a way that was almost splendid in its recklessness, seeing that they did not know but that we could go on firing for ever.

A great fellow bounded up upon the platform, and Leo struck him dead with one blow of his powerful arm, sending the knife right through him. I did the same by another, but Job missed his stroke, and I saw a brawny Amahagger grip him by the middle and whirl him off the rock. The knife not being secured by a thong fell from Job's hand as he did so, and, by a most happy accident for him, lit upon its handle on the rock, just as the body of the Amahagger, who was undermost, struck upon its point and was transfixed upon it. What happened to Job after that I am sure I do not know, but my own impression is that he lay still upon the corpse of his deceased assailant, "playing 'possum'" as the Americans say. As for myself, I was soon involved in a desperate encounter with two ruffians who, luckily for me, had left their spears behind them; and for the first time in my life the great physical power with which Nature has endowed me stood me in good stead. I had hacked at the head of one man with my hunting-knife, which was almost as big and heavy as a short sword, with such vigour, that the sharp steel had split his skull down to the eyes, and was held so fast by it that as he suddenly fell sideways the knife was twisted right out of my hand.

Then it was that the two others sprang upon me. I saw them coming, and got an arm round the waist of each, and down we all fell upon the floor of the cave together, rolling over and over. They were strong men, but I was mad with rage, and that awful lust for slaughter which will creep into the hearts of the most civilised of us when blows are flying, and life and death tremble on the turn.[18] My arms were round the two swarthy demons, and I hugged them till I heard their ribs crack and crunch up beneath my gripe.[19] They twisted and writhed like snakes, and clawed and battered at me with their fists, but I held on. Lying on my back there, so that their bodies might protect me from spear thrusts from above, I slowly crushed the life out of them, and as I did so, strange as it may seem, I thought of what the amiable Head of my College at Cambridge (who is a member of the Peace Society[20]) and my brother Fellows would say if by clairvoyance they could see me, of all men, playing such a bloody game. Soon my assailants grew faint, and almost ceased to struggle, their breath had failed them, and they were dying, but still I dared not leave them, for they died very slowly. I knew that if I relaxed my grip they would revive. The other ruffians probably thought—for we were all three lying in the shadow of the ledge —that we were all dead together, at any rate they did not interfere with our little tragedy.

I turned my head, and as I lay gasping in the throes of that awful struggle I could see that Leo was off the rock now, for the lamplight fell full upon him. He was still on his feet, but in the centre of a surging mass of struggling men, who were striving to pull him down as wolves pull down a stag. Up above them towered his beautiful pale face crowned with its bright curls (for Leo is six feet two high), and I saw that he was fighting with a desperate abandonment and energy that was at once splendid and hideous to behold. He drove his knife through one man—they were so close to him and mixed up with him that they could not get at him to kill him with their big spears, and they had no knives or sticks. The man fell, and then somehow the knife was wrenched from his hand, leaving him defenceless, and I thought the end had come. But no; with a desperate effort he broke loose from them, seized the body of the man he had just slain, and lifting it high in the air hurled it right at the mob of his assailants, so that the shock and weight of it swept some five or six of them to the earth. But in a minute they were all up again, except one, whose skull was smashed, and had once more fastened upon him. And then slowly, and with infinite labour and struggling, the wolves bore the lion down. Once even then he recovered himself, and felled an Amahagger with his fist, but it was more than man could do to hold his own for long against so many, and at last he came crashing down upon the rock floor, falling as an oak falls, and bearing with him to the earth all those who clung about him. They gripped him by his arms and legs, and then cleared off his body.

"A spear," cried a voice, "a spear to cut his throat and a vessel to catch his blood."

I shut my eyes, for I saw the man coming with a spear, and myself, I could not stir to Leo's help, for I was growing weak, and the two men on me were not yet dead, and a deadly sickness overcame me.

Then suddenly there was a disturbance, and involuntarily I opened my eyes again, and looked towards the scene of murder. The girl Ustane had thrown herself on Leo's prostrate form, covering his body with her body, and fastening her arms about his neck. They tried to drag her from him, but she twisted her legs round his, and hung on like a bulldog, or rather like a creeper to a tree, and they could not. Then they tried to stab him in the side without hurting her, but somehow she shielded him, and he was only wounded.

At last they lost patience.

"Drive the spear through the man and the woman together," said a voice, the same voice that had asked the questions at that ghastly feast, "so of a verity shall they be wed."

Then I saw the man with the weapon straighten himself for the effort. I saw the cold steel gleam on high, and once more I shut my eyes.

As I did so, I heard the voice of a man thunder out in tones that rang and echoed down the rocky ways—

"*Cease!*"

Then I fainted, and as I did so it flashed through my darkening mind that I was passing down into the last oblivion of death.

IX.
A Little Foot.

When I opened my eyes again I found myself lying on a skin mat not far from the fire round which we had been gathered for that dreadful feast. Near me lay Leo, still apparently in a swoon, and over him was bending the tall form of the girl Ustane, who was washing a deep spear wound in his side with cold water preparatory to binding it up with linen. Leaning against the wall of the cave behind her was Job, apparently uninjured, but bruised and trembling. On the other side of the fire, tossed about this way and that, as though they had thrown themselves down to sleep in some moment of absolute exhaustion, were the bodies of those whom we had killed in our frightful struggle for life.[1] I counted them: there were twelve besides the woman, and the corpse of poor Mahomed, who had died by my hand, which, the fire-stained pot at its side, was placed at the end of the irregular line. To the left a body of men were engaged in binding the arms of the survivors of the cannibals behind them, and then fastening them two and two. The villains were submitting with a look of sulky indifference upon their faces which accorded ill with the baffled fury that gleamed in their sombre eyes. In front of these men, directing the operations, stood no other than our friend Billali, looking rather tired, but particularly patriarchal with his flowing beard, and as cool and unconcerned as though he were superintending the cutting up of an ox.

Presently he turned, and perceiving that I was sitting up advanced to me, and with the utmost courtesy said that he trusted that I felt better. I answered that at present I scarcely knew how I felt, except that I ached all over.

Then he bent down and examined Leo's wound.

"It is an evil cut," he said, "but the spear has not pierced the entrails. He will recover."

"Thanks to thy arrival, my father," I answered. "In another minute we should all have been beyond the reach of recovery, for those devils of thine[2] would have slain us as they would have slain our servant," and I pointed towards Mahomed.

The old man ground his teeth, and I saw an extraordinary expression of malignity light up his eyes.

"Fear not, my son," he answered. "Vengeance shall be taken on them such as would make the flesh twist upon the bones merely to hear of it. To *She* shall they go, and her vengeance shall be worthy of her greatness. That man," pointing to Mahomed, "I tell thee that man would have died a merciful death to the death these hyæna-men[3] shall die. Tell me, I pray of thee, how it came about."

In a few words I sketched what had happened.

"Ah, so," he answered. "Thou seest, my son, here there is a custom that if a stranger comes into this country he may be slain by 'the pot,' and eaten."

"It is hospitality turned upside down," I answered feebly.[4] "In our country we entertain a stranger, and give him food to eat. Here ye eat him, and are entertained."

"It is a custom," he answered, with a shrug. "Myself I think it an evil one; but then," he added by an afterthought, "I do not like the taste of strangers, especially after they have wandered through the swamps and lived on wildfowl. When *She-who-must-be-obeyed* sent orders that ye were to be saved alive she said naught of the black man, therefore, being hyænas, these men lusted after his flesh, and the woman it was, whom thou didst rightly

slay, who put it into their evil hearts to hot-pot him. Well, they will have
their reward. Better for them would it be if they had never seen the light
than that they should stand before *She* in her terrible anger. Happy are those
of them that died by your hands.

"Ah," he went on, "it was a gallant fight that ye fought. Knowest thou
that, long-armed old baboon that thou art, thou hast crushed in the ribs
of those two who are laid out there as though they were but as the shell
on an egg? And the young one, the lion, it was a beautiful stand that he
made—one against so many—three did he slay outright, and that one there"
—and he pointed to a body that was still moving a little—"will die anon,
for his head is cracked across, and others of those who are bound are hurt.
It was a gallant fight, and thou and he have made a friend of me by it,
for I love to see a well-fought fray. But tell me, my son, the baboon—and
now I think of it thy face, too, is hairy, and altogether like a baboon's—
how was it that ye slew those with a hole in them?—Ye made a noise, they
say, and slew them—they fell down on their faces at the noise?"

I explained to him as well as I could, but very shortly—for I was terribly
wearied, and only persuaded to talk at all through fear of offending one
so powerful if I refused to do so—what were the properties of gunpowder,
and he instantly suggested that I should illustrate what I said by operating
on the person of one of the prisoners. One, he said, never would be counted,
and it would not only be very interesting to him, but would give me an
opportunity of an instalment of revenge. He was greatly astounded when
I told him that it was not our custom to avenge ourselves in cold blood,
and that we left vengeance to the law and a higher power, of which he
knew nothing. I added, however, that when I recovered I would take him
out shooting with us, and he should kill an animal for himself, and at this
he was as pleased as a child at the promise of a new toy.

Just then, Leo opened his eyes beneath the stimulus of some brandy (of
which we still had a little) that Job had poured down his throat, and our
conversation came to an end.

After this we managed to get Leo, who was in a very poor way indeed,
and only half conscious, safely off to bed, supported by Job and that brave
girl Ustane, to whom, had I not been afraid that she might resent it, I would
certainly have given a kiss for her splendid behaviour in saving my boy's
life at the risk of her own. But Ustane was not the sort of young person
with whom one would care to take liberties unless one were perfectly certain
that they would not be misunderstood, so I repressed my inclinations. Then,
bruised and battered, but with a sense of safety in my breast to which I
had for some days been a stranger, I crept off to my own little sepulchre,
not forgetting before I laid down in it to thank Providence[5] from the bottom
of my heart that it was not a sepulchre indeed, as, save for a merciful combination of events that I can only attribute to its protection, it would certainly
have been for me that night. Few men have been nearer their end and yet
escaped it than we were on that dreadful day.

I am a bad sleeper at the best of times, and my dreams that night when at last I got to rest were not of the pleasantest. The awful vision of poor Mahomed struggling to escape the red-hot pot would haunt them, and then in the background, as it were, a veiled form was always hovering, which, from time to time, seemed to draw the coverings from its body, revealing now the perfect shape of a lovely blooming woman, and now again the white bones of a grinning skeleton, and which, as it veiled and unveiled, uttered the mysterious and apparently meaningless sentence:

"That which is alive hath known death, and that which is dead yet can never die, for in the Circle of the Spirit life is naught and death is naught. Yea, all things live for ever, though at times they sleep and are forgotten."[6]

The morning came at last, but when it came I found that I was too stiff and sore to rise. About seven Job arrived, limping terribly, and with his face the colour of a rotten apple, and told me that Leo had slept fairly, but was very weak. Two hours afterwards Billali (Job called him "Billy-goat," to which, indeed, his white beard gave him some resemblance, or more familiarly "Billy"[7]) came too, bearing a lamp in his hand, his towering form reaching nearly to the roof of the little chamber. I pretended to be asleep, and through the cracks of my eyelids watched his sardonic but handsome old face. He fixed his hawk-like eyes upon me, and stroked his glorious white beard, which, by the way, would have been worth a hundred a year to any London barber as an advertisement.

"Ah!" I heard him mutter (Billali had a habit of muttering to himself), "he is ugly—ugly as the other is beautiful—a very Baboon, it was a good name. But I like the man. Strange now, at my age, that I should like a man. What says the proverb—'Mistrust all men, and slay him whom thou mistrustest overmuch; and as for women, flee from them, for they are evil, and in the end will destroy thee.' It is a good proverb, especially the last part of it: I think that it must have come down from the ancients. Nevertheless I like this Baboon, and I wonder where they taught him his tricks, and I trust that *She* will not bewitch him. Poor Baboon! he must be wearied after that fight. I will go lest I should awake him."

I waited till he had turned and was nearly through the entrance, walking softly on tiptoe, and then called after him.

"My father," I said, "is it thou?"

"Yes, my son, it is I; but let me not disturb thee. I did but come to see how thou didst fare, and to tell thee that those who would have slain thee, my Baboon, are now far on their road to *She*. *She* said that ye also were to come at once, but I fear ye cannot yet."

"Nay," I said, "not till we have recovered a little; but have me borne out into the daylight, I pray thee, my father. I love not this place."

"Ah, no," he answered, "it hath a sad air. I remember when I was a boy I found the body of a fair woman lying where thou liest now, yes, on that very bench. She was so beautiful that I was wont to creep in hither with a lamp and gaze upon her. Had it not been for her cold hands,[8] almost could I think that she slept and would one day awake, so fair and peaceful was she in her robes of white. White was she, too, and her hair was yellow and lay down her almost to the feet. There are many such still in the tombs at the place where *She* is, for those who set them there had a way I know naught of, whereby to keep their beloved out of the crumbling hand of Decay, even when Death had slain them. Ay, day by day I came hither, and gazed on her till at last—laugh not at me, stranger, for I was but a silly lad— I learned to love that dead form, that shell which once had held a life that no more is. I would creep up to her and kiss her cold face, and wonder how many men had lived and died since she was, and who had loved her and embraced her in the days that long had passed away. And, my Baboon, I think I learned wisdom from that dead one, for of a truth it taught me of the littleness of life, and the length of Death, and how all things that are under the sun go down one path, and are for ever forgotten. And so I mused, and it seemed to me that wisdom flowed into me from the dead, till one day my mother, a watchful woman, but hasty-minded, seeing I was changed, followed me, and saw the beautiful white one, and feared that I was bewitched, as, indeed, I was. So half in dread, and half in anger, she took the lamp, and standing the dead woman up against the wall even there, set fire to her hair, and she burnt fiercely, even down to the feet, for those who are thus kept burn excellently well.

"See, my son, there on the roof is yet the smoke of her burning."

I looked up doubtfully, and there, sure enough, on the roof of the sepulchre, was a peculiarly unctuous[9] and sooty mark, three feet or more across. Doubtless it had in the course of years been rubbed off the sides of the little cave, but on the roof it remained, and there was no mistaking its appearance.

"She burnt," he went on in a meditative way, "even to the feet, but the feet I came back and saved, cutting the burnt bone from them, and hid them under the stone bench there, wrapped up in a piece of linen. Surely, I remember it as though it were but yesterday. Perchance they are there, if none have found them, even to this hour. Of a truth I have not entered this chamber from that time to this very day. Stay, I will look," and, kneeling down, he groped about with his long arm in the recess under the stone bench. Presently his face brightened, and with an exclamation he pulled something forth that was caked in dust; which he shook on to the floor. It was covered with the remains of a rotting rag, which he undid, and revealed to my astonished gaze a beautifully shaped and almost white woman's foot, looking as fresh and firm as though it had but now been placed there.

"Thou seest, my son, the Baboon," he said, in a sad voice, "I spake the truth to thee, for here is yet one foot remaining. Take it, my son, and gaze upon it."

I took this cold fragment of mortality in my hand and looked at it in the light of the lamp with feelings which I cannot describe, so mixed up were they between astonishment, fear, and fascination. It was light, much lighter I should say than it had been in the living state, and the flesh to all appearance was still flesh, though about it there clung a faintly aromatic odour. For the rest it was not shrunk or shrivelled, or even black and unsightly, like the flesh of Egyptian mummies, but plump and fair, and, except where it had been slightly burnt, perfect as on the day of death—a very triumph of embalming.

Poor little foot! I set it down upon the stone bench where it had lain for so many thousand years, and wondered whose was the beauty that it had upborne through the pomp and pageantry of a forgotten civilisation —first as a merry child's, then as a blushing maid's, and lastly as a perfect woman's. Through what halls of Life had its soft step echoed, and in the end, with what courage had it trodden down the dusty ways of Death! To whose side had it stolen in the hush of night when the black slave slept upon the marble floor, and who had listened for its stealing? Shapely little foot! Well might it have been set upon the proud neck of a conqueror bent at last to woman's beauty, and well might the lips of nobles and of kings have been pressed upon its jewelled whiteness.

I wrapped up this relic of the past in the remnants of the old linen rag which had evidently formed a portion of its owner's grave-clothes, for it was partially burnt, and put it away in my Gladstone bag[10]—a strange combination, I thought. Then with Billali's help I staggered off to see Leo. I found him dreadfully bruised, worse even than myself, perhaps owing to the excessive whiteness of his skin, and faint and weak with the loss of blood from the flesh wound in his side, but for all that cheerful as a cricket, and asking for some breakfast. Job and Ustane got him on to the bottom, or rather the sacking of a litter, which was removed from its pole for that purpose, and with the aid of old Billali carried him out into the shade at the mouth of the cave, from which, by the way, every trace of the slaughter of the previous night had now been removed, and there we all breakfasted, and indeed spent that day, and most of the two following ones.

On the third morning Job and myself were practically recovered. Leo also was so much better that I yielded to Billali's often expressed entreaty, and agreed to start at once upon our journey to Kôr, which we were told was the name of the place where the mysterious *She* lived, though I still feared for its effects upon Leo, and especially lest the motion should cause his wound, which was scarcely skinned over, to break open again. Indeed, had it not been for Billali's evident anxiety to get off, which led us to suspect that some difficulty or danger might threaten us if we did not comply with it, I would not have consented to go.

X.

Speculations.

Within an hour of our finally deciding to start five litters were brought up to the door of the cave, each accompanied by four regular bearers and two spare hands, also a band of about fifty armed Amahagger, who were to form the escort and carry the baggage. Three of these litters, of course, were for us, and one for Billali, who, I was immensely relieved to hear, was to be our companion, while the fifth I presume was for the use of Ustane.

"Does the lady go with us, my father?" I asked of Billali, as he stood superintending things in general.

He shrugged his shoulders as he answered—

"If she wills. In this country the women do what they please. We worship them, and give them their way, because without them the world could not go on; they are the source of life."

"Ah," I said, the matter never having struck me quite in that light before.

"We worship them," he went on, "up to a point, till at last they get unbearable, which," he added, "they do about every second generation."[1]

"And then what do you do?" I asked, with curiosity.

"Then," he answered, with a faint smile, "we rise, and kill the old ones as an example to the young ones, and to show them that we are the strongest. My poor wife was killed in that way three years ago. It was very sad, but to tell thee the truth, my son, life has been happier since, for my age protects me from the young ones."

"In short," I replied, quoting the saying of a great man whose wisdom has not yet lightened the darkness of the Amahagger, "thou hast found thy position one of greater freedom and less responsibility."[2]

This phrase puzzled him a little at first from its vagueness, though I think my translation hit off its sense very well, but at last he saw it, and appreciated it.

"Yes, yes, my Baboon," he said, "I see it now, but all the 'responsibilities' are killed, at least some of them are, and that is why there are so few old women about just now. Well, they brought it on themselves. As for this girl," he went on, in a graver tone, "I know not what to say. She is a brave girl, and she loves the Lion (Leo); thou sawest how she clung to him, and saved his life.[3] Also, she is, according to our custom, wed to him, and has a right to go where he goes, unless," he added significantly, "*She* would say her no, for her word overrides all rights."

"And if *She* bade her leave him, and the girl refused? What then?"

"If," he said, with a shrug, "the hurricane bids the tree to bend, and it will not; what happens?"

And then, without waiting for an answer, he turned and walked to his litter, and in ten minutes from that time we were all well under way.

It took us an hour and more to cross the cup of the volcanic plain, and another half-hour or so to climb the edge on the farther side. Once there, however, the view was a very fine one.[4] Before us was a long steep slope of grassy plain, broken here and there by clumps of trees mostly of the thorn tribe. At the bottom of this gentle slope, some nine or ten miles away, we could make out a dim sea of marsh, over which the foul vapours hung like smoke about a city.[5] It was easy going for the bearers down the slopes, and by midday we had reached the borders of the dismal swamp. Here we halted to eat our midday meal, and then, following a winding and devious path, plunged into the morass. Presently the path, at any rate to our unaccustomed eyes, grew so faint as to be almost indistinguishable from those made by the aquatic beasts and birds, and it is to this day a mystery to me how our bearers found their way across the marshes. Ahead of the cavalcade marched two men with long poles, which they now and again plunged into the ground before them, the reason of this being that the nature of the soil frequently changed from causes with which I am not acquainted, so that places which might be safe enough to cross one month would certainly swallow the wayfarer the next. Never did I see a more dreary and depressing scene. Miles on miles of quagmire,[6] varied only by bright green strips of comparatively solid ground, and by deep and sullen pools fringed with tall rushes, in which the bitterns boomed and the frogs croaked incessantly: miles on miles of it without a break, unless the fever fog can be called a break. The only life in this great morass was that of the aquatic birds, and the animals that fed on them, of both of which there were vast numbers. Geese, cranes, ducks, teal, coot, snipe, and plover swarmed all around us, many being of varieties that were quite new to me, and all so tame that one could almost have knocked them over with a stick. Among these birds I especially noticed a very beautiful variety of painted snipe, almost the size of woodcock, and with a flight more resembling that bird's than an English snipe's.[7] In the pools, too, was a species of small alligator or enormous iguana, I do not know which, that fed, Billali told me, upon the waterfowl, also large quantities of a hideous black water-snake, of which the bite is very dangerous, though not, I gathered, so deadly as a cobra's or a puff adder's. The bull frogs were also very large, and with voices proportionate to their size; and as for the mosquitoes—the "musqueteers," as Job called them—they were, if possible, even worse than they had been on the river, and tormented us greatly. Undoubtedly, however, the worst feature of the swamp was the awful smell of rotting vegetation that hung about it, which was at times positively overpowering, and the malarious exhalations that accompanied it, which we were of course obliged to breathe.[8]

On we went through it all, till at last the sun sank in sullen splendour just as we reached a spot of rising ground about two acres in extent—

a little oasis of dry in the midst of the miry wilderness—where Billali announced that we were to camp. The camping, however, turned out to be
a very simple process, and consisted, in fact, in sitting down on the ground
round a scanty fire made of dry reeds and some wood that had been brought
with us. However, we made the best we could of it, and smoked and ate
with such appetite as the smell of damp, stifling heat would allow, for it
was very hot on this low land, and yet, oddly enough, chilly at times. But,
however hot it was, we were glad enough to keep near the fire, because
we found that the mosquitoes did not like the smoke. Presently we rolled
ourselves up in our blankets and tried to go to sleep, but so far as I was
concerned the bull-frogs, and the extraordinary roaring and alarming sound
produced by hundreds of snipe hovering high in the air, made sleep an impossibility, to say nothing of our other discomforts. I turned and looked at Leo,
who was next me; he was dozing, but his face had a flushed appearance
that I did not like, and by the flickering fire-light I saw Ustane, who was
lying on the other side of him, raise herself from time to time upon her
elbow, and look at him anxiously enough.

However, I could do nothing for him, for we had all already taken a
good dose of quinine, which was the only preventative we had;[9] so I lay
and watched the stars come out by thousands, till all the immense arch of
heaven was strewn with glittering points, and every point a world! Here
was a glorious sight by which man might well measure his own insignifi-
cance! Soon I gave up thinking about it, for the mind wearies easily when
it strives to grapple with the Infinite, and to trace the footsteps of the Almighty
as he strides from sphere to sphere, or deduce His purpose from His works.
Such things are not for us to know. Knowledge is to the strong, and we
are weak. Too much wisdom would perchance blind our imperfect sight,
and too much strength would make us drunk, and overweight our feeble
reason till it fell and we were drowned in the depths of our own vanity.
For what is the first result of man's increased knowledge interpreted from
Nature's book by the persistent effort of his purblind observation? Is it not
but too often to make him question the existence of his Maker, or indeed
of any intelligent purpose beyond his own? The truth is veiled,[10] because
we could no more look upon her glory than we can upon the sun. It would
destroy us. Full knowledge is not for man as man is here, for his capacities,
which he is apt to think so great, are indeed but small. The vessel is soon
filled, and, were one-thousandth part of the unutterable and silent wisdom
that directs the rolling of those shining spheres, and the Force which makes
them roll, pressed into it, it would be shattered into fragments. Perhaps in
some other place and time it may be otherwise, who can tell? Here the lot
of man born of the flesh is but to endure midst toil and tribulation, to catch
at the bubbles blown by Fate, which he calls pleasures, thankful if before
they burst they rest a moment in his hand, and when the tragedy is played
out and his hour comes to perish, to pass humbly whither he knows not.

Above me, as I lay, shone the eternal stars, and there at my feet the impish marsh-born balls of fire rolled this way and that, vapour-tossed and earth-desiring, and methought that in the two I saw a type and image of what man is, and what perchance man may one day be, if the living Force who ordained him and them should so ordain this also. Oh, that it might be ours to rest year by year upon that high level of the heart to which at times we momentarily attain! Oh, that we could shake loose the prisoned pinions of the soul and soar to that superior point, whence, like to some traveller looking out through space from Darien's giddiest peak, we might gaze with the spiritual eyes deep into Infinity![11]

What would it be to cast off this earthy robe, to have done for ever with these earthy thoughts and miserable desires; no longer, like those corpse candles,[12] to be tossed this way and that, by forces beyond our control; or which, if we can theoretically control them, we are at times driven by the exigencies of our nature to obey! Yes, to cast them off, to have done with the foul and thorny places of the world; and like to those glittering points above me, to rest on high wrapped for ever in the brightness of our better selves, that even now shines in us as fire faintly shines within those lurid balls, and lay down our littleness in that wide glory of our dreams, that invisible but surrounding Good, from which all truth and beauty comes!

These and many such thoughts passed through my mind that night. They come to torment us all at times. I say to torment, for alas! thinking can only serve to measure out the helplessness of thought. What is the purpose of our feeble crying in the awful silences of space? Can our dim intelligence read the secrets of that star-strewn sky? Does any answer come out of it? Never any at all, nothing but echoes and fantastic visions! And yet we believe that there is an answer, and that upon a time a new Dawn will come blushing down the ways of our enduring night.[13] We believe it, for its reflected beauty even now shines up continually in our hearts from beneath the horizon of the grave, and we call it Hope. Without Hope we should suffer moral death,[14] and by the help of Hope we yet may climb to Heaven, or at the worst, if she also prove but a kindly mockery given to hold us from despair, be gently lowered into the abysses of eternal sleep.

Then I fell to reflecting upon the undertaking on which we were bent, and what a wild one it was, and yet how strangely the story seemed to fit in with what had been written centuries ago upon the sherd. Who was this extraordinary woman, Queen over a people apparently as extraordinary as herself, and reigning amidst the vestiges of a lost civilisation? And what was the meaning of this story of the Fire that gave unending life? Could it be possible that any fluid or essence should exist which might so fortify these fleshy walls that they should from age to age resist the mines and batterings of decay?[15] It was possible, though not probable. The indefinite continuation of life would not, as poor Vincey said, be so marvellous a thing as the production of life and its temporary endurance.[16] And if it were true, what then? The person who found it could no doubt rule the world. He could accumulate all the wealth in the world, and all the power, and all the wisdom that is power. He might give a lifetime to the study of each art or science. Well, if that were so, and this *She* were practically immortal, which I did not for one moment believe, how was it that, with all these things at her feet, she preferred to remain in a cave amongst a society of cannibals? This surely settled the question. The whole story was monstrous, and only worthy of the superstitious days in which it was written. At any rate I was very sure that *I* would not attempt to attain unending life. I had had far too many worries and disappointments and secret bitternesses during my forty odd years of existence to wish that this state of affairs should be continued indefinitely. And yet I suppose that my life has been, comparatively speaking, a happy one.

And then, reflecting that at the present moment there was far more likelihood of our earthly careers being cut exceedingly short than of their being unduly prolonged, I at last managed to get to sleep, a fact for which anybody who reads this narrative, if anybody ever does, may very probably be thankful.

When I woke again it was just dawning, and the guard and bearers were moving about like ghosts through the dense morning mists, getting ready for our start. The fire had died quite down, and I rose and stretched myself, shivering in every limb from the damp cold of the dawn. Then I looked at Leo. He was sitting up, holding his hands to his head, and I saw that his face was flushed and his eyes bright, and yet yellow round the pupil.

"Well, Leo," I said, "how do you feel?"

"I feel as though I were going to die," he answered hoarsely. "My head is splitting, my body is trembling, and I am as sick as a cat."

I whistled, or if I did not whistle, I felt inclined to—Leo had got a sharp attack of fever. I went to Job, and asked him for the quinine, of which fortunately we had still a good supply, only to find that Job himself was not much better. He complained of pains across the back, and dizziness, and was almost incapable of helping himself. Then I did the only thing it was possible to do under the circumstances—gave them both about ten grains of quinine, and took a slightly smaller dose myself as a matter of precaution. After that I found Billali, and explained to him how matters stood, asking at the same time what he thought had best be done. He came with me, and looked at Leo and Job (whom, by the way, he had named the Pig on account of his fatness, round face, and small eyes).

"Ah," he said, when we were out of earshot, "the fever!¹⁷ I thought so. The Lion has it badly, but he is young, and he may live. As for the Pig, his attack is not so bad; it is the 'little fever' which he has; that always begins with pains across the back, it will spend itself upon his fat."

"Can they go on, my father?" I asked.

"Nay, my son, they must go on. If they stop here they will certainly die; also, they will be better in the litters than on the ground. By to-night, if all goes well, we shall be across the marsh and in good air.¹⁸ Come, let us lift them into the litters and start, for it is very bad to stand still in this morning fog. We can eat our meal as we go."

This we accordingly did, and with a heavy heart I once more set out upon our strange journey. For the first three hours all went as well as could be expected, and then an accident happened that nearly lost us the pleasure of the company of our venerable friend Billali, whose litter was leading the cavalcade. We were going through a particularly dangerous stretch of quag-mire, in which the bearers sometimes sank up to their knees. Indeed, it was a mystery to me how they contrived to carry the heavy litters at all over such ground as that which we were traversing, though the two spare hands, as well as the four regular ones, had of course to put their shoulders to the pole.

Presently, as we blundered and floundered along, there was a sharp cry, then a storm of exclamations, and, last of all, a most tremendous splash, and the whole caravan halted.

I jumped out of my litter and ran forward. About twenty yards ahead was the edge of one of those sullen peaty pools of which I have spoken, the path we were following running along the top of its bank, that, as it happened, was a steep one. Looking towards this pool, to my horror I saw that Billali's litter was floating on it, and as for Billali himself, he was nowhere to be seen. To make matters clear I may as well explain at once what had happened. One of Billali's bearers had unfortunately trodden on a basking snake, which had bitten him in the leg, whereon he had, not unnaturally, let go of the pole, and then, finding that he was tumbling down the bank, grasped at the litter to save himself. The result of this was what might have been expected. The litter was pulled over the edge of the bank, the bearers let go, and the whole thing, including Billali and the man who had been bitten, rolled into the slimy pool. When I got to the edge of the water neither of them were to be seen; indeed, the unfortunate bearer never was seen again. Either he struck his head against something, or got wedged in the mud, or possibly the snake-bite paralysed him. At any rate he vanished. But though Billali was not to be seen, his whereabouts was clear enough from the agitation of the floating litter, in the bearing cloth and curtains of which he was entangled.

"He is there! Our father is there!" said one of the men, but he did not stir a finger to help him, nor did any of the others. They simply stood and stared at the water.[19]

"Out of the way, you brutes," I shouted in English, and throwing off my hat I took a run and sprang well out into the horrid slimy-looking pool. A couple of strokes took me to where Billali was struggling beneath the cloth.

Somehow, I do not quite know how, I managed to push it free of him, and his venerable head all covered with green slime, like that of a yellowish Bacchus with ivy leaves,[20] emerged upon the surface of the water. The rest was easy, for Billali was an eminently practical individual, and had the com-mon sense not to grasp hold of me as drowning people often do, so I got him by the arm, and towed him to the bank, through the mud of which we were with difficulty dragged. Such a filthy spectacle as we presented I have never seen before or since, and it will perhaps give some idea of the almost superhuman dignity of Billali's appearance when I say that, coughing, half-drowned, and covered with mud and green slime as he was, with his beautiful beard coming to a dripping point, like a Chinaman's freshly-oiled pig-tail, he still looked venerable and imposing.[21]

"Ye dogs," he said, addressing the bearers, as soon as he had sufficiently recovered to speak, "ye left me, your father, to drown. Had it not been for this stranger, my son the Baboon, assuredly I should have drowned. Well, I will remember it," and he fixed them with his gleaming though slightly watery eye, in a way I saw that they did not like, though they tried to appear sulkily indifferent.

"As for thee, my son," the old man went on, turning towards me and grasping my hand, "rest assured that I am thy friend through good and evil. Thou hast saved my life: perchance a day may come when I shall save thine."

After that we cleaned ourselves as best we could, fished out the litter, and went on, *minus* the man who had been drowned. I do not know if it was owing to his being an unpopular character, or from native indifference and selfishness of temperament, but I am bound to say that nobody seemed to grieve much over his sudden and final disappearance, unless, perhaps, it was the men who had to do his share of the work.

XI.
The Plain of Kôr.

About an hour before sundown we at last, to my unbounded gratitude, emerged from the great belt of marsh on to land that swelled upwards in a succession of rolling waves. Just on the hither side of the crest of the first wave we halted for the night. My first act was to examine Leo's condition. It was, if anything, worse than in the morning, and a new and very distressing feature, vomiting, set in, and continued till dawn. Not one wink of sleep did I get that night, for I passed it in assisting Ustane, who was one of the most gentle and indefatigable nurses I ever saw, to wait upon Leo and Job. However, the air here was warm and genial without being too hot, and there were no mosquitoes to speak of. Also we were above the level of the marsh mist, which lay stretched beneath us like the dim smoke-pall over a city, lit up here and there by the wandering globes of fen fire. Thus it will be seen that we were, speaking comparatively, in clover.

By dawn on the following morning Leo was quite light-headed, and fancied that he was divided into halves.[1] I was dreadfully distressed, and began to wonder with a sort of sick fear what the end of the attack would be. Alas! I had heard but too much of how these attacks generally terminate. As I was wondering Billali came up and said that we must be getting on, more especially as, in his opinion, if Leo did not reach some spot where he could be quiet, and have proper nursing, within the next twelve hours, his life would only be a matter of a day or two. I could not but agree with him, so we got Leo into the litter, and started on, Ustane walking by his side to keep the flies off him, and see that he did not throw himself out on to the ground.

Within half an hour of sunrise we had reached the top of the rise of which I have spoken, and a most beautiful view broke upon our gaze. Beneath us was a rich stretch of country, verdant with grass and lovely with foliage and flowers. In the background, at a distance, so far as I could judge, of some eighteen miles from where we then stood, a huge and extraordinary mountain rose abruptly from the plain. The base of this great mountain appeared to consist of a grassy slope, but rising from this, I should say, from subsequent observation, at a height of about five hundred feet above the level of the plain, was a most tremendous and absolutely precipitous wall of bare rock, quite twelve or fifteen hundred feet in height. The shape of the mountain, which was undoubtedly of volcanic origin, was round, and of course, as only a segment of its circle was visible, it was difficult to estimate its exact size, which was enormous. I afterwards discovered that it could not cover less than fifty square miles of ground. Anything more grand and imposing than the sight presented by this great natural castle, starting in solitary grandeur from the level of the plain, I never saw, and I suppose I never shall. Its very solitude added to its majesty, and its towering cliffs seemed to kiss the sky. Indeed, generally speaking, they were clothed in clouds that lay in fleecy masses upon their broad and level battlements.

I sat up in my hammock and gazed out across the plain at this thrilling and majestic sight, and I suppose that Billali noticed it, for he brought his litter alongside.

"Behold the House of '*She-who-must-be-obeyed!*'" he said. "Had ever a queen such a throne before?"

"It is wonderful, my father," I answered. "But how do we enter? Those cliffs look hard to climb."

"Thou shalt see, my Baboon. Look now at the path below us. What thinkest thou that it is? Thou art a wise man. Come, tell me."

I looked, and saw what appeared to be the line of roadway running straight towards the base of the mountain, though it was covered with turf. There were high banks on each side of it, broken here and there, but fairly continuous on the whole, the meaning of which I did not understand. It seemed so very odd that anybody should embank a roadway.

"Well, my father," I answered, "I suppose that it is a road, otherwise I should have been inclined to say that it was the bed of a river, or rather," I added, observing the extraordinary directness of the cutting, "of a canal."

Billali—who, by the way, was none the worse for his immersion of the day before—nodded his head sagely as he replied—

"Thou art right, my son. It is a channel cut out by those who were before us in this place to carry away water. Of this am I sure: within the rocky circle of the mountain whither we journey was once a great lake. But those who were before us, by wonderful arts of which I know naught, hewed a path for the water through the solid rock of the mountain, piercing even to the bed of the lake. But first they cut the channel that thou seest across the plain. Then when at last the water burst out, it rushed down the channel that had been made to receive it, and crossed this plain till it reached the low land behind the rise, and there, perchance, it made the swamp through which we have come.[2] Then when the lake was drained dry, the people whereof I speak built a mighty city on its bed, whereof naught but ruins and the name of Kôr yet remaineth, and from age to age hewed the caves and passages that thou wilt see."

"It may be," I answered; "but if so, how is it that the lake does not fill up again with the rains and the water of the springs?"

"Nay, my son, the people were a wise people, and they left a drain to keep it clear. Seest thou the river to the right?" and he pointed to a fair-sized stream that wound away across the plain, some four miles from us. "That is the drain, and it comes out through the mountain wall where this cutting goes in. At first, perhaps, the water ran down this canal, but afterwards the people turned it, and used the cutting for a road."

"And is there then no other place where one may enter into the great mountain," I asked, "except through the drain?"

"There is a place," he answered, "where cattle and men on foot may cross with much labour, but it is secret.[3] A year mightest thou search and shouldst never find it. It is only used once a year, when the herds of cattle that have been fatting on the slopes of the mountain, and on this plain, are driven into the space within."

"And does *She* live there always?" I asked, "or does she come at times without the mountain?"

"Nay, my son, where she is, there she is."

By now we were well on to the great plain, and I was examining with delight the varied beauty of its semi-tropical flowers and trees, the latter of which grew singly, or at most in clumps of three or four, much of the timber being of large size, and belonging apparently to a variety of evergreen oak.[4] There were also many palms, some of them more than one hundred feet high, and the largest and most beautiful tree ferns that I ever saw, about which hung clouds of jewelled honeysuckers and great-winged butterflies. Wandering about among the trees or crouching in the long and feathered grass were all varieties of game, from rhinocerotes down. I saw a rhinoceros, buffalo (a large herd), eland, quagga, and sable antelope, the most beautiful of all the bucks, not to mention many smaller varieties of game, and three ostriches which scudded away at our approach like white drift before a gale.

So plentiful was the game that at last I could stand it no longer. I had a single-barrel sporting Martini with me in the litter, the "Express" being too cumbersome,[5] and espying a beautiful fat eland rubbing himself under one of the oak-like trees, I jumped out of the litter, and proceeded to creep as near to him as I could. He let me come within eighty yards, and then turned his head, and stared at me, preparatory to running away. I lifted the rifle, and taking him about midway down the shoulder, for he was side on to me, fired. I never made a cleaner shot or a better kill in all my small experience, for the great buck sprang right up into the air and fell dead. The bearers, who had all halted to see the performance, gave a murmur of surprise, an unwonted compliment from these sullen people, who never appear to be surprised at anything, and a party of the guard at once ran off to cut the animal up. As for myself, though I was longing to have a look at him, I sauntered back to my litter as though I had been in the habit of killing eland all my life, feeling that I had gone up several degrees in the estimation of the Amahagger, who looked on the whole thing as a very high-class manifestation of witchcraft. As a matter of fact, however, I had never seen an eland in a wild state before. Billali received me with enthusiasm.

"It is wonderful, my son the Baboon," he cried; "wonderful! Thou art a very great man, though so ugly. Had I not seen, surely I would never have believed. And thou sayest that thou wilt teach me to slay in this fashion?"

"Certainly, my father," I said, airily; "it is nothing."

But all the same I firmly made up my mind that when "my father" Billali began to fire I would without fail lie down or take refuge behind a tree.

After this little incident nothing happened of any note till about an hour and a half before sundown, when we arrived beneath the shadow of the towering volcanic mass that I have already described. It is quite impossible for me to describe its grim grandeur as it appeared to me while my patient bearers toiled along the bed of the ancient watercourse towards the spot where the rich brown-hued cliff shot up from precipice to precipice till its crown lost itself in cloud. All I can say is that it almost awed me by the intensity of its lonesome and most solemn greatness. On we went up the bright and sunny slope, till at last the creeping shadows from above swallowed up its brightness, and presently we began to pass through a cutting hewn in the living rock.[6] Deeper and deeper grew this marvellous work, which must, I should say, have employed thousands of men for many years. Indeed, how it was ever executed at all without the aid of blasting-powder or dynamite I cannot to this day imagine. It is and must remain one of the mysteries of that wild land. I can only suppose that these cuttings and the vast caves that had been hollowed out of the rocks they pierced were the State undertakings of the people of Kôr, who lived here in the dim lost ages of the world, and, as in the case of the Egyptian monuments, were executed by the forced labour of tens of thousands of captives, carried on through an indefinite number of centuries. But who were the people?

At last we reached the face of the precipice itself, and found ourselves looking into the mouth of a dark tunnel that forcibly reminded me of those undertaken by our nineteenth-century engineers in the construction of railway lines. Out of this tunnel flowed a considerable stream of water. Indeed, though I do not think that I have mentioned it, we had followed this stream, which ultimately developed into the river I have already described as winding away to the right, from the spot where the cutting in the solid rock commenced. Half of this cutting formed a channel for the stream, and half, which was placed on a slightly higher level—eight feet perhaps—was devoted to the purposes of a roadway. At the termination of the cutting, however, the stream turned off across the plain and followed a channel of its own. At the mouth of the cave the cavalcade was halted, and, while the men employed themselves in lighting some earthenware lamps they had brought with them, Billali, descending from his litter, informed me politely but firmly that the orders of *She* were that we were now to be blindfolded, so that we should not learn the secret of the paths through the bowels of the mountains. To this I, of course assented cheerfully enough, but Job, who was now very much better, notwithstanding the journey, did not like it at all, fancying, I believe, that it was but a preliminary step to being hot-potted. He was, however, a little consoled when I pointed out to him that there were no hot pots at hand, and, so far as I knew, no fire to heat them in. As for poor Leo, after turning restlessly for hours, he had, to my deep thankfulness, at last dropped off into a sleep or stupor, I do not know which, so there was no need to blindfold him. The blindfolding was performed by binding a piece of the yellowish linen whereof those of the Amahagger who condescended to wear anything in particular made their dresses, tightly round the eyes. This linen I afterwards discovered was taken from the tombs, and was not, as I had at first supposed, of native manufacture. The bandage was then knotted at the back of the head, and finally brought down again and the ends bound under the chin to prevent its slipping. Ustane, by the way, was also blindfolded, I do not know why, unless it was from fear that she should impart the secrets of the route to us.

This operation performed we started on once more, and soon, by the echoing sound of the footsteps of the bearers and the increased noise of the water caused by reverberation in a confined space, I knew that we were entering into the bowels of the great mountain. It was an eerie sensation, being borne along into the dead heart of the rock we knew not whither, but I was getting used to eerie sensations by this time, and by now was pretty well prepared for anything. So I lay still, and listened to the tramp, tramp of the bearers and the rushing of the water, and tried to believe that I was enjoying myself. Presently the men set up the melancholy little chant that I had heard on the first night when we were captured in the whale-boat, and the effect produced by their voices was very curious, and quite indescrib-

able. After a while the air began to get exceedingly thick and heavy, so much
so, indeed, that I felt as though I were going to choke, till at length the
litter took a sharp turn, then another and another, and the sound of the
running water ceased. After this the air got fresher again, but the turns were
continuous, and to me, blindfolded as I was, most bewildering. I tried to
keep a map of them in my mind in case it might ever be necessary for us
to try and escape by this route, but, needless to say, failed utterly. Another
half-hour or so passed, and then suddenly I became aware that we were
once more in the open air. I could see the light through my bandage and
feel its freshness on my face. A few more minutes and the caravan halted,
and I heard Billali order Ustane to remove her bandage and undo ours. Without waiting for her attentions I got the knot of mine loose, and looked out.

As I anticipated, we had passed right through the precipice, and were
now on the farther side, and immediately beneath its beetling face. The first
thing I noticed was that the cliff is not nearly so high here, not so high
I should say by five hundred feet, which proved that the bed of the lake,
or rather of the vast ancient crater in which we stood, was much above
the level of the surrounding plain. For the rest, we found ourselves in a
huge rock-surrounded cup, not unlike that of the first place where we had
sojourned, only ten times the size. Indeed, I could only just make out the
frowning line of the opposite cliffs. A great portion of the plain thus enclosed
by nature was cultivated, and fenced in with walls of stone placed there
to keep the cattle and goats, of which there were large herds about, from
breaking into the gardens. Here and there rose great grass mounds,[7] and
some miles away towards the center I thought that I could see the outline
of colossal ruins. I had no time to observe anything more at the moment,
for we were instantly surrounded by crowds of Amahagger, similar in every
particular to those with whom we were already familiar, who, though they
spoke little, pressed round us so closely as to obscure the view to a person
lying in a hammock. Then all of a sudden a number of armed men arranged
in companies, and marshalled by officers who held ivory wands in their
hands, came running swiftly towards us, having, so far as I could make out,
emerged from the face of the precipice like ants from their burrows. These
men as well as their officers were all robed in addition to the usual leopard
skin, and, as I gathered, formed the bodyguard of *She* herself.

Their leader advanced to Billali, saluted him by placing his ivory wand
transversely across his forehead, and then asked some question which I could
not catch, and Billali having answered him the whole regiment turned and
marched along the side of the cliff, our cavalcade of litters following in their
track. After going thus for about half a mile we halted once more in front
of the mouth of a tremendous cave, measuring about sixty feet[8] in height
by eighty wide, and here Billali descended finally, and requested Job and
myself to do the same. Leo, of course, was far too ill to do anything of
the sort. I did so, and we entered the great cave, into which the light of
the setting sun penetrated for some distance, while beyond the reach of the

daylight it was faintly illuminated with lamps which seemed to me to stretch away for an almost immeasurable distance, like the gas lights of an empty London street.[9] The first thing that I noticed was that the walls were covered with sculptures in bas-relief, of a sort, pictorially speaking, similar to those that I have described upon the vases;—love-scenes principally, then hunting pictures, pictures of executions, and the torture of criminals by the placing of a, presumably, red-hot pot upon the head, showing whence our hosts had derived this pleasant practice. There were very few battle-pieces, though many of duels, and men running and wrestling, and from this fact I am led to believe that this people was not much subject to attack by exterior foes, either on account of the isolation of their position or because of their great strength. Between the pictures were columns of stone characters of a formation absolutely new to me; at any rate they were neither Greek nor Egyptian, nor Hebrew, nor Assyrian—that I am sure of. They looked more like Chinese writings than any other that I am acquainted with. Near to the entrance of the cave both pictures and writing were worn away, but further in they were in many cases absolutely fresh and perfect as the day on which the sculptor had ceased work upon them.

The regiment of guards did not come further than the entrance to the cave, where they formed up to let us pass through. On entering the place itself we were, however, met by a man robed in white, who bowed humbly, but said nothing, which, as it afterwards appeared that he was a deaf mute, was not very wonderful.

Running at right angles to the great cave, at a distance of some twenty feet from the entrance was a smaller cave or wide gallery, that was pierced into the rock both to the right and to the left of the main cavern. In front of the gallery to our left stood two guards, from which circumstance I argued that it was the entrance to the apartments of *She* herself. The mouth of the right-hand gallery was unguarded, and along it the mute indicated that we were to go. Walking a few yards down this passage, which was lighted with lamps, we came to the entrance to a chamber having a curtain made of some grass material, not unlike a Zanzibar mat in appearance, hung over the doorway. This the mute drew back with another profound obeisance, and led the way into a good-sized apartment, hewn, of course, out of the solid rock, but to my great relief lighted by means of a shaft pierced in the face of the precipice. In this room was a stone bedstead, pots full of water for washing, and beautifully tanned leopard skins to serve as blankets.

Here we left Leo, who was still sleeping heavily, and with him stopped Ustane. I noticed that the mute gave her a very sharp look, as much as to say, "Who are you, and by whose orders do you come here?" Then he conducted us to another similar room which Job took, and then to two more that were respectively occupied by Billali and myself.

XII.
"She."

The first care of Job and myself, after seeing to Leo, was to wash ourselves and put on clean clothing, for what we were wearing had not been changed since the loss of the dhow. Fortunately, as I think that I have said, by far the greater part of our personal baggage had been packed into the whale-boat, and was therefore saved—and brought hither by the bearers—although all the stores laid in by us for barter and presents to the natives were lost.[1] Nearly all our clothing was made of a well-shrunk and very strong grey flannel, and excellent I found it for travelling in these places, because though a Norfolk jacket,[2] shirt, and pair of trousers of it only weighed about four pounds, a great consideration in a tropical country, where every extra ounce tells on the wearer, it was warm, and offered a good resistance to the rays of the sun, and best of all to chills, which are so apt to result from sudden changes of temperature.

Never shall I forget the comfort of the "wash and brushup," and of those clean flannels. The only thing that was wanting to complete my joy was a cake of soap, of which we had none.

Afterwards I discovered that the Amahagger, who do not reckon dirt among their many disagreeable qualities, use a kind of burnt earth for washing purposes, which, though unpleasant to the touch till one gets accustomed to it, forms a very fair substitute for soap.

By the time that I was dressed, and had combed and trimmed my black beard, the previous condition of which was certainly sufficiently unkempt to give weight to Billali's appellation for me of "Baboon," I began to feel most uncommonly hungry. Therefore I was by no means sorry when, without the slightest preparatory sound or warning, the curtain over the entrance to my cave was flung aside, and another mute, a young girl this time, announced to me by signs that I could not misunderstand—that is, by opening her mouth, and pointing down it—that there was something ready to eat. Accordingly I followed her into the next chamber, which we had not yet entered, where I found Job, who had also, to his great embarrassment, been conducted thither by a fair mute. Job never got over the advances the former lady had made towards him, and suspected every girl who came near to him of similar designs.

"These young parties have a way of looking at one, sir," he would say apologetically, "which I don't call respectable."

This chamber was twice the size of the sleeping caves, and I saw at once that it had originally served as a refectory, and also probably as an embalming room for the Priests of the Dead; for I may as well say at once these hollowed-out caves were nothing more nor less than vast catacombs, in which for tens of ages the mortal remains of the great extinct race whose monuments surrounded us had been first preserved, with an art and a completeness that has never since been equalled, and then hidden away for all time. On each side of this particular rock-chamber was a long and solid stone table, about three feet wide by three feet six in height, hewn out of the living rock, of which it had formed part, and was still attached to at the base. These tables were slightly hollowed out or curved inward, to give room for the knees of any one sitting on the stone ledge that had been cut for a bench along the side of the cave at a distance of about two feet from them. Each of them, also, was so arranged that it ended right under a shaft pierced in the rock for the admission of light and air. On examining them carefully, however, I saw that there was a difference between them that had at first escaped my attention, viz., that one of the tables, that to the left as we entered the cave, had evidently been used, not to eat upon, but for the purposes of embalming. That this was beyond all question the case was clear from five shallow depressions in the stone of the table, all shaped like a human form, with a separate place for the head to lie in, and a little bridge to support the neck, each depression being of a different size, so as to fit bodies varying in stature from a full-grown man's to a small child's, and with little holes bored at intervals to carry off fluid. And, indeed, if any further confirmation was required, we had but to look at the wall of the cave above to find it. For there, sculptured all round the apartment, and looking nearly as fresh as the day it was done, was the pictorial representation of the death, embalming, and burial of an old man with a long beard, probably an ancient king or grandee of this country.

The first picture represented his death. He was lying upon a couch which had four short curved posts at the corners coming to a knob at the end, in appearance something like a written note of music, and was evidently in the very act of expiring. Gathered round the couch were women and children weeping, the former with their hair hanging down their back. The next scene represented the embalmment of the body, which lay nude upon the table with depressions in it, similar to the one before us; probably, indeed, it was a picture of the same table. Three men were employed at the work —one superintending, one holding a funnel shaped exactly like a port wine strainer, of which the narrow end was fixed in an incision in the breast, no doubt in the great pectoral artery; while the third, who was depicted as standing straddle-legged over the corpse, held a kind of large jug high in his hand, and poured from it some steaming fluid which fell accurately into the funnel. The most curious part of this sculpture is that both the man with the funnel and the man who poured the fluid are drawn holding their noses, either I suppose because of the stench arising from the body, or more probably to keep out the aromatic fumes of the hot fluid[3] which was being forced into the dead man's veins. Another curious thing which I am unable to explain is that all three men were represented as having a band of linen tied round the face with holes in it for the eyes.

The third sculpture was a picture of the burial of the deceased. There he was, stiff and cold, clothed in a linen robe, and laid out on a stone slab such as I had slept upon at our first sojourning-place. At his head and feet burnt lamps, and by his side were placed several of the beautiful painted vases that I have described, which were perhaps supposed to be full of provisions. The little chamber was crowded with mourners, and with musicians playing on an instrument resembling a lyre, while near the foot of the corpse stood a man with a sheet, with which he was preparing to cover it from view.

These sculptures, looked at merely as works of art, were so remarkable that I make no apology for describing them rather fully. They struck me also as being of surpassing interest as representing, probably with studious accuracy, the last rites of the dead as practiced among an utterly lost people, and even then I thought how envious some antiquarian friends of my own at Cambridge would be if ever I found an opportunity of describing these wonderful remains to them. Probably they would say that I was exaggerating, notwithstanding that every page of this history must bear so much internal evidence of its truth that it would obviously have been quite impossible for me to have invented it.

To return. As soon as I had hastily examined these sculptures, which I think I omitted to mention were executed in relief, we sat down to a very excellent meal of boiled goats'-flesh, fresh milk, and cakes made of meal, the whole being served upon clean wooden platters.

When we had eaten we returned to see how Leo was getting on, Billali saying that he must now wait upon *She*, and hear her commands. On reaching Leo's room we found the poor boy in a very bad way. He had woke up from his torpor, and was altogether off his head, babbling about some boat-race on the Cam, and was inclined to be violent. Indeed, when we entered the room Ustane was holding him down. I spoke to him, and my voice seemed to soothe him; at any rate he grew much quieter, and was persuaded to swallow a dose of quinine.

I had been sitting with him for an hour, perhaps—at any rate I know that it was getting so dark that I could only just make out his head lying like a gleam of gold upon the pillow we had extemporised out of a bag covered with a blanket—when suddenly Billali arrived with an air of great importance, and informed me that *She* herself had deigned to express a wish to see me—an honour, he added, accorded to but very few. I think that he was a little horrified at my cool way of taking the honour, but the fact was that I did not feel overwhelmed with gratitude at the prospect of seeing some savage, dusky queen, however absolute and mysterious she might be, more especially as my mind was full of dear Leo, for whose life I began to have great fears. However, I rose to follow him, and as I did so I caught sight of something bright lying on the floor, which I picked up. Perhaps the reader will remember that with the potsherd in the casket was a composition scarabæus marked with a round O, a goose, and another curious hieroglyphic, the meaning of which signs is "Suten se Rā," or "Royal Son of the Sun." This scarab, which is a very small one, Leo had insisted upon having set in a massive gold ring, such as is generally used for signets, and it was this very ring that I now picked up. He had pulled it off in the paroxysm of his fever, at least I suppose so, and flung it down upon the rock-floor. Thinking that if I left it about it might get lost, I slipped it on to my own little finger, and then followed Billali, leaving Job and Ustane with Leo.

We passed down the passage, crossed the great aisle-like cave, and came to the corresponding passage on the other side, at the mouth of which the guards stood like two statues. As we came they bowed their heads in saluta-tion, and then lifting their long spears placed them transversely across their foreheads, as the leaders of the troop that had met us had done with their ivory wands. We stepped between them, and found ourselves in an exactly similar gallery to that which led to our own apartments, only this passage was, comparatively speaking, brilliantly lighted. A few paces down it we were met by four mutes—two men and two women—who bowed low and then arranged themselves, the women in front and the men behind of us, and in this order we continued our procession past several doorways hung with curtains resembling those leading to our own quarters, and which I afterwards found opened out into chambers occupied by the mutes who attended on *She*. A few paces more and we came to another doorway facing us, and not to our left like the others, which seemed to mark the termination of the passage. Here two more white, or rather yellow-robed guards were standing, and they too bowed, saluted, and let us pass through heavy curtains into a great antechamber, quite forty feet long by as many wide, in which some eight or ten women, most of them young and handsome, with yellow-ish hair, sat on cushions working with ivory needles at what had the appear-ance of being embroidery-frames. These women were also deaf and dumb. At the farther end of this great lamp-lit apartment was another doorway closed in with heavy Oriental-looking curtains, quite unlike those that hung before the doors of our own rooms, and here stood two particularly hand-some girl mutes, their heads bowed upon their bosoms and their hands crossed in an attitude of the humblest submission. As we advanced they each stretched out an arm and drew back the curtains. Thereupon Billali did a curious thing. Down he went, that venerable-looking old gentleman —for Billali is a gentleman at the bottom—down on to his hands and knees, and in this undignified position, with his long white beard trailing on the ground, he began to creep into the apartment beyond. I followed him, standing on my feet in the usual fashion. Looking over his shoulder he perceived it.

"Down, my son; down, my Baboon; down on to thy hands and knees. We enter the presence of *She*, and, if thou art not humble, of a surety she will blast thee where thou standest."

I halted, and felt scared. Indeed, my knees began to give way of their own mere motion; but reflection came to my aid. I was an Englishman, and why, I asked myself, should I creep into the presence of some savage woman as though I were a monkey in fact as well as in name? I would not and could not do it, that is, unless I was absolutely sure that my life or comfort depended upon it. If once I began to creep upon my knees I should always have to do so, and it would be a patent acknowledgment of inferiority. So, fortified by an insular prejudice against "kootooing,"[4] which has, like most of our so-called prejudices, a good deal of common sense to recommend it, I marched in boldly after Billali. I found myself in another apartment, considerably smaller than the anteroom, of which the walls were entirely hung with rich-looking curtains of the same make as those over the door, the work, as I subsequently discovered, of the mutes who sat in the antechamber and wove them in strips, which were afterwards sewn together. Also, here and there about the room, were settees of a beautiful black wood of the ebony tribe, inlaid with ivory, and all over the floor were other tapestries, or rather rugs. At the top end of this apartment was what appeared to be a recess, also draped with curtains, through which shone rays of light. There was nobody in the place except ourselves.

Painfully and slowly old Billali crept up the length of the cave, and with the most dignified stride that I could command I followed after him. But I felt that it was more or less of a failure. To begin with, it is not possible to look dignified when you are following in the wake of an old man writhing along on his stomach like a snake, and then, in order to go sufficiently slowly, either I had to keep my leg some seconds in the air at every step, or else to advance with a full stop between each stride, like Mary Queen of Scots going to execution in a play. Billali was not good at crawling, I suppose his years stood in the way, and our progress up that apartment was a very long affair. I was immediately behind him, and several times I was sorely tempted to help him on with a good kick. It is so absurd to advance into the presence of savage royalty after the fashion of an Irishman driving a pig to market, for that is what we looked like, and the idea nearly made me burst out laughing then and there. I had to work off my dangerous tendency to unseemly merriment by blowing my nose, a proceeding which filled old Billali with horror, for he looked over his shoulder, and made a ghastly face at me, and I heard him murmur, "Oh, my poor Baboon!"

At last we reached the curtains, and here Billali collapsed flat on to his stomach, with his hands stretched out before him as though he were dead, and I, not knowing what to do, began to stare about the place. But presently I clearly felt that somebody was looking at me from behind the curtains. I could not see the person, but I could distinctly feel his or her gaze, and, what is more, it produced a very odd effect upon my nerves. I was frightened, I do not know why. The place was a strange one, it is true, and looked lonely, notwithstanding its rich hangings and the soft glow of the lamps—indeed these accessories added to, rather than detracted from its loneliness, just as a lighted street at night has always a more solitary appearance than a dark one. It was so silent in the place, and there lay

Billali like one dead before the heavy curtains, through which the odour of perfume seemed to float up towards the gloom of the arched roof above. Minute grew into minute, and still there was no sign of life, nor did the curtain move; but I felt the gaze of the unknown being sinking through and through me, and filling me with a nameless terror, till the perspiration stood in beads upon my brow.

At length the curtain began to move. Who could be behind it?—some naked savage queen, a languishing Oriental beauty, or a nineteenth-century young lady, drinking afternoon tea? I had not the slightest idea, and should not have been astonished at seeing any of the three. I was getting beyond astonishment. The curtain agitated itself a little, then suddenly between its folds there appeared a most beautiful white hand (white as snow), and with long tapering fingers, ending in the pinkest nails.[5] The hand grasped the curtain, and drew it aside, and as it did so I heard a voice, I think the softest and yet most silvery voice I ever heard. It reminded me of the murmur of a brook.

"Stranger," said the voice in Arabic, but much purer and more classical Arabic than the Amahagger talk—"stranger, wherefore art thou so much afraid?"

Now I flattered myself that in spite of my inward terrors I had kept a very fair command of my countenance, and was, therefore, a little astonished at this question. Before I had made up my mind how to answer it, however, the curtain was drawn, and a tall figure stood before us. I say a figure, for not only the body, but also the face was wrapped up in soft white, gauzy material in such a way as at first sight to remind me most forcibly of a corpse in its grave-clothes. And yet I do not know why it should have given me that idea, seeing that the wrappings were so thin that one could distinctly see the gleam of the pink flesh beneath them. I suppose it was owing to the way in which they were arranged, either accidentally, or more probably by design. Anyhow, I felt more frightened than ever at this ghost-like apparition, and my hair began to rise upon my head as the feeling crept over me that I was in the presence of something that was not canny. I could, however, clearly distinguish that the swathed mummy-like form before me was that of a tall and lovely woman, instinct with[6] beauty in every part, and also with a certain snake-like grace which I had never seen anything to equal before. When she moved a hand or foot her entire frame seemed to undulate, and the neck did not bend, it curved.

"Why art thou so frightened, stranger?" asked the sweet voice again —a voice which seemed to draw the heart out of me, like the strains of softest music. "Is there that about me that should affright a man? Then surely are men changed from what they used to be!" And with a little coquettish movement she turned herself, and held up one arm, so as to show all her loveliness and the rich hair of raven blackness that streamed in soft ripples down her snowy robes, almost to her sandalled feet.

"It is thy beauty that makes me fear, oh Queen," I answered humbly, scarcely knowing what to say, and I thought that as I did so I heard old Billali, who was still lying prostrate on the floor, mutter, "Good, my Baboon, good."

"I see that men still know how to beguile us women with false words. Ah, stranger," she answered, with a laugh that sounded like distant silver bells, "thou wast afraid because mine eyes were searching out thine heart, therefore wast thou afraid. Yet being but a woman, I forgive thee for the lie, for it was courteously said. And now tell me how came ye hither to this land of the dwellers among caves—a land of swamps and evil things and dead old shadows of the dead? What came ye for to see? How is it that ye hold your lives so cheap as to place them in the hollow of the hand of *Hiya*, into the hand of '*She-who-must-be-obeyed*?' Tell me also how come ye to know the tongue I talk. It is an ancient tongue, that sweet child of the old Syriac.[7] Liveth it yet in the world? Thou seest I dwell among the caves and the dead, and naught know I of the affairs of men, nor have I cared to know. I have lived, oh stranger, with my memories, and my memories are in a grave that mine hands hollowed, for truly hath it been said that the child of man maketh his own path evil;" and her beautiful voice quivered, and broke in a note as soft as any wood-bird's. Suddenly her eye fell upon the sprawling frame of Billali, and she seemed to recollect herself.

"Ah! thou art there, old man. Tell me how it is that things have gone wrong in thine household. Forsooth, it seems that these my guests were set upon. Ay, and one was nigh to being slain by the hot-pot to be eaten of those brutes, thy children, and had not the others fought gallantly they too had been slain, and not even I could have called back the life which had been loosed from the body. What means it, old man? What hast thou to say that I should not give thee over to those who execute my vengeance?"

Her voice had risen in her anger, and it rang clear and cold against the rocky walls. Also I thought I could see her eyes flash through the gauze that hid them. I saw poor Billali, whom I had believed to be a very fearless person, positively quiver with terror at her words.

"Oh 'Hiya!' oh *She!*" he said, without lifting his white head from the floor. "Oh *She*, as thou art great be merciful, for I am now as ever thy servant to obey. It was no plan or fault of mine, oh *She*, it was those wicked ones who are called my children. Led on by a woman whom thy guest the Pig had scorned, they would have followed the ancient custom of the land, and eaten the fat black stranger who came hither with these thy guests the Baboon and the Lion who is sick, thinking that no word had come from thee about the Black one. But when the Baboon and the Lion saw what they would do, they slew the woman, and slew also their servant to save him from the horror of the pot. Then those evil ones, ay, those children of the Wicked One who lives in the Pit, they went mad with the lust of blood, and flew at the throats of the Lion and the Baboon and the Pig. But gallantly they fought. Oh *Hiya!* they fought like very men, and slew many, and held their own, and then I came and saved them, and the evildoers have I sent on hither to Koˆr to be judged of thy greatness, oh *She*! and here they are."

"Ay, old man, I know it, and to-morrow will I sit in the great hall and do justice upon them, fear not. And for thee, I forgive thee, though hardly. See that thou dost keep thine household better. Go."

Billali rose upon his knees with astonishing alacrity, bowed his head thrice, and, his white beard sweeping the ground, crawled down the apartment as he had crawled up it, till he finally vanished through the curtains, leaving me, not a little to my alarm, alone with this terrible but most fascinating person.

XIII.
Ayesha Unveils.[1]

"There," said *She*, "he has gone, the white-bearded old fool! Ah, how little knowledge does a man acquire in his life. He gathereth it up like water, but like water it runneth through his fingers, and yet, if his hands be but wet as though with dew, behold a generation of fools call out, 'See, he is a wise man!' Is it not so? But how call they thee? 'Baboon,' he says," and she laughed; "but that is the fashion of these savages who lack imagination, and fly to the beasts they resemble for a name. How do they call thee in thine own country, stranger?"

"They call me Holly, oh Queen," I answered.

"'Holly,'" she answered, speaking the word with difficulty, and yet with a most charming accent, "and what is 'Holly?'"

"'Holly' is a prickly tree," I said.

"So. Well, thou hast a prickly and yet a tree-like look. Strong art thou, and ugly, but, if my wisdom be not at fault, honest at the core, and a staff to lean on. Also one who thinks. But stay, oh Holly, stand not there, enter with me and be seated by me. I would not see thee crawl before me like those slaves. I am aweary of their worship and their terror; sometimes when they vex me I could blast them for very sport, and to see the rest turn white, even to the heart." And she held the curtain aside with her ivory hand to let me pass in.

I entered, shuddering. This woman was very terrible. Within the curtains was a recess, about twelve feet by ten, and in the recess was a couch and a table whereon stood fruit and sparkling water. By it, at its end, was a vessel like a font cut in carved stone, also full of pure water. The place was softly lit with lamps formed out of the beautiful vessels of which I have spoken, and the air and curtains were laden with a subtle perfume. Perfume too seemed to emanate from the glorious hair and white clinging vestments of *She* herself.[2] I entered the little room, and there stood uncertain.

"Sit," said *She*, pointing to the couch. "As yet thou hast no cause to fear me. If thou hast cause, thou shalt not fear for long, for I shall slay thee. Therefore let thy heart be light."

I sat down on the foot of the couch near to the font-like basin of water, and *She* sank down softly on to the other end.

"Now, Holly," she said, "how comest thou to speak Arabic? It is my own dear tongue, for Arabian am I by my birth, even 'al Arab al Ariba' (an Arab of the Arabs), and of the race of our father Yârab, the son of Kâhtan, for in that fair and ancient city Ozal was I born, in the province of Yaman the Happy. Yet does thou not speak it as we used to speak. Thy talk doth lack the music of the sweet tongue of the tribes of Hamyar which I was wont to hear. Some of the words too seemed changed, even as among these Amahagger, who have debased and defiled its purity, so that I must speak with them in what is to me another tongue."*[3]

"I have studied it," I answered, "for many years. Also the language is spoken in Egypt and elsewhere."

"So it is still spoken, and there is yet an Egypt? And what Pharaoh sits upon the throne? Still one of the spawn of the Persian Ochus, or are the Achæmenians gone, for far is it to the days of Ochus."[4]

"The Persians have been gone from Egypt for nigh two thousand years, and since then the Ptolemies, the Romans, and many others have flourished and held sway upon the Nile, and fallen when their time was ripe," I said, aghast.[5] "What canst thou know of the Persian Artaxerxes?"

She laughed, and made no answer, and again a cold chill went through me. "And Greece," she said, "is there still a Greece? Ah, I loved the Greeks. Beautiful were they as the day, and clever, but fierce at heart and fickle, notwithstanding."

"Yes," I said, "there is a Greece; and, just now, is it once more a people. Yet the Greeks of to-day are not what the Greeks of the old time were, and Greece herself is but a mockery of the Greece that was."[6]

"So! The Hebrews, are they yet at Jerusalem? And does the Temple that the wise king[7] built stand, and if so what God do they worship therein? Is their Messiah come, of whom they preached so much and prophesied so loudly and doth He rule the earth?"

---

*Yârab the son of Kâhtan, who lived some centuries before the time of Abraham, was the father of the ancient Arabs, and gave its name Araba to the country. In speaking of herself as "al Arab al Ariba," *She* no doubt meant to convey that she was of the true Arab blood as distinguished from the naturalized Arabs, the descendants of Ishmæl, the son of Abraham and Hagar, who were known as "al Arab al mostáreba." The dialect of the Koreish was usually called the clear or "perspicuous" Arabic, but the Hamaritic dialect approached nearer to the purity of the mother Syriac.—L.H.H.

"The Jews are broken and gone, and the fragments of their people strew the world, and Jerusalem is no more. As for the temple that Herod built —"

"Herod!" she said. "I know not Herod.[8] But go on."

"The Romans burnt it, and the Roman eagles flew across its ruins, and now Judæa is a desert."

"So, so! They were a great people, those Romans, and went straight to their end—ay, they sped to it like Fate, or like their own eagles on their prey!—and left peace behind them."

"Solitudinem faciunt, pacem appellant," I suggested.[9]

"Ah, thou canst speak the Latin tongue, too!" she said, in surprise. "It hath a strange ring in my ears after all these days, and it seems to me that thy accent does not fall as the Romans put it. Who was it wrote that? I know not the saying, but it is a true one of that great people.[10] It seems that I have found a learned man—one whose hands have held the water of the world's knowledge. Knowest thou Greek also?"

"Yes, oh Queen, and something of Hebrew, but not to speak them well. They are all dead languages now."

She clapped her hands in childish glee. "Of a truth, ugly tree that thou art, thou growest the fruits of wisdom, oh Holly," she said; "but of those Jews whom I hated, for they called me 'heathen' when I would have taught them my philosophy—did their Messiah come, and doth He rule the world?"

"Their Messiah came," I answered with reverence; "but He came poor and lowly, and they would have none of Him.[11] They scourged Him, and crucified Him upon a tree, but yet His words and His works live on, for He was the Son of God, and now of a truth He doth rule half the world, but not with an Empire of the World."

"Ah, the fierce-hearted wolves," she said, "the followers of Sense and many gods—greedy of gain and faction-torn.[12] I can see their dark faces yet. So they crucified their Messiah? Well can I believe it. That He was a Son of the Living Spirit would be naught to them, if indeed He was so, and of that we will talk afterwards. They would care naught for any God if He came not with pomp and power. They, a chosen people, a vessel of Him they call Jehovah, ay, and a vessel of Baal, and a vessel of Astoreth, and a vessel of the gods of the Egyptians—a high-stomached people, greedy of aught that brought them wealth and power. So they crucified their Messiah because He came in lowly guise—and now are they scattered about the earth? Why, if I remember, so said one of their prophets[13] that it should be. Well, let them go—they broke my heart, those Jews, and made me look with evil eyes across the world, ay, and drove me to this wilderness, this place of a people that was before them. When I would have taught them wisdom in Jerusalem they stoned me, ay, at the Gate of the Temple those white-bearded hypocrites and Rabbis hounded the people on to stone me! See, here is the mark of it to this day!" and with a sudden move she pulled up the gauzy wrapping on her rounded arm, and pointed to a little scar that showed red against its milky beauty.

I shrank back horrified.

"Pardon me, oh Queen!" I said, "but I am bewildered. Nigh upon two thousand years have rolled across the earth since the Jewish Messiah hung upon His cross at Golgotha. How then canst thou have taught thy philosophy to the Jews before He was? Thou art a woman, and no spirit. How can a woman live two thousand years? Why dost thou befool me, oh Queen?"

She leaned back on the couch, and once more I felt the hidden eyes playing upon me and searching out my heart.

"Oh man!" she said at last, speaking very slowly and deliberately, "it seems that there are still things upon the earth of which thou knowest naught. Dost thou still believe that all things die, even as those very Jews believed? I tell thee that naught dies. There is no such thing as Death, though there be a thing called Change. See," and she pointed to some sculptures on the rocky wall. "Three times two thousand years[14] have passed since the last of the great race that hewed those pictures fell before the breath of the pestilence which destroyed them, yet are they not dead. E'en now they live; perchance their spirits are drawn toward us at this very hour," and she glanced round. "Of a surety it sometimes seems to me that my eyes can see them."

"Yes, but to the world they are dead."

"Ay, for a time; but even to the world are they born again and again. I, yes I, Ayesha**—for that, stranger, is my name—I say to thee that I wait now for one I loved to be born again, and here I tarry till he finds me, knowing of a surety that hither he will come, and that here, and here only, shall he greet me.[16] Why, dost thou believe that I, who am all powerful, I, whose loveliness is more than the loveliness of the Grecian Helen, of whom they used to sing, and whose wisdom is wider, ay, far more wide and deep than the wisdom of Solomon the Wise,—I, who know the secrets of the earth and its riches, and can turn all things to my uses,— I, who have even for a while overcome Change, that ye call Death,—why, I say, oh stranger, dost thou think that I herd here with barbarians lower than the beasts?"

"I know not," I said humbly.

"Because I wait for him I love. My life has perchance been evil, I know not—for who can say what is evil and what good?—so I fear to die even if I could die, which I cannot until mine hour comes, to go and seek him where he is; for between us there might rise a wall I could not climb, at least, I dread it. Surely easy would it be also to lose the way in seeking in those great spaces wherein the planets wander on for ever. But the day will come, it may be when five thousand more years have passed, and are lost and melted into the vault of Time, even as the little clouds melt into the gloom of night, or it may be to-morrow, when he, my love, shall be

**Pronounced Assha.—L.H.H.[15]

born again, and then, following a law that is stronger than any human plan, he shall find me *here*, where once he knew me, and of a surety his heart will soften towards me, though I sinned against him; ay, even though he know me not again, yet will he love me, if only for my beauty's sake."

For a moment I was dumbfounded, and could not answer. The matter was too overpowering for my intellect to grasp.

"But even so, oh Queen," I said at last, "even if we men be born again and again, that is not so with thee, if thou speakest truly." Here she looked up sharply, and once more I caught the flash of those hidden eyes; "thou," I went on hurriedly, "who hast never died?"

"That is so," she said; "and it is so because I have, half by chance and half by learning, solved one of the great secrets of the world. Tell me, stranger: life is—why therefore should not life be lengthened for a while? What are ten or twenty or fifty thousand years in the history of life? Why in ten thousand years scarce will the rain and storms lessen a mountain top by a span in thickness?[17] In two thousand years these caves have not changed, nothing has changed but the beasts, and man, who is as the beasts. There is naught that is wonderful about the matter, couldst thou but understand. Life is wonderful, ay, but that it should be a little lengthened is not wonderful. Nature hath her animating spirit as well as man, who is Nature's child, and he who can find that spirit, and let it breathe upon him, shall live with her life. He shall not live eternally, for Nature is not eternal, and she herself must die, even as the nature of the moon hath died. She herself must die, I say, or rather change and sleep till it be time for her to live again. But when shall she die? Not yet, I ween, and while she lives, so shall he who hath all her secret live with her. All I have it not, yet have I some, more perchance than any who were before me. Now, to thee I doubt not that this thing is a great mystery, therefore I will not overcome thee with it now. Another time will I tell thee more if the mood be on me, though perchance I shall never speak thereof again. Dost thou wonder how I knew that ye were coming to this land, and so saved your heads from the hot-pot?"

"Ay, oh Queen," I answered, feebly.

"Then gaze upon that water," and she pointed to the font-like vessel, and then, bending forward, held her hand over it.

I rose and gazed, and instantly the water darkened. Then it cleared, and I saw as distinctly as I ever saw anything in my life—I saw, I say, our boat upon that horrible canal. There was Leo lying at the bottom asleep in it, with a coat thrown over him to keep off the mosquitoes, in such a fashion as to hide his face, and myself, Job, and Mahomed towing on the bank.

I started back aghast, and cried out that it was magic, for I recognised the whole scene—it was one which had actually occurred.

"Nay, nay; oh, Holly," she answered, "it is no magic, that is a fiction of ignorance. There is no such thing as magic, though there is such a thing as a knowledge of the secrets of Nature. That water is my glass; in it I see what passes if I care to summon up the pictures, which is not often. Therein I can show thee what thou wilt of the past, if it be anything that hath to do with this country and with what I have known, or anything that thou, the gazer, hast known. Think of a face if thou wilt, and it shall be reflected from thy mind upon the water. I know not all the secret yet—I can read nothing in the future. But it is an old secret; I did not find it. In Arabia and in Egypt the sorcerers knew it centuries gone. So one day I chanced to bethink me of that old canal—some twenty ages since I sailed upon it, and I was minded to look thereon again. So I looked, and there I saw the boat and three men walking, and one, whose face I could not see, but a youth of noble form, sleeping in the boat, and so I sent and saved ye. And now farewell. But stay, tell me of this youth—the Lion, as the old man calls him. I would look upon him, but he is sick, thou sayest—sick with the fever, and also wounded in the fray."

"He is very sick," I answered, sadly; "canst thou do nothing for him, oh Queen! who knowest so much?"

"Of a surety I can. I can cure him; but why speakest thou so sadly? Dost thou love the youth? Is he perchance thy son?"

"He is my adopted son, oh Queen! Shall he be brought in before thee?"

"Nay. How long hath the fever taken him?"

"This is the third day."

"Good; then let him lie another day. Then will he perchance throw it off by his own strength, and that is better than that I should cure him, for my medicine is of a sort to shake the life in its very citadel. If, however, by to-morrow night, at that hour when the fever first took him, he doth not begin to mend, then will I come to him and cure him. Stay, who nurses him?"

"Our white servant, him whom Billali names the Pig; also," and here I spoke with some little hesitation, "a woman named Ustane, a very handsome woman of this country, who came and embraced him when first she saw him, and hath stayed by him ever since, as I understand is the fashion of thy people, oh Queen."

"My people! speak not to me of my people," she answered hastily; "these slaves are no people of mine, they are but dogs to do my bidding till the day of my deliverance comes; and, as for their customs, naught have I to do with them. Also, call me not Queen—I am sick of flattery and titles —call me Ayesha, the name hath a sweet sound in mine ears, it is an echo from the past. As for this Ustane, I know not. I wonder if it be she against whom I was warned, and whom I in turn did warn? Hath she—stay I will see;" and, bending forward, she passed her hand over the font of water and gazed intently into it. "See," she said, quietly, "is that the woman?"

I looked into the water, and there, mirrored upon its placid surface, was the silhouette of Ustane's stately face. She was bending forward, with a look of infinite tenderness upon her features, watching something beneath her, and with her chestnut locks falling on to her right shoulder.

"It is she," I said, in a low voice, for once more I felt much disturbed at this most uncommon sight. "She watches Leo asleep."

"Leo!" said Ayesha, in an absent voice; "why, that is 'lion' in the Latin tongue. The old man hath named happily for once. It is very strange," she went on, speaking to herself, "very. So like—but it is not possible!" With an impatient gesture she passed her hand over the water once more. It darkened, and the image vanished silently and mysteriously as it had risen, and once more the lamplight, and the lamplight only, shone on the placid surface of that limpid, living mirror.

"Hast thou aught to ask me before thou goest, oh Holly?" she said, after a few moments' reflection. "It is but a rude life that thou must live here, for these people are savages, and know not the ways of cultivated man. Not that I am troubled thereby, for behold my food," and she pointed to the fruit upon the little table. "Naught but fruit doth ever pass my lips —fruit and cakes of flour, and a little water.[18] I have bidden my girls to wait upon thee. They are mutes, thou knowest, deaf are they and dumb, and therefore the safest of servants, save to those who can read their faces and their signs. I bred them so—it hath taken many centuries and much trouble; but at last I have triumphed.[19] Once I succeeded before, but the race was too ugly, so I let it die away; but now, as thou seest, they are otherwise. Once, too, I reared a race of giants, but after a while Nature would no more of it, and it died away. Hast thou aught to ask of me?"

"Ay, one thing, oh Ayesha," I said boldly; but feeling by no means as bold as I trust I looked. "I would gaze upon thy face."

She laughed out in her bell-like notes. "Bethink thee, Holly," she answered; "bethink thee. It seems that thou knowest the old myths of the gods of Greece. Was there not one Actæon[20] who perished miserably because he looked on too much beauty? If I show thee my face, perchance thou wouldst perish miserably also; perchance thou wouldst eat out thy heart in impotent desire; for know I am not for thee—I am for no man, save one, who hath been, but is not yet."

"As thou wilt, Ayesha," I said. "I fear not thy beauty. I have put my heart away from such vanities as woman's loveliness, that passeth like a flower."

"Nay, thou errest," she said; "that does *not* pass. My beauty endures even as I endure; still if thou wilt, oh rash man, have thy will; but blame not me if passion mount thy reason, as the Egyptian breakers used to mount a colt, and guide it whither thou wilt not. Never may the man to whom my beauty hath been unveiled put it from his mind, and therefore even with these savages do I go veiled, lest they vex me, and I should slay them. Say, wilt thou see?"

"I will," I answered, my curiosity overpowering me.

She lifted her white and rounded arms—never had I seen such arms before—and slowly, very slowly withdrew some fastening beneath her hair. Then all of a sudden the long, corpse-like wrapping fell from her to the

ground, and my eyes travelled up her form, now only robed in a garb of
clinging white that did but serve to show its perfect and imperial shape,
instinct with a life that was more than life, and with a certain serpent-like
grace that was more than human. On her little feet were sandals, fastened
with studs of gold. Then came ankles more perfect than ever sculptor dreamed
of. About the waist her white kirtle was fastened by a double-headed snake
of solid gold,[21] above which her gracious form swelled up in lines as pure
as they were lovely, till the kirtle ended on the snowy argent of her breast,
whereon her arms were folded. I gazed above them at her face, and—I
do not exaggerate—shrank back blinded and amazed. I have heard of the
beauty of celestial beings, now I saw it; only this beauty, with all its awful
loveliness and purity, was *evil*—at least, at the time, it struck me as evil.
How am I to describe it? I cannot—simply I cannot! The man does not
live whose pen could convey a sense of what I saw. I might talk of the
great changing eyes of deepest, softest black, of the tinted face, of the broad
and noble brow, on which the hair grew low, and delicate, straight features.
But, beautiful, surpassingly beautiful as they all were, her loveliness did not
lie in them. It lay rather, if it can be said to have had any fixed abiding
place, in a visible majesty, in an imperial grace, in a godlike stamp of softened
power, which shone upon that radiant countenance like a living halo. Never
before had I guessed what beauty made sublime could be—and yet, the
sublimity was a dark one—the glory was not all of heaven—though
none the less was it glorious. Though the face before me was that of a young
woman of certainly not more than thirty years, in perfect health, and the
first flush of ripened beauty, yet it had stamped upon it a look of unutterable
experience, and of deep acquaintance with grief and passion. Not even
the lovely smile that crept about the dimples of her mouth could hide this
shadow of sin and sorrow. It shone even in the light of the glorious
eyes, it was present in the air of majesty, and it seemed to say: "Behold
me, lovely as no woman was or is, undying and half-divine; memory
haunts me from age to age, and passion leads me by the hand—evil have
I done, and with sorrow have I made acquaintance from age to age,
and from age to age evil I shall do, and sorrow shall I know till my redemption comes."

Drawn by some magnetic force which I could not resist, I let my eyes
rest upon her shining orbs, and felt a current pass from them to me that
bewildered and half-blinded me.

She laughed—ah, how musically! and nodded her little head at me
with an air of sublimated coquetry that would have done credit to a Venus
Victrix.[22]

"Rash man!" she said; "like Actæon, thou hast had thy will; be careful
lest, like Actæon, thou too dost perish miserably, torn to pieces by the ban-
hounds of thine own passions. I, too, oh Holly, am a virgin goddess, not
to be moved of any man, save one, and it is not thou. Say, hast thou seen
enough!"

"I have looked on beauty, and I am blinded," I said hoarsely, lifting my hand to cover up my eyes.

"So! what did I tell thee? Beauty is like the lightning; it is lovely, but it destroys—especially trees, oh Holly!" and again she nodded and laughed.

Suddenly, she paused, and through my fingers I saw an awful change come over her countenance. Her great eyes suddenly fixed themselves into an expression in which horror seemed to struggle with some tremendous hope arising through the depths of her dark soul. The lovely face grew rigid, and the gracious willowy form seemed to erect itself.

"Man," she half whispered, half hissed, throwing back her head like a snake about to strike—"Man, whence hadst thou that scarab on thy hand? Speak, or by the Spirit of Life I will blast thee where thou standest!" and she took one light step towards me, and from her eyes there shone such an awful light—to me it seemed almost like a flame—that I fell, then and there, on the ground before her, babbling confusedly in my terror.

"Peace," she said, with a sudden change of manner, and speaking in her former soft voice, "I did affright thee! Forgive me! But at times, oh Holly, the almost infinite mind grows impatient of the slowness of the very finite, and am I tempted to use my power out of vexation—very nearly wast thou dead, but I remembered—. But the scarab—about the scarabæus!"

"I picked it up," I gurgled feebly, as I got on to my feet again, and it is a solemn fact that my mind was so disturbed that at the moment I could remember nothing else about the ring except that I had picked it up in Leo's cave.

"It is very strange," she said with a sudden access of woman-like trembling and agitation which seemed out of place in this awful woman—"but once I knew a scarab like that. It—hung round the neck—of one I loved," and she gave a little sob, and I saw that after all she was only a woman, although she might be a very old one.

"There," she went on, "it must be one like to it, and yet never did I see one like to it, for thereto hung a history, and he who wore it prized it much.*** But the scarab that I knew was not set thus in the bezel of a ring. Go now, Holly, go, and, if thou canst, try to forget that thou hast of thy folly looked upon Ayesha's beauty," and, turning from me, she flung herself on her couch, and buried her face in the cushions.

As for me, I stumbled from her presence, and I do not remember how I reached my own cave.[23]

***I am informed by a renowned and most learned Egyptologist, to whom I have submitted this very interesting and beautifully finished scarab, "Suten se Rā," that he has never seen one resembling it. Although it bears a title frequently given to Egyptian royalty, he is of opinion that it is not necessarily the cartouche of a Pharaoh, on which either the throne or personal name of the monarch is generally inscribed. What the history of this particular scarab may have been we can now, unfortunately, never know, but I have little doubt but that it played some part in the tragic story of the Princess Amenartas and her lover Kallikrates, the forsworn priest of Isis.—EDITOR.

XIV.
A Soul in Hell.

It was nearly ten o'clock at night when I cast myself down upon my bed, and began to gather my scattered wits, and reflect upon what I had seen and heard. But the more I reflected the less I could make of it. Was I mad, or drunk, or dreaming, or was I merely the victim of a gigantic and most elaborate hoax? How was it possible that I, a rational man, not unacquainted with the leading scientific facts of our history, and hitherto an absolute and utter disbeliever in all the hocus-pocus which in Europe goes by the name of the supernatural, could believe that I had within the last few minutes been engaged in conversation with a woman two thousand and odd years old? The thing was contrary to the experience of human nature, and absolutely and utterly impossible. It must be a hoax, and yet, if it were a hoax, what was I to make of it? What, too, was to be said of the figures on the water, of the woman's extraordinary acquaintance with the remote past, and her ignorance, or apparent ignorance, of any subsequent history? What, too, of her wonderful and awful loveliness? This, at any rate, was a patent fact, and beyond the experience of the world. No merely mortal woman could shine with such a supernatural radiance. About that she had, at any rate, been in the right—it was not safe for any man to look upon such beauty. I was a hardened vessel in such matters, having, with the exception of one painful experience of my green and tender youth, put the softer sex (I sometimes think that this is a misnomer) almost entirely out of my thoughts. But now, to my intense horror, I *knew* that I could never put away the vision of those glorious eyes; and, alas! the very *diablerie*[1] of the woman, whilst it horrified and repelled, attracted in even a greater degree. A person with the experience of two thousand years at her back, with the command of such tremendous powers, and the knowledge of a mystery that could hold off death, was certainly worth falling in love with, if ever woman was. But, alas! it was not a question of whether or no she was worth it, for so far as I could judge, not being versed in such matters, I, a fellow of my college, noted for what my acquaintances are pleased to call my misogyny, and a respectable man now well on in middle life, had fallen absolutely and hopelessly in love with this white sorceress. Nonsense; it must be nonsense! She had warned me fairly, and I had refused to take the warning. Curses on the fatal curiosity that is ever prompting man to draw the veil from woman, and curses on the natural impulse that begets it! It is the cause of half— ay, and more than half—of our misfortunes. Why cannot man be content to live alone and be happy, and let the women live alone and be happy too? But perhaps they would not be happy, and I am not sure that we should either. Here was a nice state of affairs. I, at my age, to fall a victim to this modern Circe! But then she was not modern, at least she said not. She was almost as ancient as the original Circe.[2]

I tore my hair, and jumped up from my couch, feeling that if I did not do something I should go off my head. What did she mean about the scarabæus too? It was Leo's scarabæus, and had come out of the old coffer that Vincey had left in my rooms nearly one-and-twenty years before. Could it be, after all, that the whole story was true, and the writing on the sherd was *not* a forgery, or the invention of some crack-brained, long-forgotten individual? And if so, could it be that *Leo* was the man that *She* was waiting for—the dead man who was to be born again! Impossible! The whole thing was gibberish! Who ever heard of a man being born again?[3]

But if it were possible that a woman could exist for two thousand years, this might be possible also—anything might be possible. I myself might, for aught I knew, be a reincarnation of some other forgotten self, or perhaps the last of a long line of ancestral selves. Well, *vive la guerre!*[4] why not? Only, unfortunately, I had no recollection of these previous conditions. The idea was so absurd to me that I burst out laughing, and, addressing the sculptured picture of a grim-looking warrior on the cave wall, called out to him aloud, "Who knows, old fellow?—perhaps I was your contemporary. By Jove! perhaps I was you and you are I," and then I laughed again at my own folly, and the sound of my laughter rang dismally along the vaulted roof, as though the ghost of the warrior had uttered the ghost of a laugh.[5]

Next I bethought me that I had not been to see how Leo was, so, taking up one of the lamps which was burning at my bedside, I slipped off my shoes and crept down the passage to the entrance of his sleeping cave. The draught of the night air was lifting his curtain to and fro gently, as though spirit hands were drawing and redrawing it. I slid into the vault-like apartment, and looked round. There was a light by which I could see that Leo was lying on the couch, tossing restlessly in his fever, but asleep. At his side, half-lying on the floor, half-leaning against the stone couch, was Ustane. She held his hand in one of hers, but she too was dozing, and the two made a pretty, or rather a pathetic, picture. Poor Leo! his cheek was burning red, there were dark shadows beneath his eyes, and his breath came heavily. He was very, very ill; and again the horrible fear seized me that he might die, and I be left alone in the world. And yet if he lived he would perhaps be my rival with Ayesha; even if he were not the man, what chance should I, middle-aged and hideous, have against his bright youth and beauty? Well, thank heaven! my sense of right was not dead. *She* had not killed that yet; and, as I stood there, I prayed to Heaven in my heart that my boy, my more than son, might live—ay, even if he proved to be the man.

Then I went back as softly as I had come, but still I could not sleep; the sight and thought of dear Leo lying there so ill had but added fuel to the fire of my unrest. My wearied body and overstrained mind awakened all my imagination into preternatural activity. Ideas, visions, almost inspira-

tions, floated before it with startling vividness. Most of them were grotesque
enough, some were ghastly, some recalled thoughts and sensations that had
for years been buried in the *de'bris* of my past life. But, behind and above
them all, hovered the shape of that awful woman, and through them gleamed
the memory of her entrancing loveliness. Up and down the cave I strode
—up and down.

Suddenly I observed, what I had not noticed before, that there was a
narrow aperture in the rocky wall. I took up the lamp and examined it;
the aperture led to a passage. Now, I was still sufficiently sensible to remember
that it is not pleasant, in such a situation as ours was, to have passages
running into one's bedchamber from no one knows where. If there are passages, people can come up them; they can come up when one is asleep.
Partly to see where it went to, and partly from a restless desire to be doing
something, I followed the passage. It led to a stone stair, which I descended;
the stair ended in another passage, or rather tunnel, also hewn out of the
bed-rock, and running, so far as I could judge, exactly beneath the gallery
that led to the entrance of our rooms, and across the great central cave.
I went on down it; it was as silent as the grave, but still, drawn by some
sensation or attraction that I cannot define, I followed on, my stockinged
feet falling without noise on the smooth and rocky floor. When I had trav-
ersed some fifty yards of space, I came to another passage running at right
angles, and here an awful thing happened to me: the sharp draught caught
my lamp and extinguished it, leaving me in utter darkness in the bowels
of that mysterious place. I took a couple of strides forward so as to clear
the bisecting tunnel, being terrible afraid lest I should turn up it in the dark
if once I got confused as to the direction, and then paused to think. What
was I to do? I had no match; it seemed awful to attempt that long journey
back through the utter gloom, and yet I could not stand there all night,
and, if I did, probably it would not help me much, for in the bowels of
the rock it would be as dark at midday as at midnight. I looked back over
my shoulder—not a sight or a sound. I peered forward down the darkness:
surely, far away, I saw something like the faint glow of fire. Perhaps it was
a cave where I could get a light—at any rate, it was worth investigating.
Slowly and painfully I crept along the tunnel, keeping my hand against its
wall, and feeling at every step with my foot before I put it down, fearing
lest I should fall into some pit. Thirty paces—there was a light, a broad
light that came and went shining through curtains! Fifty paces—it was close
at hand! Sixty—oh, great heaven!

I was at the curtains, and they did not hang close, so I could see clearly
into the little cavern beyond them. It had all the appearance of being a tomb,
and was lit up by a fire that burnt in its center with a whitish flame and
without smoke. Indeed, there to the left, was a stone shelf with a little ledge
to it three inches or so high, and on the shelf lay what I took to be a corpse;
at any rate, it looked like one, with something white thrown over it. To
the right was a similar shelf, on which lay some broidered[6] coverings. Over

the fire bent the figure of a woman; she was sideways to me and facing
the corpse, wrapped in a dark mantle that hid her like a nun's cloak. She
seemed to be staring at the flickering flame. Suddenly, as I was trying to
make up my mind what to do, with a convulsive movement that somehow
gave an impression of despairing energy, the woman rose to her feet and
cast the dark cloak from her.

It was *She* herself!

She was clothed, as I had seen her when she unveiled, in the kirtle
of clinging white, cut low upon her bosom, and bound in at the waist with
the barbaric double-headed snake, and, as before, her rippling black hair fell
in heavy masses down her back. But her face was what caught my eye,
and held me as in a vice, not this time by the force of its beauty, but by
the power of fascinated terror. The beauty was still there, indeed, but the
agony, the blind passion, and the awful vindictiveness displayed upon those
quivering features, and in the tortured look of the upturned eyes, were such
as surpass my powers of description.

For a moment she stood still, her hands raised high above her head,
and as she did so the white robe slipped from her down to her golden girdle,
baring the blinding loveliness of her form. She stood there, her fingers
clenched, and the awful look of malevolence gathered and deepened on her
face.

Suddenly, I thought of what would happen if she discovered me, and
the reflection made me turn sick and faint. But, even if I had known that
I must die if I stopped, I do not believe that I could have moved, for I was
absolutely fascinated. But still I knew my danger. Supposing she should hear
me, or see me through the curtain, supposing I even sneezed, or that her
magic told her that she was being watched—swift indeed would be my
doom.

Down came the clenched hands to her sides, then up again above her
head, and, as I am a living and honourable man, the white flame of the
fire leapt up after them, almost to the roof, throwing a fierce and ghastly
glare upon *She* herself, upon the white figure beneath the covering, and every
scroll and detail of the rockwork.

Down came the ivory arms again, and as they did so she spoke, or
rather hissed, in Arabic, in a note that curdled my blood, and for a second
stopped my heart.

"Curse her, may she be everlastingly accursed."

The arms fell and the flame sank. Up they went again, and the broad
tongue of fire shot up after them; then again they fell.

"Curse her memory—accursed be the memory of the Egyptian."

Up again, and again down.

"Curse her, the daughter of the Nile, because of her beauty."

"Curse her, because her magic hath prevailed against me."

"Curse her, because she held my beloved from me."

And again the flame dwindled and shrank.

She put her hands before her eyes, and, abandoning the hissing tone, cried aloud:—

"What is the use of cursing?—she prevailed, and she is gone."

Then she recommenced with an even more frightful energy.

"Curse her where she is. Let my curses reach her where she is and disturb her rest."

"Curse her through the starry spaces. Let her shadow be accursed."

"Let my power find her even there."

"Let her hear me even there. Let her hide herself in the blackness."

"Let her go down into the pit of despair, because I shall one day find her."

Again the flame fell, and again she covered her eyes with her hands.

"It is of no use—no use," she wailed; "who can reach those who sleep? Not even I can reach them."

Then once more she began her unholy rites.

"Curse her when she shall be born again. Let her be born accursed.

"Let her be utterly accursed from the hour of her birth until sleep finds her.

"Yea, then, let her be accursed; for then shall I overtake her with my vengeance, and utterly destroy her."

And so on. The flame rose and fell, reflecting itself in her agonised eyes; the hissing sound of her terrible maledictions, and no words of mine can convey how terrible they were, ran round the walls and died away in little echoes, and the fierce light and deep gloom alternated themselves on the white and dreadful form stretched upon that bier of stone.

But at length she seemed to wear herself out and ceased. She sat herself down upon the rocky floor, shook the dense cloud of her beautiful hair over her face and breast, and began to sob terribly in the torture of a heartrending despair.

"Two thousand years," she moaned; "two thousand years have I waited and endured; but though century doth still creep on to century, and time give place to time, the sting of memory hath not lessened, the light of hope doth not shine more bright. Oh! to have lived two thousand years, with all my passion eating at my heart, and with my sin ever before me. Oh, that for me life cannot bring forgetfulness! Oh, for the weary years that have been and are yet to come, and evermore to come, endless and without end!

"My love! my love! my love! Why did that stranger bring thee back to me after this sort? For five hundred years I have not suffered thus. Oh, if I sinned against thee have I not wiped away the sin? When wilt thou come back to me who have all, and yet without thee have naught! What is there that I can do? What? What? What? And perchance she—perchance that Egyptian doth abide with thee where thou art, and mock my memory. Oh, why could I not die with thee, I who slew thee? Alas, that I cannot die! Alas! Alas!" and she flung herself prone upon the ground, and sobbed and wept till I thought her heart must burst.

Suddenly she ceased, raised herself to her feet, rearranged her robe, and tossing back her long locks impatiently, swept across to where the figure lay upon the stone.

"Oh Kallikrates," she cried, and I trembled at the name, "I must look upon thy face again, though it be agony. It is a generation since I looked upon thee whom I slew—slew with mine own hand," and with trembling fingers she seized the corner of the sheet-like wrapping that covered the form upon the stone bier, and then paused. When she spoke again, it was in a kind of awed whisper, as though her idea were terrible even to herself.

"Shall I raise thee," she said, apparently addressing the corpse, "so that thou standest there before me, as of old? I *can* do it," and she held out her hands over the sheeted dead, while her whole frame became rigid and terrible to see, and her eyes grew fixed and dull. I shrank in horror behind curtain, my hair stood up upon my head, and, whether it was my imagination or a fact I am unable to say, but I thought that the quiet form beneath the covering began to quiver, and the winding sheet to lift as though it lay on the breast of one who slept. Suddenly she withdrew her hands, and the motion of the corpse seemed to me to cease.

"To what purpose?" she said, gloomily. "Of what good is it to recall the semblance of life when I cannot recall the spirit? Even if thou stoodest before me thou wouldst not know me, and couldst but do what I bid thee. The life in thee would be *my* life, and not *thy* life, Kallikrates."

For a moment she stood there brooding, and then cast herself down on her knees beside the form, and began to press her lips against the sheet, and weep. There was something so horrible about the sight of this awe-inspiring woman letting loose her passion on the dead[7]—so much more horrible even than anything that had gone before—that I could no longer bear to look at it, and, turning, began to creep, shaking as I was in every limb, slowly along the pitch-dark passage, feeling in my trembling heart that I had seen a vision of a Soul in Hell.

On I stumbled, I scarcely know how. Twice I fell, once I turned up the bisecting passage, but fortunately found out my mistake in time. For twenty minutes or more I crept along, till at last it occurred to me that I must have passed the little stair by which I descended. So, utterly exhausted, and nearly frightened to death, I sank down at length there on the stone flooring, and sank into oblivion.

When I came to I noticed a faint ray of light in the passage just behind me. I crept to it, and found it was the little stair down which the weak dawn was stealing. Passing up it, I gained my chamber in safety, and, flinging myself on the couch, was soon lost in slumber, or rather stupor.

XV.
Ayesha Gives Judgment.

The next thing that I remember was opening my eyes and perceiving the form of Job, who had now practically recovered from his attack of fever. He was standing in the ray of light that pierced into the cave from the outer air, shaking out my clothes as a makeshift for brushing them, which he could not do because there was no brush, and then folding them up neatly and laying them on the foot of the stone couch. This done, he got my travelling dressing-case out of the Gladstone bag, and opened it ready for my use. First he stood it on the foot of the couch also, then, being afraid, I suppose, that I should kick it off, he placed it on a leopard skin on the floor, and stood back a step or two to observe the effect. It was not satisfactory, so he shut up the bag, turned it on end, and, having rested it against the foot of the couch, placed the dressing-case on it. Next he looked at the pots full of water, which constituted our washing apparatus. "Ah!" I heard him murmur, "no hot water in this beastly place. I suppose these poor creatures only use it to boil each other in," and he sighed deeply.

"What is the matter, Job?" I said.

"Beg pardon, sir," he said, touching his hair.[1] "I thought you were asleep, sir; and I am sure you seem as though you want it. One might think from the look of you that you had been having a night of it."

I only groaned by way of answer. I had, indeed, been having a night of it, such as I hope never to have again.

"How is Mr. Leo, Job?"

"Much the same, sir. If he don't soon mend, he'll end, sir; and that's all about it; though I must say that that there savage, Ustane, do do her best for him, almost like a baptised Christian. She is always hanging round and looking after him, and if I ventures to interfere it's awful to see her; her hair seems to stand on end, and she curses and swears away in her heathen talk—at least I fancy she must be cursing, from the look of her."

"And what do you do then?"

"I make her a perlite[2] bow, and I say, Young woman, your position is one that I don't quite understand, and can't recognise. Let me tell you that I has a duty to perform to my master as is incapacitated by illness, and that I am going to perform it until I am incapacitated too,' but she don't take no heed, not she—only curses and swears away worse than ever. Last night she put her hand under that sort of nightshirt she wears and whips out a knife with a kind of curl in the blade, so I whips out my revolver, and we walks round and round each other till at last she bursts out laughing. It isn't nice treatment for a Christian man to have to put up with from a savage, however handsome she may be, but it is what people must expect as is *fools* enough" (Job laid great emphasis on the "fools") "to come to such a place to look for things no man is meant to find. It's a judgment on us, sir—that's my view; and I, for one, is of opinion that the judgment isn't half done yet, and when it is done we shall be done too, and just stop in these beastly caves with the ghosts and the corpseses for once and all. And now, sir, I must be seeing about Mr. Leo's broth, if that wild cat will let me; and, perhaps, you would like to get up, sir, because it's past nine o'clock."

Job's remarks were not of an exactly cheering order to a man who had passed such a night as I had; and, what is more, they had the weight of truth. Taking one thing with another, it appeared to me to be an utter impossibility that we should escape from the place where we were. Supposing that Leo recovered, and supposing that *She* would let us go, which was exceedingly doubtful, and that she did not "blast" us in some moment of vexation, and that we were not hot-potted by the Amahagger, it would be quite impossible for us to find our way across the network of marshes which, stretching for scores and scores of miles, formed a stronger and more impassable fortification round the various Amahagger households than any that could be built or designed by man. No, there was but one thing to do—face it out; and, speaking for my own part, I was so intensely interested in the whole weird story that, so far as I was concerned, notwithstanding the shattered state of my nerves, I asked nothing better, even if my life paid forfeit to my curiosity. What man for whom physiology[3] has charms could forbear to study such a character as that of this Ayesha when the opportunity of doing so presented itself? The very terror of the pursuit added to its fascination, and besides, as I was forced to own to myself even now in the sober light of day, she herself had attractions that I could not forget. Not even the dreadful sight which I had witnessed during the night could drive that folly from my mind; and, alas! that I should have to admit it, it has not been driven thence to this hour.

After I had dressed myself I passed into the eating, or rather embalming chamber, and had some food, which was as before brought to me by the girl mutes. When I had finished I went and saw poor Leo, who was quite off his head,[4] and did not even know me. I asked Ustane how she thought he was; but she only shook her head and began to cry a little. Evidently her hopes were small; and I then and there made up my mind that, if it were in any way possible, I would get *She* to come and see him. Surely she would cure him if she chose—at any rate she said she could. While I was in the room Billali entered, and also shook his head.

"He will die at night," he said.

"God forbid, my father," I answered, and turned away with a heavy heart.

"*She-who-must-be-obeyed* commands thy presence, my Baboon," said the old man as soon as we got to the curtain; "but, oh my dear son, be more careful. Yesterday I made sure in my heart that *She* would blast thee when thou didst not crawl upon thy stomach before her. She is sitting in the great hall even now to do justice upon those who would have smitten thee and the Lion. Come on, my son; come swiftly."

I turned, and followed him down the passage, and when we reached the great central cave saw that many Amahagger, some robed, and some merely clad in the sweet simplicity of a leopard skin, were hurrying along it. We mingled with the throng, and walked up the enormous and, indeed, almost interminable cave. All the way its walls were elaborately sculptured, and every twenty paces or so passages opened out of it at right angles, leading, Billali told me, to tombs, hollowed in the rock by "the people who were before." Nobody visited those tombs now, he said; and I must say that my heart rejoiced when I thought of the opportunities of antiquarian research which opened out before me.

At last we came to the head of the cave, where there was a rock daïs almost exactly similar to the one on which we had been so furiously attacked, a fact that proved to me that these daïs must have been used as altars, probably for the celebration of religious ceremonies, and more especially of rites connected with the interment of the dead. On either side of this daïs were passages leading, Billali informed me, to other caves full of dead bodies. "Indeed," he added, "the whole mountain is full of dead, and nearly all of them are perfect."

In front of the daïs were gathered a great number of people of both sexes, who stood staring about in their peculiar gloomy fashion, which would have reduced Mark Tapley[5] himself to misery in about five minutes. On the daïs was a rude chair of black wood inlaid with ivory, having a seat made of grass fibre, and a footstool formed of a wooden slab attached to the framework of the chair.

Suddenly there was a cry of "Hiya! Hiya!" ("*She! She!*") and thereupon the entire crowd of spectators instantly precipitated itself upon the ground, and lay still as though it were individually and collectively stricken dead, leaving me standing there like some solitary survivor of a massacre. As it did so a long string of guards began to defile from a passage to the left, and ranged themselves on either side of the daïs. Then followed about a score of male mutes, then as many women mutes bearing lamps, and then a tall white figure, swathed from head to foot, in whom I recognised *She* herself. She mounted the daïs and sat down upon the chair, and spoke to me in *Greek*, I suppose because she did not wish those present to understand what she said.

"Come hither, oh Holly," she said, "and sit thou at my feet, and see me do justice on those who would have slain thee. Forgive me if my Greek doth halt like a lame man; it is so long since I have heard the sound of it that my tongue is stiff, and will not bend rightly to the words."

I bowed, and, mounting the daïs, sat down at her feet.

"How hast thou slept, my Holly?" she asked.

"I slept not well, oh Ayesha!" I answered with perfect truth, and with an inward fear that perhaps she knew how I had passed the heart of the night.

"So," she said, with a little laugh; "I, too, have not slept well. Last night I had dreams, and methinks that thou didst call them to me, oh Holly."

"Of what didst thou dream, Ayesha?" I asked, indifferently.

"I dreamed," she answered, quickly, "of one I hate and one I love," and then, as though to turn the conversation, she addressed the captain of her guard in Arabic: "Let the men be brought before me."

The captain bowed low, for the guard and her attendants did not prostrate themselves, but had remained standing, and departed with his underlings down a passage to the right.

Then came a silence. *She* leaned her swathed head upon her hand and appeared to be lost in thought, while the multitude before her continued to grovel upon their stomachs, only screwing their heads round a little so as to get a view of us with one eye. It seemed that their Queen so rarely appeared in public that they were willing to undergo this inconvenience, and even graver risks, to have the opportunity of looking on her, or rather on her garments, for no living man there except myself had ever seen her face. At last we caught sight of the waving of lights, and heard the tramp of men coming along the passage, and in filed the guard, and with them the survivors of our would-be murderers, to the number of twenty or more, on whose countenances a natural expression of sullenness struggled with the terror that evidently filled their savage hearts. They were ranged in front of the daïs, and would have cast themselves down on the floor of the cave like the spectators, but *She* stopped them.

"Nay," she said in her softest voice, "stand; I pray you stand. Perchance the time will soon be when ye shall grow weary of being stretched out," and she laughed melodiously.

I saw a cringe of terror run along the rank of the doomed wretches, and, wicked villains as they were, I felt sorry for them. Some minutes, perhaps two or three, passed before anything fresh occurred, during which *She* appeared from the movement of her head—for, of course, we could not see her eyes—to be slowly and carefully examining each delinquent. At last she spoke, addressing herself to me in a quiet and deliberate tone.

"Dost thou, oh my guest, recognise these men?"

"Ay, oh Queen, nearly all of them," I said, and I saw them glower at me as I said it.

"Then tell to me, and this great company, the tale whereof I have heard."

Thus adjured, I, in as few words as I could, related the history of the cannibal feast, and of the attempted torture of our poor servant. The narrative was received in perfect silence, both by the accused and by the audience, and also by *She* herself. When I had done, Ayesha called upon Billali by name, and, lifting his head from the ground, but without rising, the old man confirmed my story. No further evidence was taken.

"Ye have heard," said *She* at length, in a cold, clear voice, very different from her usual tones—indeed, it was one of the most remarkable things about this extraordinary creature that her voice had the power of suiting itself in a wonderful manner to the mood of the moment. "What have ye to say, ye rebellious children, why vengeance should not be done upon you?"[6]

For some time there was no answer, but at last one of the men, a fine, broad-chested fellow, well on in middle-life, with deep-graven features and an eye like a hawk's, spoke, and said that the orders that they had received were not to harm the white men; nothing was said of their black servant, so, egged on thereto by a woman who was now dead, they proceeded to try to hot-pot him after the ancient and honourable custom of their country, with a view of eating him in due course. As for their attack upon ourselves, it was made in an access of sudden fury, and they deeply regretted it. He ended by humbly praying that mercy might be extended to them; or, at least, that they might be banished into the swamps, to live or die as it might chance; but I saw it written on his face that he had but little hope of mercy.

Then came a pause, and the most intense silence reigned over the whole scene, which, illuminated as it was by the flicker of the lamps striking out broad patterns of light and shadow upon the rocky walls, was as strange as any I ever saw, even in that unholy land. Upon the ground before the daïs were stretched scores of the corpselike forms of the spectators, till at last the long lines of them were lost in the gloomy background. Before this outstretched audience were the knots of evil-doers, trying to cover up their natural terrors with a brave appearance of unconcern. On the right and left stood the silent guards, robed in white and armed with great spears and daggers, and men and women mutes watching with hard curious eyes. Then, seated in her barbaric chair above them all, with myself at her feet, was the veiled white woman, whose loveliness and awesome power seemed to visibly shine about her like a halo, or rather like the glow from some unseen light. Never have I seen her veiled shape look more terrible than it did in that space, while she gathered herself up for vengeance.

At last it came.

"Dogs and serpents," *She* began in a low voice that gradually gathered power as she went on, till the place rang with it. "Eaters of human flesh,[7] two things have ye done. First ye have attacked these strangers, being white men, and would have slain their servant, and for that alone death is your reward. But that is not all. Ye have dared to disobey me. Did I not send my word unto you by Billali, my servant, and the father of your household? Did I not bid you to hospitably entertain these strangers, whom now ye have striven to slay, and whom, had not they been brave and strong beyond the strength of men, ye would cruelly have murdered? Hath it not been taught to you from childhood that the law of *She* is an ever fixed law, and that he who breaketh it by so much as one jot or tittle shall perish? And is not my lightest word a law? Have not your fathers taught you this, I say, whilst as yet ye were but children? Do ye not know that as well might ye bid these great caves to fall upon you, or the sun to cease its journeying, as to hope to turn me from my courses, or make my word light or heavy, according to your minds. Well do ye know it, ye Wicked Ones. But ye are all evil—evil to the core—the wickedness bubbles up in you like a fountain in the spring-time. Were it not for me, generations since had ye ceased to be, for of your own evil way had ye destroyed each other. And now, because ye have done this thing, because ye have striven to put these men, my guests, to death, and yet more because ye have dared to disobey my word, this is the doom that I doom you to. That ye be taken to the cave of torture,* and given over to the tormenters, and that on the going down of to-morrow's sun those of you who yet remain alive be slain, even as ye would have slain the servant of this my guest."

She ceased, and a faint murmur of horror ran round the cave. As for the victims, as soon as they realized the full hideousness of their doom, their stoicism forsook them, and they flung themselves down upon the ground, and wept and implored for mercy in a way that was dreadful to behold. I, too, turned to Ayesha, and begged her to spare them, or at least to mete out their fate in some less awful way. But she was hard as adamant about it.

"My Holly," she said, again speaking in Greek, which, to tell the truth, although I have always been considered a better scholar of that language than most men, I found it rather difficult to follow, chiefly because of the change in the fall of the accent. Ayesha, of course, talked with the accent of her contemporaries, whereas we have only tradition and the modern accent to guide us as to the exact pronunciation. "My Holly, it cannot be. Were I to show mercy to those wolves, your lives would not be safe among this people for a day. Thou knowest them not. They are tigers to lap blood, and even now they hunger for your lives. How thinkest thou that I rule this people? I have but a regiment of guards to do my bidding, therefore it is not by force. It is by terror. My empire is of the imagination. Once in a generation mayhap I do as I have done but now, and slay a score by torture. Believe not that I would be cruel, or take vengeance on anything so low. What can it profit me to be avenged on such as these? Those who live long, my Holly, have no passions, save where they have interests. Though I may seem to slay in wrath, or because my mood is crossed, it is not so. Thou hast seen how in the heavens the little clouds blow this way and that without a cause, yet behind them is the great wind sweeping on its path whither it listeth. So is it with me, oh Holly. My moods and changes are

*"The cave of torture." I afterwards saw this dreadful place, also a legacy from the prehistoric people who lived in Kôr. The only objects in the cave itself were slabs of rock arranged in various positions to facilitate the operations of the torturers. Many of these slabs, which were of a porous stone, were stained quite dark with the blood of ancient victims that had soaked into them. Also in the centre of the room was a place for a furnace, with a cavity wherein to heat the historic pot. But the most dreadful thing about the cave was that over each slab was a sculptured illustration of the appropriate torture being applied. These sculptures were so awful that I will not harrow the reader by attempting a description of them.—L.H.H.

the little clouds, and fitfully these seem to turn; but behind them ever blows the great wind of my purpose. Nay, the men must die; and die as I have said." Then, suddenly turning to the captain of the guard:—

"As my word is, so be it!"[8]

XVI.
The Tombs of Kôr.

After the prisoners had been removed Ayesha waved her hand, and the spectators turned round, and began to crawl off down the cave like a scattered flock of sheep. When they were a fair distance from the daïs, however, they rose and walked away, leaving the Queen and myself alone, with the exception of the mutes and the few remaining guards, most of whom had departed with the doomed men. Thinking this a good opportunity, I asked *She* to come and see Leo, telling her of his serious condition; but she would not, saying that he certainly would not die before the night, as people never died of that sort of fever except at nightfall or dawn. Also she said that it would be better to let the sickness spend its course as much as possible before she cured it. Accordingly, I was rising to leave, when she bade me follow her, as she would talk with me, and show me the wonders of the caves.

I was too much involved in the web of her fatal fascinations to say her no, even if I had wished, which I did not. She rose from her chair, and, making some signs to the mutes, descended from the daïs. Thereon four of the girls took lamps, and ranged themselves two in front and two behind us, but the others went away, as also did the guards.

"Now," she said, "wouldst thou see some of the wonders of this place, oh Holly? Look upon this great cave. Sawest thou ever the like? Yet was it, and many more like it, hollowed by the hands of the dead race that once lived here in the city on the plain. A great and a wonderful people must they have been, those men of Kôr, but, like the Egyptians, they thought more of the dead than of the living. How many men, thinkest thou, working for how many years, did it need to the hollowing out this cave and all the galleries thereof?"[1]

"Tens of thousands," I answered.

"So, oh Holly. This people was an old people before the Egyptians were. A little can I read of their inscriptions, having found the key thereto—and, see thou here, this was one of the last of the caves that they hollowed," and, turning to the rock behind her, she motioned the mutes to hold up

the lamps. Carven over the daïs was the figure of an old man seated in
a chair, with an ivory rod in his hand. It struck me at once that his features
were exceedingly like those of the man who was represented as being embalmed in the chamber where we took our meals. Beneath the chair, which,
by the way, was shaped exactly like the one in which Ayesha had sat to
give judgment, was a short inscription in the extraordinary characters of
which I have already spoken, but which I do not remember sufficient of
to illustrate. It looked more like Chinese writing than any other that I am
acquainted with. This inscription Ayesha proceeded, with some difficulty and
hesitation, to read aloud and translate. It ran as follows:—

*"In the year four thousand two hundred and fifty-nine[2] from the founding
of the City of imperial Kôr was this cave (or burial place) completed by Tisno,
King of Kôr, the people thereof and their slaves having laboured thereat for three
generations, to be a tomb for their citizens of rank who shall come after. May
the blessing of the heaven above the heaven rest upon their work, and make the
sleep of Tisno, the mighty monarch, the likeness of whose features is graven above,
a sound and happy sleep till the day of awakening,* and also the sleep of his servants,
and of those of his race who, rising up after him, shall yet lay their heads as
low."*

"Thou seest, oh Holly," she said, "this people founded the city, of which
the ruins yet cumber the plain yonder, four thousand years before[3] this cave
was finished. Yet, when first mine eyes beheld it two thousand years ago,
was it even as it is now. Judge, therefore, how old must that city have been!
And now, follow thou me, and I will show thee after what fashion this great
people fell when the time was come for it to fall," and she led the way
down to the centre of the cave, stopping at a spot where a round rock had
been let into a kind of large manhole in the flooring, accurately filling it
just as the iron plates fill the spaces in the London pavements down which
the coals are thrown. "Thou seest," she said. "Tell me, what is it?"

"Nay, I know not," I answered; whereon she crossed to the left-hand
side of the cave (looking towards the entrance) and signed to the mutes
to hold up the lamps. On the wall was something painted with a red pigment
in similar characters to those hewn beneath the sculpture of Tisno, King
of Kôr. This inscription she proceeded to translate to me, the pigment still
being quite fresh enough to show the form of the letters. It ran as follows:—

*"I, Junis, a priest of the Great Temple of Kôr, write this upon the rock of
the burying-place in the year four thousand eight hundred and three from the
founding of Kôr.[4] Kôr is fallen! No more shall the mighty feast in her halls, no
more shall she rule the world, and her navies go out to commerce with the world.
Kôr is fallen! and her mighty works and all the cities of Kôr, and all the harbours
that she built and the canals that she made, are for the wolf and the owl and*

---

*This phrase is remarkable, as seeming to indicate a belief in a future state.—EDITOR.

the wild swan, and the barbarian who comes after. Twenty and five moons ago did a cloud settle upon Kôr, and the hundred cities of Kôr, and out of the cloud came a pestilence that slew her people, old and young, one with another, and spared not. One with another they turned black and died—the young and the old, the rich and the poor, the man and the woman, the prince and the slave. The pestilence slew and slew, and ceased not by day or by night, and those who escaped from the pestilence were slain of the famine. No longer could the bodies of the children of Kôr be preserved according to the ancient rites, because of the number of the dead, therefore were they hurled into the great pit beneath the cave, through the hole in the floor of the cave. Then, at last, a remnant of this the great people, the light of the whole world, went down to the coast and took ship and sailed northwards; and now am I, the Priest Junis, who write this, the last man left alive of this great city of men, but whether there be any yet left in the other cities I know not. This do I write in misery of heart before I die, because Kôr the Imperial is no more, and because there are none to worship in her temple, and all her palaces are empty, and her princes and her captains and her traders and her fair women have passed off the face of the earth."[5]

I gave a sigh of astonishment—the utter desolation depicted in this rude scrawl was so overpowering. It was terrible to think of this solitary survivor of a mighty people recording its fate before he too went down into darkness. What must the old man have felt as, in ghastly terrifying solitude, by the light of one lamp feebly illumining a little space of gloom, he in a few brief lines daubed the history of his nation's death upon the cavern wall? What a subject for the moralist, or the painter, or indeed for any one who can think!

"Doth it not occur to thee, oh Holly," said Ayesha, laying her hand upon my shoulder, "that those men who sailed North may have been the fathers of the first Egyptians?"

"Nay, I know not," I said; "it seems that the world is very old."

"Old?—Yes, it is old indeed. Time after time have nations, ay, and rich and strong nations, learned in the arts, been and passed away and been forgotten, so that no memory of them remains. This is but one of several; for Time eats up the works of man, unless, indeed, he digs in caves like the people of Kôr, and then mayhap the sea swallows them, or the earthquake shakes them in. Who knows what hath been on the earth, or what shall be? There is no new thing under the sun, as the wise Hebrew wrote long ago.[6] Yet were not these people utterly destroyed, as I think. Some few remained in the other cities, for their cities were many. But the barbarians from the south, or perchance my people, the Arabs, came down upon them, and took their women to wife, and the race of the Amahagger that is now is a bastard brood of the mighty sons of Kôr,[7] and behold it dwelleth in the tombs with its fathers' bones.** But I know not: who can know? My

---

**The name of the race Ama-hagger would seem to indicate a curious mingling of races such

arts cannot pierce so far into the blackness of Time's night. A great people were they. They conquered till none were left to conquer, and then they dwelt at ease within their rocky mountain walls, with their man servants and their maid servants, their minstrels, their sculptors, and their concubines, and traded and quarrelled, and ate and hunted and slept and made merry till their time came. But come, I will show thee the great pit beneath the cave whereof the writing speaks. Never shall thine eyes witness such another sight."

Accordingly I followed her to a side passage opening out of the main cave, then down a great number of steps, and along an underground shaft which cannot have been less than sixty feet beneath the surface of the rock, and was ventilated by curious borings that ran upward, I do not know where. Suddenly the passage ended, and she halted and bade the mutes hold up the lamps, and, as she had prophesied, I saw a scene such as I was not likely to see again.[8] We were standing in an enormous pit, or rather on the brink of it, for it went down deeper—I don't know how much—than the level on which we stood, and was edged in with a low wall of rock. So far as I could judge, this pit was about the size of the space beneath the dome of St. Paul's in London, and when the lamps were held up I saw that it was nothing but one vast charnel-house, being literally full of thousands of human skeletons, which lay piled up in an enormous gleaming pyramid, formed by the slipping down of the bodies at the apex as fresh ones were dropped in from above. Anything more appalling than this jumbled mass of the remains of a departed race I cannot imagine, and what made it even more dreadful was that in this dry air a considerable number of the bodies had simply become desiccated with the skin still on them, and now, fixed in every conceivable position, stared at us out of the mountain of white bones, grotesquely horrible caricatures of humanity. In my astonishment I uttered an ejaculation, and the echoes of my voice, ringing in the vaulted space, disturbed a skull that had been accurately balanced for many thousands of years near the apex of the pile. Down it came with a run, bounding along merrily towards us, and of course bringing an avalanche of other bones after it, till at last the whole pit rattled with their movement, even as though the skeletons were getting up to greet us.[9]

"Come," I said, "I have seen enough. These are the bodies of those who died of the great sickness, is it not so?" I added, as we turned away.

"Yea. The people of Kôr ever embalmed their dead, as did the Egyptians, but their art was greater than the art of the Egyptians, for, whereas the Egyptians disembowelled and drew the brain, the people of Kôr injected fluid into the veins, and thus reached every part. But stay, thou shalt see," and

as might easily have occurred in the neighbourhood of the Zambezi. The prefix "Ama" is common to the Zulu and kindred races, and signifies "people," while "hagger" is an Arabic word meaning a stone.—EDITOR.

she halted at haphazard at one of the little doorways opening out of the passage along which we were walking, and motioned to the mutes to light us in. We entered into a small chamber similar to the one in which I had slept at our first stopping-place, only instead of one there were two stone benches or beds in it. On the benches lay figures covered with yellow linen,*** on which a fine and impalpable dust had gathered in the course of ages, but nothing like to the extent that one would have anticipated, for in these deep-hewn caves there is no material to turn to dust. About the bodies on the stone shelves and floor of the tomb were many painted vases, but I saw very few ornaments or weapons in any of the vaults.

"Uplift the cloths, oh Holly," said Ayesha, but when I put out my hand to do so I drew it back again. It seemed like sacrilege, and, to speak the truth, I was awed by the dread solemnity of the place, and of the presences before us. Then, with a little laugh at my fears she drew them herself, only to discover other and yet finer cloths lying over the forms upon the stone bench. These also she withdrew, and then for the first time for thousands upon thousands of years did living eyes look upon the face of that chilly dead. It was a woman; she might have been thirty-five years of age, or perhaps a little less, and had certainly been beautiful. Even now her calm clear-cut features, marked out with delicate eyebrows and long eyelashes which threw little lines of the shadow of the lamplight upon the ivory face, were wonderfully beautiful. There, robed in white, down which her blue-black hair was streaming, she slept her last long sleep, and on her arm, its face pressed against her breast, there lay a little babe. So sweet was the sight, although so awful, that I confess it without shame—I could scarcely withhold my tears. It took me back across the dim gulf of the ages to some happy home in dead Imperial Kôr, where this winsome lady girt about with beauty had lived and died, and dying taken her last-born with her to the tomb. There they were before us, mother and babe, the white memories of a forgotten human history speaking more eloquently to the heart than could any written record of their lives. Reverently I replaced the grave-cloths, and, with a sigh that flowers so fair should, in the purpose of the Everlasting, have only bloomed to be gathered to the grave, I turned to the body on the opposite shelf, and gently unveiled it. It was that of a man in advanced life, with a long grizzled beard, and also robed in white, probably the husband of the lady, who, after surviving her many years, came at last to sleep once more for good and all beside her.

We left the place and entered others. It would be too long to describe the many things I saw in them. Each one had its occupants, for the five hundred and odd years that had elapsed between the completion of the cave and the

---

***All the linen that the Amahagger wore was taken from the tombs, which accounted for its yellow hue. If it was well washed, however, and properly rebleached, it acquired its former snowy whiteness, and was the softest and best linen I ever saw.—L.H.H.

destruction of the race had evidently sufficed to fill these catacombs, number-less as they were, and all appeared to have been undisturbed since the day when they were placed there. I could fill a book with the description of them, but to do so would only be to repeat what I have said, with variations.

Nearly all the bodies, so masterly was the art with which they had been treated, were as perfect as on the day of death thousands of years before. Nothing came to injure them in the deep silence of the living rock: they were beyond the reach of heat and cold and damp, and the aromatic drugs with which they had been saturated were evidently practically everlasting in their effect. Here and there, however, we saw an exception, and in these cases, although the flesh looked sound enough externally, if one touched it it fell in, and revealed the fact that the figure was but a pile of dust. This arose, Ayesha told me, from these particular bodies having, either owing to haste in the burial or other causes, been soaked in the preservative,**** instead of its being injected into the substance of the flesh.

About the last tomb we visited I must, however, say one word, for its contents spoke even more eloquently to the human sympathies than those of the first. It had but two occupants, and they lay together on a single shelf. I withdrew the grave cloths, and there, clasped heart to heart, were a young man and a blooming girl. Her head rested on his arm, and his lips were pressed against her brow. I opened the man's linen robe, and there over his heart was a dagger-wound, and beneath the girl's fair breast was a like cruel stab, through which her life had ebbed away. On the rock above was an inscription in three words. Ayesha translated it. It was *Wedded in Death*.

What was the life-history of these two, who, of a truth, were beautiful in their lives, and in their death were not divided?[10]

I closed my eyelids, and imagination, taking up the thread of thought, shot its swift shuttle back across the ages, weaving a picture on their blackness so real and vivid in its detail that I could almost for a moment think that I had triumphed o'er the Past, and that my spirit's eyes had pierced the mystery of Time.

I seemed to see this fair girl form—the yellow hair streaming down

****Ayesha afterwards showed me the tree from the leaves of which this ancient preservative was manufactured. It is a low bush-like tree, that to this day grows in wonderful plenty upon the sides of the mountains, or rather upon the slopes leading up to the rocky walls. The leaves are long and narrow, a vivid green in colour, but turning a bright red in the autumn, and not unlike those of a laurel in general appearance. They have little smell when green, but if boiled the aromatic odour from them is so strong that one can hardly bear it. The best mixture, however, was made from the roots, and among the people of Kôr there was a law, which Ayesha showed me alluded to on some of the inscriptions, to the effect that on pain of heavy penalties no one under a certain rank was to be embalmed with the drugs prepared from the roots. The object and effect of this was, of course, to preserve the trees from extermination, the sale of the leaves and roots was a Government monopoly, and from it the Kings of Kôr derived a large proportion of their private revenue.—L.H.H.

her, glittering against her garments snowy white, and the bosom that was whiter than the robes, even dimming with its lustre her ornaments of burnished gold. I seemed to see the great cave filled with warriors, bearded and clad in mail, and, on the lighted daïs where Ayesha had given judgment, a man standing, robed, and surrounded by the symbols of his priestly office. And up the cave there came one clad in purple, and before him and behind him came minstrels and fair maidens, chanting a wedding song. White stood the maid against the altar, fairer than the fairest there—purer than a lily, and more cold than the dew that glistens in its heart. But as the man drew near she shuddered. Then out of the press and throng there sprang a dark-haired youth, and put his arm about this long-forgotten maid, and kissed her pale face in which the blood shot up like lights of the red dawn across the silent sky. And next there was turmoil and uproar, and a flashing of swords, and they tore the youth from her arms, and stabbed him, but with a cry she snatched the dagger from his belt, and drove it into her snowy breast, home to the heart, and down she fell, and then, with cries and wailing, and every sound of lamentation, the pageant rolled away from the arena of my vision, and once more the past shut to its book.

Let him who reads forgive the intrusion of a dream into a history of fact. But it came so home to me—I saw it all so clear in a moment, as it were; and, besides, who shall say what proportion of fact, past, present, or to come, may lie in the imagination? What is imagination? Perhaps it is the shadow of the intangible truth, perhaps it is the soul's thought.

In an instant the whole thing had passed through my brain, and *She* was addressing me.

"Behold the lot of man," said the veiled Ayesha, as she drew the winding sheets back over the dead lovers, speaking in a solemn, thrilling voice, which accorded well with the dream that I had dreamed, "to the tomb, and to the forgetfulness that hides the tomb, must we all come at last! Ay, even I who live so long. Even for me, oh Holly, thousands upon thousands of years hence; thousands of years after thou hast gone through the gate and been lost in the mists, a day will dawn whereon I shall die, and be even as thou art and these are. And then what will it avail that I have lived a little longer, holding off death by the knowledge I have wrung from Nature, since at last I too must die? What is a span of ten thousand years, or ten times ten thousand years, in the history of time? It is as naught—it is as the mists that roll up in the sunlight; it fleeth away like an hour of sleep or a breath of the Eternal Spirit. Behold the lot of man! Certainly it shall overtake us, and we shall sleep. Certainly, too, we shall awake and live again, and again shall sleep, and so on and on, through periods, spaces, and times, from æon unto æon, till the world is dead, and the worlds beyond the worlds are dead,[11] and naught liveth save the Spirit that is Life. But for us twain and for these dead ones shall the end of ends be Life, or shall it be Death? As yet Death is but Life's Night, but out of the night is the Morrow born

again, and doth again beget the Night. Only when Day and Night, and Life
and Death, are ended and swallowed up in that from which they came,
what shall be our fate, oh Holly? Who can see so far? Not even I!"

And then, with a sudden change of tone and manner—

"Hast thou seen enough, my stranger guest, or shall I show thee more
of the wonders of these tombs that are my palace halls? If thou wilt, I can
lead thee to where Tisno, the mightiest and most valorous King of Kôr, in
whose day these caves were ended, lies in a pomp that seems to mock at
nothingness, and bid the empty shadows of the past do homage to his sculptured vanity!"

"I have seen enough, oh Queen," I answered. "My heart is overwhelmed
by the power of the present Death. Mortality is weak, and easily broken
down by a sense of the companionship that waits upon its end. Take me
hence, oh Ayesha!"

XVII.
The Balance Turns.

In a few minutes, following the lamps of the mutes, which, held out from
the body as a bearer holds water in a vessel, had the appearance of floating
down the darkness by themselves, we came to a stair which led us to *She's*
ante-room, the same that Billali had crept up upon all fours on the previous
day. Here I would have bid the Queen adieu, but she would not.

"Nay," she said, "enter with me, oh Holly, for of a truth thy conversation
pleaseth me. Think, oh Holly: for two thousand years have I had none to
converse with save slaves and my own thoughts, and though of all this thinking hath much wisdom come, and many secrets been made plain, yet am
I weary of my thoughts, and have come to loathe mine own society, for
surely the food that memory gives to eat is bitter to the taste, and it is only
with the teeth of hope that we can bear to bite it. Now, though thy thoughts
are green and tender, as becometh one so young, yet are they those of a
thinking brain, and in truth thou dost bring back to my mind certain of
those old philosophers with whom in days bygone I have disputed at Athens,
and at Becca in Arabia,[1] for thou hast the same crabbed air and dusty look,
as though thou hadst passed thy days in reading ill-writ Greek, and been
stained dark with the grime of manuscripts. So draw the curtain, and sit
here by my side, and we will eat fruit, and talk of pleasant things. See,
I will again unveil to thee. Thou hast brought it on thyself, oh Holly; fairly

have I warned thee—and thou shalt call me beautiful as even those old philosophers were wont to do. Fie upon them, forgetting their philosophy!"

And without more ado she stood up and shook the white wrappings from her, and came forth shining and splendid like some glittering snake when she has cast her slough; ay, and fixed her wonderful eyes upon me —more deadly than any Basilisk's[2]—and pierced me through and through with their beauty, and sent her light laugh ringing through the air like chimes of silver bells.

A new mood was on her, and the very colour of her mind seemed to change beneath it. It was no longer torture-torn and hateful, as I had seen it when she was cursing her dead rival by the leaping flames, no longer icily terrible as in the judgment-hall, no longer rich, and sombre, and splendid, like a Tyrian cloth,[3] as in the dwellings of the dead. No, her mood now was that of Aphrodité[4] triumphing. Life—radiant, ecstatic, wonderful— seemed to flow from her and around her. Softly she laughed and sighed, and swift her glances flew. She shook her heavy tresses, and their perfume filled the place; she struck her little sandalled foot upon the floor, and hummed a snatch of some old Greek epithalamium.[5] All the majesty was gone, or did but lurk and faintly flicker through her laughing eyes, like light- ning seen through sunlight. She had cast off the terror of the leaping flame, the cold power of judgment that was even now being done, and the wise sadness of the tombs—cast them off and put them behind her, like the white shroud she wore, and now stood out the incarnation of lovely tempting womanhood, made more perfect—and in a way more spiritual—than ever woman was before.

"So, my Holly, sit there where thou canst see me. It is by thine own wish, remember—again I say, blame me not if thou dost wear away thy little span with such a sick pain at the heart that thou wouldst fain have died before ever thy curious eyes were set upon me. There, sit so, and tell me, for in truth I am inclined for praises—tell me, am I not beautiful? Nay, speak not so hastily; consider well the point; take me feature by feature, forgetting not my form, and my hands and feet, and my hair, and the white- ness of my skin, and then tell me truly, hast thou ever known a woman who in aught, ay, in one little portion of her beauty, in the curve of an eyelash even, or the modelling of a shell-like ear, is justified to hold a light before my loveliness? Now, my waist! Perchance thou thinkest it too large, but of a truth it is not so; it is this golden snake that is too large, and doth not bind it as it should. It is a wise snake, and knoweth that it is ill to tie in the waist.[6] But see, give me thy hands—so—now press them round me, there, with but a little force, thy fingers touch, oh Holly."

I could bear it no longer. I am but a man, and she was more than a woman. Heaven knows what she was—I do not! But then and there I fell upon my knees before her, and told her in a sad mixture of languages —for such moments confuse the thoughts—that I worshipped her as never woman was worshipped, and that I would give my immortal soul to marry her, which at that time I certainly would have done, and so, indeed, would any other man, or all the race of men rolled into one. For a moment she looked a little surprised, and then she began to laugh, and clap her hands in glee.

"Oh, so soon, oh Holly!" she said. "I wondered how many minutes it would need to bring thee to thy knees. I have not seen a man kneel before me for so many days, and, believe me, to a woman's heart the sight is sweet, ay, wisdom and length of days take not from that dear pleasure which is our sex's only right.

"What wouldst thou?—what wouldst thou? Thou dost not know what thou doest. Have I not told thee that I am not for thee? I love but one, and thou art not the man. Ah Holly, for all thy wisdom—and in a way thou art wise—thou art but a fool running after folly. Thou wouldst look into mine eyes—thou wouldst kiss me. Well, if it pleaseth thee, *look*," and she bent herself towards me, and fixed her dark and thrilling orbs upon my own; "ay, and *kiss*, too, if thou wilt, for, thanks be given to the scheme of things, kisses leave no marks, except upon the heart. But if thou dost kiss, I tell thee of a surety wilt thou eat out thy breast with love of me, and die!" and she bent yet further towards me till her soft hair brushed my brow, and her fragrant breath played upon my face, and made me faint and weak. Then of a sudden, even as I stretched out my arms to clasp, she straightened herself, and a quick change passed over her. Reaching out her hand, she held it over my head, and it seemed to me that something flowed from it that chilled me back to common sense, and a knowledge of propriety and the domestic virtues.

"Enough of this wanton play," she said with a touch of sternness. "Listen, Holly. Thou art a good and honest man, and I fain would spare thee; but, oh! it is so hard for woman to be merciful. I have said I am not for thee, therefore let thy thoughts pass by me like an idle wind, and the dust of thy imagination sink again into the depths—well, of despair, if thou wilt. Thou dost not know me, Holly. Hadst thou seen me but ten hours past when my passion seized me, thou hadst shrunk from me in fear and trembling. I am of many moods, and, like the water in that vessel, I reflect many things; but they pass, my Holly; they pass, and are forgotten. Only the water is the water still, and I still am I, and that which maketh the water maketh it, and that which maketh me maketh me, nor can my quality be altered. Therefore, pay no heed to what I seem, seeing that thou canst not know what I am. If thou troublest me again I will veil myself, and thou shalt behold my face no more."

I rose, and sank on the cushioned couch beside her, yet quivering with emotion, though for a moment my mad passion had left me, as the leaves of a tree quiver still, although the gust be gone that stirred them. I did not dare to tell her that I *had* seen her in that deep and hellish mood, muttering incantations to the fire in the tomb.

"So," she went on, "now eat some fruit; believe me, it is the only true food for man.[7] Oh, tell me of the philosophy of that Hebrew Messiah, who came after me, and who thou sayest doth now rule Rome, and Greece, and Egypt, and the barbarians beyond. It must have been a strange philosophy that He taught, for in my day the peoples would have naught of our philosophies. Revel and lust and drink, blood and cold steel, and the shock of men gathered in the battle—these were the canons of their creeds."

I had recovered myself a little by now, and, feeling bitterly ashamed of the weakness into which I had been betrayed, I did my best to expound to her the doctrines of Christianity, to which, however, with the single exception of our conception of Heaven and Hell, I found that she paid but faint attention, her interest being all directed towards the Man who taught them. Also I told her that among her own people, the Arabs, another prophet, one Mohammed, had arisen and preached a new faith, to which many millions of mankind now adhered.

"Ah!" she said; "I see—two new religions! I have known so many, and doubtless there have been many more since I knew aught beyond these caves of Kôr. Mankind asks ever of the skies to vision out what lies behind them. It is terror for the end, and but a subtler form of selfishness—this it is that breeds religions. Mark, my Holly, each religion claims the future for its followers; or, at the least, the good thereof. The evil is for those benighted ones who will have none of it; seeing the light the true believers worship, as the fishes see the stars, but dimly. The religions come and the religions pass, and civilisations come and pass, and naught endures but the world and human nature. Ah! if man would but see that hope is from within and not from without—that he himself must work out his own salvation! He is there, and within him is the breath of life and a knowledge of good and evil as good and evil is to him. Thereon let him build and stand erect, and not cast himself before the image of some unknown God, modelled like his poor self, but with a bigger brain to think the evil thing, and a longer arm to do it."

I thought to myself, which shows how old such reasoning is, being, indeed, one of the recurring quantities of theological discussion, that her argument sounded very like some that I have heard in the nineteenth century, and in other places than the caves of Kôr, and with which, by the way, I totally disagree, but I did not care to try and discuss the question with her.[8] To begin with, my mind was too weary with all the emotions through which I had passed, and, in the second place, I knew that I should get the worst of it. It is weary work enough to argue with an ordinary materialist, who hurls statistics and whole strata of geological facts at your head, whilst you can only buffet him with deductions and instincts and the snowflakes of faith, that are, alas! so apt to melt in the hot embers of our troubles. How little chance, then, should I have against one whose brain was supernaturally sharpened, and who had two thousand years of experience, besides all manner of knowledge of the secrets of Nature at her command! Feeling that she would be more likely to convert me than I should to convert her, I thought it best to leave the matter alone, and so sat silent. Many a time since then have I bitterly regretted that I did so, for thereby I lost the only opportunity I can remember having had of ascertaining what Ayesha *really* believed, and what her "philosophy" was.

"Well, my Holly,"[9] she continued, "and so those people of mine have also found a prophet, a false prophet thou sayest, for he is not thine own, and, indeed, I doubt it not. Yet in my day was it otherwise, for then we Arabs had many gods. Allât there was, and Saba, the Host of Heaven, Al Uzza, and Manah the stony one, for whom the blood of victims flowed, and Wadd and Sawâ, and Yaghûth the Lion of the dwellers in Yaman, and Yâûk the Horse of Morad, and Nasr the Eagle of Hamyar; ay, and many more. Oh, the folly of it all, the shame and the pitiful folly! Yet when I rose in wisdom and spoke thereof, surely they would have slain me in the name of their outraged gods. Well, so hath it ever been—but, my Holly, art thou weary of me already, that thou dost sit so silent? Or dost thou fear lest I should teach thee my philosophy?—for know I have a philosophy. What would a teacher be without her own philosophy? and if thou dost vex me overmuch beware! for I will have thee learn it, and thou shalt be my disciple, and we twain will found a faith that shall swallow up all others. Faithless man! And but half an hour since thou wast upon thy knees—the posture does not suit thee, Holly,—swearing that thou didst love me. What shall we do?—Nay, I have it. I will come and see this youth, the Lion, as the old man Billali calls him, who came with thee, and who is so sick. The fever must have run its course by now, and if he is about to die I will recover him. Fear not, my Holly, I shall use no magic. Have I not told thee that there is no such thing as magic, though there is such a thing as understanding and applying the forces which are in Nature? Go now, and presently, when I have made the drug ready, I will follow thee."*

Accordingly I went, only to find Job and Ustane in a great state of grief, declaring that Leo was in the throes of death, and that they had been searching for me everywhere. I rushed to the couch, and glanced at him: clearly he was dying. He was senseless, and breathing heavily, but his lips were quivering, and every now and again a little shudder ran down his frame. I knew enough of doctoring to see that in another hour he would be beyond the reach of earthly help,—perhaps in another five minutes. How I cursed my selfishness and the folly that had kept me lingering by Ayesha's side while my dear boy lay dying! Alas and alas! how easily the best of us are lighted down to evil by the gleam of a woman's eyes! What a wicked wretch

---

*Ayesha was a great chemist, indeed chemistry appears to have been her only amusement and occupation. She had one of the caves fitted up as a laboratory, and although her appliances were necessarily rude, the results that she attained were, as will become clear in the course of this narrative, sufficiently surprising.—L.H.H

was I! Actually, for the last half-hour I had scarcely thought of Leo, and this, be it remembered, of the man who for twenty years had been my dearest companion, and the chief interest of my existence. And now, perhaps, it was too late!

I wrung my hands, and glanced round. Ustane was sitting by the couch, and in her eyes burnt the dull light of despair. Job was blubbering—I am sorry I cannot name his distress by any more delicate word—audibly in the corner. Seeing my eye fixed upon him, he went outside to give way to his grief in the passage. Obviously the only hope lay in Ayesha. She, and she alone—unless, indeed, she was an impostor, which I could not believe—could save him. I would go and implore her to come. As I started to do so, however, Job came flying into the room, his hair literally standing on end with terror.

"Oh, God help us, sir!" he ejaculated in a frightened whisper, "here's a corpse a-coming sliding down the passage!"

For a moment I was puzzled, but presently, of course, it struck me that he must have seen Ayesha, wrapped in her grave-like garment, and been deceived by the extraordinary undulating smoothness of her walk into a belief that she was a white ghost gliding towards him. Indeed, at that very moment the question was settled, for Ayesha herself was in the apartment, or rather cave. Job turned, and saw her sheeted form, and then, with a convulsive howl of "Here it comes!" sprang into a corner, and jammed his face against the wall, and Ustane, guessing whose the dread presence must be, prostrated herself upon her face.

"Thou comest in a good time, Ayesha," I said, "for my boy lies at the point of death."

"So," she said, softly; "provided he be not dead, it is no matter, for I can bring him back to life, my Holly. Is that man there thy servant, and is that the method wherewith thy servants greet strangers in thy country?"

"He is frightened of thy garb—it hath a death-like air," I answered.

She laughed.

"And the girl? Ah, I see now. It is she of whom thou didst speak to me. Well, bid them both to leave us, and we will see to this sick Lion of thine. I love not that underlings should perceive my wisdom."

Thereon I told Ustane in Arabic and Job in English both to leave the room; an order which the latter obeyed readily enough, and was glad to obey, for he could not in any way subdue his fear. But it was otherwise with Ustane.

"What does *She* want?" she whispered, divided between her fear of the terrible Queen and her anxiety to remain near Leo. "It is surely the right of a wife to be near her husband when he dieth. Nay, I will not go, my lord the Baboon."

"Why doth not that woman leave us, my Holly?" asked Ayesha, from the other end of the cave, where she was engaged in carelessly examining some of the sculptures on the wall.

"She is not willing to leave Leo," I answered, not knowing what to say. Ayesha wheeled round, and pointing to the girl Ustane, said one word, and one only, but it was quite enough, for the tone in which it was said meant volumes.

"Go!"

And then Ustane crept past her on her hands and knees, and went.

"Thou seest, my Holly," said Ayesha, with a little laugh, "it was needful that I should give these people a lesson in obedience. That girl went nigh to disobeying me, but then she did not learn this morn how I treat the disobedient. Well, she has gone; and now let me see the youth," and she glided towards the couch on which Leo lay, with his face in the shadow and turned towards the wall.

"He hath a noble shape," she said, as she bent over him to look upon his face.

Next second her tall and willowy form was staggering back across the room, as though she had been shot or stabbed, staggering back till at last she struck the cavern wall, and then there burst from her lips the most awful and unearthly scream that I ever heard in all my life.

"What is it, Ayesha?" I cried. "Is he dead?"

She turned, and sprang towards me like a tigress.

"Thou dog!" she said, in her terrible whisper, which sounded like the hiss of a snake, "why didst thou hide this from me?" And she stretched out her arm, and I thought that she was about to slay me.

"What?" I ejaculated, in the most lively terror; "what?"

"Ah!" she said, "perchance thou didst not know. Learn, my Holly, learn: there lies—there lies my lost Kallikrates. Kallikrates, who has come back to me at last, as I knew he would, as I knew he would;" and she began to sob and to laugh, and generally to conduct herself like any other lady who is a little upset, murmuring, "Kallikrates, Kallikrates."

"Nonsense," thought I to myself, but I did not like to say it; and, indeed, at that moment I was thinking of Leo's life, having forgotten everything else in that terrible anxiety. What I feared now was that he should die whilst she was "carrying on."

"Unless thou art able to help him, Ayesha," I put in, by way of a reminder, "thy Kallikrates will soon be far beyond thy calling. Surely he dieth even now."

"True," she said, with a start. "Oh, why did I not come before! I am unnerved—my hand trembles, even mine—and yet it is very easy. Here, thou Holly, take this phial," and she produced a tiny jar of pottery from the folds of her garment, "and pour the liquid in it down his throat. It will cure him if he be not dead. Swift, now! Swift! The man dies!"

I glanced towards him; it was true enough, Leo was in his death-struggle. I saw his poor face turning ashen, and heard the breath begin to rattle in his throat. The phial was stoppered with a little piece of wood. I drew it with my teeth, and a drop of the fluid within flew out upon my tongue.

It had a sweet flavour, and for a second made my head swim, and a mist gather before my eyes, but happily the effect passed away as swiftly as it had arisen.

When I reached Leo's side he was plainly expiring—his golden head was slowly turning from side to side, and his mouth was slightly open. I called to Ayesha to hold his head, and this she managed to do, though the woman was quivering from head to foot, like an aspen-leaf or a startled horse. Then, forcing the jaw a little more open, I poured the contents of the phial into his mouth. Instantly a little vapour arose from it, as happens when one disturbs nitric acid, and this sight did not increase my hopes, already faint enough, of the efficacy of the treatment.

One thing, however, was certain, the death-throes ceased—at first I thought because he had got beyond them, and crossed the awful river.[10] His face turned to a livid pallor, and his heart-beats, which had been feeble enough before, seemed to die away altogether—only the eyelid still twitched a little. In my doubt I looked up at Ayesha, whose head-wrapping had slipped back in her excitement when she went reeling across the room. She was still holding Leo's head, and with a face as pale as his own, watching his countenance with such an expression of agonised anxiety as I had never seen before. Clearly she did not know if he would live or die. Five minutes slowly passed, and I saw that she was abandoning hope; her lovely oval face seemed to fall in and grow visibly thinner beneath the pressure of a mental agony whose pencil drew black lines about the hollows of her eyes. The coral faded even from her lips, till they were as white as Leo's face, and quivered pitifully. It was shocking to see her: even in my own grief I felt for hers.

"Is it too late?" I gasped.

She hid her face in her hands, and made no answer, and I too turned away. But as I did so I heard a deep-drawn breath, and looking down perceived a line of colour creeping up Leo's face, then another and another, and then, wonder of wonders, the man we had thought dead turned over on his side.

"Thou seest," I said in a whisper.

"I see," she answered, hoarsely. "He is saved. I thought we were too late—another moment—one little moment more—and he had been gone!" and she burst into an awful flood of tears, sobbing as though her heart would break, and yet looking lovelier than ever as she did it. At last she ceased.

"Forgive me, my Holly—forgive me for my weakness," she said. "Thou seest after all I am a very woman. Think—now think of it. This morning didst thou speak of the place of torment appointed by this new religion of thine. Hell or Hades thou didst call it—a place where the vital essence lives and retains an individual memory, and where all the errors and faults of judgment, and unsatisfied passions and the unsubstantial terrors of the mind wherewith it hath at any time had to do, come to mock and haunt and gibe and wring the heart for ever and for ever with the vision of its own hopelessness. Thus, even thus, have I lived for full two thousand years —for some six and sixty generations, as ye reckon time—in a Hell, as thou callest it—tormented by the memory of a crime, tortured day and night with an unfulfilled desire—without companionship, without comfort, without death, and led on only down my dreary road by the marsh lights of Hope, which, though they flickered here and there, and now glowed strong, and now were not, yet, as my skill told me, would one day lead unto my deliverer.

"And then—think of it still, oh Holly, for never shalt thou hear such another tale, or see such another scene, nay, not even if I give thee ten thousand years of life—and thou shalt have it in payment if thou wilt— think: at last my deliverer came—he for whom I had watched and waited through the generations—at the appointed time he came to seek me, as I knew that he must come, for my wisdom could not err, though I knew not when or how. Yet see how ignorant I was! See how small my knowledge, and how faint my strength! For hours he lay here sick unto death, and I felt it not—I who had waited for him for two thousand years—I knew it not. And then at last I see him, and, behold, my chance is gone but by a hair's breadth even before I have it, for he is in the very jaws of death, whence no power of mine can draw him. And if he die, surely must the Hell be lived through once more—once more must I face the weary centuries, and wait, and wait till the time in its fulness shall bring my Beloved back to me. And then thou gavest him the medicine, and that five minutes dragged along before I knew if he would live or die, and I tell thee that all the sixty generations that are gone were not so long as that five minutes. But they passed at length, and still he showed no sign, and I knew that if the drug works not then, so far as I have had knowledge, it works not at all. Then thought I that he was once more dead, and all the tortures of all the years gathered themselves into a single venomed spear, and pierced me through and through, because again I had lost Kallikrates! And then, when all was done, behold! he sighed, behold! he lived, and I knew that he would live, for none die on whom the drug takes hold. Think of it now, my Holly— think of the wonder of it! He will sleep for twelve hours and then the fever will have left him!"

She stopped, and laid her hand upon the golden head, and then bent down and kissed his brow with a chastened abandonment of tenderness that would have been beautiful to behold had not the sight cut me to the heart—for I was jealous!

XVIII.
Go, Woman!

Then followed a silence of a minute or so, during which *She* appeared, if one might judge from the almost angelic rapture of her face—for she looked angelic sometimes—to be plunged in a happy ecstasy. Suddenly, however, a new thought struck her, and her expression became the very reverse of angelic.

"Almost had I forgotten," she said, "that woman, Ustane. What is she to Kallikrates—his servant, or—" and she paused, and her voice trembled.

I shrugged my shoulders. "I understand that she is wed to him according to the custom of the Amahagger," I answered; "but I know not."

Her face grew dark as a thunder-cloud. Old as she was, Ayesha had not outlived jealousy.

"Then there is an end," she said; "she must die, even now!"

"For what crime?" I asked, horrified; "she is guilty of naught that thou art not guilty of thyself, oh Ayesha. She loves the man, and he has been pleased to accept her love: where, then, is her sin?"

"Truly, oh Holly, thou art foolish," she answered, almost petulantly. "Where is her sin? Her sin is that she stands between me and my desire. Well, I know that I can take him from her—for dwells there a man upon this earth, oh Holly, who could resist me if I put out my strength? Men are faithful for so long only as temptations pass them by. If the temptation be but strong enough, then will the man yield, for every man, like every rope, hath his breaking strain, and passion is to men what gold and power are to women—the weight upon their weakness. Believe me, ill will it go with mortal women in that heaven of which thou speakest, if only the spirits be more fair, for their lords will never turn to look upon them, and their Heaven will become their Hell. For man can be bought with woman's beauty, if it be but beautiful enough; and woman's beauty can be ever bought with gold, if only there be gold enough. So was it in my day, and so it will be to the end of time. The world is a great mart, my Holly, where all things are for sale to him who bids the highest in the currency of our desires."

These remarks, which were as cynical as might have been expected from a woman of Ayesha's age and experience,[1] jarred upon me, and I answered, testily, that in our heaven there was no marriage or giving in marriage.[2]

"Else would it not be heaven, dost thou mean?" she put in. "Fie upon thee, Holly, to think so ill of us poor women! Is it, then, marriage that marks the line between thy heaven and thy hell? but enough of this. This is no time for disputing and the challenge of our wits. Why dost thou always dispute? Art thou also a philosopher of these latter days? As for this woman, she must die; for, though I can take her lover from her, yet, while she lived, might he think tenderly of her, and that I cannot away with. No other woman shall dwell in my Lord's thoughts; my empire shall be all my own. She hath had her day, let her be content; for better is an hour with love than a century of loneliness—now the night shall swallow her."

"Nay, nay," I cried, "it would be a wicked crime; and from a crime naught comes but what is evil. For thine own sake, do not this deed."

"Is it, then, a crime, oh foolish man, to put away that which stands between us and our ends?[3] Then is our life one long crime, my Holly; for day by day we destroy that we may live, since in this world none save the strongest can endure. Those who are weak must perish; the earth is to the strong, and the fruits thereof. For every tree that grows a score shall wither, that the strong one may take their share. We run to place and power over the dead bodies of those who fail and fall; ay, we win the food we eat from out the mouths of starving babes. It is the scheme of things. Thou sayest, too, that a crime breeds evil, but therein thou dost lack experience; for out of crimes come many good things, and out of good grows much evil. The cruel rage of the tyrant may prove a blessing to thousands who come after him, and the sweet-heartedness of a holy man may make a nation slaves. Man doeth this and doeth that from the good or evil of his heart; but he knoweth not to what end his moral sense doth prompt him; for when he striketh he is blind to where the blow shall fall, nor can he count the airy threads that weave the web of circumstance. Good and evil, love and hate, night and day, sweet and bitter, man and woman, heaven above and the earth beneath—all these things are necessary, one to the other, and who knows the end of each? I tell thee that there is a hand of Fate that twines them up to bear the burden of its purpose, and all things are gathered in that great rope to which all things are needful. Therefore doth it not become us to say this thing is evil and this good, or the dark is hateful and the light lovely; for to other eyes than ours the evil may be the good and the darkness more beautiful than the day, or all alike be fair. Hearest thou, my Holly?"

I felt it was hopeless to argue against casuistry of this nature, which, if it were carried to its logical conclusion, would absolutely destroy all morality, as we understand it. But her talk gave me a fresh thrill of fear; for what may not be possible to a being who, unconstrained by human law, is also absolutely unshackled by a moral sense of right and wrong, which, however partial and conventional it may be, is yet based, as our conscience tells us, upon the great wall of individual responsibility that marks off mankind from the beasts?

But I was deeply anxious to save Ustane, whom I liked and respected, from the dire fate that overshadowed her at the hands of her mighty rival. So I made one more appeal.

"Ayesha," I said, "thou art too subtle for me; but thou thyself hast told me that each man should be a law unto himself, and follow the teaching of his heart. Hath thy heart no mercy towards her whose place thou wouldst take? Bethink thee, as thou sayest—though to me the thing is incredible —he whom thou desirest has returned to thee after many ages, and but now thou hast, as thou sayest also, wrung him from the jaws of death. Wilt thou celebrate his coming by the murder of one who loved him, and whom perchance he loved—one, at the least, who saved his life for thee when the spears of thy slaves would have made an end thereof? Thou sayest also that in past days thou didst grievously wrong this man, that with thine own hand thou didst slay him because of the Egyptian Amenartas whom he loved."

"How knowest thou that, oh stranger? How knowest thou that name? I spoke it not to thee," she broke in with a cry, catching at my arm.

"Perchance I dreamed it," I answered; "strange dreams do hover about these caves of Kôr. It seems that the dream was, indeed, a shadow of the truth. What came to thee of thy mad crime?—two thousand years of waiting, was it not? And now wouldst thou repeat the history? Say what thou wilt, I tell thee that evil will come of it; for to him who doeth, at the least, good breeds good and evil evil, even though in after days out of evil cometh good. Offences must needs come; but woe to him by whom the offence cometh. So said that Messiah of whom I spoke to thee, and it was truly said. If thou slayest this innocent woman, I say unto thee that thou shalt be accursed, and pluck no fruit from thine ancient tree of love. Also, what thinkest thou? How will this man take thee red-handed from the slaughter of her who loved and tended him?"

"As to that," she answered, "I have already answered thee. Had I slain thee as well as her, yet should he love me, Holly, because he could not help himself therefrom any more than thou couldst save thyself from dying, if by chance I slew thee, oh Holly. And yet maybe there is truth in what thou dost say; for in some way it presseth on my mind. If it may be, I will spare this woman; for have I not told thee that I am not cruel for the sake of cruelty? I love not to see suffering, or to cause it. Let her come before me—quick now, before my mood changes," and she hastily covered her face with its gauzy wrapping.

Well pleased to have succeeded even to this extent, I passed out into the passage and called to Ustane, whose white garment I caught sight of some yards away, huddled up against one of the earthenware lamps that were placed at intervals along the tunnel. She rose, and ran towards me.

"Is my lord dead? Oh, say not he is dead," she cried, lifting her noble-looking face, all stained as it was with tears, up to me with an air of infinite beseeching that went straight to my heart.

"Nay, he lives," I answered. "*She* hath saved him. Enter."

She sighed deeply, entered, and fell upon her hands and knees, after the custom of the Amahagger people, in the presence of the dread *She*.

"Stand," said Ayesha, in her coldest voice, "and come hither."

Ustane obeyed, standing before her with bowed head.

Then came a pause, which Ayesha broke.

"Who is this man?" she said, pointing to the sleeping form of Leo.

"The man is my husband," she answered in a low voice.

"Who gave him to thee for a husband?"

"I took him according to the custom of our country, oh *She*."

"Thou hast done evil, woman, in taking this man, who is a stranger. He is not a man of thine own race, and the custom fails.[4] Listen: perchance thou didst this thing through ignorance, therefore, woman, do I spare thee, otherwise hadst thou died. Listen again. Go from hence back to thine own place, and never dare to speak to or set thine eyes upon this man again. He is not for thee. Listen a third time. If thou breakest this my law, that moment thou diest. Go."

But Ustane did not move.

"Go, woman!"

Then she looked up, and I saw that her face was torn with passion.

"Nay, oh *She*, I will not go," she answered in a choked voice; "the man is my husband, and I love him—I love him, and I will not leave him. What right hast thou to command me to leave my husband?"

I saw a little quiver pass down Ayesha's frame, and shuddered myself, fearing the worst.

"Be pitiful," I said in Latin;[5] "it is but Nature working."

"I am pitiful," she answered coldly in the same language; "had I not been pitiful she had been dead even now." Then, addressing Ustane: "Woman, I say to thee, go, before I destroy thee where thou art!"

"I will not go! He is mine—mine!" she cried in anguish. "I took him, and I saved his life! Destroy me, then, if thou hast the power! I will not give thee my husband—never—never!"

Ayesha made a movement so swift that I could scarcely follow it, but it seemed to me that she lightly struck the poor girl on the head with her hand. I looked at Ustane, and then staggered back in horror, for there upon her hair, right across her bronze-like tresses, were three finger-marks *white as snow*. As for the girl herself, she had put her hands to her head, and was looking dazed.

"Great heavens!" I said, perfectly aghast at this dreadful manifestation of inhuman power; but *She* did but laugh a little.

"Thou thinkest, poor ignorant fool," she said to the bewildered woman, "that I have not power to slay. Stay, there lies a mirror," and she pointed to Leo's round shaving-glass that had been arranged by Job with other things upon his portmanteau; "give it to this woman, my Holly, and let her see that which lies across her hair, and whether or no I have power to slay."

I picked up the glass, and held it before Ustane's eyes. She gazed, then felt at her hair, then gazed again, and then sank upon the ground with a sort of sob.

"Now, wilt thou go, or must I strike a second time?" asked Ayesha, in mockery. "Look, I have set my seal upon thee so that I may know thee till thy hair is all as white as it. If I see thy face again, be sure, too, that thy bones shall soon be whiter than my mark upon thy hair."

Utterly awed and broken down, the poor creature rose, and, marked with that awful mark, crept from the room, sobbing bitterly.

"Look not so frighted, my Holly," said Ayesha, when she had gone. "I tell thee I deal not in magic—there is no such thing. 'Tis only a force that thou dost not understand. I marked her to strike terror to her heart, else must I have slain her. And now I will bid my servants bear my Lord Kallikrates to a chamber near mine own, that I may watch over him, and be ready to greet him when he wakes; and thither, too, shalt thou come, my Holly, and the white man, thy servant. But one thing remember at thy peril. Naught shalt thou say to Kallikrates as to how this woman went, and as little as may be of me. Now, I have warned thee!" and she slid away to give her orders, leaving me more absolutely confounded than ever. Indeed, so bewildered was I, and racked and torn with such a succession of various emotions, that I began to think that I must be going mad. However, perhaps fortunately, I had but little time to reflect, for presently the mutes arrived to carry the sleeping Leo and our possessions across the central cave, so for a while all was bustle. Our new rooms were situated immediately behind what we used to call Ayesha's boudoir—the curtained space where I had first seen her. Where she herself slept I did not then know, but it was somewhere quite close.

That night I passed in Leo's room, but he slept through it like the dead, never once stirring. I also slept fairly well, as, indeed, I needed to do, but my sleep was full of dreams of all the horrors and wonders I had undergone. Chiefly, however, I was haunted by that frightful piece of *diablerie* by which Ayesha left her finger-marks upon her rival's hair. There was something so terrible about her swift, snake-like movement, and the instantaneous blanching of that three-fold line, that, if the results to Ustane had been much more tremendous, I doubt if they would have impressed me so deeply. To this day I often dream of that awful scene, and see the weeping woman, bereaved, and marked like Cain, cast a last look at her lover, and creep from the presence of her dread Queen.

Another dream that troubled me originated in the huge pyramid of bones. I dreamed that they all stood up and marched past me in thousands and tens of thousands—in squadrons, companies, and armies—with the sunlight shining through their hollow ribs. On they rushed across the plain to Kôr, their imperial home; I saw the drawbridges fall before them, and heard their bones clank through the brazen gates. On they went, up the splendid streets, on past fountains, palaces, and temples such as the eye of man never saw. But there was no man to greet them in the market-place, and no woman's face appeared at the windows—only a bodiless voice went before them, calling: "*Fallen is Imperial Kôr!—fallen!—fallen!—fallen!*" On, right through the city, marched those gleaming phalanxes, and the rattle of their bony tread echoed through the silent air as they pressed grimly on. They passed through the city and climbed the wall, and marched along the great roadway that was made upon the wall, till at length they once more reached the drawbridge. Then, as the sun was sinking, they returned again towards their sepulchre, and luridly his light shone in the sockets of their empty eyes, throwing gigantic shadows of their bones, that stretched away, and crept and crept like huge spider's legs as their armies wound across the plain. Then they came to the cave, and once more one by one flung themselves in unending files through the hole into the pit of bones, and I awoke, shuddering, to see *She*, who had evidently been standing between my couch and Leo's, glide like a shadow from the room.

After this I slept again, soundly this time, till morning, when I awoke much refreshed, and got up. At last the hour drew near at which, according to Ayesha, Leo was to awake, and with it came *She* herself, as usual, veiled.

"Thou shalt see, oh Holly," she said; "presently shall he awake in his right mind, the fever having left him."

Hardly were the words out of her mouth, when Leo turned round and stretched out his arms, yawned, opened his eyes, and, perceiving a female form bending over him, threw his arms round her and kissed her, mistaking her, perhaps, for Ustane. At any rate, he said, in Arabic, "Hullo, Ustane, why have you tied your head up like that? Have you got the toothache?" and then, in English, "I say, I'm awfully hungry. Why, Job, you old son of a gun, where the deuce have we got to now—eh?"

"I am sure I wish I knew, Mr. Leo," said Job, edging suspiciously past Ayesha, whom he still regarded with the utmost disgust and horror, being by no means sure that she was not an animated corpse; "but you mustn't talk, Mr. Leo, you've been very ill, and given us a great deal of hanxiety,[6] and, if this lady," looking at Ayesha, "would be so kind as to move, I'll bring you your soup."

This turned Leo's attention to the "lady," who was standing by in perfect silence. "Hullo!" he said; "that is not Ustane—where is Ustane?"

Then, for the first time, Ayesha spoke to him, and her first words were a lie. "She has gone from hence upon a visit," she said; "and, behold, in her place am I here as thine handmaiden."

Ayesha's silver notes seemed to puzzle Leo's half-awakened intellect, as also did her corpse-like wrappings. However, he said nothing at the time, but drank off his soup greedily enough, and then turned over and slept again till the evening. When he woke for the second time he saw me, and began to question me as to what had happened, but I had to put him off as best I could till the morrow, when he awoke almost miraculously better. Then I told him something of his illness and of my doings, but as Ayesha was present I could not tell him much except that she was the Queen of the country, and well-disposed towards us, and that it was her pleasure to go veiled; for, though of course I spoke in English, I was afraid that she might

understand what we were saying from the expression of our faces, and besides, I remembered her warning.

On the following day Leo got up almost entirely recovered. The flesh
wound in his side was healed, and his constitution, naturally a vigorous
one, had shaken off the exhaustion consequent on his terrible fever with
a rapidity that I can only attribute to the effects of the wonderful drug which
Ayesha had given to him, and also to the fact that his illness had been too
short to reduce him very much. With his returning health came back full
recollection of all his adventures up to the time when he had lost consciousness in the marsh, and of course of Ustane also, to whom I discovered he
had grown considerably attached. Indeed, he overwhelmed me with questions about the poor girl, which I did not dare to answer, for after Leo's
first awakening *She* had sent for me, and again warned me solemnly that
I was to reveal nothing of the story to him, delicately hinting that if I did
it would be the worse for me. She also, for the second time, cautioned me
not to tell Leo anything more than I was obliged about herself, saying that
she would reveal herself to him in her own time.

Indeed, her whole manner changed. After all that I had seen I had expected that she would take the earliest opportunity of claiming the man
she believed to be her old-world lover, but this, for some reason of her own,
which was at the time quite inscrutable to me, she did not do. All that she
did was to attend to his wants quietly, and with a humility which was in
striking contrast with her former imperious bearing, addressing him always
in a tone of something very like respect, and keeping him with her as much
as possible. Of course his curiosity was as much excited about this mysterious
woman as my own had been, and he was particularly anxious to see her
face, which I had, without entering into particulars, told him was as lovely
as her form and voice. This in itself was enough to raise the expectations
of any young man to a dangerous pitch, and, had it not been that he had
not as yet completely shaken off the effects of illness, and was much troubled
in his mind about Ustane, of whose affection and brave devotion he spoke
in touching terms, I have no doubt that he would have entered into her
plans, and fallen in love with her by anticipation. As it was, however, he
was simply wildly curious, and also, like myself, considerably awed, for,
though no hint had been given to him by Ayesha of her extraordinary age,
he not unnaturally came to identify her with the woman spoken of on the
potsherd. At last, quite driven into a corner by his continual questions, which
he showered on me while he was dressing on this third morning, I referred
him to Ayesha, saying, with perfect truth, that I did not know where Ustane
was. Accordingly, after Leo had eaten a hearty breakfast, we adjourned into
She's presence, for her mutes had orders to admit us at all hours.

She was, as usual, seated in what, for want of a better term, we called
her boudoir, and, on the curtains being drawn she rose from her couch and,
stretching out both hands, came forward to greet us, or rather Leo; for I,

as may be imagined, was now quite left in the cold. It was a pretty sight to see her veiled form gliding towards the sturdy young Englishman, dressed in his grey flannel suit; for, though he is half a Greek in blood, Leo is, with the exception of his hair, one of the most English-looking men I ever saw. He has nothing of the supple form or slippery manner of the modern Greek about him, though I presume that he got his remarkable personal beauty from his foreign mother, whose portrait he resembles not a little. He is very tall and big-chested, and yet not awkward, as so many big men are, and his head is set upon him in such a fashion as to give him a proud and vigorous air, which was well translated in his Amahagger name of the "Lion."

"Greeting to thee, my young stranger lord," she said in her softest voice. "Right glad am I to see thee upon thy feet. Believe me, had I not saved thee at the last, never wouldst thou have stood upon those feet again. But the danger is done, and it shall be my care"—and she flung a world of meaning into the words—"that it doth return no more."[7]

Leo bowed to her, and then, in his best Arabic, thanked her for all her kindness and courtesy in caring for one unknown to her.

"Nay," she answered softly, "ill could the world spare such a man. Beauty is too rare upon it. Give me no thanks, who am made happy by thy coming."

"Humph! old fellow," said Leo aside to me in English, "the lady is very civil. We seem to have tumbled into clover. I hope that you have made the most of your opportunities. By Jove! what a pair of arms she has got!"

I nudged him in the ribs to make him keep quiet, for I caught sight of a gleam from Ayesha's veiled eyes, which were regarding me curiously.

"I trust," went on Ayesha, "that my servants have attended well upon thee; if there can be comfort in this poor place, be sure it waits on thee. Is there aught that I can do for thee more?"

"Yes, oh *She*," answered Leo hastily. "I would fain know whither the young lady who was looking after me has gone to."

"Ah," said Ayesha; "the girl—yes, I saw her. Nay, I know not; she said that she would go, I know not whither. Perchance she will return, perchance not. It is wearisome waiting on the sick, and these savage women are fickle."

Leo looked both sulky and distressed at this intelligence.

"It's very odd," he said to me in English; and then, addressing *She*, "I cannot understand," he said; "the young lady and I—well—in short, we had a regard for each other."

Ayesha laughed a little very musically, and then turned the subject.

XIX.
"Give Me a Black Goat!"

The conversation after this was of such a desultory order that I do not quite recollect it. For some reason, perhaps from a desire to keep her identity and character in reserve, Ayesha did not talk freely, as she usually did. Presently, however, she informed Leo that she had arranged a dance that night for our amusement. I was astonished to hear this, as I fancied that the Amahagger were much too gloomy a folk to indulge in any such frivolity; but, as will presently more clearly appear, it turned out that an Amahagger dance has little in common with such fantastic festivities in other countries, savage or civilised. Then, as we were about to withdraw, she suggested that Leo might like to see some of the wonders of the caves, and as he gladly assented thither we departed, accompanied by Job and Billali. To describe our visit would only be to repeat a great deal of what I have already said. The tombs we entered were indeed different, for the whole rock was a honey-comb of sepulchres,* but the contents were nearly always similar. Afterwards we visited the pyramid of bones that had haunted my dreams on the previous night, and from thence went down a long passage to one of the great vaults occupied by the bodies of the poorer citizens of Imperial Kôr. These bodies were not nearly so well preserved as were those of the wealthier classes.[1] Many of them had no linen covering on them, also they were buried from five hundred to one thousand in a single large vault, the corpses in some instances being thickly piled one upon another, like a heap of slain.

Leo was of course intensely interested in this stupendous and unequalled sight, which was, indeed, enough to awake all the imagination a man had in him into the most active life. But to poor Job it did not prove attractive. His nerves—already seriously shaken by what he had undergone since we had arrived in this terrible country—were, as may be imagined, still further disturbed by the spectacle of these masses of departed humanity, whereof the forms still remained perfect before his eyes, though their voices were for ever lost in the eternal silence of the tomb. Nor was he comforted when Old Billali, by way of soothing his evident agitation, informed him that he should not be frightened of these dead things, as he would soon be like them himself.[2]

"There's a nice thing to say of a man, sir," he ejaculated, when I trans-

---

*For a long while it puzzled me to know what could have been done with the enormous quantities of rock that must have been dug out of these vast caves; but I afterwards discovered that it was for the most part built into the walls and palaces of Kôr, and also used to line the reservoirs and sewers.—L.H.H.

lated this little remark; "but there, what can one expect of an old man-eating savage? Not but what I dare say he's right," and Job sighed.

When we had finished inspecting the caves, we returned and had our meal, for it was now past four in the afternoon, and we all—especially Leo—needed some food and rest. At six o'clock we, together with Job, waited on Ayesha, who set to work to terrify our poor servant still further by showing him pictures on the pool of water in the font-like vessel.[3] She learnt from me that he was one of seventeen children, and then bid him think of all his brothers and sisters, or as many of them as he could, gathered together in his father's cottage. Then she told him to look in the water, and there, reflected from its stilly[4] surface, was that dead scene of many years gone by, as it was recalled to our retainer's brain. Some of the faces were clear enough, but some were mere blurs and splotches, or with one feature grossly exaggerated; the fact being that, in these instances, Job had been unable to recall the exact appearances of the individuals, or remembered them only by a peculiarity of his tribe, and the water could only reflect what he saw with his mind's eye. For it must be remembered that *She's* power in this matter was strictly limited; she could apparently, except in very rare instances, only photograph upon the water what was actually in the mind of some one present, and then only by his will. But, if she was personally acquainted with a locality she could, as in the case of ourselves and the whale-boat, throw its reflection upon the water, and also, it seems, the reflection of anything extraneous that was passing there at the time. This power, however, did not extend to the minds of others. For instance, she could show me the interior of my college chapel, as I remembered it, but not as it was at the moment of reflection; for, where other people were concerned, her art was strictly limited to the facts or memories present to *their* consciousness at the moment. So much was this so that when we tried, for her amusement, to show her pictures of noted buildings, such as St. Paul's or the Houses of Parliament, the result was most imperfect; for, of course, though we had a good general idea of their appearance, we could not recall all the architectural details, and therefore the minutiæ necessary to a perfect reflection were wanting. But Job could not be got to understand this, and, so far from accepting a natural explanation of the matter, which was after all, though strange enough in all conscience, nothing more than an instance of glorified and perfected telepathy, he set the whole thing down as a manifestation of the blackest magic. I shall never forget the howl of terror which he uttered when he saw the more or less perfect portraits of his long-scattered brethren staring at him from the quiet water, or the merry peal of laughter with which Ayesha greeted his consternation. As for Leo, he did not altogether like it either, but ran his fingers through his yellow curls, and remarked that it gave him the creeps.

After about an hour of this amusement, in the latter part of which Job did *not* participate, the mutes by signs indicated that Billali was waiting for an audience. Accordingly he was told to "crawl up," which he did as awk-

wardly as usual, and announced that the dance was ready to begin if *She*
and the white strangers would be pleased to attend. Shortly afterwards we
all rose, and, Ayesha having thrown a dark cloak (the same, by the way,
that she had worn when I saw her cursing by the fire) over her white wrappings, we started. The dance was to be held in the open air, on the smooth
rocky plateau in front of the great cave, and thither we made our way. About
fifteen paces from the mouth of the cave we found three chairs placed, and
here we sat and waited, for as yet no dancers were to be seen. The night
was almost, but not quite, dark, the moon not having risen as yet, which
made us wonder how we should be able to see the dancing.

"Thou wilt presently understand," said Ayesha, with a little laugh, when
Leo asked her; and we certainly did. Scarcely were the words out of her
mouth when from every point we saw dark forms rushing up, each bearing
with him what we at first took to be an enormous flaming torch. Whatever
they were, they were burning furiously, for the flames stood out a yard or
more behind each bearer. On they came, fifty or more of them, carrying
their flaming burdens and looking like so many devils from hell. Leo was
the first to discover what these burdens were.

"Great heaven!" he said, "they are corpses on fire!"

I stared and stared again—he was perfectly right—the torches that
were to light our entertainment were human mummies from the caves!

On rushed the bearers of the flaming corpses, and, meeting at a spot
about twenty paces in front of us, built their ghastly burdens crossways into
a huge bonfire. Heavens! how they roared and flared! No tar barrel could
have burnt as those mummies did. Nor was this all. Suddenly I saw one
great fellow seize a flaming human arm that had fallen from its parent frame,
and rush off into the darkness. Presently he stopped, and a tall streak of
fire shot up into the air, illumining the gloom, and also the lamp from which
it sprang. That lamp was the mummy of a woman tied to a stout stake let
into the rock, and he had fired her hair. On he went a few paces and touched
a second, then a third, and a fourth, till at last we were surrounded on
all three sides by a great ring of bodies flaring furiously, the material with
which they were preserved having rendered them so inflammable that the
flames would literally spout out of the ears and mouth in tongues of fire
a foot or more in length.

Nero illuminated his gardens with live Christians soaked in tar,[5] and
we were now treated to a similar spectacle, probably for the first time since
his day, only happily our lamps were not living ones.

But, although this element of horror was fortunately wanting, to describe
the awful and hideous grandeur of the spectacle thus presented to us is,
I feel, so absolutely beyond my poor powers that I scarcely dare attempt
it. To begin with, it appealed to the moral as well as the physical susceptibili-
ties. There was something very terrible, and yet very fascinating, about the
employment of the remote dead to illumine the orgies of the living; in itself
the thing was a satire, both on the living and the dead. Cæsar's dust—

or is it Alexander's?—may stop a bunghole,[6] but the functions of these dead Cæsars of the past was to light up a savage fetish dance. To such base uses may we come, of so little account may we be in the minds of the eager multitudes that we shall breed, many of whom, so far from revering our memory, will live to curse us for begetting them into such a world of woe.

Then there was the physical side of the spectacle, and a weird and splendid one it was. Those old citizens of Kôr burnt as, to judge from their sculptures and inscriptions, they had lived, very fast, and with the utmost liberality. What is more, there were plenty of them. As soon as ever a mummy had burnt down to the ankles, which it did in about twenty minutes, the feet were kicked away, and another one put in its place. The bonfire was kept going on the same generous scale, and its flames shot up, with a hiss and a crackle, twenty or thirty feet into the air, throwing great flashes of light far out into the gloom, through which the dark forms of the Amahagger flitted to and fro like devils replenishing the infernal fires. We all stood and stared aghast—shocked, and yet fascinated at so strange a spectacle, and half-expecting to see the spirits those flaming forms had once enclosed come creeping from the shadows to work vengeance on their desecrators.

"I promised thee a strange sight, my Holly," laughed Ayesha, whose nerves alone did not seem to be affected; "and, behold, I have not failed thee. Also, it hath its lesson. Trust not to the future, for who knows what the future may bring! Therefore, live for the day, and endeavour not to escape the dust which seems to be man's end.[7] What thinkest thou those long-forgotten nobles and ladies would have felt had they known that they should one day flare to light the dance or boil the pot of savages? But see, here come the dancers; a merry crew—are they not? The stage is lit—now for the play."

As she spoke, we perceived two lines of figures, one male and the other female, to the number of about a hundred, each advancing round the human bonfire, arrayed only in the usual leopard and buck skins. They formed up, in perfect silence, in two lines, facing each other between us and the fire, and then the dance—a sort of infernal and fiendish cancan—began.[8] To describe it is quite impossible, but, though there was a good deal of tossing of legs and double-shuffling, it seemed to our untutored minds to be more of a play than a dance, and, as usual with this dreadful people, whose minds seem to have taken their colour from the caves in which they live, and whose jokes and amusements are drawn from the inexhaustible stores of preserved mortality with which they share their homes, the subject appeared to be a most ghastly one. I know that it represented an attempted murder first of all, and then the burial alive of the victim and his struggling from the grave, each act of the abominable drama, which was carried on in perfect silence, being rounded off and finished with a furious and most revolting dance round the supposed victim, who writhed upon the ground in the red light of the bonfire.

Presently, however, this pleasing piece was interrupted. Suddenly there was a slight commotion, and a large powerful woman, whom I had noted as one of the most vigorous of the dancers, came, made mad[9] and drunken with unholy excitement, bounding and staggering towards us, shrieking out as she came:—

"I want a Black Goat, I must have a Black Goat, bring me a Black Goat!" and down she fell upon the rocky floor foaming and writhing, and shrieking for a Black Goat, about as hideous a spectacle as can well be conceived.

Instantly most of the dancers came up and got round her, though some still continued their capers in the background.

"She has got a Devil," called out one of them.[10] "Run and get a black goat. There, Devil, keep quiet! keep quiet! You shall have the goat presently. They have gone to fetch it, Devil."

"I want a Black Goat, I must have a Black Goat!" shrieked the foaming rolling creature again.

"All right, Devil, the goat will be here presently; keep quiet, there's a good Devil!"

And so on till the goat, taken from a neighbouring *kraal*,[11] did at last arrive, being dragged bleating on to the scene by its horns.

"Is it a Black One, is it a Black One?" shrieked the possessed.

"Yes, yes, Devil, as black as night," then aside, "keep it behind thee, don't let the Devil see that it has got a white spot on its rump and another on its belly. In one minute, Devil. There, cut his throat quick. Where is the saucer?"

"The Goat! the Goat! the Goat! Give me the blood of my black goat! I must have it, don't you see I must have it? Oh! oh! oh! give me the blood of the goat."

At this moment a terrified *bah!* announced that the poor goat had been sacrificed, and the next minute a woman ran up with a saucer full of the blood. This the possessed creature, who was then raving and foaming her wildest, seized and *drank*, and was instantly recovered, and without a trace of hysteria, or fits, or being possessed, or whatever dreadful thing it was she was suffering from. She stretched her arms, smiled faintly, and walked quietly back to the dancers, who presently withdrew in a double line as they had come, leaving the space between us and the bonfire deserted.

I thought that the entertainment was now over, and, feeling rather queer, was about to ask *She* if we could rise, when suddenly what at first I took to be a baboon came hopping round the fire, and was instantly met upon the other side by a lion, or rather a human being dressed in a lion's skin. Then came a goat, then a man wrapped in an ox's hide, with the horns wobbling about in a ludicrous way. After him followed a blesbok, then an impala, then a koodoo, then more goats, and many other animals, including a girl sewn up in the shining scaly hide of a boa constrictor, several yards of which trailed along the ground behind her.[12] When all the beasts had collected they began to dance about in a lumbering, unnatural fashion, and to imitate the sounds produced by the respective animals they represented, till the whole air was alive with roars and bleating and the hissing of snakes. This went on for a long time, till, getting tired of the pantomime, I asked Ayesha if there would be any objection to Leo and myself walking round to inspect the human torches, and, as she had nothing to say against it, we started, striking round to the left. After looking at one or two of the flaming bodies we were about to return, thoroughly disgusted with the grotesque weirdness of the spectacle, when our attention was attracted by one of the dancers, a particularly active leopard, that had separated itself from its fellow-beasts, and was whisking about in our immediate neighbourhood, but gradually drawing into a spot where the shadow was darkest, equidistant between two of the flaming mummies. Drawn by curiosity, we followed it, when suddenly it darted past us into the shadows beyond, and as it did so erected itself and whispered, "Come," in a voice that we both recognised as that of Ustane. Without waiting to consult me Leo turned and followed her into the outer darkness, and I, feeling sick enough at heart, went after them. The leopard crawled on for about fifty paces—a sufficient distance to be quite beyond the light of the fire and torches—and then Leo came up with it, or, rather, with Ustane.

"Oh, my lord," I heard her whisper, "so I have found thee! Listen. I am in peril of my life from 'She-who-must-be-obeyed.' Surely the Baboon has told thee how she drove me from thee? I love thee, my lord, and thou art mine according to the custom of the country. I saved thy life! My Lion, wilt thou cast me off now?"

"Of course not," ejaculated Leo; "I have been wondering whither thou hadst gone. Let us go and explain matters to the Queen."

"Nay, nay, she would slay us. Thou knowest not her power—the Baboon there, he knoweth, for he saw. Nay, there is but one way: if thou wilt cleave to me, thou must flee with me across the marshes even now, and then perchance we may escape."

"For Heaven's sake, Leo," I began, but she broke in—

"Nay, listen not to him. Swift—be swift—death is in the air we breathe. Even now, mayhap, *She* heareth us," and without more ado she proceeded to back her arguments by throwing herself into his arms. As she did so the leopard's head slipped from her hair, and I saw the three white finger-marks upon it, gleaming faintly in the starlight. Once more realising the desperate nature of the position, I was about to interpose, for I knew that Leo was not too strong-minded where women were concerned, when—oh! horror! —I heard a little silvery laugh behind me. I turned round, and there was *She* herself, and with her Billali and two male mutes. I gasped and nearly sank to the ground, for I knew that such a situation must result in some dreadful tragedy, of which it seemed exceedingly probable to me that I should be the first victim. As for Ustane, she untwined her arms and covered her eyes with her hands, while Leo, not knowing the full terror of the position, merely coloured up,[13] and looked as foolish as a man caught in such a trap would naturally do.

XX.
Triumph.

Then followed a moment of the most painful silence that I ever endured. It was broken by Ayesha, who addressed herself to Leo.

"Nay, now, my lord and guest," she said, in her softest tones, which yet had the ring of steel about them, "look not so bashful. Surely the sight was a pretty one—the leopard and the lion!"

"Oh, hang it all!" said Leo, in English.

"And thou, Ustane," she went on, "surely I should have passed thee by, had not the light fallen on the white across thy hair," and she pointed to the bright edge of the rising moon which was now appearing above the horizon. "Well! well! the dance is done—see, the tapers have burnt down, and all things end in silence and in ashes. So thou thoughtest it a fit time for love, Ustane, my servant—and I, dreaming not that I could be disobeyed, thought thee already far away."

"Play not with me," moaned the wretched woman; "slay me, and let there be an end."

"Nay, why? It is not well to go so swift from the hot lips of love down to the cold mouth of the grave," and she made a motion to the mutes, who instantly stepped up and caught the girl by either arm. With an oath Leo sprang upon the nearest, and hurled him to the ground, and then stood over him with his face set, and his fist ready.

Again Ayesha laughed. "It was well thrown, my guest; thou hast a strong arm for one who so late was sick. But now out of thy courtesy I pray thee let that man live and do my bidding. He shall not harm the girl; the night air grows chill, and I would welcome her in mine own place. Surely she whom thou dost favour shall be favoured of me also."

I took Leo by the arm, and pulled him from the prostrate mute, and he, half bewildered, obeyed the pressure. Then we all set out for the cave across the plateau, where a pile of white human ashes was all that remained of the fire that had lit the dancing, for the dancers had vanished.

In due course we gained Ayesha's boudoir—all too soon, it seemed to me, having a sad presage of what was to come lying heavy on my heart.

Ayesha seated herself upon her cushions, and, having dismissed Job and Billali, by signs bade the mutes tend the lamps and retire—all save one girl, who was her favourite personal attendant. We three remained standing, the unfortunate Ustane a little to the left of the rest of us.

"Now, oh Holly," Ayesha began, "how came it that thou who didst hear my words bidding this evil-doer"—and she pointed to Ustane—"to go from hence—thou at whose prayer I did weakly spare her life—how came it, I say, that thou wast a sharer in what I saw tonight? Answer, and for thine own sake, I say, speak all the truth, for I am not minded to hear lies upon this matter!"

"It was by accident, oh Queen," I answered. "I knew naught of it."

"I do believe thee, oh Holly," she answered, coldly, "and well it is for thee that I do—then does the whole guilt rest upon her."

"I do not find any guilt therein," broke in Leo. "She is not another man's wife, and it appears that she has married me according to the custom of this awful place, so who is the worse? Any way, madam," he went on, "whatever she has done I have done too, so if she is to be punished let me be punished also; and I tell thee," he went on, working himself up into a fury, "that if thou biddest one of those deaf and dumb villains to touch her again I will tear him to pieces!" And he looked as though he meant it.

Ayesha listened in icy silence, and made no remark. When he had finished, however, she addressed Ustane.

"Hast thou aught to say, woman?¹ Thou silly straw, thou feather, who didst think to float towards thy passion's petty ends, even against the great wind of my will! Tell me, for I fain would understand. Why didst thou this thing?"

And then I think I saw the most tremendous exhibition of moral courage and intrepidity that it is possible to conceive. For the poor doomed girl, knowing what she had to expect at the hands of her terrible Queen, knowing, too, from bitter experience, how great was her adversary's power, yet gathered herself together, and out of the very depths of her despair drew materials to defy her.

"I did it, oh *She*," she answered, drawing herself up to the full of her stately height, and throwing back the panther skin from her head, "because my love is stronger than the grave. I did it because my life without this man whom my heart chose would be but a living death. Therefore did I risk my life, and, now that I know that it is forfeit to thine anger, yet am I glad that I did risk it, and pay it away in the risking, ay, because he embraced me once, and told me that he loved me yet."

Here Ayesha half rose from her couch, and then sank down again.

"I have no magic," went on Ustane, her rich voice ringing strong and full, "and I am not a Queen, nor do I live for ever, but a woman's heart is heavy to sink through waters, however deep, oh Queen! and a woman's eyes are quick to see—even through thy veil, oh Queen!

"Listen: I know it, thou dost love this man thyself, and therefore wouldst thou destroy me who stand across thy path. Ay, I die—I die, and go into the darkness, nor know I whither I go. But this I know. There is a light shining in my breast, and by that light, as by a lamp, I see the truth and the future that I shall not share unroll itself before me like a scroll. When first I knew my lord" and she pointed to Leo, "I knew also that death would be the bridal gift he gave me—it rushed upon me of a sudden, but I turned not back, being ready to pay the price, and, behold, death is here! And now, even as I knew that, so do I, standing on the steps of doom, know that thou shalt not reap the profit of thy crime. Mine he is, and though thy beauty shine like a sun among the stars, mine shall he remain for thee. Never here in this life shall he look thee in the eyes and call thee spouse. Thou too art doomed, I see"—and her voice rang like the cry of an inspired prophetess; "ah, I see—"

Then came an answering cry of mingled rage and terror. I turned my head. Ayesha had risen, and was standing with her outstretched hand pointing at Ustane, who had suddenly stopped speaking. I gazed at the poor woman, and as I gazed there came upon her face that same, woful, fixed expression of terror that I had seen once before when she had broken out into her wild chant. Her eyes grew large, her nostrils dilated, and her lips blanched.

Ayesha said nothing, she made no sound, she only drew herself up, stretched out her arm, and, her tall veiled frame quivering like an aspen leaf, appeared to look fixedly at her victim. Even as she did so Ustane put her hands to her head, uttered one piercing scream, turned round twice, and then fell backwards with a thud—prone upon the floor. Both Leo and myself rushed to her—she was stone dead—blasted into death by some mysterious electric agency or overwhelming will-force whereof the dread *She* had command.

For a moment Leo did not quite realise what had happened. But, when he did, his face was awful to see. With a savage oath he rose from beside the corpse, and, turning, literally sprang at Ayesha. But she was watching, and, seeing him come, stretched out her hand again, and he went staggering back towards me, and would have fallen, had I not caught him. Afterwards he told me that he felt as though he had suddenly received a violent blow in the chest, and, what is more, utterly cowed, as if all the manhood had been taken out of him.

Then Ayesha spoke. "Forgive me, my guest," she said softly, addressing him, "if I have shocked thee with my justice."

"Forgive thee, thou fiend!" roared poor Leo, wringing his hands in his rage and grief, "Forgive thee, thou murderess! By Heaven I will kill thee if I can!"

"Nay, nay," she answered, in the same soft voice, "thou dost not understand—the time has come for thee to learn. *Thou* art my love, my Kallikrates, my Beautiful, my Strong! For two thousand years, Kallikrates, have I waited for *thee*, and now at length thou hast come back to me; and as for this woman," pointing to the corpse, "she stood between me and thee, and therefore have I laid her in the dust, Kallikrates."

"It is an accursed lie!" said Leo. "My name is not Kallikrates! I am Leo Vincey; my ancestor was Kallikrates—at least, I believe he was."

"Ah, thou sayest it—thine ancestor was Kallikrates, and thou, even thou, art Kallikrates reborn, come back—and mine own dear lord!"

"I am not Kallikrates, and as for being thy lord, or having aught to do with thee, I had sooner be the lord of a fiend from hell, for she would be better than thou."

"Sayest thou so—sayest thou so, Kallikrates? Nay, but thou hast not seen me for so long a time that no memory remains. Yet am I very fair, Kallikrates!"

"I hate thee, murderess, and I have no wish to see thee. What is it to me how fair thou art? I hate thee, I say."

"Yet within a very little space shalt thou creep to my knee, and swear that thou dost love me," answered Ayesha, with a sweet, mocking laugh. "Come, there is no time like the present time, here before this dead girl who loved thee, let us put it to the proof.

"Look now on me, Kallikrates!" and with a sudden motion she shook her gauzy covering from her, and stood forth in her low kirtle and her snaky zone,[2] in her glorious, radiant beauty and her imperial grace, rising from her wrappings, as it were, like Venus from the wave,[3] or Galatea from her marble,[4] or a beatified spirit from the tomb. She stood forth, and fixed her deep and glowing eyes upon Leo's eyes, and I saw his clenched fists unclasp, and his set and quivering features relax beneath her gaze. I saw his wonder and astonishment grow into admiration, and then into fascination, and the more he struggled the more I saw the power of her dread beauty fasten on him and take possession of his senses, drugging them, and drawing the heart out of him. Did I not know the process? Had not I, who was twice his age, gone through it myself? Was I not going through it afresh even then, although her sweet and passionate gaze was not for me? Yes, alas, I was! Alas, that I should have to confess that at that very moment I was rent by mad and furious jealousy. I could have flown at him, shame upon me! The woman had confounded and almost destroyed my moral sense, as she was bound to confound all who looked upon her superhuman loveliness.[5] But—I do not quite know how—I got the better of myself, and once more turned to see the climax of the tragedy.

"Oh, great Heaven!" gasped Leo, "art thou a woman?"

"A woman in truth—in very truth—and thine own spouse, Kallikrates!" she answered, stretching out her rounded ivory arms towards him, and smiling, ah, so sweetly!

He looked and looked, and slowly I perceived that he was drawing nearer to her. Suddenly his eye fell upon the corpse of poor Ustane, and he shuddered and stopped.

"How can I?" he said, hoarsely. "Thou art a murderess; she loved me."

Observe, he was already forgetting that he had loved her.

"It is naught," she murmured, and her voice sounded sweet as the night-wind passing through the trees. "It is naught at all. If I have sinned, let my beauty answer for my sin. If I have sinned, it is for love of thee: let my sin, therefore, be put away and forgotten;" and once more she stretched out her arms and whispered *"Come,"* and then in another few seconds it was over.[6]

I saw him struggle—I saw him even turn to fly; but her eyes drew him more strongly than iron bonds, and the magic of her beauty and concentrated will and passion entered into him and overpowered him—ay, even there, in the presence of the body of the woman who had loved him well enough to die for him. It sounds horrible and wicked enough, but he should not be too greatly blamed, and be sure his sin will find him out. The temptress who drew him into evil was more than human, and her beauty was greater than the loveliness of the daughters of men.[7]

I looked up again, and now her perfect form lay in his arms, and her lips were pressed against his own; and thus, with the corpse of his dead love for an altar, did Leo Vincey plight his troth to her red-handed murderess —plight it for ever and a day. For those who sell themselves into a like dominion, paying down the price of their own honour, and throwing their soul into the balance to sink the scale to the level of their lusts, can hope for no deliverance here or hereafter. As they have sown, so shall they reap and reap, even when the poppy flowers of passion have withered in their hands, and their harvest is but bitter tares, garnered in satiety.[8]

Suddenly, with a snake-like motion, she seemed to slip from his embrace, and then again broke out into her low laugh of triumphant mockery.

"Did I not tell thee that within a little space thou wouldst creep to my knee, oh Kallikrates! And surely the space has not been a great one!"

Leo groaned in shame and misery; for though he was overcome and stricken down, he was not so lost as to be unaware of the depth of the degradation to which he had sunk. On the contrary, his better nature rose up in arms against his fallen self, as I saw clearly enough later on.

Ayesha laughed again, and then quickly veiled herself, and made a sign to the girl mute, who had been watching the whole scene with curious startled eyes. The girl left, and presently returned, followed by two male mutes, to whom the Queen made another sign. Thereon they all three seized the body of poor Ustane by the arms, and dragged it heavily down the cavern and away through the curtains at the end. Leo watched it for a little while, and then covered his eyes with his hand, and it, too, to my excited fancy, seemed to watch us as it went.

"There passes the dead past," said Ayesha, solemnly, as the curtains shook and fell back into their places, when the ghastly procession had vanished behind them. And then, with one of those extraordinary transitions of which I have already spoken, she again threw off her veil, and broke out, after the ancient and poetic fashion of the dwellers in Arabia,* into

---

*Among the ancient Arabians the power of poetic declamation, either in verse or prose, was held in the highest honour and esteem, and he who excelled in it was known as "Khâteb," or Orator. Every year a general assembly was held at which the rival poets repeated their compositions, when those poems which were judged to be the best were, so soon as the knowledge of the art of writing became general, inscribed on silk in letters of gold, and publicly exhibited, being known as "Al Modhahabât," or golden verses. In the poem given above by Mr. Holly, Ayesha evidently followed the traditional poetic manner of her people, which was to embody

a pæan of triumph or epithalamium, which, wild and beautiful as it was, is exceedingly difficult to render into English, and ought by rights to be sung to the music of a cantata, rather than written and read.[9] It was divided into two parts—one descriptive or definitive, and the other personal; and, as nearly as I can remember, ran as follows:—

Love is like a flower in the desert.

It is like the aloe of Arabia that blooms but once and dies; it blooms in the salt emptiness of Life, and the brightness of its beauty is set upon the waste as a star is set upon a storm.

It hath the sun above that is the Spirit, and above it blows the air of its own divinity.

At the echoing of a step, Love blooms, I say; I say Love blooms, and bends her beauty down to him who passeth by.

He plucketh it, yea, he plucketh the red cup that is full of honey, and beareth it away; away across the desert, away till the flower be withered, away till the desert be done.

There is only one perfect flower in the wilderness of Life.

That flower is Love!

There is only one fixed star in the mists of our wandering.

That star is Love!

There is only one hope in our despairing night.

That hope is Love!

All else is false. All else is shadow moving upon water. All else is wind and vanity.

Who shall say what is the weight or the measure of Love?

It is born of the flesh, it dwelleth in the spirit. From each does it draw its comfort.

For beauty it is as a star.

Many are its shapes, but all are beautiful, and none know where the star rose, or the horizon where it shall set.

Then, turning to Leo, and laying her hand upon his shoulder, she went on in a fuller and more triumphant tone, speaking in balanced sentences that gradually grew and swelled from idealised prose into pure and majestic verse:—

Long have I loved thee, oh, my love; yet has my love not lessened.

Long have I waited for thee, and behold my reward is at hand—is here!

Far away I saw thee once, and thou wast taken from me.

Then in a grave sowed I the seed of patience, and shone upon it with the sun of hope, and watered it with tears of repentance, and breathed on it with

their thoughts in a series of somewhat disconnected sentences, each remarkable for its beauty and the grace of its expression.—EDITOR

the breath of my knowledge. And now, lo! it hath sprung up, and borne fruit.
Lo! out of the grave hath it sprung. Yea, from among the dry bones and ashes
of the dead.

I have waited and my reward is with me.

I have overcome Death, and Death hath brought back to me him that was
dead.

Therefore do I rejoice, for fair is the future.
Green are the paths that we shall tread across the everlasting meadows.
The hour is at hand. Night hath fled away into the valleys.
The dawn kisseth the mountain tops.
Soft shall we live, my love, and easy shall we go,
Crowned shall we be with the diadem of Kings.[10]
Worshipping and wonder struck all peoples of the world,
Blinded shall fall before our beauty and our might.
From time unto times shall our greatness thunder on,
Rolling like a chariot through the dust of endless days.
Laughing shall we speed in our victory and pomp,
Laughing like the Daylight as he leaps along the hills.
Onward, still triumphant to a triumph ever new!
Onward, in our power to a power unattained!
Onward, never weary, clad with splendour for a robe!
Till accomplished be our fate, and the night is rushing down.

She paused in her strange and most thrilling allegorical chant, of which
I am, unfortunately, only able to give the burden, and that feebly enough,
and then said—

"Perchance thou dost not believe my word, Kallikrates—perchance
thou thinkest that I do delude thee, and that I have not lived these many
years, and that thou hast not been born again to me.[11] Nay, look not so
—put away that pale cast of doubt,[12] for oh be sure herein can error find
no foothold! Sooner shall the suns forget their course and the swallow miss
her nest, than my soul shall swear a lie and be led astray from thee,
Kallikrates. Blind me, take away mine eyes, and let the darkness utterly
fence me in, and still mine ears would catch the tone of thine unforgotten
voice, striking more loud against the portals of my sense than can the call
of brazen-throated clarions:—stop up mine hearing also, and let a thousand
touch me on the brow, and I would name thee out of all:—yea, rob me
of every sense, and see me stand deaf and blind, and dumb, and with nerves
that cannot weigh the value of a touch, yet would my spirit leap within
me like a quickening child and cry unto my heart, behold Kallikrates! behold,
thou watcher, the watches of thy night are ended! behold thou who seekest
in the night season, thy morning Star ariseth."

She paused awhile and then continued, "But stay, if thy heart is yet
hardened against the mighty truth and thou dost require a further pledge

of that which thou dost find too deep to understand, even now shall it be given to thee, and to thee also, oh my Holly. Bear each one of you a lamp, and follow after me whither I shall lead you."

Without stopping to think—indeed, speaking for myself, I had almost abandoned the function in circumstances under which to think seemed to be absolutely useless, since thought fell hourly helpless against a black wall of wonder—we took the lamps and followed her. Going to the end of her "boudoir," she raised a curtain and revealed a little stair of the sort that is so common in these dim caves of Kôr. As we hurried down the stair I observed that the steps were worn in the centre to such an extent that some of them had been reduced from seven and a half inches, at which I guessed their original height, to about three and a half. Now, all the other steps that I had seen in the caves were practically unworn, as was to be expected, seeing that the only traffic which ever passed upon them was that of those who bore a fresh burden to the tomb. Therefore this fact struck my notice with that curious force with which little things do strike us when our minds are absolutely overwhelmed by a sudden rush of powerful sensations; beaten flat, as it were, like a sea beneath the first burst of a hurricane, so that every little object on the surface starts into an unnatural prominence.

At the bottom of the staircase I stood and stared at the worn steps, and Ayesha, turning, saw me.

"Wonderest thou whose are the feet that have worn away the rock, my Holly?" she asked. "They are mine—even mine own light feet! I can remember when these stairs were fresh and level, but for two thousand years and more have I gone down hither day by day, and see, my sandals have worn out the solid rock!"

I made no answer, but I do not think that anything that I had heard or seen brought home to my limited understanding so clear a sense of this being's overwhelming antiquity as that hard rock hollowed out by her soft white feet. How many hundreds of thousands of times must she have passed up and down that stair to bring about such a result?

The stair led to a tunnel, and a few paces down the tunnel was one of the usual curtain-hung doorways, a glance at which told me that it was the same where I had been a witness of that terrible scene by the leaping flame. I recognised the pattern of the curtain, and the sight of it brought the whole event vividly before my eyes, and made me tremble even at its memory. Ayesha entered the tomb (for it was a tomb), and we followed her—I, for one, rejoicing that the mystery of the place was about to be cleared up, and yet afraid to face its solution.

XXI.

The Dead and Living Meet.

"See now the place where I have slept for these two thousand years," said Ayesha, taking the lamp from Leo's hand and holding it above her head. Its rays fell upon a little hollow in the floor, where I had seen the leaping flame, but the fire was out now. They fell upon the white form stretched there beneath its wrappings upon its bed of stone, upon the fretted carving of the tomb, and upon another shelf of stone opposite the one on which the body lay, and separated from it by the breadth of the cave.

"Here," went on Ayesha, laying her hand upon the rock—"here have I slept night by night for all these generations, with but a cloak to cover me. It did not become me that I should lie soft when my spouse yonder," and she pointed to the rigid form, "lay stiff in death. Here night by night have I slept in his cold company—till, thou seest, this thick slab, like the stairs down which we passed, has worn thin with the tossing of my form —so faithful have I been to thee even in thy space of sleep, Kallikrates. And now, mine own, thou shalt see a wonderful thing—living, thou shalt behold thyself dead—for well have I tended thee during all these years, Kallikrates. Art thou prepared?"

We made no answer, but gazed at each other with frightened eyes, the whole scene was so dreadful and so solemn. Ayesha advanced, and laid her hand upon the corner of the shroud, and once more spoke.

"Be not affrighted," she said; "though the thing seem wonderful to thee —all we who live have thus lived before; nor is the very shape that holds us a stranger to the sun! Only we know it not, because memory writes no record, and earth hath gathered in the earth she lent us, for none have saved our glory from the grave. But I, by my arts and by the arts of those dead men of Kôr which I have learned, have held thee back, oh Kallikrates, from the dust, that the waxen stamp of beauty on thy face should ever rest before mine eyes. 'Twas a mask that memory might fill, serving to fashion out thy presence from the past, and give it strength to wander in the habitations of my thought, clad in a mummery of life that stayed my appetite with visions of dead days.

"Behold now, let the Dead and Living meet! Across the gulf of Time they still are one. Time hath no power against Identity, though sleep the merciful hath blotted out the tablets of our mind, and with oblivion sealed the sorrows that else would hound us from life to life, stuffing the brain with gathered griefs till it burst in the madness of uttermost despair. Still are they one, for the wrappings of our sleep shall roll away as thunder clouds before the wind; the frozen voices of the past shall melt in music like mountain snows beneath the sun; and the weeping and the laughter of the lost hours shall be heard once more most sweetly echoing up the cliffs of immeasurable time.

"Ay, the sleep shall roll away, and the voices shall be heard, when down the completed chain,[1] whereof our each existence is a link, the lightning of the Spirit hath passed to work out the purpose of our being; quickening and fusing those separated days of life,[2] and shaping them to a staff whereon we may safely lean as we wend to our appointed fate.

"Therefore, have no fear, Kallikrates, when thou—living, and but lately born—shalt look upon thine own departed self, who breathed and died so long ago. I do but turn one page in thy Book of Being, and show thee what is writ thereon.

"*Behold*!"

With a sudden motion she drew the shroud from the cold form, and let the lamplight play upon it. I looked, and then shrank back terrified; since, say what she might in explanation, the sight was an uncanny one—for her explanations were beyond the grasp of our finite minds, and when they were stripped from the mists of vague esoteric philosophy, and brought into conflict with the cold and horrifying fact, did not do much to break its force. For there, stretched upon the stone bier before us, robed in white and perfectly preserved, was what appeared to be the body of Leo Vincey. I stared from Leo, standing *there* alive, to Leo lying *there* dead, and could see no difference; except, perhaps, that the body on the bier looked older. Feature for feature they were the same, even down to the crop of little golden curls, which was Leo's most uncommon beauty. It even seemed to me, as I looked, that the expression on the dead man's face resembled that which I had sometimes seen upon Leo's when he was plunged into profound sleep. I can only sum up the closeness of the resemblance by saying that I never saw twins so exactly similar as that dead and living pair.

I turned to see what effect was produced upon Leo by the sight of his dead self, and found it to be one of partial stupefaction. He stood for two or three minutes staring, and said nothing, and when at last he spoke it was only to ejaculate—

"Cover it up, and take me away."

"Nay, wait, Kallikrates," said Ayesha, who, standing with the lamp raised above her head, flooding with its light her own rich beauty and the cold wonder of the death-clothed form upon the bier, resembled an inspired Sibyl[3] more than a woman, as she rolled out her majestic sentences with a grandeur and a freedom of utterance which I am, alas! quite unable to reproduce.

"Wait, I would show thee something, that no tittle of my crime may be hidden from thee. Do thou, oh Holly, open the garment on the breast of the dead Kallikrates, for perchance my lord may fear to touch himself."

I obeyed with trembling hands. It seemed a desecration and an unhallowed thing to touch that sleeping image of the live man by my side. Presently his broad chest was bare, and there upon it, right over the heart, was a wound, evidently inflicted with a spear.

"Thou seest, Kallikrates," she said. "Know then that it was *I* who slew thee: in the Place of Life *I* gave thee death. I slew thee because of the Egyptian Amenartas, whom thou didst love, for by her wiles she held thy heart, and her I could not smite as but now I smote the woman, for she was too strong for me. In my haste and bitter anger I slew thee, and now for all these days have I lamented thee, and waited for thy coming. And thou hast come, and none can stand between thee and me, and of a truth now for death I will give thee life—not life eternal, for that none can give, but life and youth that shall endure for thousands upon thousands of years, and with it pomp, and power, and wealth, and all things that are good and beautiful, such as have been to no man before thee, nor shall be to any man who comes after. And now one thing more, and thou shalt rest and make ready for the day of thy new birth. Thou seest this body, which was thine own. For all these centuries it hath been my cold comfort and my companion, but now I need it no more, for I have thy living presence, and it can but serve to stir up memories of that which I would fain forget. Let it therefore go back to the dust from which I held it.

"Behold! I have prepared against this happy hour!" And going to the other shelf or stone ledge, which she said had served her for a bed, she took from it a large vitrified double-handled vase, the mouth of which was tied up with a bladder. This she loosed, and then, having bent down and gently kissed the white forehead of the dead man, she undid the vase, and sprinkled its contents carefully over the form, taking, I observed, the greatest precautions against any drop of them touching us or herself, and then poured out what remained of the liquid upon the chest and head. Instantly a dense vapour arose, and the cave was filled with choking fumes that prevented us from seeing anything while the deadly acid (for I presume it was some tremendous preparation of that sort) did its work. From the spot where the body lay came a fierce fizzing and cracking sound, which ceased, however, before the fumes had cleared away. At last they were all gone, except a little cloud that still hung over the corpse. In a couple of minutes more this too had vanished, and, wonderful as it may seem, it is a fact that on the stone bench that had supported the mortal remains of the ancient Kallikrates for so many centuries there was now nothing to be seen but a few handfuls of smoking white powder. The acid had utterly destroyed the body, and even in places eaten into the stone. Ayesha stooped down, and, taking a handful of this powder in her grasp, threw it into the air, saying at the same time, in a voice of calm solemnity—

"Dust to dust!—the past to the past!—the dead to the dead!—Kallikrates is dead, and is born again!"

The ashes floated noiselessly to the rocky floor, and we stood in awed silence and watched them fall, too overcome for words.

"Now leave me," she said, "and sleep if ye may. I must watch and think, for to-morrow night we go hence, and the time is long since I trod the path that we must follow."

Accordingly we bowed, and left her.

As we passed to our own apartment, I peeped into Job's sleeping place, to see how he fared, for he had gone away just before our interview with the murdered Ustane, quite prostrated by the terrors of the Amahagger festivity. He was sleeping soundly, good honest fellow that he was, and I rejoiced to think that his nerves, which, like those of the most uneducated people, were far from strong, had been spared the closing scenes of this dreadful day. Then we entered our own chamber, and here at last poor Leo, who, ever since he had looked upon that frozen image of his living self, had been in a state not far removed from stupefaction, burst out into a torrent of grief. Now that he was no longer in the presence of the dread *She*, his sense of the awfulness of all that had happened, and more especially of the wicked murder of Ustane, who was bound to him by ties so close, broke upon him like a storm, and lashed him into an agony of remorse and terror which was painful to witness. He cursed himself—he cursed the hour when we had first seen the writing on the sherd, which was being so mysteriously verified, and bitterly he cursed his own weakness. Ayesha he dared not curse —who dared speak evil of such a woman, whose consciousness, for aught we knew, was watching us at the very moment?

"What am I to do, old fellow?" he groaned, resting his head against my shoulder in the extremity of his grief. "I let her be killed—not that I could help that, but within five minutes I was kissing her murderess over her body. I am a degraded brute, but I cannot resist that" (and here his voice sank) "that awful sorceress. I know I shall do it again to-morrow; I know that I am in her power for always; if I never saw her again I should never think of anybody else during all my life; I must follow her as a needle follows a magnet; I would not go away now if I could; I could not leave her, my legs would not carry me, but my mind is still clear enough, and in my mind I hate her—at least, I think so. It is all so horrible; and that—that body! What can I make of it? It was *I*! I am sold into bondage, old fellow, and she will take my soul as the price of herself!"

Then, for the first time, I told him that I was in a but very little better position, and I am bound to say that, notwithstanding his own infatuation, he had the decency to sympathise with me. Perhaps he did not think it worth while being jealous, realising that he had no cause so far as the lady was concerned. I went on to suggest that we should try to run away, but we soon rejected the project as futile, and, to be perfectly honest, I do not believe that either of us would really have left Ayesha even if some superior power had suddenly offered to convey us from these gloomy caves and set us down in Cambridge. We could no more have left her than a moth can leave the light that destroys it. We were like confirmed opium-eaters:[4] in our moments of reason we well knew the deadly nature of our pursuit, but we certainly were not prepared to abandon its terrible delights.

No man who once had seen *She* unveiled, and heard the music of her voice, and drunk in the bitter wisdom of her words, would willing give up the sight for a whole sea of placid joys. How much more, then, was this likely to be so when, as in Leo's case, to put myself out of the question, this extraordinary creature declared her utter and absolute devotion, and gave what appeared to be proofs of its having lasted for some two thousand years?

No doubt she was a wicked person, and no doubt she had murdered Ustane when she stood in her path, but then she was very faithful, and by a law of nature man is apt to think but lightly of a woman's crimes, especially if that woman be beautiful, and the crime be committed for the love of him.

And then, for the rest, when had such a chance ever come to a man before as that which now lay in Leo's hand? True, in uniting himself to this dread woman, he would place his life under the influence of a mysterious creature of evil tendencies,* but then that would be likely enough to happen to him in any ordinary marriage. On the other hand, however, no ordinary marriage could bring him such awful beauty—for awful is the only word that can describe it—such divine devotion, such wisdom, and command over the secrets of nature, and the place and power that they must win, or, lastly, the royal crown of unending youth, if indeed she could give that. No, on the whole, it is not wonderful that, though Leo was plunged in bitter shame and grief, such as any gentleman would have felt under the circumstances, he was not ready to entertain the idea of running away from his extraordinary fortune.

My own opinion is that he would have been mad if he had done so.

---

*After some months of consideration of this statement I am bound to confess that I am not quite satisfied of its truth. It is perfectly true that Ayesha committed a murder, but I shrewdly suspect that were we endowed with the same absolute power, and if we had the same tremendous interest at stake, we should be very apt to do likewise under parallel circumstances. Also, it must be remembered that she looked on it as an execution for disobedience under a system which made the slightest disobedience punishable by death. Putting aside this question of murder, her evil-doing resolves itself into the expression of views and the acknowledgment of motives which are contrary to our preaching if not to our practice. Now at first sight this might be fairly taken as a proof of an evil nature, but when we come to consider the great antiquity of the individual it becomes doubtful if it was anything more than the natural cynicism which arises from age and bitter experience, and the possession of extraordinary powers of observation. It is a well known fact that very often, putting the period of boyhood out of the question, the older we grow the more cynical and hardened we get; indeed many of us are only saved by timely death from utter moral petrifaction if not moral corruption. No one will deny that a young man is on the average better than an old one, for he is without that experience of the order of things that in certain thoughtful dispositions can hardly fail to produce cynicism, and that disregard of acknowledged methods and established custom which we call evil. Now the oldest man upon the earth was but a babe compared to Ayesha, and the wisest man upon the earth was not one-third as wise. And the fruit of her wisdom was this, that there was but one thing worth living for, and that was Love in its highest sense, and to gain that good thing she was not prepared to stop at trifles. This is really the sum of her evil doings, and it must be remembered, on the other hand, that, whatever may be thought of them, she had some virtues developed to a degree very uncommon in either sex—constancy for instance. —L.H.H.

But then I confess that my statement on the matter must be accepted with qualifications. I am in love with Ayesha myself to this day, and I would rather have been the object of her affection for one short week than that of any other woman in the world for a whole lifetime. And let me add that, if anybody who doubts this statement, and thinks me foolish for making it, could have seen Ayesha draw her veil and flash out in beauty on his gaze, his view would exactly coincide with my own. Of course, I am speaking of any *man*. We never had the advantage of a lady's opinion of Ayesha, but I think it quite possible that she would have regarded the Queen with dislike, would have expressed her disapproval in some more or less pointed manner, and ultimately have got herself blasted.

For two hours or more Leo and I sat with shaken nerves and frightened eyes, and talked over the miraculous events through which we were passing. It seemed like a dream or a fairy tale, instead of the solemn, sober fact. Who would have believed that the writing on the potsherd was not only true, but that we should live to verify its truth, and that we two seekers should find her who was sought, patiently awaiting our coming in the tombs of Kôr? Who would have thought that in the person of Leo this mysterious woman should, as she believed, discover the being whom she awaited from century to century, and whose former earthly habitation she had till this very night preserved? But so it was. In the face of all we had seen it was difficult for us as ordinary reasoning men any longer to doubt its truth, and therefore at last, with humble hearts and a deep sense of the impotence of human knowledge, and the insolence of its assumption that denies that to be possible which it has no experience of, we laid ourselves down to sleep, leaving our fates in the hands of that watching Providence which had thus chosen to allow us to draw the veil of human ignorance, and reveal to us for good or evil some glimpse of the possibilities of life.

XXII.
Job Has a Presentiment.

It was nine o'clock on the following morning when Job, who still looked scared and frightened, came in to call me, and at the same time breathe his gratitude at finding us alive in our beds, which it appeared was more than he had expected. When I told him of the awful end of poor Ustane he was even more grateful at our survival, and much shocked, though Ustane had been no favourite of his, or he of hers, for the matter of that. She called him "pig" in bastard Arabic, and he called her "hussy" in good English, but these amenities were forgotten in the face of the catastrophe that had overwhelmed her at the hands of her Queen.

"I don't want to say anything as mayn't be agreeable, sir," said Job, when he had finished exclaiming at my tale, "but it's my opinion that that there She is the old gentleman himself,[1] or perhaps his wife, if he has one, which I suppose he has, for he couldn't be so wicked all by himself. The Witch of Endor[2] was a fool to her, sir; bless you, she would make no more of raising every gentleman in the Bible out of these here beastly tombs than I should of growing cress on an old flannel.[3] It's a country of devils, this is, sir, and she's the master one of the lot; and if ever we get out of it it will be more than I expect to do. I don't see no way out of it. That witch isn't likely to let a fine young man like Mr. Leo go."

"Come," I said, "at any rate she saved his life."

"Yes, and she'll take his soul to pay for it. She'll make him a witch, like herself. I say it's wicked to have anything to do with those sort of people. Last night, sir, I lay awake and read in my little Bible that my poor old mother gave me about what is going to happen to sorceresses and them sort, till my hair stood on end.[4] Lord, how the old lady would stare if she saw where her Job had got to!"

"Yes, it's a queer country, and queer people too, Job," I answered, with a sigh, for, though I am not superstitious like Job, I admit to a natural shrinking (which will not bear investigation) from the things that are above Nature.

"You are right, sir," he answered, "and if you won't think me very foolish, I should like to say something to you now that Mr. Leo is out of the way"—(Leo had got up early and gone for a stroll)—"and that is that I know it is the last country as ever I shall see in this world. I had a dream last night, and I dreamed that I saw my old father with a kind of night-shirt on him, something like these folks wear when they want to be in particular full-dress, and a bit of that feathery grass in his hand, which he may have gathered on the way, for I saw lots of it yesterday about three hundred yards from the mouth of this beastly cave.

"'Job,' he said to me, solemn like, and yet with a kind of satisfaction shining through him, more like a Methody parson[5] when he has sold a neighbour a marked horse[6] for a sound one and cleared twenty pounds by the job than anything I can think on, 'Job, time's up, Job; but I never did expect to have to come and hunt you out in this 'ere place, Job. Such ado as I have had to nose you up; it wasn't friendly to give your poor old father such a run, let alone that a wonderful lot of bad characters hail from this place Kôr.'"

"Regular cautions,"[7] I suggested.

"Yes, sir—of course, sir, that's just what he said they was—'cautions, downright scorchers'—sir,[8] and I'm sure I don't doubt it, seeing what I know of them and their hot-potting ways," went on Job, sadly. "Anyway, he was sure that time was up, and went away saying that we should see more than we cared for of each other soon, and I suppose he was a-thinking of the fact that father and I never could hit it off together for longer nor three days, and I daresay that things will be similar when we meet again."

"Surely," I said, "you don't think that you are going to die because you dreamed you saw your old father; if one dies because one dreams of one's father, what happens to a man who dreams of his mother-in-law?"

"Ah, sir, you're laughing at me," said Job; "but, you see, you didn't know my old father. If it had been anybody else—my Aunt Mary, for instance, who never made much of a job[9]—I should not have thought so much of it; but my father was that idle,[10] which he shouldn't have been with seventeen children, that he would never have put himself out to come here just to see the place. No, sir; I know that he meant business. Well, sir, I can't help it; I suppose every man must go some time or other, though it is a hard thing to die in a place like this, where Christian burial isn't to be had for its weight in gold. I've tried to be a good man, sir, and do my duty honest, and if it wasn't for the supercilus[11] kind of way in which father carried on last night—a sort of sniffing at me as it were, as though he hadn't no opinion of my references and testimonials—I should feel easy enough in my mind. Any way, sir, I've been a good servant to you and Mr. Leo, bless him!—why, it seems but the other day that I used to lead him about the streets with a penny whip;[12]—and if ever you get out of this place—which, as father didn't allude to you, perhaps you may— I hope you will think kindly of my whitened bones, and never have anything more to do with Greek writing on flower-pots, sir, if I may make so bold as to say so."

"Come, come, Job," I said seriously, "this is all nonsense, you know. You mustn't be silly enough to go getting such ideas into your head. We've lived through some queer things, and I hope that we may go on doing so."

"No, sir," answered Job, in a tone of conviction that jarred on me unpleasantly, "it isn't nonsense. I'm a doomed man, and I feel it, and a wonderful uncomfortable feeling it is, sir, for one can't help wondering how it's going to come about. If you are eating your dinner you think of poison and it goes against your stomach, and if you are walking along these dark rabbit-burrows you think of knives, and Lord, don't you just shiver about the back! I ain't particular, sir, provided it's sharp, like that poor girl, who, now that she's gone, I am sorry to have spoke hard on, though I don't approve of her morals in getting married, which I consider too quick to be decent. Still, sir," and poor Job turned a shade paler as he said it, "I do hope it won't be that hot-pot game."

"Nonsense," I broke in angrily, "nonsense!"

"Very well, sir," said Job, "it isn't my place to differ from you, sir, but if you happen to be going anywhere, sir, I should be obliged if you could manage to take me with you, seeing that I shall be glad to have a friendly face to look at when the time comes, just to help one through, as it were. And now, sir, I'll be getting the breakfast," and he went, leaving me in a very uncomfortable state of mind. I was deeply attached to old Job, who was one of the best and honestest men I have ever had to do with in any class of life, and really more of a friend than a servant, and the mere idea of anything happening to him brought a lump into my throat. Beneath all his ludicrous talk I could see that he himself was quite convinced that something was going to happen, and though in most cases these convictions turn out to be utter moonshine—and this particular one especially was to be amply accounted for by the gloomy and unaccustomed surroundings in which its victim was placed—still it did more or less carry a chill to my heart, as any dread that is obviously a genuine object of belief is apt to do, however absurd the belief may be. Presently the breakfast arrived, and with it Leo, who had been taking a walk outside the cave—to clear his mind, he said—and very glad I was to see both, for they gave me a respite from my gloomy thoughts. After breakfast we went for another walk, and watched some of the Amahagger sowing a plot of ground with the grain from which they make their beer. This they did in scriptural fashion—a man with a bag made of goat's hide fastened round his waist walking up and down the plot and scattering the seed as he went.[13] It was a positive relief to see one of these dreadful people do anything so homely and pleasant as sow a field, perhaps because it seemed to link them, as it were, with the rest of humanity.

As we were returning Billali met us, and informed us that it was *She*'s pleasure that we should wait upon her, and accordingly we entered her presence, not without trepidation, for Ayesha was certainly an exception to the rule.[14] Familiarity with her might and did breed passion and wonder and horror, but it certainly did *not* breed contempt.

We were as usual shown in by the mutes, and after these had retired Ayesha unveiled, and once more bade Leo embrace her, which, notwithstanding his heart-searchings of the previous night, he did with more alacrity and fervour than in strictness courtesy required.

She laid her white hand on his head, and looked him fondly in the eyes. "Dost thou wonder, my Kallikrates," she said, "when thou shalt call me all thine own, and when we shall of a truth be for one another and to one another?[15] I will tell thee. First, must thou be even as I am, not immortal indeed, for that I am not, but so cased and hardened against the attacks of Time that his arrows shall glance from the armour of thy vigorous life as the sunbeams glance from water. As yet I may not mate with thee, for thou and I are different, and the very brightness of my being would burn thee up, and perchance destroy thee. Thou couldst not even endure to look upon me for too long a time lest thine eyes should ache, and thy senses swim, and therefore" (with a little nod) "shall I presently veil myself again." (This by the way she did not do.) No: listen, thou shalt not be tried beyond endurance, for this very evening, an hour before the sun goes down, shall we start hence, and by to-morrow's dark, if all goes well, and the road is not lost to me, which I pray it may not be, shall we stand in the place of Life, and thou shalt bathe in the fire, and come forth glorified, as no man ever was before thee, and then, Kallikrates, shalt thou call me wife, and I will call thee husband."

Leo muttered something in answer to this astonishing statement, I do not know what, and she laughed a little at his confusion, and went on.

"And thou, too, oh Holly; on thee also will I confer this boon, and then of a truth shalt thou be evergreen, and this will I do—well, because thou hast pleased me, Holly, for thou art not altogether a fool, like most of the sons of men, and because, though thou hast a school of philosophy as full of nonsense as those of the old days, yet hast thou not forgotten how to turn a pretty phrase about a lady's eyes.'"

"Hulloa, old fellow!" whispered Leo, with a return of his old cheerfulness, "have you been paying compliments? I should never have thought it of you!"

"I thank thee, oh Ayesha," I replied, with as much dignity as I could command, "but if there be such a place as thou dost describe, and if in this strange place there can be found a fiery virtue that can hold off Death when he comes to pluck us by the hand, yet would I none of it. For me, oh Ayesha, the world has not proved so soft a nest that I would lie in it for ever. A stony-hearted mother is our earth, and stones are the bread she gives her children for their daily food. Stones to eat and bitter water for their thirst, and stripes for tender nurture. Who would endure this for many lives? Who would so load up his back with memories of lost hours and loves, and of his neighbour's sorrows that he cannot lessen, and wisdom that brings not consolation? Hard is it to die, because our delicate flesh doth shrink back from the worm it will not feel, and from that unknown which the winding-sheet doth curtain from our view. But harder still, to my fancy, would it be to live on, green in the leaf and fair, but dead and rotten at the core, and feel that other secret worm of recollection gnawing ever at the heart."

"Bethink thee, Holly," she said; "yet doth long life and strength and beauty beyond measure mean power and all things that are dear to man."

"And what, oh Queen," I answered, "are those things that are dear to man? Are they not bubbles? Is not ambition but an endless ladder by which no height is ever climbed till the last unreachable rung is mounted? For height leads on to height, and there is no resting-place upon them, and rung doth grow upon rung, and there is no limit to the number. Doth not wealth satiate and become nauseous, and no longer serve to satisfy or pleasure, or to buy an hour's ease of mind? And is there any end to wisdom that we may hope to reach it? Rather, the more we learn, shall we not thereby be able only to better compass out our ignorance? Did we live ten thousand years could we hope to solve the secrets of the suns, and the space beyond the suns, and of the Hand that hung them in the heavens? Would not our wisdom be but as a gnawing hunger calling our consciousness day by day to a knowledge of the empty craving of our souls? Would it not be but as a light in one of these great caverns, that, though bright it burn, and brighter yet, doth but the more serve to show the depths of the gloom around it? And what good thing is there beyond that we may gain by length of days?"

"Nay, my Holly, there is love—love which makes all things beautiful, and doth breathe divinity into the very dust we tread. With love shall life roll gloriously on from year to year, like the voice of some great music that hath power to hold the hearer's heart poised on eagles' wings above the sordid shame and folly of the earth."

"It may be so," I answered; "but if the loved one prove a broken reed to pierce us, or if the love be loved in vain—what then? Shall a man grave[16] his sorrows upon a stone when he hath but need to write them on the water? Nay, oh *She*, I will live my day and grow old with my generation, and die my appointed death, and be forgotten. For I do hope for an immortality to which the little span that perchance thou canst confer will be but as a finger's length laid against the measure of the great world; and, mark this! the immortality to which I look, and which my faith doth promise to me, shall be free from the bonds that here must tie my spirit down. For, while the flesh endures, sorrow and evil and the scorpion whips of sin must endure also; but when the flesh hath fallen from us, then shall the spirit shine forth clad in the brightness of eternal good, and for its common air shall breathe so rare an ether of most noble thoughts that the highest aspiration of our manhood, or the purest incense of a maiden's prayer, would prove too earthly gross to float therein."

"Thou lookest high," answered Ayesha, with a little laugh, "and speakest clearly as a trumpet and with no uncertain sound. And yet methinks that but now didst thou talk of 'that Unknown' from which the winding-sheet doth curtain us. But perchance, thou seest with the eye of Faith, gazing on this brightness, that is to be, through the painted glass of thy imagination. Strange are the pictures of the future that mankind can thus draw with this brush of faith and this many-coloured pigment of imagination! Strange, too, that no one of them doth agree with another! I could tell thee—but there, what is the use? why rob a fool of his bauble? Let it pass, and I pray, oh Holly, that when thou dost feel old age creeping slowly toward thyself, and the confusion of senility making havoc in thy brain, thou mayest not bitterly regret that thou didst cast away the imperial boon I would have given to thee. But so it hath ever been; man can never be content with that which his hand can pluck. If a lamp be in his reach to light him through the darkness, he must needs cast it down because it is no star. Happiness danceth ever a pace before him, like the marsh-fires in the swamps, and he must catch the fire, and he must hold the star! Beauty is naught to him, because there are lips more honey-sweet; and wealth is naught, because others can weigh him down with heavier shekels; and fame is naught, because there have been greater men than he. Thyself thou saidst it, and I turn thy words against thee. I believe it not, and I think thee a fool, my Holly, to throw away the lamp."

I made no answer, for I could not—especially before Leo—tell her that since I had seen her face I knew that it would always be before my eyes, and that I had no wish to prolong an existence which must always be haunted and tortured by her memory, and by the last bitterness of unsatisfied love. But so it was, and so, alas, is it to this hour!

"And now," went on *She*, changing her tone and the subject together, "tell me, my Kallikrates, for as yet I know it not, how came ye to seek me here? Yesternight thou didst say that Kallikrates—him who thou sawest —was thine ancestor. How was it? Tell me—thou dost not speak over-much!"

Thus adjured, Leo told her the wonderful story of the casket and of the potsherd that, written on by his ancestress, the Egyptian Amenartas, had been the means of guiding us to her. Ayesha listened intently, and, when he had finished, spoke to me.

"Did I not tell thee one day, when we did talk of good and evil, oh Holly—it was when my beloved lay so ill—that out of good came evil, and out of evil good,—that they who sowed knew not what the crop should be, nor he who struck where the blow should fall? See, now: this Egyptian Amenartas, this royal child of the Nile who hated me, and whom even now I hate, for in a way she did prevail against me—see, now, she herself hath been the very means to bring her lover to mine arms! For her sake I slew him, and now, behold, through her he hath come back to me! She would have done me evil, and sowed her seeds that I might reap tares, and behold she hath given me more than all the world can give, and there is a strange square for thee to fit into thy circle of good and evil, oh Holly![17]

"And so," she went on after a pause—"and so she bade her son destroy me if he might, because I slew his father. And thou, my Kallikrates, art the father, and in a sense thou art likewise the son; and wouldst thou avenge thy wrong, and the wrong of that far-off mother of thine, upon me, oh Kallikrates? See," and she slid to her knees, and drew the white corsage still further down her ivory bosom—"see, here beats my heart, and there by thy side is a knife, heavy, and long, and sharp, the very knife to slay an erring woman with. Take it now, and be avenged. Strike, and strike home! —so shalt thou be satisfied, Kallikrates, and go through life a happy man, because thou hast paid back the wrong, and obeyed the mandate of the past."

He looked at her, and then stretched out his hand and lifted her to her feet.

"Rise, Ayesha," he said sadly; "well thou knowest that I cannot strike thee, no, not even for the sake of her whom thou slewest but last night. I am in thy power, and a very slave to thee. How can I kill thee?—sooner should I slay myself."

"Almost dost thou begin to love me, Kallikrates," she answered smiling. "And now tell me of thy country—'tis a great people, is it not? with an empire like that of Rome! Surely thou wouldst return thither, and it is well, for I mean not that thou shouldst dwell in these caves of Kôr. Nay, when once thou art even as I am, we will go hence—fear not but that I shall find a path—and then shall we journey to this England of thine, and live as it becometh us to live. Two thousand years have I waited for the day when I should see the last of these hateful caves and this gloomy-visaged folk, and now it is at hand, and my heart bounds up to meet it like a child's towards its holiday. For thou shalt rule this England"—

"But we have a queen already," broke in Leo, hastily.

"It is naught, it is naught," said Ayesha; "she can be overthrown."[18]

At this we both broke out into an exclamation of dismay, and explained that we should as soon think of overthrowing ourselves.

"But here is a strange thing," said Ayesha, in astonishment; "a queen whom her people love! Surely the world must have changed since I dwelt in Kôr."

Again we explained that it was the character of monarchs that had changed, and that the one under whom we lived was venerated and beloved by all right-thinking people in her vast realms. Also, we told her that real power in our country rested in the hands of the people, and that we were in fact ruled by the votes of the lower and least educated classes of the community.

"Ah," she said, "a democracy—then surely there is a tyrant, for I have long since seen that democracies, having no clear will of their own, in the end set up a tyrant, and worship him."

"Yes," I said, "we have our tyrants."[19]

"Well," she answered, resignedly, "we can at any rate destroy these tyrants, and Kallikrates shall rule the land."[20]

I instantly informed Ayesha that in England "blasting" was not an amusement that could be indulged in with impunity, and that any such attempt would meet with the consideration of the law and probably end upon a scaffold.

"The law," she laughed with scorn, "the law! Canst thou not understand, oh Holly, that I am above the law, and so shall my Kallikrates be also? All human law will be to us as the north wind to a mountain. Does the wind bend the mountain, or the mountain the wind?[21]

"And now leave me, I pray thee, and thou too, my own Kallikrates, for I would get me ready against our journey, and so must ye both, and your servant also. But bring no great quantity of things with thee, for I trust that we shall be but three days gone. Then shall we return hither, and I will make a plan whereby we can bid farewell for ever to these sepulchres of Kôr. Yea, surely thou mayst kiss my hand!"

So we went, I, for one, meditating deeply on the awful nature of the problem that now opened out before us. The terrible *She* had evidently made up her mind to go to England, and it made me absolutely shudder to think what would be the result of her arrival there. What her powers were I knew, and I could not doubt but that she would exercise them to the full. It might be possible to control her for a while, but her proud, ambitious spirit would be certain to break loose and avenge itself for the long centuries of its solitude. She would, if necessary, and if the power of her beauty did not unaided prove equal to the occasion, blast her way to any end she set before her, and, as she could not die, and for aught I knew could not even be killed,* what was there to stop her? In the end she would, I had little doubt, assume absolute rule over the British dominions, and probably over the whole earth, and, though I was sure that she would speedily make ours the most glorious and prosperous empire that the world has ever seen, it would be at the cost of a terrible sacrifice of life.[22]

The whole thing sounded like a dream or some extraordinary invention of a speculative brain, and yet it was a fact—a wonderful fact—of which the whole world would soon be called on to take notice. What was the meaning of it all? After much thinking I could only conclude that this marvellous creature, whose passion had kept her for so many centuries chained as it were, and comparatively harmless, was now about to be used by Providence as a means to change the order of the world, and possibly, by the building up of a power that could no more be rebelled against or questioned than the decrees of Fate, to change it materially for the better.

XXIII.
The Temple of Truth.

Our preparations did not take us very long. We put a change of clothing apiece and some spare boots into my Gladstone bag, also we took our revolvers and an express rifle each, together with a good supply of ammunition, a precaution to which, under Providence, we subsequently owed our lives over and over again.[1] The rest of our gear, together with our heavy rifles, we left behind us.

A few minutes before the appointed time we once more attended in Ayesha's boudoir, and found her also ready, her dark cloak thrown over her winding-sheetlike wrappings.

"Are ye prepared for the great venture?" she said.

"We are," I answered, "though for my part, Ayesha, I have no faith in it."

---

*I regret to say that I was never able to ascertain if *She* was invulnerable against the accidents of life. Presumably this was so, else some misadventure would have been sure to put an end to her in the course of so many centuries. True, she offered to let Leo slay her, but very probably this was only an experiment to try his temper and mental attitude towards her. Ayesha never gave way to impulse without some valid object.—L.H.H.

"Ah, my Holly," she said, "thou art of a truth like those old Jews—of whom the memory vexes me so sorely—unbelieving, and hard to accept that which they have not known. But thou shalt see; for unless my mirror yonder lies," and she pointed to the font of crystal water, "the path is yet open as it was of old time. And now let us start upon the new life which shall end—who knoweth where?"

"Ah," I echoed, "who knoweth where?" and we passed down into the great central cave, and out into the light of day. At the mouth of the cave we found a single litter with six bearers, all of them mutes, waiting, and with them I was relieved to see our old friend Billali, for whom I had conceived a sort of affection. It appeared that for reasons not necessary to explain at length, Ayesha had thought it best that, with the exception of herself, we should proceed on foot, and this we were nothing loth to do, after our long confinement in these caves, which, however suitable they might be for sarcophagi—a singularly inappropriate word, by the way, for these particular tombs, which certainly did not consume the bodies given to their keeping[2]—were depressing habitations for breathing mortals like ourselves. Either by accident or by the orders of *She*, the space in front of the cave where we had beheld that awful dance was perfectly clear of spectators. Not a soul was to be seen, and consequently I do not believe that our departure was known to anybody, except perhaps the mutes who waited on *She*, and they were, of course, in the habit of keeping what they saw to themselves.

In a few minutes' time we were stepping out sharply across the great cultivated plain or lake bed, framed like a vast emerald in its setting of frowning cliff, and had another opportunity of wondering at the extraordinary nature of the site chosen by these old people of Kôr for their capital, and at the marvellous amount of labour, ingenuity, and engineering skill that must have been brought into requisition by the founders of the city to drain so huge a sheet of water, and to keep it clear of subsequent accumulations. It is, indeed, so far as my experience goes, an unequalled instance of what man can do in the face of nature, for in my opinion such achievements as the Suez Canal or even the Mont Cenis Tunnel do not approach this ancient undertaking in magnitude and grandeur of conception.

When we had been walking for about half an hour, enjoying ourselves exceedingly in the delightful cool which about this time of the day always appeared to descend upon the great plain of Kôr, and which in some degree atoned for the want of any land or sea breeze—for all wind was kept off by the rocky mountain wall—we began to get a clear view of what Billali had informed us were the ruins of the great city. And even from that distance we could see how wonderful those ruins were, a fact which with every step we took became more evident. The town was not very large if compared to Babylon or Thebes, or other cities of remote antiquity; perhaps its outer wall contained some twelve square miles of ground, or a little more. Nor had the walls, so far as we could judge when we reached them, been very high, probably not more than forty feet, which was about their present height where they had not through the sinking of the ground, or some such cause, fallen into ruin. The reason of this, no doubt, was that the people of Kôr, being protected from any outside attack by far more tremendous ramparts than any that the hand of man could rear, only required them for show and to guard against civil discord. But on the other hand they were as broad as they were high, built entirely of dressed stone, hewn, no doubt, from the vast caves, and surrounded by a great moat about sixty feet in width, some reaches of which were still filled with water. About ten minutes before the sun finally sank we reached this moat, and passed down and through it, clambering across what evidently were the piled-up fragments of a great bridge in order to do so, and then with some little difficulty over the slope of the wall to its summit. I wish that it lay within the power of my pen to give some idea of the grandeur of the sight that then met our view. There, all bathed in the red glow of the sinking sun, were miles upon miles of ruins—columns, temples, shrines, and the palaces of kings, varied with patches of green bush. Of course, the roofs of these buildings had long since fallen into decay and vanished, but owing to the extreme massiveness of the style of building, and to the hardness and durability of the rock employed, most of the party walls and great columns still remained standing.*

Straight before us stretched away what had evidently been the main thoroughfare of the city, for it was very wide, wider than the Thames Embankment,[3] and regular. Being, as we afterwards discovered, paved, or rather built, throughout of blocks of dressed stone, such as were employed in the walls, it was but little overgrown even now with grass and shrubs that could get no depth of soil to live in. What had been the parks and gardens, on the contrary, were now dense jungle. Indeed, it was easy even from a distance to trace the course of the various roads by the burnt-up appearance of the scanty grass that grew upon them. On either side of this great thoroughfare were vast blocks of ruins, each block, generally speaking, being separated from its neighbour by a space of what had once, I suppose, been garden-ground, but was now dense and tangled bush. They were all built of the same coloured stone, and most of them had pillars, which was as much as we could make out in the fading light as we passed swiftly up the main road, that I believe I am right in saying no living foot had pressed for thousands of years.**

---

*In connection with the extraordinary state of preservation of these ruins after so vast a lapse of time—at least, six thousand years—it must be remembered that Kôr was not burnt or destroyed by an enemy or an earthquake, but deserted, owing to the action of a terrible plague. Consequently the houses were left unharmed; also the climate of the plain is remarkably fine and dry, and there is very little rain or wind, as a result of which these relics have only to contend against the unaided action of time, that works but slowly upon such massive blocks of masonry.—L.H.H.

**Billali told me that the Amahagger believe that the site of the city is haunted, and could not be persuaded to enter it upon any consideration. Indeed, I could see that he himself did not at all like doing so, and was only consoled by the reflection that he was under the direct protec-

Presently we came to an enormous pile, which we rightly took to be a temple covering at least eight acres of ground,[4] and apparently arranged in a series of courts, each one enclosing another of smaller size, on the principle of a Chinese nest of boxes, the courts being separated one from the other by rows of huge columns. And, while I think of it, I may as well state a remarkable thing about the shape of these columns, which resembled none that I have ever seen or heard of, being fashioned with a kind of waist in the centre, and swelling out above and below. At first we thought that this shape was meant to roughly symbolise or suggest the female form, as was a common habit amongst the ancient religious architects of many creeds.[5] On the following day, however, as we went up the slopes of the mountain, we discovered a large quantity of the most stately looking palms, of which the trunks grew exactly in this shape, and I have now no doubt but that the first designer of those columns drew his inspiration from the graceful bends of those very palms, or rather of their ancestors, which then, some eight or ten thousand years ago as now, beautified the slopes of the mountain, that had once formed the shores of the volcanic lake.[6]

At the *façade* of this huge temple, which, I should imagine, is almost as large as that of El-Karnac, at Thebes,[7] some of the largest columns, which I measured, being between eighteen to twenty feet in diameter at the base, by about seventy[8] feet in height, our little procession was halted, and Ayesha descended from her litter.

"There was a spot here, Kallikrates," she said to Leo, who had run up to help her down, "where one might sleep. Two thousand years ago did thou and I and that Egyptian asp rest therein, but since then have I not set foot here, nor any man, and perchance it has fallen," and, followed by the rest of us, she passed up a vast flight of broken and ruined steps into the outer court, and looked round into the gloom. Presently she seemed to recollect, and, walking a few paces along the wall to the left, halted.

"It is here," she said, and at the same time beckoned to the two mutes, who were loaded with provisions and our little belongings, to advance. One of them came forward, and, producing a lamp, lit it from his brazier (for the Amahagger when on a journey nearly always carried with them a little lighted brazier, from which to provide fire). The tinder of this brazier was made of broken fragments of mummy carefully damped, and, if the admixture of moisture was properly managed, this unholy compound would smoulder away for hours.*** As soon as the lamp was lit we entered the place

---

tion of *She*. It struck Leo and myself as very curious that a people which has no objection to living amongst the dead, with whom their familiarity has perhaps bred contempt, and even using their bodies for purposes of fuel, should be terrified at approaching the habitations that these very departed had occupied when alive. After all, however, it is only a savage inconsistency. —L.H.H.

***After all we are not much in advance of the Amahagger in these matters. "Mummy," that is pounded ancient Egyptian, is I believe, a pigment much used by artists, and especially by those of them who direct their talents to the reproduction of the works of the old masters.— EDITOR.[9]

before which Ayesha had halted. It turned out to be a chamber hollowed
in the thickness of the wall, and, from the fact of there still being a massive
stone table in it, I should think that it had probably served as a living-room,
perhaps for one of the door-keepers of the great temple.

Here we stopped, and after cleaning the place out and making it as
comfortable as circumstances and the darkness would permit, we ate some
cold meat, at least Leo, Job, and I did, for Ayesha, as I think I have said
elsewhere, never touched anything except cakes of flour, fruit and water.
While we were still eating, the moon, which was at her full, rose above
the mountain-wall, and began to flood the place with silver.

"Wot[10] ye why I have brought you here to-night, my Holly?" said Ayesha, leaning her head upon her hand and watching the great orb as she
rose, like some heavenly queen, above the solemn pillars of the temple. "I
brought you—nay, it is strange, but knowest thou, Kallikrates, that thou
liest at this moment upon the very spot where thy dead body lay when
I bore thee back to those caves of Kôr so many years ago? It all returns
to my mind now. I can see it, and horrible is it to my sight!" and she shuddered.

Here Leo jumped up and hastily changed his seat. However the reminis-
cence might affect Ayesha, it clearly had few charms for him.

"I brought you," went on Ayesha presently, "that ye might look upon
the most wonderful sight that ever the eye of man beheld—the full moon
shining over ruined Kôr. When ye have done your eating—I would that
I could teach thee to eat naught but fruit, Kallikrates, but that will come
after thou hast laved in the fire. Once I, too, ate flesh like a brute beast.
When ye have done we will go out, and I will show you this great temple
and the God whom men once worshipped therein."

Of course we got up at once, and started. And here again my pen fails
me. To give a string of measurements and details of the various courts of
the temple would only be wearisome, supposing that I had them, and yet
I know not how I am to describe what we saw, magnificent as it was even
in its ruin, almost beyond the power of realisation. Court upon dim court,
row upon row of mighty pillars—some of them (especially at the gateways)
sculptured from pedestal to capital—space upon space of empty chambers
that spoke more eloquently to the imagination than any crowded streets.
And over all, the dead silence of the dead, the sense of utter loneliness,
and the brooding spirit of the Past! How beautiful it was, and yet how drear!
We did not dare to speak aloud. Ayesha herself was awed in the presence
of an antiquity compared to which even her length of days was but a little
thing; we only whispered, and our whispers seemed to run from column
to column, till they were lost in the quiet air. Bright fell the moonlight on
pillar and court and shattered wall, hiding all their rents and imperfections
in its silver garment, and clothing their hoar majesty with the peculiar glory
of the night. It was a wonderful sight to see the full moon looking down
on the ruined fane[11] of Kôr. It was a wonderful thing to think for how many

thousands of years the dead orb above and the dead city below had gazed thus upon each other, and in the utter solitude of space poured forth each to each the tale of their lost life and long-departed glory. The white light fell, and minute by minute the quiet shadows crept across the grass-grown courts like the spirits of old priests haunting the habitations of their worship —the white light fell, and the long shadows grew till the beauty and grandeur of the scene and the untamed majesty of its present Death seemed to sink into our very souls, and speak more loudly than the shouts of armies[12] concerning the pomp and splendour that the grave had swallowed, and even memory had forgotten.

"Come," said Ayesha, after we had gazed and gazed, I know not for how long, "and I will show you the stony flower of Loveliness and Wonder's very crown, if yet it stands to mock time with its beauty and fill the heart of man with longing for that which is behind the veil," and, without waiting for an answer, she led us through two more pillared courts into the inner shrine of the old fane.

And there, in the centre of the inmost court, that might have been some fifty yards square, or a little more, we stood face to face with what is perhaps the grandest allegorical work of Art that the genius of her children has ever given to the world.[13] For in the exact centre of the court, placed upon a thick square slab of rock, was a huge round ball of dark stone, some twenty feet[14] in diameter, and standing on the ball was a colossal winged figure of a beauty so entrancing and divine that when I first gazed upon it, illuminated and shadowed as it was by the soft light of the moon, my breath stood still, and for an instant my heart ceased its beating.

The statue was hewn from marble so pure and white that even now, after all those ages, it shone as the moonbeams danced upon it, and its height was, I should say, a trifle over twenty feet. It was a winged figure of a woman of such marvellous loveliness and delicacy of form that the size seemed rather to add to than to detract from its so human and yet more spiritual beauty. She was bending forward and poising herself upon her half-spread wings as though to preserve her balance as she leant. Her arms were outstretched like those of some woman about to embrace one she dearly loved, while her whole attitude gave an impression of the tenderest beseeching. Her perfect and most gracious form was naked, save—and here came the extraordinary thing—the face, which was thinly veiled, so that we could only trace the marking of her features. A gauzy veil was thrown round and about the head, and of its two ends one fell down across her left breast, which was outlined beneath it, and one, now broken, streamed away upon the air behind her.

"Who is she?" I asked, as soon as I could take my eyes off the statue.

"Canst thou not guess, oh Holly?" answered Ayesha. "Where then is thy imagination? It is Truth standing on the World, and calling to its children to unveil her face. See what is writ upon the pedestal. Without doubt it is taken from the book of the Scriptures of these men of Kôr," and she led the way to the foot of the statue, where an inscription of the usual Chinese-looking hieroglyphics was so deeply graven as to be still quite legible, at least to Ayesha. According to her translation it ran thus:—

"Is there no man that will draw my veil and look upon my face, for it is very fair? Unto him who draws my veil shall I be, and peace will I give him, and sweet children of knowledge and good works.

And a voice cried, 'Though all those who seek after thee desire thee, behold! Virgin art thou, and Virgin shalt thou go till Time be done. No man is there born of woman who may draw thy veil and live, nor shall be. By Death only can thy veil be drawn, oh Truth!'

And Truth stretched out her arms and wept, because those who sought her might not find her, nor look upon her face to face."

"Thou seest," said Ayesha, when she had finished translating, "Truth was the Goddess of the people of old Kôr, and to her they built their shrines, and her they sought; knowing that they should never find, still sought they."

"And so," I added sadly, "do men seek to this very hour, but they find not; and, as this Scripture saith, nor shall they; for in Death only is Truth found."

Then with one more look at the veiled and spiritualised loveliness—which was so perfect and so pure that one might almost fancy that the light of a living spirit shone through the marble prison to lead man on to high and ethereal thoughts—this poet's dream of beauty frozen into stone, which I never shall forget while I live, we turned and went back through the vast moonlit courts to the spot whence we had started. I never saw the statue again, which I the more regret, because on the great ball of stone representing the World whereon the figure stood, lines were drawn, that probably, had there been light enough, we should have discovered to be a map of the Universe as it was known to the people of Kôr. It is at any rate suggestive of some scientific knowledge that these long-dead worshippers of Truth had recognized the fact that the globe is round.[15]

XXIV.
Walking the Plank.

Next day the mutes woke us before the dawn; and by the time that we had got the sleep out of our eyes, and gone through a perfunctory wash at a spring which still welled up into the remains of a marble basin in the centre of the North quadrangle of the vast outer court, we found *She* standing by the litter ready to start, while old Billali and the two bearer mutes were busy collecting the baggage. As usual, Ayesha was veiled like the marble Truth (by the way, I wonder if she originally got the idea of covering up her beauty from that statue?). I noticed, however, that she seemed very depressed, and had none of that proud and buoyant bearing which would have betrayed her among a thousand women of the same stature, even if they had been veiled like herself. She looked up as we came—for her head was bowed—and greeted us. Leo asked her how she had slept.

"Ill, my Kallikrates," she answered, "ill. This night have strange and hideous dreams come creeping through my brain, and I know not what they may portend. Almost do I feel as though some evil overshadowed me; and yet how can evil touch me? I wonder," she went on with a sudden outbreak of womanly tenderness, "I wonder if, should aught happen to me, so that I slept awhile and left thee waking, thou wouldst think gently of me? I wonder, my Kallikrates, if thou wouldst tarry till I came again, as for so many centuries I have tarried for thy coming?" Then, without waiting for an answer, she went on: "Come, let us be setting forth, for we have far to go, and before another day is born in yonder blue should we stand in the place of Life."

In five minutes we were once more on our way through the vast ruined city, which loomed at us on either side in the grey dawning in a way that was at once grand and oppressive. Just as the first ray of the rising sun shot like a golden arrow athwart this storied desolation we gained the further gateway of the outer wall, and having given one more glance at the hoar and pillared majesty through which we had journeyed, and (with the exception of Job, for whom ruins had no charms) breathed a sigh of regret that we had not had more time to explore it, passed through the great moat, and on to the plain beyond.

As the sun rose so did Ayesha's spirits, till by breakfasttime they had regained their normal level, and she laughingly set down her previous depression to the associations of the spot where she had slept.

"These barbarians declare that Kôr is haunted," she said, "and of a truth I do believe their saying, for never did I know so ill a night save once. I remember it now. It was on that very spot when thou didst lie dead at my feet, Kallikrates. Never will I visit it again; it is a place of evil omen."

After a very brief halt for breakfast we pressed on with such good will that by two o'clock in the afternoon we were at the foot of the vast wall of rock that formed the lip of the volcano, and which at this point towered up precipitously above us for fifteen hundred or two thousand feet.[1] Here we halted, certainly not to my astonishment, for I did not see how it was possible that we should go any further.

"Now," said Ayesha, as she descended from her litter, "doth our labour but commence, for here do we part with these men, and henceforward must we bear ourselves;" and then, addressing Billali, "do thou and these slaves remain here, and abide our coming. By to-morrow at the midday shall we be with thee—if not, wait."

Billali bowed humbly, and said that her august bidding should be obeyed if they stopped there till they grew old.

"And this man, oh Holly," said *She*, pointing to Job; "best is it that he should tarry also, for if his heart be not high and his courage great, perchance some evil might overtake him. Also, the secrets of the place whither we go are not fit for common eyes."

I translated this to Job, who instantly and earnestly entreated me, almost with tears in his eyes, not to leave him behind. He said that he was sure that he could see nothing worse than he had already seen, and that he was terrified to death at the idea of being left alone with those "dumb folk," who, he thought, would probably take the opportunity to hot-pot him.

I translated what he said to Ayesha, who shrugged her shoulders, and answered, "Well, let him come, it is naught to me; on his own head be it; and he will serve to bear the lamp and this," and she pointed to a narrow plank, some sixteen feet in length, which had been bound above the long bearing-pole of her hammock, as I had thought to make curtains spread out better, but, as it now appeared, for some unknown purpose connected with our extraordinary undertaking.

Accordingly, the plank, which, though tough, was very light, was given to Job to carry, and also one of the lamps. I slung the other on to my back, together with a spare jar of oil, while Leo loaded himself with the provisions and some water in a kid's skin. When this was done *She* bade Billali and the six bearer mutes to retreat behind a grove of flowering magnolias about a hundred yards away, and remain there under pain of death till we had vanished. They bowed humbly, and went, and, as he departed, old Billali gave me a friendly shake of the hand, and whispered that he had rather that it was I than he who was going on this wonderful expedition with *"She-who-must-be-obeyed,"* and upon my word I felt inclined to agree with him. In another minute they were gone, and then, having briefly asked us if we were ready, Ayesha turned, and gazed up the towering cliff.

"Goodness me, Leo," I said, "surely we are not going to climb that precipice!"

Leo shrugged his shoulders, being in a condition of half-fascinated, half-expectant mystification, and as he did so, Ayesha with a sudden move began to climb the cliff, and of course we had to follow her. It was perfectly marvellous to see the ease and grace with which she sprang from rock to rock, and swung herself along the ledges. The ascent was not, however, so difficult as it seemed, although there were one or two nasty places where it did not do to look behind you, the fact being that the rock still sloped here, and was not absolutely precipitous as it was higher up. In this way we, with no great labour, mounted to the height of some fifty feet above our last standing place, the only really troublesome thing to manage being Job's board, and in doing so drew some fifty or sixty paces to the left of our starting-point, for we went up like a crab, sideways. Presently we reached a ledge,

narrow enough at first, but which widened as we followed it, and moreover
sloped inwards like the petal of a flower, so that as we followed it we gradually got into a kind of rut or fold of rock that grew deeper and deeper, till
at last it resembled a Devonshire lane in stone, and hid us perfectly from
the gaze of anybody on the slope below, if there had been anybody to gaze.
This lane (which appeared to be a natural formation) continued for some
fifty or sixty paces, and then suddenly ended in a cave, also natural, running
at right angles to it. I am sure it was a natural cave, and not hollowed by
the hand of man, because of its irregular and contorted shape and course,
which gave it the appearance of having been blown bodily in the mountain
by some frightful eruption of gas following the line of the least resistance.[2]
All the caves hollowed by the ancients of Koˆr, on the contrary, were cut
out with the most perfect regularity and symmetry. At the mouth of this
cave Ayesha halted, and bade us light the two lamps, which I did, giving
one to her and keeping the other myself. Then, taking the lead, she advanced
down the cavern, picking her way with great care, as indeed it was necessary
to do, for the floor was most irregular—strewn with boulders like the bed
of a stream, and in some places pitted with deep holes, in which it would
have been easy to break one's leg.

This cavern we pursued for twenty minutes or more, it being, so far
as I could form a judgment—owing to its numerous twists and turns no
easy task—about a quarter of a mile long.

At last, however, we halted at its farther end, and whilst I was still
trying to pierce the gloom a great gust of air came tearing down it, and
extinguished both the lamps.

Ayesha called to us, and we crept up to her, for she was a little in front,
and were rewarded with a view that was positively appalling in its gloom
and grandeur. Before us was a mighty chasm in the black rock, jagged and
torn and splintered through it in a far past age by some awful convulsion
of Nature, as though it had been cleft by stroke upon stroke of the lightning.
This chasm, which was bounded by a precipice on the hither, and presumably,
though we could not see it, on the farther side also, may have measured
any width across, but from its darkness I do not think that it can have been
very broad. It was impossible to make out much of its outline, or how far
it ran, for the simple reason that the point where we were standing was
so far from the upper surface of the cliff, at least fifteen hundred or two
thousand feet, that only a very dim light struggled down to us from above.
The mouth of the cavern that we had been following gave on to a most
curious and tremendous spur of rock, which jutted out in mid air into the
gulf before us, for a distance of some fifty yards, coming to a sharp point
at its termination, and resembling nothing that I can think of so much as
the spur upon the leg of a cock in shape. This huge spur was attached only
to the parent precipice at its base, which was, of course, enormous, just
as the cock's spur is attached to its leg. Otherwise it was utterly unsupported.

"Here must we pass," said Ayesha. "Be careful lest giddiness overcome you, or the wind sweep you into the gulf beneath, for of a truth it hath no bottom;" and, without giving us any further time to get scared, she started walking along the spur, leaving us to follow her as best we might. I was next to her, then came Job, painfully dragging his plank, while Leo brought up the rear. It was a wonderful sight to see this intrepid woman gliding fearlessly along that dreadful place. For my part, when I had gone but a very few yards, what between the pressure of the air and the awful sense of the consequences that a slip would entail, I found it necessary to go down on my hands and knees and crawl, and so did the other two.

But Ayesha never condescended to this. On she went, leaning her body against the gusts of wind, and never seeming to lose her head or her balance.

In a few minutes we had crossed some twenty paces of this awful bridge, which got narrower at every step, and then all of a sudden a great gust came tearing along the gorge. I saw Ayesha lean herself against it, but the strong draught got under her dark cloak, and tore it from her, and away it went down the wind flapping like a wounded bird. It was dreadful to see it go, till it was lost in the blackness. I clung to the saddle of rock, and looked round, while, like a living thing, the great spur vibrated with a humming sound beneath us. The sight was a truly awesome one. There we were poised in the gloom between earth and heaven. Beneath us were hundreds upon hundreds of feet of emptiness that gradually grew darker, till at last it was absolutely black, and at what depth it ended is more than I can guess. Above was space upon space of giddy air, and far, far away a line of blue sky. And down this vast gulf upon which we were pinnacled the great draught dashed and roared, driving clouds and misty wreaths of vapour before it, till we were nearly blinded, and utterly confused.

The whole position was so tremendous and so absolutely unearthly, that I believe it actually lulled our sense of terror, but to this hour I often see it in my dreams, and at its mere phantasy[3] wake up covered with cold sweat.

"On! on!" cried the white form before us, for now the cloak had gone *She* was robed in white, and looked more like a spirit riding down the gale than a woman; "On, or ye will fall and be dashed to pieces. Keep your eyes fixed upon the ground, and closely hug the rock."

We obeyed her, and crept painfully along the quivering path, against which the wind shrieked and wailed as it shook it, causing it to murmur like a vast tuning-fork. On we went, I do not know for how long, only gazing round now and again, when it was absolutely necessary, until at last we saw that we were on the very tip of the spur, a slab of rock, little larger than an ordinary table, and that throbbed and jumped like any over-engined steamer.[4] There we lay, clinging to the ground, and looked about us, while Ayesha stood leaning out against the wind, down which her long hair streamed, and, absolutely heedless of the hideous depth that yawned beneath, pointed before her. Then we saw why the narrow plank had been provided, which Job and I had painfully dragged along between us. Before us was an empty space, on the other side of which was something, as yet we could not see what, for here—either owing to the shadow of the opposite cliff, or from some other cause—the gloom was that of night.

"We must wait awhile," called Ayesha; "soon there will be light."

At the moment I could not imagine what she meant. How could more light than there was ever come to this dreadful spot? While I was still wondering, suddenly, like a great sword of flame, a beam from the setting sun pierced the Stygian gloom, and smote upon the point of rock whereon we lay, illumining Ayesha's lovely form with an unearthly splendour. I only wish I could describe the wild and marvellous beauty of that sword of fire, laid across the darkness and rushing mist-wreaths of the gulf.[5] How it got there I do not to this moment know, but I presume there was some cleft or hole in the opposing cliff, through which it pierced when the setting orb was in a direct line therewith. All I can say is, that the effect was the most wonderful that I ever saw. Right through the heart of the darkness that flaming sword was stabbed, and where it lay there was the most surpassingly vivid light, so vivid that even at a distance we could see the grain of the rock, while, outside of it—yes, within a few inches of its keen edge—was naught but clustering shadows.

And now, by this ray of light, for which *She* had been waiting, and timed our arrival to meet, knowing that at this season for thousands of years it has always struck thus at sunset, we saw what was before us. Within eleven or twelve feet of the very tip of the tongue-like rock whereon we stood there arose, presumably from the far bottom of the gulf, a sugarloaf-shaped cone, of which the summit was exactly opposite to us. But had there been a summit only it would not have helped us much, for the nearest point of its circumference was some forty feet from where we were. On the lip of this summit, however, which was circular and hollow, rested a tremendous flat boulder, something like a glacier stone—perhaps it was one, for all I know to the contrary—and the end of this boulder approached to within twelve feet or so of us. This huge rock was nothing more or less than a gigantic rocking-stone, accurately balanced upon the edge of the cone or miniature crater, like a half-crown[6] on the rim of a wine glass; for, in the fierce light that played upon it and us, we could see it oscillating in the gusts of wind.

"Quick!" said Ayesha, "the plank—we must cross while the light endures; presently it will be gone."

"Oh, Lord, sir!" groaned Job, "surely she don't mean us to walk across that there place on that there thing," as in obedience to my direction he pushed the long board towards me.

"That's it, Job," I halloaed in ghastly merriment, though the idea of walking the plank was no pleasanter to me than to him.

I pushed the board on to Ayesha, who deftly ran it across the gulf so that one end of it rested on the rocking stone, the other remaining on the extremity of the trembling spur. Then placing her foot upon it to prevent it from being blown away, she turned to me.

"Since last I was here, oh Holly," she called, "the support of the moving stone hath lessened somewhat, so that I am not certain if it will bear our weight and fall or no. Therefore will I cross the first, because no harm will come unto me," and, without further ado, she trod lightly but firmly across the frail bridge, and in another second was standing safe upon the heaving stone.

"It is safe," she called. "See, hold thou the plank! I will stand on the farther side of the stone so that it may not overbalance with your greater weights. Now, come, oh Holly, for presently the light will fail us."

I struggled to my knees, and if ever I felt terrified in my life it was then, and I am not ashamed to say that I hesitated and hung back.

"Surely thou art not afraid," this strange creature called in a lull of the gale, from where she stood poised like a bird on the highest point of the rocking-stone. "Make way then for Kallikrates."

This settled me; it is better to fall down a precipice and die than be laughed at by such a woman; so I clenched my teeth, and in another instant I was on that horrible, narrow, bending plank, with bottomless space beneath and around me. I have always hated a great height, but never before did I realise the full horrors of which such a position is capable. Oh, the sickening sensation of that yielding board resting on the two moving supports! I grew dizzy, and thought that I must fall; my spine *crept*; it seemed to me that I was falling, and my delight at finding myself sprawling upon that stone, which rose and fell beneath me like a boat in a swell, cannot be expressed in words. All I know is that briefly, but earnestly enough, I thanked Providence for preserving me so far.

Then came Leo's turn, and, though he looked rather queer, he came across like a rope-dancer.[7] Ayesha stretched out her hand to clasp his own, and I heard her say, "Bravely done, my love—bravely done! The old Greek spirit lives in thee yet!"

And now only poor Job remained on the farther side of the gulf. He crept up to the plank, and yelled out, "I can't do it, sir. I shall fall into that beastly place."

"You must," I remember saying with inappropriate facetiousness—"you must, Job, it's as easy as catching flies." I suppose that I must have said it to satisfy my conscience, because although the expression conveys a wonderful idea of facility, as a matter of fact I know no more difficult operation in the whole world than catching flies—that is, in warm weather, unless, indeed, it is catching mosquitoes.

"I can't, sir—I can't, indeed."

"Let the man come, or let him stop and perish there. See, the light is dying! In a moment it will be gone!" said Ayesha.

I looked. She was right. The sun was passing below the level of the hole or cleft in the precipice through which the ray reached us.

"If you stop there, Job, you will die alone," I called; "the light is going."

"Come, be a man Job," roared Leo; "it's quite easy."

Thus adjured, the miserable Job, with a most awful yell, precipitated himself face downwards on the plank—he did not dare, small blame to him, to try to walk it, and commenced to draw himself across in little jerks, his poor legs hanging down on either side into the nothingness beneath.

His violent jerks at the frail board made the great stone, which was only balanced on a few inches of rock, oscillate in a most dreadful manner, and, to make matters worse, when he was half-way across the flying ray of lurid light suddenly went out just as though a lamp had been extinguished in a curtained room, leaving the whole howling wilderness of air black with darkness.

"Come on, Job, for God's sake," I shouted in an agony of fear, while the stone, gathering motion with every swing, rocked so violently that it was difficult to hang on to it. It was a truly awful position.

"Lord have mercy on me!" cried poor Job from the darkness. "Oh, the plank's slipping!" and I heard a violent struggle, and thought that he was gone.

But at that moment his outstretched hand, clasping in agony at the air, met my own, and I hauled—ah, how I did haul, putting out all the strength that it has pleased Providence to give me in such abundance—and to my joy in another minute Job was gasping on the rock beside me. But the plank! I felt it slip, and heard it knock against a projecting knob of rock, and it was gone.

"Great Heavens!" I exclaimed. "How are we going to get back?"

"I don't know," answered Leo, out of the gloom.

"'Sufficient to the day is the evil thereof.' I am thankful enough to be here."

But Ayesha merely called to me to take her hand and creep after her.

X X V.
The Spirit of Life.

I did as I was bid, and in fear and trembling felt myself guided over the edge of the stone. I sprawled my legs out, but could touch nothing.

"I am going to fall!" I gasped.

"Nay, let thyself go, and trust to me," answered Ayesha.

Now, if the position is considered, it will be easily understood that this was a greater demand upon my confidence than was justified by my knowledge of Ayesha's character. For all I knew she might be in the very act of consigning me to a horrible doom. But in life we sometimes have to lay our faith upon strange altars, and so it was now.

"Let thyself go!" she cried, and, having no choice, I did.

I felt myself slide a pace or two down the sloping surface of the rock, and then pass into the air, and the thought flashed through my brain that I was lost. But no! In another instant my feet struck against a rocky floor, and I felt that I was standing on something solid, and out of reach of the wind, which I could hear singing away overhead. As I stood there thanking Heaven for these small mercies, there was a slip and a scuffle, and down came Leo alongside of me.

"Hulloa, old fellow!" he called out, "are you there? This is getting interesting, is it not?"[1]

Just then, with a terrific yell, Job arrived right on the top of us, knocking us both down. By the time that we had struggled to our feet again Ayesha was standing among us, and bidding us light the lamps, which fortunately remained uninjured, as also did the spare jar of oil.

I got out my box of wax matches,[2] and they struck as merrily, there, in that awful place, as they could have done in a London drawing-room.

In a couple of minutes both the lamps were alight and revealed a curious scene. We were huddled up together in a rocky chamber, some ten feet square,[3] and scared enough we looked; that is, except Ayesha, who was standing calmly with her arms folded, and waiting for the lamps to burn up.[4] The chamber appeared to be partly natural, and partly hollowed out of the top of the cone. The roof of the natural part was formed of the swinging stone, and that of the back part of the chamber, which sloped downwards, was hewn from the live rock. For the rest, the place was warm and dry —a perfect haven of rest compared to the giddy pinnacle above, and the quivering spur that shot out to meet it in mid-air.

"So!" said *She*, "safely have we come, though once I feared that the rocking stone would fall with you, and precipitate you into the bottomless deeps beneath, for I do believe that the cleft goeth down to the very womb of the world.[5] The rock whereon the stone resteth hath crumbled beneath the swinging weight. And now that he," nodding towards Job, who was sitting on the floor, feebly wiping his forehead with a red cotton pocket-handkerchief, "whom they rightly call the 'Pig,' for as a pig is he stupid, hath let fall the plank, it will not be easy to return across the gulf, and to that end must I make a plan. But now rest a while, and look upon this place. What think ye that it is?"

"We know not," I answered.

"Wouldst thou believe, oh Holly, that once a man did choose this airy nest for a daily habitation, and did here endure for many years; leaving it only but one day in every twelve[6] to seek food and water and oil that the people brought, more than he could carry, and laid as an offering in the mouth of the tunnel through which he passed hither?"[7]

We looked up wonderingly, and she continued—

"Yet, so it was. There was a man—Noot, he named himself—who, though he lived in the latter days, had of the wisdom of the sons of Kôr. A hermit was he, and a philosopher, and greatly skilled in the secrets of Nature, and he it was who discovered the Fire that I shall show you, which is Nature's blood and life, and also that he who bathed therein, and breathed thereof, should live while Nature lives. But like unto thee, oh Holly, this man, Noot, would not turn his knowledge to account. "Ill," he said, "was it for man to live, for man was born to die." Therefore did he tell his secret to none, and therefore did he come and live here, where the seeker after Life must pass, and was revered of the Amahagger of the day as holy, and a hermit. And when first I came to this country—knowest thou how I came, Kallikrates? Another time will I tell thee, it is a strange tale—I heard of this philosopher, and waited for him when he came to fetch his food, and returned with him hither, though greatly did I fear to tread the gulf. Then did I beguile him with my beauty and my wit, and flatter him with my tongue, so that he led me down and showed me the Fire, and told me the secrets of the Fire, but he would not suffer me to step therein, and, fearing lest he should slay me, I refrained, knowing that the man was very old, and soon would die. And I returned, having learned from him all that he knew of the wonderful Spirit of the World, and that was much, for the man was wise and very ancient, and by purity and abstinence, and the contemplations of his innocent mind, had worn thin the veil between that which we see and the great invisible truths, the whisper of whose wings at times we hear as they sweep through the gross air of the world. Then—it was but very few days after, I met thee, my Kallikrates, who hadst wandered hither with the beautiful Egyptian Amenartas, and I learned to love for the first and last time, once and for ever, so that it entered into my mind to come hither with thee, and receive the gift of Life for thee and me. Therefore came we, with that Egyptian who would not be left behind, and, behold, we found the old man Noot lying but newly dead. *There* he lay, and his white beard covered him like a garment," and she pointed to a spot near where I was sitting; "but surely he hath long since crumbled into dust, and the wind hath borne his ashes hence."

Here I put out my hand and felt in the dust, and presently my fingers touched something. It was a human tooth, very yellow, but sound. I held it up and showed it to Ayesha, who laughed.

"Yes," she said, "it is his without a doubt. Behold what remaineth of Noot and the wisdom of Noot—one little tooth! And yet that man had all life at his command, and for his conscience' sake would have none of it. Well, he lay there newly dead, and we descended whither I shall lead you, and then, gathering up all my courage, and courting death that I might perchance win so glorious a crown of life, I stepped into the flames, and behold! life such as ye can never know until ye feel it also, flowed into me, and I came forth undying, and lovely beyond imagining. Then did I stretch out mine arms to thee, Kallikrates, and bid thee take thine immortal bride, and behold, as I spoke, thou, blinded by my beauty, didst turn from me, and throw thine arms about the neck of Amenartas. And then a great fury filled me, and made me mad, and I seized the javelin that thou didst bear, and stabbed thee, so that there, at my very feet, in the place of Life, thou didst groan and go down into death.[8] I knew not then that I had strength to slay with mine eyes and by the power of my will, therefore in my madness slew I with the javelin.*

And when thou wast dead, ah! I wept, because I was undying and thou wast dead. I wept there in the place of Life so that had I been mortal any more my heart had surely broken. And she, the swart Egyptian—she cursed me by her gods. By Osiris did she curse me and by Isis, by Nephthys and by Anubis, by Sekhet, the cat-headed, and by Set, calling down evil on me, evil and everlasting desolation.[10] Ah! I can see her dark face now lowering o'er me like a storm, but she could not hurt me, and I—I know not if I could hurt her. I did not try; it was naught to me then; so together we bore thee hence. And afterwards I sent her—the Egyptian—away through the swamps, and it seems that she lived to bear a son and to write the tale that should lead thee, her husband, back to me, her rival and thy murderess.

"Such is the tale, my love, and now is the hour at hand that shall set a crown upon it. Like all things on the earth, it is compounded of evil and good—more of evil than of good, perchance; and writ in letters of blood. It is the truth; naught have I hidden from thee, Kallikrates. And now one thing before the final moment of thy trial. We go down into the presence of Death, for Life and Death are very near together, and—who knoweth? —that might happen which should separate us for another space of waiting.[11] I am but a woman, and no prophetess, and I cannot read the future. But this I know—for I learned it from the lips of the wise man Noot—that my life is but prolonged and made more bright. It cannot live for aye.[12] Therefore, before we go, tell me, oh Kallikrates, that of a truth thou dost forgive me, and dost love me from thy heart. See Kallikrates: much evil have I done—perchance it was evil but two nights gone to strike that girl who loved thee cold in death—but she disobeyed me and angered me, proph-

---

*It will be observed that Ayesha's account of the death of Kallikrates differs materially from that written on the potsherd by Amenartas. The writing on the sherd says, "Then in her rage did she smite him *by her magic,* and he died." We never ascertained which was the correct version, but it will be remembered that the body of Kallikrates had a spear-wound in the breast, which seems conclusive, unless, indeed, it was inflicted after death. Another thing that we never ascertained was *how* the two women—*She* and the Egyptian Amenartas—were able to bear the corpse of the man they both loved across the dread gulf and along the shaking spur. What a spectacle the two distracted creatures must have presented in their grief and loveliness as they toiled along that awful place with the dead man between them! Probably however the passage was easier then.—L.H.H.[9]

esying misfortune to me, and I smote. Be careful when power comes to thee also, lest thou too shouldst smite in thine anger or thy jealousy, for unconquerable strength is a sore weapon in the hands of erring man. Yea, I have sinned—out of the bitterness born of a great love have I sinned—but yet do I know the good from the evil, nor is my heart altogether hardened. Thy love, Kallikrates, shall be the gate of my redemption, even as aforetime my passion was the path down which I ran to evil. For deep love unsatisfied is the hell of noble hearts and a portion[13] for the accursed, but love that is mirrored back more perfect from the soul of our desired doth fashion wings to lift us above ourselves, and make us what we might be. Therefore, Kallikrates, take me by the hand, and lift my veil with no more fear than though I were some peasant girl, and not the wisest and most beauteous woman in this wide world, and look me in the eyes, and tell me that thou dost forgive me with all thine heart, and that with all thine heart thou dost worship me."

She paused, and the strange tenderness in her voice seemed to hover round us like a memory. I know that the sound of it moved me more even than her words, it was so very human—so very womanly. Leo, too, was strangely touched. Hitherto he had been fascinated against his better judgment, something as a bird is fascinated by a snake, but now I think that all this passed away, and he realised that he really loved this strange and glorious creature, as, alas! I loved her also. At any rate, I saw his eyes fill with tears, and he stepped swiftly to her and undid the gauzy veil, and then took her by the hand, and, gazing into her deep eyes, said aloud—

"Ayesha, I love thee with all my heart, and so far as forgiveness is possible I forgive thee the death of Ustane. For the rest, it is between thee and thy Maker; I know naught of it. I only know that I love thee as I never loved before, and that I will cleave to thee to the end."

"Now," answered Ayesha, with proud humility, "now when my lord doth speak thus royally and give with so free a hand, it cannot become me to lag behind in words, and be beggared of my generosity. Behold!" and she took his hand and placed it upon her shapely head, and then bent herself slowly down till one knee for an instant touched the ground—"Behold! in token of submission do I bow me to my lord! Behold!" and she kissed him on the lips, "in token of my wifely love do I kiss my lord. Behold!" and she laid her hand upon his heart, "by the sin I sinned, by my lonely centuries of waiting wherewith it was wiped out, by the great love wherewith I love, and by the Spirit—the Eternal Thing that doth beget all life, from whom it ebbs, to whom it doth return again—I swear:—

"I swear, even in this first most holy hour of completed Womanhood,[14] that I will abandon Evil and cherish Good. I swear that I will be ever guided by thy voice in the straightest path of Duty. I swear that I will eschew Ambition, and through all my length of endless days set Wisdom over me as a guiding star to lead me unto Truth and a knowledge of the Right. I swear also that I will honour and will cherish thee, Kallikrates, who hath been swept by the wave of time back into my arms, ay, till the very end, come it soon or late. I swear—nay, I will swear no more, for what are words? Yet shalt thou learn that Ayesha hath no false tongue.

"So I have sworn, and thou, my Holly, art witness to my oath. Here, too, are we wed, my husband,[15] with the gloom for bridal canopy—wed till the end of all things; here do we write our marriage vows upon the rushing winds which shall bear them up to heaven, and round and continually round this rolling world.

"And for a bridal gift I crown thee with my beauty's starry crown, and enduring life, and wisdom without measure, and wealth that none can count. Behold! the great ones of the earth shall creep about thy feet, and its fair women shall cover up their eyes because of the shining glory of thy countenance, and its wise ones shall be abased before thee. Thou shalt read the hearts of men as an open writing, and hither and thither shalt thou lead them as thy pleasure listeth. Like that old Sphinx of Egypt shalt thou sit aloft from age to age, and ever shall they cry to thee to solve the riddle of thy greatness that doth not pass away, and ever shalt thou mock them with thy silence!

"Behold! once more I kiss thee, and by that kiss I give to thee dominion over sea and earth, over the peasant in his hovel, over the monarch in his palace halls, and cities crowned with towers, and those who breathe therein. Where'er the sun shakes out his spears, and the lonesome waters mirror up the moon, where'er storms roll, and Heaven's painted bows arch in the sky—from the pure North clad in snows, across the middle spaces of the world, to where the amorous South, lying like a bride upon her blue couch of seas, breathes in sighs made sweet with the odour of myrtles— there shall thy power pass and thy dominion find a home. Nor sickness, nor icy-fingered fear, nor sorrow, and pale waste of form and mind hovering ever o'er humanity, shall so much as shadow thee with the shadow of their wings. As a God shalt thou be, holding good and evil in the hollow of thy hand, and I, even I, I humble myself before thee. Such is the power of Love, and such is the bridal gift I give unto thee, Kallikrates, my Lord and Lord of All."

"And now it is done; now for thee I loose my virgin zone;[16] and come storm, come shine, come good, come evil, come life, come death, it never, never can be undone. For, of a truth, that which is, is, and, being done, is done for aye, and cannot be altered. I have said——Let us hence, that all things may be accomplished in their order;" and, taking one of the lamps, she advanced towards the end of the chamber that was roofed in by the swaying stone, where she halted.

We followed her, and perceived that in the wall of the cone there was a stair, or, to be more accurate, that some projecting knobs of rock had been so shaped as to form a good imitation of a stair. Down this Ayesha began to climb, springing from step to step, like a chamois,[17] and after her we followed with less grace. When we had descended some fifteen or sixteen steps we found that they ended in a tremendous rocky slope, running first outwards and then inwards—like the slope of an inverted cone, or tunnel. The slope was very steep, and often precipitous, but it was nowhere impassable, and by the light of the lamps we went down it with no great difficulty, though it was gloomy work enough travelling on thus, no one of us knew whither, into the dead heart of a volcano. As we went, however, I took the precaution of noting our route as well as I could; and this was not so very difficult, owing to the extraordinary and most fantastic shape of the rocks that were strewn about, many of which in that dim light looked more like the grim faces carven upon mediæval gargoyles than ordinary boulders.

For a long time we travelled on thus, half an hour I should say, till, after we had descended for many hundreds of feet, I perceived that we were reaching the point of the inverted cone. In another minute we were there, and found that at the very apex of the funnel was a passage, so low and narrow that we had to stoop as we crept along it in Indian file. After some fifty yards of this creeping, the passage suddenly widened into a cave, so huge that we could see neither the roof nor the sides. We only knew that it was a cave by the echo of our tread and the perfect quiet of the heavy air. On we went for many minutes in absolute awed silence, like lost souls in the depths of Hades,[18] Ayesha's white and ghost-like form flitting in front of us, till once more the place ended in a passage which opened into a second cavern much smaller than the first. Indeed, we could clearly make out the arch and stony banks of this second cave, and, from their rent and jagged appearance, discovered that, like the first long passage down which we had passed through the cliff before we reached the quivering spur, it had, to all appearance, been torn in the bowels of the rock by the terrific force of some explosive gas. At length this cave ended in a third passage, through which gleamed a faint glow of light.

I heard Ayesha give a sigh of relief as this light dawned upon us.

"It is well," she said; "prepare to enter the very womb of the Earth, wherein she doth conceive the Life that ye see brought forth in man and beast—ay, and in every tree and flower."

Swiftly she sped along, and after her we stumbled as best we might, our hearts filled like a cup with mingled dread and curiosity. What were we about to see? We passed down the tunnel; stronger and stronger the light beamed, reaching us in great flashes like the rays from a lighthouse, as one by one they are thrown wide upon the darkness of the waters. Nor was this all, for with the flashes came a soul-shaking sound like that of thunder and of crashing trees. Now we were through it, and—oh, heavens!

We stood in a third cavern, some fifty feet in length by perhaps as great a height, and thirty wide. It was carpeted with fine white sand, and its walls had been worn smooth by the action of I know not what. The cavern was not dark like the others, it was filled with a soft glow of rose-coloured light, more beautiful to look on than anything that can be conceived. But at first we saw no flashes, and heard no more of the thunderous sound. Presently, however, as we stood in amaze,[19] gazing at the marvellous sight, and wondering whence the rosy radiance flowed, a dread and beautiful thing happened. Across the far end of the cavern, with a grinding and crashing noise—a noise so dreadful and awe-inspiring that we all trembled, and Job actually sank to his knees—there flamed out an awful cloud or pillar of fire,[20] like a rainbow, many-coloured, and like the lightning bright. For a space, perhaps forty seconds, it flamed and roared thus, turning slowly round and round, and then by degrees the terrible noise ceased, and with the fire it passed away—I know not where—leaving behind it the same rosy glow that we had first seen.[21]

"Draw near, draw near!" cried Ayesha, with a voice of thrilling exultation. "Behold the very Fountain and Heart of Life as it beats in the bosom of the great world. Behold the substance from which all things draw their energy, the bright Spirit of the Globe, without which it cannot live, but must grow cold and dead as the dead moon. Draw near, and wash you in the living flames, and take their virtue into your poor frames in all its virgin strength—not as it now feebly glows within your bosoms, filtered thereto through all the fine strainers of a thousand intermediate lives, but as it is here in the very fount and seat of earthly Being."

We followed her through the rosy glow up to the head of the cave, till at last we stood before the spot where the great pulse beat and the great flame passed. And as we went we became sensible of a wild and splendid exhilaration, of a glorious sense of such a fierce intensity of Life that the most buoyant moments of our strength seemed flat and tame and feeble beside it. It was the mere effluvium of the flame, the subtle ether that it cast off as it passed, working on us, and making us feel strong as giants and swift as eagles.

We reached the head of the cave, and gazed at each other in the glorious glow, and laughed aloud—even Job laughed, and he had not laughed for a week—in the lightness of our hearts and the divine intoxication of our brains. I know that I felt as though all the varied genius of which the human intellect is capable had descended upon me. I could have spoken in blank verse of Shakespearian beauty, all sorts of great ideas flashed through my mind; it was as though the bonds of my flesh had been loosened, and left the spirit free to soar to the empyrean[22] of its native power. The sensations that poured in upon me are indescribable. I seemed to live more keenly, to reach to a higher joy, and sip the goblet of a subtler thought than ever it had been my lot to do before. I was another and most glorified self, and all the avenues of the Possible were for a space laid open to the footsteps of the Real.

Then, suddenly, whilst I rejoiced in this splendid vigour of a new-found self, from far, far away there came a dreadful muttering noise, that grew and grew to a crash and a roar, which combined in itself all that is terrible and yet splendid in the possibilities of sound. Nearer it came, and nearer yet, till it was close upon us, rolling down like all the thunder-wheels of heaven behind the horses of the lightning. On it came, and with it came the glorious blinding cloud of many-coloured light, and stood before us for a space, turning, as it seemed to us, slowly round and round, and then, accompanied by its attendant pomp of sound, passed away I know not whither.

So astonishing was the wondrous sight that one and all of us, save *She*, who stood up and stretched her hands towards the fire, sank down before it, and hid our faces in the sand.

When it was gone, Ayesha spoke.

"Now, Kallikrates," she said, "the mighty moment is at hand. When the great flame comes again thou must stand in it. First throw aside thy garments, for it will burn them, though thee it will not hurt. Thou must stand in the flame while thy senses will endure, and when it embraces thee suck the fire down into thy very heart, and let it leap and play around thy every part, so that thou lose no moiety of its virtue. Hearest thou me, Kallikrates?"

"I hear thee, Ayesha," answered Leo, "but, of a truth—I am no coward —but I doubt me of that raging flame. How know I that it will not utterly destroy me, so that I lose myself and lose thee also? Nevertheless will I do it," he added.

Ayesha thought for a minute, and then said—

"It is not wonderful that thou shouldst doubt. Tell me, Kallikrates: if thou seest me stand in the flame and come forth unharmed, wilt thou enter also?"

Yes," he answered, "I will enter, even if it slay me. I have said that I will enter now."

"And that will I also," I cried.

"What, my Holly!" she laughed, aloud; "methought that thou wouldst naught of length of days. Why, how is this?"

"Nay, I know not," I answered, "but there is that in my heart that calleth me to taste of the flame, and live."

"It is well," she said. "Thou art not altogether lost in folly. See now, I will for the second time bathe me in this living bath. Fain would I add to my beauty and my length of days if that be possible. If it be not possible, at the least it cannot harm me.[23]

"Also," she continued, after a momentary pause, "is there another and a deeper cause why I would once again dip me in the flame. When first I tasted of its virtue full was my heart of passion and of hatred of that Egyptian Amenartas, and therefore, despite my strivings to be rid thereof, have passion and hatred been stamped upon my soul from that sad hour to this. But now it is otherwise. Now is my mood a happy mood, and filled am I with the purest part of thought, and so would I ever be. Therefore, Kallikrates, will I once more wash and make me pure and clean, and yet more fit for thee. Therefore also, when thou dost in turn stand in the fire, empty all thy heart of evil, and let soft contentment hold the balance of thy mind.

Shake loose thy spirit's wings, and take thy stand upon the utter verge of holy contemplation; ay, dream upon thy mother's kiss, and turn thee towards the vision of the highest good that hath ever swept on silver wings across the silence of thy dreams. For from the germ of what thou art in that dread moment shall grow the fruit of what thou shalt be for all unreckoned time.

"Now prepare thee, prepare! even as though thy last hour were at hand, and thou wast about to cross to the Land of Shadows, and not through the Gates of Glory into the realms of Life made beautiful. Prepare, I say!"

XXVI.
What We Saw.

Then came a few moments' pause, during which Ayesha seemed to be gathering up her strength for the fiery trial, while we clung to each other, and waited in utter silence.

At last from far far away, came the first murmur of sound, that grew and grew till it began to crash and bellow in the distance. As she heard it, Ayesha swiftly threw off her gauzy wrapping, loosened the golden snake from her kirtle, and then, shaking her lovely hair about her like a garment, beneath its cover slipped the kirtle off, and replaced the snaky belt around her and outside the masses of falling hair. There she stood before us as Eve might have stood before Adam, clad in nothing but her abundant locks, held round her by the golden band; and no words of mine can tell how sweet she looked—and yet how divine. Nearer and nearer came the thunder wheels of fire, and as they came she pushed one ivory arm through the dark masses of her hair and flung it round Leo's neck.

"Oh, my love, my love," she murmured, "wilt thou ever know how I have loved thee!" and she kissed him on the forehead, and then went and stood in the pathway of the flame of Life.

There was, I remember, to my mind something very touching about her words and that embrace upon the forehead. It was like a mother's kiss, and seemed to convey a benediction with it.

On came the crashing, rolling noise, and the sound of it was as the sound of a forest being swept flat by a mighty wind, and then tossed up like so much grass, and thundered down a mountain-side. Nearer and nearer it came; now flashes of light, forerunners of the revolving pillar of flame, were passing like arrows through the rosy air; and now the edge of the pillar itself appeared. Ayesha turned towards it, and stretched out her arms to greet it. On it came very slowly, and lapped her round with flame. I saw the fire run up her form. I saw her lift it with both her hands as though it were water, and pour it over her head. I even saw her open her mouth and draw it down into her lungs, and a dread and wonderful sight it was.

Then she paused, and stretched out her arms, and stood there quite still, with a heavenly smile upon her face, as though she were the very Spirit of the Flame.

The mysterious fire played up and down her dark and rolling locks, twining and twisting itself through and around them like threads of golden lace; it gleamed upon her ivory breast and shoulder, from which the hair had slipped aside; it slid along her pillared throat and delicate features, and seemed to find a home in the glorious eyes that shone and shone, more brightly even than the spiritual essence.

Oh, how beautiful she looked there in the flame! No angel out of heaven could have worn a greater loveliness. Even now my heart faints before the recollection of it, as she stood and smiled at our awed faces, and I would give half my remaining time upon this earth to see her once like that again.

But suddenly—more suddenly than I can describe—a kind of change came over her face, a change which I could not define, or explain, but none the less a change. The smile vanished, and in its place there came a dry, hard look; the rounded face seemed to grow pinched, as though some great anxiety were leaving its impress upon it. The glorious eyes, too, lost their light, and, as I thought, the form its perfect shape and erectness.

I rubbed my eyes, thinking that I was the victim of some hallucination, or that the refraction from the intense light produced an optical delusion; and, as I did so, the flaming pillar slowly twisted and thundered off whithersoever it passes to in the bowels of the great earth, leaving Ayesha standing where it had been.

As soon as it was gone, she stepped forward to Leo's side—it seemed to me that there was no spring in her step—and stretched out her hand to lay it on his shoulder. I gazed at her arm. Where was its wonderful roundness and beauty? It was getting thin and angular. And her face—by Heaven! —*her face was growing old before my eyes!* I suppose that Leo saw it also; certainly he recoiled a step or two.

"What is it, my Kallikrates?" she said, and her voice—what was the matter with those deep and thrilling notes? They were quite high and cracked.

"Why, what is it—what is it?" she said, confusedly. "I feel dazed. Surely the quality of the fire hath not altered. Can the principle of Life alter? Tell me, Kallikrates, is there aught wrong with my eyes? I see not clear," and she put her hand to her head and touched her hair—and oh, *horror of horrors!* —it all fell upon the floor.[1]

"Oh, *look!—look!—look!*" shrieked Job, in a shrill falsetto of terror, his eyes nearly dropping out of his head, and foam upon his lips. "*Look! —look!—look!* she's shrivelling up! she's turning into a monkey!" and down he fell upon the ground, foaming and gnashing in a fit.

True enough—I faint even as I write it in the living presence of that terrible recollection—she *was* shrivelling up; the golden snake that had encircled her gracious form slipped over her hips and to the ground; smaller and smaller she grew; her skin changed colour, and in place of the perfect whiteness of its lustre it turned dirty brown and yellow, like an old piece of withered parchment. She felt at her head; the delicate hand was nothing but a claw now, a human talon like that of a badly-preserved Egyptian mummy, and then she seemed to realise what kind of change was passing over her, and she shrieked—ah, she shrieked!—she rolled upon the floor and shrieked!

Smaller she grew, and smaller yet, till she was no larger than a monkey. Now the skin was puckered into a million wrinkles, and on the shapeless face was the stamp of unutterable age. I never saw anything like it; nobody ever saw anything like the frightful age that was graven on that fearful countenance, no bigger now than that of a two-months' child, though the skull remained the same size, or nearly so, and let all men pray they never may, if they wish to keep their reason.

At last she lay still, or only feebly moving. She who, but two minutes before had gazed upon us the loveliest, noblest, most splendid woman the world has ever seen, she lay still before us, near the masses of her own dark hair, no larger than a big monkey, and hideous—ah, too hideous for words. And yet, think of this—at that very moment I thought of it— it was the *same* woman!

She was dying: we saw it, and thanked God—for while she lived she could feel, and what must she have felt? She raised herself upon her bony hands, and blindly gazed around her, swaying her head slowly from side to side as a tortoise does. She could not see, for her whitish eyes were covered with a horny film. Oh, the horrible pathos of the sight! But she could still speak.

"Kallikrates," she said, in husky, trembling notes. "Forget me not, Kallikrates. Have pity on my shame; I shall come again, and shall once more be beautiful, I swear it—it is true! *Oh-h-h-*" and she fell upon her face, and was still.

On the very spot where more than twenty centuries before she had slain Kallikrates the priest, she herself fell down and died.[2]

Overcome with the extremity of horror, we too, fell on the sandy floor of that dread place, and swooned away.

• • • • •

I know not how long we remained thus. Many hours, I suppose. When at last I opened my eyes, the other two were still outstretched upon the floor. The rosy light yet beamed like a celestial dawn, and the thunder-wheels of the Spirit of Life yet rolled upon their accustomed track, for as I awoke the great pillar was passing away. There, too, lay the hideous little monkey frame, covered with crinkled yellow parchment, that once had been the glorious *She*. Alas! it was no hideous dream—it was an awful and unparalleled fact!

What had happened to bring this shocking change about? Had the nature of the life-giving Fire changed? Did it, perhaps, from time to time send forth an essence of Death instead of an essence of Life? Or was it that the frame once charged with its marvellous virtue could bear no more, so that were the process repeated—it mattered not at what lapse of time—the two impregnations neutralised each other, and left the body on which they acted as it was before it ever came into contact with the very essence of Life? This, and this alone, would account for the sudden and terrible ageing of Ayesha, as the whole length of her two thousand years took effect upon her. I have not the slightest doubt myself but that the frame now lying before me was just what the frame of a woman would be if by any extraordinary means life could be preserved in her till she at length died at the age of two-and-twenty centuries.

But who can tell what had happened? There was the fact. Often since that awful hour I have reflected that it requires no great stretch of imagination to see the finger of Providence in the matter. Ayesha locked up in her living tomb waiting from age to age for the coming of her lover worked but a small change in the order of the World. But Ayesha strong and happy in her love, clothed in immortal youth and goddess beauty, and the wisdom of the centuries, would have revolutionised society, and even perchance have changed the destiny of Mankind. Thus she opposed herself against the eternal law, and, strong though she was, by it was swept back to nothingness—swept back with shame and hideous mockery!

For some minutes I lay faintly turning these terrors over in my mind, while my physical strength came back to me, which it quickly did in that buoyant atmosphere. Then I bethought me of the others, and staggered to my feet, to see if I could arouse them. But first I took up Ayesha's kirtle and the gauzy scarf with which she had been wont to hide her dazzling loveliness from the eyes of men, and, averting my head so that I might not look upon it, covered up that dreadful relic of the glorious dead, that shocking epitome of human beauty and human life. I did this hurriedly, fearing lest Leo should recover, and see it again.

Then, stepping over the perfumed masses of dark hair that lay upon the sand, I stopped down by Job, who was lying upon his face, and turned him over. As I did so his arm fell back in a way that I did not like, and which sent a chill through me, and I glanced sharply at him. One look was enough. Our old and faithful servant was dead. His nerves, already shattered by all he had seen and undergone, had utterly broken down beneath this last dire sight, and he had died of terror, or in a fit brought on by terror. One had only to look at his face to see it.

It was another blow; but perhaps it may help people to understand how overwhelmingly awful was the experience through which we had passed —we did not feel it much at the time. It seemed quite natural that the poor old fellow should be dead. When Leo came to himself, which he did with a groan and trembling of the limbs about ten minutes afterwards, and I told him that Job was dead, he merely said, "*Oh!*" And, mind you, this was from no heartlessness, for he and Job were much attached to each other; and he often talks of him now with the deepest regret and affection. It was only that his nerves would bear no more. A harp can give out but a certain quantity of sound, however heavily it is smitten.

Well, I set myself to recovering Leo, who, to my infinite relief, I found was not dead, but only fainting, and in the end I succeeded, as I have said, and he sat up; and then I saw another dreadful thing. When we entered that awful place his curling hair had been of the ruddiest gold, now it was turning grey, and by the time we gained the outer air it was snow white. Besides, he looked twenty years older.

"What is to be done, old fellow?" he said in a hollow, dead sort of voice, when his mind had cleared a little, and a recollection of what had happened forced itself upon it.

"Try and get out, I suppose," I answered; "that is, unless you would like to go in there," and I pointed to the column of fire that was once more rolling by.

"I would go in if I were sure that it would kill me," he said with a little laugh. "It was my cursed hesitation that did this. If I had not been doubtful she might never have tried to show me the road. But I am not sure. The fire might have the opposite effect upon me. It might make me immortal; and, old fellow, I have not the patience to wait a couple of thousand years for her to come back again as she did for me. I had rather die when my hour comes—and I should fancy that it isn't far off either— and go my ways to look for her. Do you go in if you like."

But I merely shook my head, my excitement was as dead as ditch-water, and my distaste for the prolongation of my mortal span had come back upon me more strongly than ever. Besides, we neither of us knew what the effects of the fire might be. The result upon *She* had not been of an encouraging nature, and of the exact causes that produced that result we were, of course, ignorant.

"Well, my boy," I said, "we can't stop here till we go the way of those two," and I pointed to the little heap under the white garment and to the stiffening corpse of poor Job. "If we are going we had better go. But, by the way, I expect that the lamps have burnt out," and I took one up and looked at it, and sure enough it had.

"There is some more oil in the vase," said Leo indifferently, "if it is not broken, at least."

I examined the vessel in question—it was intact. With a trembling hand I filled the lamps—luckily there was still some of the linen wick unburnt. Then I lit them with one of our wax matches. While I did so we heard the pillar of fire approaching once more as it went on its never-ending journey, if, indeed, it was the same pillar that passed and repassed in a circle.

"Let's see it come once more," said Leo; "we shall never look upon its like again in this world."

It seemed a bit of idle curiosity, but somehow I shared it, and so we waited till, turning slowly round upon its own axis, it had flamed and thundered by; and I remember wondering for how many thousands of years this same phenomenon had been taking place in the bowels of the earth, and for how many more thousands it would continue to take place. I wondered also if any mortal eyes would ever again mark its passage, or any mortal ears be thrilled and fascinated by the swelling volume of its majestic sound. I do not think that they will. I believe that we are the last human beings who will ever see that earthly sight. Presently it had gone, and we too turned to go.

But before we did so we each took Job's cold hand in ours and shook it. It was a rather ghastly ceremony, but it was the only means in our power of showing our respect to the faithful dead and of celebrating his obsequies. The heap beneath the white garment we did not uncover. We had no wish to look upon that terrible sight again. But we went to the pile of rippling hair that had fallen from her in the agony of that hideous change which was worse than a thousand natural deaths, and each of us drew from it a shining lock, and these locks we still have, the sole memento that is left to us of Ayesha as we knew her in the fulness of her grace and glory. Leo pressed the perfumed hair to his lips.

"She called to me not to forget her," he said hoarsely; "and swore that we should meet again. By Heaven! I never will forget her. Here I swear that, if we live to get out of this, I will not for all my days have anything to say to another living woman, and that wherever I go I will wait for her as faithfully as she waited for me."

"Yes," I thought to myself, "if she comes back as beautiful as we knew her. But supposing she came back *like that!*"*

Well, and then we went. We went, and left those two in the presence of the very well and spring of Life, but gathered to the cold company of Death. How lonely they looked as they lay there, and how ill-assorted! That little heap had been for two thousand years the wisest, loveliest, proudest creature—I can hardly call her woman—in the whole universe. She had been wicked, too, in her way; but, alas! such is the frailty of the human

---

*What a terrifying reflection it is, by the way, that nearly all our deep love for women who are not our kindred depends—at any rate, in the first instance—upon their personal appearance. If we lost them, and found them again dreadful to look on, though otherwise they were the very same, should we still love them?—L.H.H.[3]

heart, her wickedness had not detracted from her charm. Indeed, I am by no means certain that it did not add to it. It was after all of a grand order, there was nothing mean or small about Ayesha.[4]

And poor Job, too! His presentiment had come true, and there was an end of him. Well, he has a strange burial-place—no Norfolk hind[5] ever had a stranger, or ever will; and it is something to lie in the same sepulchre with the poor remains of the imperial *She.*

We looked our last upon them and the indescribable rosy glow in which they lay, and then with hearts far too heavy for words we left them, and crept thence broken-down men—so broken down that we even renounced the chance of practically immortal life, because all that made life valuable had gone from us, and we knew even that to prolong our days indefinitely would only be to prolong our sufferings. For we felt—yes, both of us— that having once looked Ayesha in the eyes, we could not forget her for ever and ever while memory and identity remained. We both loved her now and for all time, she was stamped and carven on our hearts, and no other woman or interest could ever raze that splendid die. And I—there lies the sting—I had and have no right to think thus of her. As she told me, I was naught to her, and never shall be through the unfathomed depth of Time, unless, indeed, conditions alter, and a day comes at last when two men may love one woman, and all three be happy in the fact. It is the only hope of my broken-heartedness, and a rather faint one. Beyond it I have nothing. I have paid down this heavy price, all that I am worth here and hereafter, and that is my sole reward. With Leo it is different, and often and often I bitterly envy him his happy lot, for if *She* was right, and her wisdom and knowledge did not fail her at the last, which, arguing from the precedent of her own case, I think most unlikely, he has some future to look forward to. But I have none, and yet—mark the folly and the weakness of the human heart, and let him who is wise learn wisdom from it—yet I would not have it otherwise. I mean that I am content to give what I have given and must always give, and take in payment those crumbs that fall from my mistress's table, the memory of a few kind words, the hope one day in the far undreamed future of a sweet smile or two of recognition, a little gentle friendship, and a little show of thanks for my devotion to her—and Leo.

If that does not constitute true love, I do not know what does, and all I have to say is that it is a very bad state of mind for a man on the wrong side of middle age to fall into.

XXVII.
We Leap.

We passed through the caves without trouble, but when we came to the slope of the inverted cone two difficulties stared us in the face. The first of these was the laborious nature of the ascent, and the next the extreme difficulty of finding our way. Indeed, had it not been for the mental notes that I had fortunately taken of the shape of various rocks, I am sure that we never should have managed it at all, but have wandered about in the dreadful womb of the volcano—for I suppose it must once have been something of the sort—until we died of exhaustion and despair. As it was we went wrong several times, and once nearly fell into a huge crack or crevasse. It was terrible work creeping about in the dense gloom and awful stillness from boulder to boulder, and examining it by the feeble light of the lamps to see if I could recognise its shape. We rarely spoke, our hearts were too heavy for speech, we simply stumbled about, falling sometimes and cutting ourselves, in a rather dogged sort of way. The fact was that our spirits were utterly crushed, and we did not greatly care what happened to us. Only we felt bound to try and save our lives whilst we could, and indeed a natural instinct prompted us to it. So for some three or four hours, I should think —I cannot tell exactly how long, for we had no watch left that would go —we blundered on. During the last two hours we were completely lost, and I began to fear that we had got into the funnel of some subsidiary cone, when at last I suddenly recognised a very large rock which we had passed in descending but a little way from the top. It is a marvel that I should have recognised it, and, indeed, we had already passed it going at right angles to the proper path, when something about it struck me, and I turned back and examined it in an idle sort of way, and, as it happened, this proved our salvation.

After this we gained the rocky natural stair without much further trouble, and in due course found ourselves back in the little chamber where the benighted Noot had lived and died.[1]

But now a fresh terror stared us in the face. It will be remembered that owing to Job's fear and awkwardness, the plank upon which we had crossed from the huge spur to the rocking-stone had been whirled off into the tremendous gulf below.

How were we to cross without the plank?

There was only one answer—we must try and *jump* it, or else stop there till we starved. The distance in itself was not so very great, between eleven and twelve feet[2] I should think, and I have seen Leo jump over twenty when he was a young fellow at college; but then, think of the conditions. Two weary, worn-out men, one of them on the wrong side of forty, a rocking-stone to take off from, a trembling point of rock some few feet across to land upon, and a bottomless gulf to be cleared in a raging gale! It was bad enough, God knows, but when I pointed out these things to Leo, he put the whole matter in a nutshell by replying that, merciless as the choice was, we must choose between the certainty of a lingering death in the chamber and the risk of a swift one in the air. Of course, there was no arguing against this, but one thing was clear, we could not attempt that leap in the dark; the only thing to do was to wait for the ray of light which pierced through the gulf at sunset. How near to or how far from sunset we might be, neither of us had the faintest notion; all we did know was, that when at last the light came it would not endure more than a couple of minutes at the outside, so that we must be prepared to meet it. Accordingly, we made up our minds to creep on to the top of the rocking-stone and lie there in readiness. We were the more easily reconciled to this course by the fact that our lamps were once more nearly exhausted—indeed, one had gone out bodily, and the other was jumping up and down as the flame of a lamp does when the oil is done. So, by the aid of its dying light, we hastened to crawl out of the little chamber and clamber up the side of the great stone.

As we did so the light went out.

The difference in our position was a sufficiently remarkable one. Below, in the little chamber, we had only heard the roaring of the gale overhead —here, lying on our faces on the swinging stone, we were exposed to its full force and fury, as the great draught drew first from this direction and then from that, howling against the mighty precipice and through the rocky cliffs like ten thousand despairing souls. We lay there hour after hour in terror and misery of mind so deep that I will not attempt to describe it, and listened to the wild storm-voices of that Tartarus,[3] as, set to the deep undertone of the spur opposite against which the wind hummed like some awful harp, they called to each other from precipice to precipice. No night-mare dreamed by man, no wild invention of the romancer, can ever equal the living horror of that place, and the weird crying of those voices of the night, as we clung like shipwrecked mariners to a raft, and tossed on the black, unfathomed wilderness of air. Fortunately the temperature was not a low one; indeed, the wind was warm, or we should have perished. So, we clung and listened, and while we were stretched out upon the rock a thing happened which was so curious and suggestive in itself, though doubt-less a mere coincidence, that, if anything, it added to, rather than deducted from, the burden on our nerves.

It will be remembered that when Ayesha was standing on the spur, be-fore we crossed to the stone, the wind tore her cloak from her, and whirled it away into the darkness of the gulf, we could not see whither. Well— I hardly like to tell the story; it is so strange. As we lay there upon the rocking-stone, this very cloak came floating out of the black space, like a memory from the dead, and fell on Leo—so that it covered him nearly from head to foot. We could not at first make out what it was, but soon discovered by its feel, and then poor Leo, for the first time, gave way, and I heard him sobbing there upon the stone. No doubt the cloak had been caught upon some pinnacle of the cliff, and was thence blown hither by a chance gust; but still, it was a most curious and touching incident.

Shortly after this, suddenly, without the slightest previous warning, the great red knife of light came stabbing the darkness through and through—struck the swaying stone on which we were, and rested its sharp point upon the spur opposite.

"Now for it," said Leo, "now or never."

We rose and stretched ourselves, and looked at the cloud-wreaths stained the colour of blood by that red ray as they tore through the sickening depths beneath, and then at the empty space between the swaying stone and the quivering rock, and, in our hearts, despaired, and prepared for death. Surely we could not clear it—desperate though we were.

"Who is to go first?" said I.

"Do you, old fellow," answered Leo. "I will sit upon the other side of the stone to steady it. You must take as much run as you can, and jump high; and God have mercy on us, say I."

I acquiesced with a nod, and then I did a thing I had never done since Leo was a little boy. I turned and put my arm round him, and kissed him on the forehead. It sounds rather French, but as a fact I was taking my last farewell of a man whom I could not have loved more if he had been my own son twice over.

"Good-bye, my boy," I said, "I hope that we shall meet again, wherever it is that we go to."

The fact was I did not expect to live another two minutes.

Next I retreated to the far side of the rock, and waited till one of the chopping gusts of wind got behind me, and then I ran the length of the huge stone,[4] some three or four and thirty feet, and sprang wildly out into the dizzy air. Oh! the sickening terrors that I felt as I launched myself at that little point of rock, and the horrible sense of despair that shot through my brain as I realised that I had *jumped short*! But so it was, my feet never touched the point, they went down into space, only my hands and body came in contact with it. I gripped at it with a yell, but one hand slipped, and I swung right round, holding by the other, so that I faced the stone from which I had sprung. Wildly I stretched up with my left hand, and this time managed to grasp a knob of rock, and there I hung in the fierce red light, with thousands of feet of empty air beneath me. My hands were holding to either side of the underpart of the spur, so that its point was touching my head. Therefore, even if I could have found the strength, I could not pull myself up. The most that I could do would be to hang for about a minute, and then drop down, down into the bottomless pit. If any man can imagine a more hideous position, let him speak! All I know is that the torture of that half-minute nearly turned my brain.

I heard Leo give a cry, and then suddenly saw him in mid air springing up and out like a chamois. It was a splendid leap that he took under the influence of his terror and despair, clearing the horrible gulf as though it were nothing, and landing well on to the rocky point, he threw himself upon his face, to prevent his pitching off into the depths. I felt the spur above me shake beneath the shock of his impact, and as it did so I saw the huge rocking-stone, that had been violently depressed by him as he sprang, fly back when relieved of his weight till, for the first time during all these centuries, it got beyond its balance, and fell with a most awful crash right into the rocky chamber which had once served the philosopher Noot for a hermitage, and, I have no doubt, for ever sealed the passage the leads to the Place of Life with some hundreds of tons of rock.

All this happened in a second, and curiously enough, notwithstanding my terrible position, I noted it involuntarily, as it were. I even remember thinking that no human being would go down that dread path again.

Next instant I felt Leo seize me by the right wrist with both hands. By lying flat on the point of rock he could just reach me.

"You must let go and swing yourself clear," he said in a calm and collected voice, "and then I will try and pull you up, or we will both go together. Are you ready?"

By way of answer I let go, first with my left hand and then with the right, and, as a consequence, swayed out clear of the overshadowing rock, my weight hanging upon Leo's arms. It was a dreadful moment. He was a very powerful man, I knew, but would his strength be equal to lifting me up till I could get a hold on the top of the spur, when owing to his position he had so little purchase?

For a few seconds I swung to and fro, while he gathered himself for the effort, and then I heard his sinews cracking above me, and felt myself lifted up as though I were a little child, till I got my left arm round the rock, and my chest was resting on it. The rest was easy; in two or three more seconds I was up, and we were lying panting side by side, trembling like leaves, and with the cold perspiration of terror pouring from our skins.

And then, as before, the light went out like a lamp.

For some half-hour we lay thus without speaking a word, and then at length began to creep along the great spur as best we might in the dense gloom. As we drew towards the face of the cliff, however, from which the spur sprung out like a spike from a wall, the light increased, though only a very little, for it was night overhead. After that the gusts of wind decreased, and we got along rather better, and at last reached the mouth of the first cave or tunnel. But now a fresh trouble stared us in the face: our oil was gone, and the lamps were, no doubt, crushed to powder beneath the fallen rocking-stone. We were even without a drop of water to stay our thirst, for we had drunk the last in the chamber of Noot. How were we to see to make our way through this last boulder-strewn tunnel?

Clearly all that we could do was to trust to our sense of feeling, and attempt the passage in the dark, so in we crept, fearing that if we delayed to do so our exhaustion would overcome us, and we should probably lie down and die where we were.

Oh, the horrors of that last tunnel! The place was strewn with rocks, and we fell over them, and knocked ourselves up against them till we were bleeding from a score of wounds. Our only guide was the side of the cavern, which we kept touching, and so bewildered did we grow in the darkness that we were several times seized with the terrifying thought that we had turned, and were travelling the wrong way. On we went, feebly, and still more feebly, for hour after hour, stopping every few minutes to rest, for our strength was spent. Once we fell asleep, and, I think, must have slept for some hours, for, when we woke, our limbs were quite stiff, and the blood from our blows and scratches had caked, and was hard and dry upon our skin. Then we dragged ourselves on again, till at last, when despair was entering into our hearts, we once more saw the light of day, and found ourselves outside the tunnel in the rocky fold on the outer surface of the cliff that, it will be remembered, led into it.

It was early morning—that we could tell by the feel of the sweet air and the look of the blessed sky, which we had never hoped to see again. It was, so near as we knew, an hour after sunset when we entered the tunnel, so it followed that it had taken us the entire night to crawl through that dreadful place.

"One more effort, Leo," I gasped, "and we shall reach the slope where Billali is, if he hasn't gone. Come, don't give way," for he had cast himself upon his face. He rose, and, leaning on each other, we got down that fifty feet or so of cliff—somehow, I have not the least notion how. I only remember that we found ourselves lying in a heap at the bottom, and then once more began to drag ourselves along on our hands and knees towards the grove where *She* had told Billali to wait her re-arrival, for we could not walk another foot. We had not gone fifty yards in this fashion when suddenly one of the mutes emerged from some trees on our left, through which, I presume, he had been taking a morning stroll, and came running up to see what sort of strange animals we were. He stared, and stared, and then held up his hands in horror, and nearly fell to the ground. Next, he started off as hard as he could for the grove some two hundred yards away. No wonder that he was horrified at our appearance, for we must have been a shocking sight. To begin, Leo with his golden curls turned a snowy white, his clothes nearly rent from his body, his worn face and his hands a mass of bruises, cuts, and blood-encrusted filth, was a sufficiently alarming spectacle, as he painfully dragged himself along the ground, and I have no doubt that I was little better to look on. I know that two days afterwards when I inspected my face in some water I scarcely recognised myself. I have never been famous for beauty, but there was something beside ugliness stamped upon my features that I have never got rid of until this day, something resembling that wild look with which a startled person wakes from deep sleep more than anything else that I can think of. And really it is not to be wondered at. What I do wonder at is that we escaped at all with our reason.

Presently to my intense relief, I saw old Billali hurrying towards us, and even then I could scarcely help smiling at the expression of consternation on his dignified countenance.

"Oh, my Baboon! my Baboon!" he cried, "my dear son, is it indeed thee and the Lion? Why his mane that was ripe as corn is white like the snow. Whence come ye? and where is the Pig, and where too *She-who-must-be-obeyed*?"

"Dead, both dead," I answered; "but ask not questions; help us, and give us food and water, or we too shall die before thine eyes. Seest thou not that our tongues are black for want of water? How, then, can we talk?"

"Dead!" he gasped, "impossible. *She* who never dies—dead, how can it be?" and then, perceiving, I think, that his face was being watched by the mutes who had come running up, he checked himself, and motioned to them to carry us to the camp, which they did.

Fortunately when we arrived some broth was boiling on the fire, and with this Billali fed us, for we were too weak to feed ourselves, thereby I firmly believe saving us from death by exhaustion. Then he bade the mutes wash the blood and grime from us with wet cloths, and after that we were laid down upon piles of aromatic grass, and instantly fell into the dead sleep of absolute exhaustion of mind and body.

XXVIII.
Over the Mountain.[1]

The next thing I recollect is a feeling of the most dreadful stiffness, and a sort of vague idea passing through my half-awakened brain that I was a carpet that had just been beaten. I opened my eyes, and the first thing they fell on was the venerable countenance of our old friend, Billali, who was seated by the side of the improvised bed upon which I was sleeping, and thoughtfully stroking his long beard. The sight of him at once brought back to my mind a recollection of all that we had recently passed through, which was accentuated by the vision of poor Leo lying opposite to me, his face knocked almost to a jelly, and his beautiful crowd of curls turned from yellow to white,* and I shut my eyes again and groaned.

---

*Curiously enough, Leo's hair has lately been to some extent regaining its colour—that is to say, it is now a yellowish grey, and I am not without hopes that it will in time come quite right.—L.H.H.[2]

"Thou hast slept long, my Baboon," said old Billali.

"How long, my father?" I asked.

"A round of the sun and a round of the moon, a day and a night hast thou slept, and the Lion also. See, he sleepeth yet."

"Blessed is sleep," I answered, "for it swallows up recollection."

"Tell me," he said, "what hath befallen you, and what is this strange story of the death of Her who dieth not. Bethink thee, my son: if this be true, then is thy danger and the danger of the Lion very great—nay, almost is the pot red wherewith ye shall be potted, and the stomachs of those who shall eat ye are already hungry for the feast. Knowest thou not that these Amahagger, my children, these dwellers in the caves, hate ye? They hate ye as strangers, they hate ye more because of their brethren whom *She* put to the torment for your sake. Assuredly, if once they learn that there is naught to fear from Hiya, from the terrible One-who-must-be-obeyed, they will slay ye by the pot. But let me hear thy tale, my poor Baboon."

Thus adjured, I set to work and told him—not everything, indeed, for I did not think it desirable to do so, but sufficient for my purpose, which was to make him understand that *She* was really no more, having fallen into some fire, and, as I put it—for the real thing would have been incomprehensible to him—been burnt up. I also told him some of the horrors we had undergone in effecting our escape, and these produced a great impression on him. But I clearly saw that he did not believe in the report of Ayesha's death. He believed indeed that we thought that she was dead, but his explanation was that it had suited her to disappear for a while. Once, he said, in his father's time, she had done so for twelve[3] years, and there was a tradition in the country that many centuries back no one had seen her for a whole generation, when she suddenly reappeared, and destroyed a woman who had assumed the position of Queen. I said nothing to this, but only shook my head, sadly. Alas! I knew too well that Ayesha would appear no more, or at any rate that Billali would never see her again.

"And now," concluded Billali, "what wouldst thou do, my Baboon?"

"Nay," I said, "I know not, my father. Can we not escape from this country?"

He shook his head.

"It is very difficult. By Kôr ye cannot pass, for ye would be seen, and as soon as those fierce ones found that ye were alone, well," and he smiled significantly, and made a movement as though he were placing a hat on his head. "But there is a way over the cliff whereof I once spake to thee, where they drive the cattle out to pasture. Then beyond the pastures are three days' journey through the marshes, and after that I know not, but I have heard that seven days' journey from thence is a mighty river, which floweth to the black water. If ye could come thither, perchance ye might escape, but how can ye come thither?"

"Billali," I said, "once, thou knowest, I did save thy life. Now pay back the debt, my father, and save me mine and my friend's, the Lion's. It shall

be a pleasant thing for thee to think of when thine hour comes, and something to set in the scale against the evil doing of thy days, if perchance thou
hast done any evil. Also, if thou be right, and if *She* doth but hide herself,
surely when she comes again she shall reward thee."

"My son the Baboon," answered the old man, "think not that I have
an ungrateful heart. Well do I remember how thou didst rescue me when
those dogs stood by to see me drown. Measure for measure will I give thee,
and if thou canst be saved, surely I will save thee. Listen: by dawn to-morrow
be prepared, for litters shall be here to bear ye away across the mountains,
and through the marshes beyond. This will I do, saying that it is the word
of *She* that it be done, and he who obeyeth not the word of *She* food is
he for the hyænas. Then when ye have crossed the marshes, ye must strike
with your own hands, so that perchance, if good fortune go with you, ye
may live to come to that black water whereof ye told me. And now, see,
the Lion wakes, and ye must eat the food I have made ready for you."

Leo's condition when once he was fairly aroused proved not to be
so bad as might have been expected from his appearance, and we both of
us managed to eat a hearty meal, which indeed we needed sadly enough.
After this we limped down to the spring and bathed, and then came back
and slept again till evening, when we once more ate enough for five. Billali
was away all that day, no doubt making arrangements about litters and bearers, for we were awakened in the middle of the night by the arrival of a
considerable number of men in the little camp.

At dawn the old man himself appeared, and told us that he had by
using *She's* dreaded name, though with some difficulty, succeeded in getting
the necessary men and two guides to conduct us across the swamps, and
that he urged us to start at once, at the same time announcing his intention
of accompanying us, so as to protect us against treachery. I was much touched
by this act of kindness on the part of that wily old barbarian towards two
utterly defenceless strangers. A three—or in his case, for he would have
to return, six-days' journey through those deadly swamps was no light undertaking for a man of his age, but he consented to do it cheerfully in order
to promote our safety. It shows that even among those dreadful Amahagger
—who are certainly with their gloom and their devilish and ferocious rites
by far the most terrible savages that I ever heard of—there are people
with kindly hearts. Of course self-interest may have had something to do
with it. He may have thought that *She* would suddenly reappear and demand
an account of us at his hands, but still, allowing for all deductions, it was
a great deal more than we could expect under the circumstances, and I can
only say that I shall for as long as I live cherish a most affectionate remem-
brance of my nominal parent, old Billali.

Accordingly, after swallowing some food, we started in the litters, feeling,
so far as our bodies went, wonderfully like our old selves after our long
rest and sleep. I must leave the condition of our minds to the imagination.

Then came a terrible pull up the cliff. Sometimes the ascent was natural, more often it was a zig-zag roadway cut, no doubt, in the first instance by the old inhabitants of Kôr. The Amahagger say they drive their spare cattle over it once a year to pasture outside; all I know is that those cattle must be uncommonly active on their feet. Of course the litters were useless here, so we had to walk.

By mid-day, however, we reached the great flat top of that mighty wall of rock, and grand enough the view was from it, with the plain of Kôr, in the centre of which we could clearly make out the pillared ruins of the Temple of Truth to the one side, and the boundless and melancholy marsh on the other. This wall of rock, which had no doubt once formed the lip of the crater, was about a mile and a half thick, and still covered with clinker.[4] Nothing grew there, and the only thing to relieve our eyes were occasional pools of rain-water (for rain had lately fallen) wherever there was a little hollow. Over the flat crest of this mighty rampart we went, and then came the descent, which, if not so difficult a matter as the getting up, was still sufficiently break-neck, and took us till sunset. That night, however, we camped in safety upon the mighty slopes that rolled away to the marsh beneath.

On the following morning, about eleven o'clock, began our dreary journey across those awful seas of swamps which I have already described.

For three whole days, through stench and mire, and the all prevailing flavour of fever, did our bearers struggle along, till at length we came to open rolling ground quite uncultivated, and mostly treeless, but covered with game of all sorts, which lies beyond that most desolate, and without guides utterly impracticable, district. And here on the following morning we bade farewell, not without some regret, to old Billali, who stroked his white beard and solemnly blessed us.

"Farewell, my son the Baboon," he said, "and farewell to thee too, oh Lion. I can do no more to help you. But if ever ye come to your country, be advised, and venture no more into lands that ye know not, lest ye come back no more, but leave your white bones to mark the limit of your journeyings. Farewell once more; often shall I think of you, nor wilt thou forget me, my Baboon, for though thy face is ugly thy heart is true." And then he turned and went, and with him went the tall and sullen-looking bearers, and that was the last that we saw of the Amahagger. We watched them winding away with the empty litters like a procession bearing dead men from a battle, till the mists from the marsh gathered round them and hid them, and then, left utterly desolate in the vast wilderness, we turned and gazed around us and at each other.

Three weeks or so before four men had entered the marshes of Kôr, and now two of us were dead, and the other two had gone through adventures and experiences so strange and terrible that death himself hath not a more fearful countenance. Three weeks—and only three weeks! Truly time should be measured by events, and not by the lapse of hours. It seemed like thirty years since we saw the last of our whale-boat.

"We must strike out for the Zambesi, Leo," I said, "but God knows if we shall ever get there."

Leo nodded. He had become very silent of late, and we started with nothing but the clothes we stood in, a compass, our revolvers and express rifles, and about two hundred rounds of ammunition, and so ended the history of our visit to the ancient ruins of mighty and imperial Kôr.

As for the adventures that subsequently befell us, strange and varied as they were, I have, after deliberation, determined not to record them here. In these pages I have only tried to give a short and clear account of an occurrence which I believe to be unprecedented, and this I have done, not with a view to immediate publication, but merely to put on paper while they are yet fresh in our memories the details of our journey and its result, which will, I believe, prove interesting to the world if ever we determine to make them public. This, as at present advised, we do not intend should be done during our joint lives.

For the rest, it is of no public interest, resembling as it does the experience of more than one Central African traveller. Suffice it to say, that we did, after incredible hardships and privations, reach the Zambesi, which proved to be about a hundred and seventy miles south of where Billali left us.[5] There we were for six months imprisoned by a savage tribe, who believed us to be supernatural beings, chiefly on account of Leo's youthful face and snow-white hair. From these people we ultimately escaped, and, crossing the Zambesi, wandered off southwards, where, when on the point of starvation, we were sufficiently fortunate to fall in with a half-caste Portuguese elephant-hunter who had followed a troop of elephants farther inland than he had ever been before. This man treated us most hospitably, and ultimately through his assistance we, after innumerable sufferings and adventures, reached Delagoa Bay, more than eighteen months from the time when we emerged from the marshes of Kôr, and the very next day managed to catch one of the steamboats[6] that run round the Cape to England. Our journey home was a prosperous one, and we set our foot on the quay at Southampton exactly two years from the date of our departure upon our wild and seemingly ridiculous quest, and I now write these last words with Leo leaning over my shoulder in my old room in my college, the very same into which some two-and-twenty years ago my poor friend Vincey came stumbling on the memorable night of his death, bearing the iron chest with him.

And that is the end of this history so far as it concerns science and the outside world. What its end will be as regards Leo and myself is more than I can guess at. But we feel that is not reached yet. A story that began more than two thousand years ago may stretch a long way into the dim and distant future.[7]

Is Leo really a reincarnation of the ancient Kallikrates of whom the inscription tells? Or was Ayesha deceived by some strange hereditary resemblance? The reader must form his own opinion on this as on many other matters. I have mine, which is that she made no such mistake.

Often I sit alone at night, staring with the eyes of the mind into the blackness of unborn time, and wondering in what shape and form the great drama will be finally developed, and where the scene of its next act will be laid. And when that *final* development ultimately occurs, as I have no doubt it must and will occur, in obedience to a fate that never swerves and a purpose that cannot be altered, what will be the part played therein by that beautiful Egyptian Amenartas, the Princess of the royal race of the Pharaohs, for the love of whom the Priest Kallikrates broke his vows to Isis, and, pursued by the inexorable vengeance of the outraged Goddess, fled down the coast of Libya to meet his doom at Kôr?[8]

NOTES

Numbered notes are by the editor of the present critical edition. Asterisked notes appearing on the text pages are by Haggard. Wherever "Editor" appears in the asterisked notes, it refers to Haggard's fictional editor. The following abbreviations have been used:

MS = Haggard's original manuscript of *She*
GS = the *Graphic* serialization of 1886–87
1st ed. = the first edition published by Longmans in January 1887
1888 ed. = the New Edition of 1888, on which the text of this critical edition is based

1. Andrew Lang was the influential classical scholar and critic who first championed Haggard's work. Lang had developed the theory that the works of Homer were the product of a barbarous and primitive people. It followed that they would be better understood by comparing them to the myths and tales of present-day "primitive" peoples. This idea led Lang to take an interest in Zulu mythology as recorded by the Anglican missionary Henry Callaway. When Lang read *King Solomon's Mines*, he was impressed by Haggard's use of Zulu material and hailed the author as a writer who could reinvigorate English prose as Greek literature had been invigorated by Homer and other early bards. Haggard was flattered by Lang's attention and they soon formed a firm friendship, which led eventually to collaboration on a novel, *The World's Desire* (1891). Haggard seems to have seen in Lang a literary father figure comparable to his mentor in South African affairs, Theophilus Shepstone. Haggard especially valued Lang's classical scholarship. It is not inconceivable that Lang was part of the inspiration for the fictional scholar-adventurer Horace Holly, the narrator of *She*. While GS was in preparation, Haggard sent a copy of the novel to Lang and asked permission to dedicate it to him. Lang wrote back on July 12, 1886, that "it is one of the most astonishing romances I ever read." He also suggested several modifications, which Haggard incorporated in 1st ed.

2. MS has "author."

3. In MS, the time is set at five years ago and the college acquaintance is given as a brother rather than as a friend. Haggard did have older brothers who went to Cambridge. As a younger son he was denied this opportunity. The Latin tag, which does not appear in MS or in GS, suggests that Haggard harbored feelings of inferiority about his inadequate education.

4. In Greek mythology Charon is the boatman who ferries souls across the river Styx in Hades.

5. Haggard himself had been jilted when he was a young man and never really recovered from the experience.

6. MS date is May 1, 1886.

7. Both MS and GS refer to an introduction made through the "Editor's" brother.

8. This reference may be either to the fictional Allan Quatermain, who was pre-

sented as the narrator of Haggard's only previous central African adventure, *King Solomon's Mines*, or to Haggard himself. Given the brotherless condition ascribed to Quatermain, Haggard is more likely. Either way it is worth noting the description that follows: "partly true, and partly an effort of the imagination."

9. MS reads "We are going away again, this time to Thibet, and anticipate that our sojourn there will be a long one." Haggard was deliberately vague about geography to avoid being convicted of falsehood by knowledgeable readers. At the same time, he felt that a setting on this earth lent credibility to otherwise fantastic stories. Later in life he complained that the progress of terrestrial exploration was depriving writers like himself of locations and accurately prophesied that future writers of "romance" would have to resort to other planets ("'Elephant Smashing' and 'Lion Shooting,'" *African Review* 3[June 9, 1894]:762–63.) The sequel set in Tibet (*Ayesha, or the Return of She*) did not come until 1905.

10. Although "Editor" assures readers below that the identities have been disguised, Haggard does little or nothing to indicate that this has been done. The sherd, which he elaborately contrived to add verisimilitude to the story, bears the names Vindex and Vincey. Plays on the names Leo and Holly recur throughout the story.

11. MS: "marvellous creature."

12. MS: "Horace Holly."

13. The lawyers' names and the references to sherd, scarab, and parchments are not in MS. Haggard added them later to enhance verisimilitude.

14. Tibet.

15. MS does refrain from comments. The extensive speculations in this paragraph and the postscript were added in GS. The influence of Lang can be seen clearly in the P.S. of "Editor." On July 25, 1886, Lang wrote to Haggard: "There is a difficulty about Leo. He is not made a very interesting person. Probably he was only a fine animal. Anyhow that can't be helped now [the manuscript was already in the process of being serialized] and never could perhaps. I dare say Kallikrates was no better" (quoted by Haggard in *Days of My Life*, 1:247).

I. MY VISITOR.

1. Paragraph added prior to GS.

2. MS: "degree," not "fellowship." The change illustrates the efforts Haggard made to overcome his unfamiliarity with university life. Many Oxford and Cambridge fellowships provide lifetime membership in a college along with entitlement to room and board.

3. MS: "in the glass reflected," a play on the word *reflect* in the previous sentence. Haggard either had second thoughts or allowed a copy editor to alter his meaning.

4. MS: "Swart," not "Short."

5. Cain, first son of Adam and Eve in Genesis, had a mark set upon him for murdering his brother Abel.

6. MS and GS: "Darwin's theory," i.e., Darwin's theory of evolution, which postulated a distant kinship between man and the great apes.

7. MS and GS add "and I cursed her and fled." This addition reflects Haggard's own bitter memories of being jilted at about the same age.

8. This footnote was added after GS. In MS Haggard used the spelling Callicrates.

9. This account recapitulates the growth of civilization as Haggard understood it: a passing of the torch of greatness from the Egyptians to the Greeks to the Romans to the Franks and finally to the English. The idea of recapitulation was a major force in many areas of thought in the nineteenth century. See Stephen J. Gould, *Ontogeny and Phylogeny* (London, 1977).

10. Slang term for a servant in a college of Cambridge University. In MS Haggard wrote "man."

II. THE YEARS ROLL BY.

1. The late-Victorian treatment of suicide by coroner's courts is examined at length in Olive Anderson, *Suicide in Victorian and Edwardian England* (Oxford, 1987).

2. As there is no other indication of Vincey's first two names, what "M. L." might stand for is left for conjecture.

3. British government bonds, the safest of all possible investments, paying 3 percent interest. As the income from Holly's half of the estate is estimated at £1,000 a year, Vincey's legacy would have amounted to nearly £70,000 a very substantial fortune in those times.

4. Courts of Chancery, under the jurisdiction of Britain's lord chancellor, could take orphans and other disadvantaged children under their protection.

5. In all other instances, the name is given as L. Horace Holly. The name does not appear in this space in GS or 1st ed. Haggard found it much easier to write legal forms than to describe life at Cambridge because he trained as a lawyer. Nevertheless, he held lawyers in low regard, as instanced in the next sentence and in his novelette, *Mr. Meeson's Will* (1888).

6. MS mentions neither Holly's jealousy nor his misogny and gives a more prosaic account of the reasons for hiring a male assistant: "it was not until I had shown them [the college authorities] the will and thereby clearly demonstrated to them that it was not my own [child] that they would consent to this and then the consent was only dependent on my promising that no female nurse would be allowed to take up her quarters in the college. This I did with some difficulty." The theme of fierce single-sex attachments and jealousy of rivals of the opposite sex appears in a great many of Haggard's works.

7. Slang expression for sarcastic banter or jeers.

8. MS: "enough to save his honours that was all." This indicates a second-class honours degree, not a disgraceful result for a conscientious student, and much better than the "gentleman's third" which Haggard might have ascribed to Leo. The qualities of brilliance mentioned in the previous paragraph do not quite accord with the diminished results suggested in the final version.

9. At this time lawyers were not trained by professional courses at a university. Aspiring barristers and solicitors attached themselves to one of the London Inns of Court. That is where Leo would have had his dinners.

III. THE SHERD OF AMENARTAS.

1. MS title: "The Writing on the Sherd."

2. Sèvres ware was the famous porcelain produced by the royal potteries established by Louis XV in 1740; it was produced in the town of Sèvres from 1756 onward. Jean Paul Marat (1743–93) rose to prominence in the French Revolution and led the Cordeliers faction until he was assassinated in his bath by Charlotte Corday. Haggard's coupling of contradictory political symbols with images of breaking and assassination suggests in a somewhat puzzling form the broken love affairs and murders by women that arc related in this and later chapters.

3. Set off an explosion.

4. Wards are the indentations in locks and keys that prevent other keys from opening the mechanism. To "shoot" in this context simply means to open.

5. In MS, the casket was golden and ten, not twelve, inches square.

6. MS: "Accurate translation of the Greek Writing on the Potsherd." Haggard wrote the inscription in English and completed the novel before attempting to have the words put into ancient languages and antique characters. In March 1886 he commissioned a rendering of the inscription into classical Greek from H. A. Holden, who had been headmaster of Ipswich Grammar School when Haggard was a pupil there

(*Days of My Life*, 1:251). Uncial writing is characterized by more curves than are found in the square capital letters used in ancient Roman inscriptions.

7. MS: "from the end of the fourteenth or the commencement of the sixteenth century." Haggard stated that the job of producing the medieval Latin and Old English versions was done by his "friend Dr. Raven who was a very great authority on monkish Latin and medieval English" (*Days of My Life*, 1:251).

8. MS description of the potsherd differs in size, color, and other particulars. The description obviously was rewritten to fit the fake potsherd that Haggard used to produce the colored frontispiece that appears in 1st ed. Every writer of fantasy who seeks verisimilitude needs devices to make incredible things believable, but few have taken so much trouble as Haggard. Inspired by Stevenson's use of a pirate's map in *Treasure Island*, he used an old map to guide Allan Quatermain's party to Kukuanaland in *King Solomon's Mines*. Moreover, he personally prepared a map and went to great lengths to make it appear authentic. In the case of the Sherd of Amenartas he took more extreme measures. Besides commissioning scholars to concoct translations, he and his sister-in-law made up a sherd, which he claimed was good enough to fool experts (*Days of My Life*, 1:248).

9. A Greek pot used to hold liquids.

10. The *scarabæus sacer* was the stone representation of the sacred scarab beetle of ancient Egypt.

11. "Suten se Rā" not in MS.

12. MS and GS add "died 20 May 1856," the year of Haggard's birth.

13. "Love conquers all."

14. MS: "I, Amenartas, of the Royal House of Hor, a Pharaoh of Egypt, wife of Callicrates (the Strong & Beautiful). . . ."

15. MS: "crabbed," not "uncial."

16. MS says, "The translation was a little free but quite accurate." In GS this is changed to "The translation was, as I discovered on further investigation, both accurate and elegant." MS then proceeds without any Greek or further descriptions of the sherd to the paragraph beginning "Perfectly bewildered, I turned. . . . " GS also omits the Greek but does include the description that follows concerning other symbols on the convex side of the sherd. Haggard's elaboration of the Greek and the further description of the sherd reflect both the help he received from Lang and the effort he made to present Holly as a credible Cambridge scholar.

17. A cartouche is an oval figure enclosing the name and title of an Egyptian king; but the cartouche had not been "already mentioned."

18. Here, in place of the long passages concerning the later Roman and medieval inscriptions on the sherd, MS reads:

"Then followed many signatures most of them illegible & some repetition of the sentence 'to thee, my son' till at length the signature took the form, Vindex & other Latin names, through all of which the idea, vengeance was in one way or another preserved, shewing the fact that at that time the family had migrated to Rome. There were some six or eight of these signatures & then came one with the date 800 after it in Roman figures. Next there was a gap of no less than six centuries, if one may except a rude cross in the form, of a sword hilt probably made by some illiterate old Crusader. The following entry in crabbed Latin signed Johannes de Vincey 1445, ran thus, 'This wonderful relic was brought over from Normandy by my ancestor & my father was almost persuaded to destroy it by a holy priest who sayst it is a magical device of the Devils 7 broke it in two but I saved it & mended it."

19. This linguistic speculation is undercut by the "Editor's" introduction, which claims that names have been altered to conceal the identity of Leo Vincey and Horace Holly.

20. MS does not include this document, but it is required to explain how, after the "dark ages" when Greek could not be read, the Vincey family was able to renew the quest.

21. Because the punctuation is sometimes ancient and sometimes modern, this rendition cannot possibly be treated as a facsimile. Haggard omitted an *s* in *ipsa* in the last line of the paragraph (corrected in later editions) and put modern versions of the double *ss* in the final paragraph. Some of these were corrected later.

IV. THE SQUALL.

1. A small, single-masted vessel used in the seas between India and Africa.

2. The word *Arab* has frequently been misused to refer to black Muslims on the East Coast of Africa who speak Swahili. There were incursions of real Arabs in the eighteenth and nineteenth centuries. Haggard, who had not visited the Swahili coast, probably falls into the common error in this passage.

3. This sentence is not in MS. "Monsoon" refers to the prevailing winds that dominate weather patterns from Africa to the Philippines. The winds run in one direction for about half of each year, then in the other. This pattern enables craft such as dhows, which are not good at tacking against the wind, to serve as long-distance trading vessels.

4. "Gentry" is used ironically here, introducing the subject of race for the first time. The ironical attribution of aristocratic names to black slaves was common in plantation economies in the nineteenth and earlier centuries. Classifying East African blacks as gentry, that is, people of gentle birth, is a similar example of patronizing attitudes among whites who considered themselves racially superior.

5. MS says simply "in the north of England" and GS says "Dundee, in the North of England." Why Haggard should wish to be more precise about a matter on which he had apparently no knowledge is a mystery.

6. To protect the boat against the wood worm.

7. Neither this sentence nor the previous two sentences are in the MS. They do not add verisimilitude as the reader has no reason to expect Holly or Vincey to have special knowledge of either Arab captains or the sailing capacities of their vessels.

8. A jocular reference to the old superstition that the moon can induce insanity.

9. MS: "manure," not "muck." The juxtaposition of black, filthy manure and bad smell is common in racist language. The symbolic undercurrents of this usage are explored in Winthrop Jordan, *White over Black* (Chapel Hill, 1968), and Joel Kovel, *White Racism* (New York, 1984).

10. A haulyard, or halyard, is a rope or tackle used for raising and lowering parts of the sail apparatus. *Yard* and *parrel* are likewise nautical terms used to indicate respectively the spar at the base of a sail and the rope, chain, or collar that attaches it to the mast.

11. The wave had broken over the poop of the vessel, temporarily submerging it.

12. Haggard equips his Muslim sailor with a crescent-shaped weapon, probably a scimitar; in chap. VI, Mohamed's weapon is called a sword.

13. Rowed a boat on the Cam River, which flows through Cambridge.

14. The driving force of the waves and currents.

15. Each swears in his own way.

16. This paragraph was cited by a reviewer as a particularly flagrant example of Haggard's tendency to write purple prose (*Pall Mall Gazette*, January 4, 1885, 5). Yet he passed up the opportunity to alter it in the revisions of 1888. He was either indifferent to the criticism or generally happy with the way this paragraph fit the

general concept of the chapter— a passage through death ("teeth of hell," "avenging ghosts," Leo's apparent drowning) to rebirth on a calm sea that heaves like a woman's breast.

V. THE HEAD OF THE ETHIOPIAN.

1. 1st ed.: "old genelman." MS and GS use the capitals, which more clearly indicate that Job is referring to Satan. J. E. Scott, *A Bibliography of the Works of Sir Henry Rider Haggard 1856–1925* (London, 1947), 37, lists "genelman" as a spelling mistake. Whatmore's more recent *H. Rider Haggard: A Bibliography* correctly guesses Haggard's intention.

2. Acts 14:2.

3. MS, GS, and 1st ed.: "with us from the Army and Navy Stores," a London department store that still exists.

4. MS version of this footnote places the site at the island of Lamu, 300 miles *north* of Zanzibar, where such remains are to be found in abundance, though no scholar now believes them to have Persian origins. The change made for 1st ed. fits better with Haggard's fictional geography but lessens its credibility in other respects. The relationship of Egyptian civilization and material culture to the rest of Africa has been a matter of vigorous controversy for more than a century. Some Africanists have argued that Egyptian culture was influenced by black societies south of the Sahara; in particular the institution of divine kingship has been singled out as a common phenomenon in African societies. See Cheikh Anta Diop, *Antériorité des civilisations nègres: Mythe ou vérité* (Paris, 1967). On the other hand, the white minority regime that held power in Zimbabwe (formerly Southern Rhodesia) until 1980 encouraged the view that all stone ruins found in sub-Saharan Africa were the product of non-African settlement colonies founded by Phoenicians or other Mediterranean peoples. This view was first formulated in Haggard's day and led to considerable speculation about where the seaports might have been to service those inland colonies. This passage offers Haggard's fictional solution to the problem. The John Kirk referred to in the footnote accompanied David Livingstone on his Zambezi expedition and later served many years as British consul at Zanzibar. The allusion suggests that the journals of Livingstone and other members of the expedition may have been the source of some geographical and zoological details included in this chapter.

5. By the time Haggard wrote, quinine had been proved to offer effective protection against malaria; yellow fever and black water fever were still life-threatening. The reference to clouds of poisonous vapor in the previous paragraph reflects the prevailing opinion that "effluvia," or bad air (French, *mal air*) rising from stagnant water, caused all sorts of illness. The role of the mosquito in transmitting disease had not yet been discovered.

6. Sport of nature. MS and GS use "freak."

7. See note 5 above.

8. As in *King Solomon's Mines* and *Allan Quatermain*, Haggard here introduces his characters to the unknown regions of Africa through big game hunting. This ploy creates an atmosphere of danger and tests the moral fiber of the protagonists. Quite apart from its literary function it reflects the nineteenth-century view that Africa was a continent abundant in flora and fauna that could be endlessly exploited.

9. The express rifle was designed for hunting rather than for military purposes. It fired a bullet with high initial velocity and a very flat trajectory.

10. Haggard's intention is to locate his story in a primordial landscape unrelated to chronological time. That is why his Englishmen are "out of tone."

11. MS and GS: "fifty yards."

12. Mad in the sense of being driven crazy.

13. A typical piece of upper-class English slang mingling the pedantic "Avuncular" with the colloquial "ain't."

14. Job, the servant, would have come from the English class that dropped initial *h's* from words such as *he* and *heard* and assigned them to words that lacked them, such as *eat* and *eel*. This habit, drummed out of him by the requirements of his position, would, Haggard suggests, return in moments of stress or danger.

VI. AN EARLY CHRISTIAN CEREMONY.

1. The early Christian ceremony referred to is the custom believers had of embracing when they met, as Ustane embraces Leo near the end of this chapter.

2. Presumably Haggard contemplates the preservation of the lion pelts for later stuffing and display, which would require preservation with arsenic soap or alum salts and saltpeter. The preparation of a crocodile hide for sale would have diverted the adventurers from their quest. Haggard uses the word *alligator* interchangeably with *crocodile*. Strictly speaking, the alligator is a reptile of the Western Hemisphere not found in Africa.

3. Haggard knew biltong from his South African experience and makes frequent reference to it in the Allan Quatermain books. The dried meat (called "jerky" in the American West) is exceptionally tough but long lasting. An academic from Cambridge would not at this time have been likely to know the term.

4. The Zanzibar coast at this time included all the districts claimed by the sultan of Zanzibar, a strip extending all the way to the northwestern border of the present state of Kenya. Haggard's Ozy has disappeared from modern maps, being regarded simply as part of the Tana delta. The region has abundant ruins attesting to the part it played in Indian Ocean trade from Roman times onward, but the ancient canal system mentioned here is a speculation unsupported by the findings of modern archaeology.

5. The iguana is not found in Africa. Haggard's African experience did not prevent his slipping into this kind of error, most famously in *Nada the Lily*, in which wolves play a prominent role.

6. The foremost element of the bow that divides the water as the vessel moves forward.

7. For much of the nineteenth century this debilitating combination of quinine and laxatives was used by African travelers to stave off any sort of fever. David Livingstone swore by it, notwithstanding the sickness and death that often overtook those who faithfully adhered to his simple prescription. The quinine was effective only against malaria; the purgatives were effective against nothing but constipation.

8. The convention of using antiquated English to convey an impression of foreignness was well established by Haggard's day. Eighteenth-century poets had been charmed by the fake medieval poetry forged by James Macpherson and Thomas Chatterton, and from that time on, writers conveyed distance in time as well as tongue by the use of language borrowed loosely from Chaucer, Shakespeare, and the King James Version of the Bible. Haggard uses a peppering of *thee's* and *ye's* to achieve both effects. For a model of classical Arabic rendered in English, Haggard is likely to have turned to Fitzgerald's *Rubiyat* rather than Burton's *Arabian Nights*, which appeared only a few months before Haggard sat down to write. He made so many mistakes in grammar in MS, however, that it is likely that he was guided by his memory of the language of the Bible and Walter Scott's historical novels, rather than by any text he had at hand.

9. The first rendering of this name in MS is "Her-who-must-be-obeyed"; it was changed to "She" after the first few references. How She had known four days before that "white men are coming" is explained in chap. XIII.

10. The light color of these men is introduced to indicate their mixed descent, both from the ancient people said in later chapters to have once thrived here and from Africans. Haggard, like many other writers of his era, was prone to use color as a way of judging a people's place on an imaginary evolutionary ladder ascending from "savage" to "civilized."

11. Slang for a strange situation.

12. This passage alludes to the plan revealed in chap. VIII to make Mohamed the centerpiece of a cannibal feast. There is an apparent inconsistency, however, in that the barbarous suggestion comes from Billali, who in chap. IX claims to have been ignorant of the intention to roast the Arab.

13. A covered stretcher (litter) mounted on poles formerly used to carry people in the Orient.

14. MS: "North African Arab," not "East African Somali."

15. MS: "too white," not "too dark."

16. Charged or filled with; MS has "clothed in."

17. *Mammon* is used here in its original New Testament sense to personify worldliness.

18. MS: "As-Kati," not "Amahagger." Haggard's eventual choice of *Amahagger* is odd, considering that he describes this people's language as a form of Arabic. His first choice of *As-Kati*—suggesting Astarte, the highest deity of the Phoenicians and also goddess of beauty—would have been linguistically far more appropriate. An alternative derivation of As-kati is from Askari—the name given to the fearsome slave raiders of nineteenth-century East Africa. Given the magical powers and supernatural beauty of She, it would also have been dramatically appropriate. *Amahagger* suggests a plural formed according to the rules of grammar in the Bantu family of languages. For example, the plural of *Zulu*, the name of a people whom Haggard knew well, is *Amazulu*. Swahili, which developed from a lingua franca spoken in East Africa, is grounded in Bantu grammar but has a vocabulary containing many words of Arabic origin. It could not be readily understood by a scholar of Arabic such as Haggard presents Horace Holly to be. The Arabic origin of the language is reiterated in chap. XIII, which suggests another derivation of *Amahagger*. Ayesha (She) insists that she is of pure Arab descent, unlike the Koreish, who were thought to be descended from the union mentioned in the Old Testament between Abraham and his wife's Egyptian servant Hagar. Genesis relates that Hagar and her son Ishmael were later sent into the Egyptian wilderness. Thus *Amahagger* might be rendered as a hypothetical Bantu-based word meaning "people of Hagar." In chap. XVI, the second footnote, which first appeared in 1st ed., gives an alternative explanation, suggesting that the Amahagger are the product of a mixture of the lost white civilization of Kôr with Africans. In that footnote Haggard says the word *hagger* means "rock" in Arabic. Thus "People of the Rocks" would be people of the ruins. This too makes sense inasmuch as the Zimbabwe ruins, which Haggard did know about, were so called because the word *Zimbabwe* recorded by early Portuguese adventurers meant "stone."

19. MS renders this variously as "Hompté" and "Dompté." In GS it is changed to "Billali," which strongly suggests the Babylonian god Baal and fits very well with the earlier description of this character as an "ancient Mammon of Unrighteousness." The change to "Billali" makes the name more like those in Bantu languages. It is also reminiscent of the Arabic term for sub-Saharan Africa: *Bildad es Sudan*, "land of the blacks."

20. The rocky defile is often used by Haggard to mark a passage into the land where fantastic things happen. In *King Solomon's Mines* it is a mountain pass that opens the way to Kukuanaland. In *Allan Quatermain* it is a river between huge cliffs that leads to the lost civilization. That Holly dozes off before entering the

rocky defile emphasizes the dreamlike nature of the landscape that lies beyond. The valley that is next revealed as resembling a Roman amphitheater with pastoral animals looks backward to visions of Arcadia in classical literature and forward to the visions of science fiction writers such as Arthur Conan Doyle and Edgar Wallace, whose settings in *Lost World* and *King Kong* are approached in the same fashion.

21. MS adds that Mohamed had been blindfolded before he was forced on this run. Since we have already been told that no other strangers had been known to come this way and they were not specially barred, this blindfolding is a quite unnecessary precaution against the valley's being found again. It emphasizes the point made in note 20 above that Haggard presents this valley as a place that cannot be approached in full consciousness.

22. Earlier (cf. note 15) they are presented as darker than Arabs. MS reads "nearly as dark as Mohamed." Haggard's Victorian editor was as sensitive to the importance of skin color as the author himself.

23. MS gives the name as "Ukase" until chap. XVII, when Haggard begins to use "Ustane." This word in African languages would be pronounced "Oostahnee." In most film versions of *She*, it is mispronounced "Oostain."

24. This kind of cultural relativism can be dated back to Montaigne and even earlier authors. In Haggard's own era it was being powerfully reinforced by new discoveries and comparative ethnography. See, for example, the way in which the explorer Richard Burton used the example of female conscript armies in Dahomey to comment on the situation of women in his own country, in *A Mission to Gelele, King of Dahomey* (London, 1864), vol. 2, 66. Haggard's comments on jealousy and the defects of marriage, found repeated in most of his "realistic" novels, indicate his dissatisfactions with his own marital situation. See Etherington, *Rider Haggard*. Haggard toned down the irony of his comments by changing the last line from MS's "justifies all things."

VII. USTANE SINGS.

1. MS and GS: "Miss Ustane." The removal of the ironic honorific "Miss" suggests that when Ustane was first introduced she was given a common, even humourous African character by Haggard, who later assigned her the noblest traits of love and loyalty.

2. The galleries, whose former use was as burial places, strongly suggest that Haggard's inspiration here derived from the early Christian catacombs at Rome, an idea that is reinforced by the title of the previous chapter ("An Early Christian Ceremony"). Catacombs according to legend had once served as places of habitation and were known to have been used by Jews in earlier times. Non-Christian catacombs were known on the African continent at Alexandria in Egypt.

3. The use of milk and goats would have been impossible in a real African landscape of the type Haggard describes here. The swamps below would nourish the tse-tse fly and the disease trypanosomiasis, which is deadly to ordinary domestic animals.

4. The origin of the phrase "She-who-must-be-obeyed" can be traced to Haggard's childhood. The family nurse called a rag doll by that name; it was used to terrify the young children of the household into obedience. Speculation about the inspirations for this character is summarized in Etherington, *Rider Haggard*, 86–90.

5. This footnote implies that tobacco is native to Africa, which is not the case. Except for varieties found in New Caledonia and Australia, all known tobacco originated in the Western Hemisphere and was introduced elsewhere after the fifteenth century.

6. Haggard's description of lamps seems intended, like many other descriptive

passages in this section, to suggest that elements of a superior technology remained in use among the primitive Amahagger. The terracotta lamps with wicks projecting through holes were typical of oil lamps in use among the ancient Greeks and Romans.

7. The description of the slab resembles strongly the so-called table tombs of the Roman catacombs.

8. Haggard resorts to his characteristic practice of approaching the objects of his adventurer's quests through sleep or unconsciousness—in this case a sleep in a sepulchre haunted by dreams of death. In twentieth-century science fiction the journey to other worlds in space ships is frequently made in a state of suspended animation; see, for instance, the three astronauts en route to Jupiter in Stanley Kubrick's film of Arthur C. Clarke's novel *2001: A Space Odyssey*. For the confirmation of Holly's suspicions, see chap. IX.

9. MS includes a paragraph, subsequently deleted, implying that Ustane slept with Leo that night.

10. MS simply says "one of the young women." The change to a woman "no longer quite young" employs a cliché of Victorian comedy, found for example in the operettas of Gilbert and Sullivan. In this scene, however, Haggard takes the point beyond comedy by introducing us to a society in which women are always the initiators of romance. This introduces something that science fiction and African anthropology had in common. Both appealed to readers eager to be titillated by tales of people whose morality diverged sharply from or even reversed the conventions of European respectability.

11. Job's discomfiture is increased by the Victorian convention that servants should indicate no interest in sex while at work; transgression could bring instant dismissal. Job's mention of his "character" in the next sentence refers to the references, known as "characters," which a servant would bring from previous employers.

12. Slang expression meaning "out of the way" or "totally absent."

13. Keeping a look-out.

14. Haggard, whose ancestors were Norfolk farming gentry and who was in the process of establishing himself on the Norfolk estate of Ditchingham at the time this book was written, missed no opportunity to show off his agricultural knowledge. Polled cattle are very short horned strains produced by intensive breeding and valued for their capacity to fatten quickly. The Norfolk red-poll was less celebrated in Haggard's time than the Suffolk polled red, or Suffolk Dun as it was commonly known.

15. Iron smelting is associated with Bantu-speaking peoples throughout the southern part of the African continent, but the reversal of the usual sexual division of labor described here is not. Zulu soldiers had a part to play in maintaining agriculture and Dahomean women served in the army, but anthropologically Haggard's Amahagger do not resemble any African people. His African environment is not chosen for verisimilitude but rather to provide a remote arena for the workings of his imagination.

16. Kôr bears no similarity to any known archaeological site. There are strong suggestions, however, that names used in ancient Egypt and in the Sudan stimulated the author's invention. MS identifies Amenartas, writer of the sherd described in chap. III, as the daughter of "Hor, a Pharaoh." There was a *Hakor* who was a pharaoh not long before Nekhtnebf II, during whose reign Amenartas's supposed flight south into the wilds of Africa occurred. And *Kordofan* is an interior province of the Sudan whose name and location Haggard may also have found suggestive. Historical scholarship in Haggard's era frequently ascribed cultural traits and technological accomplishments of Africans south of the Sahara to influences emanating from ancient Egypt. More recent scholars have speculated extensively on cultural traffic that may have flowed in the other direction.

17. The so-called will-o'-the-wisp, or ignis fatuus.

18. Haggard strongly implies that the Amahagger were color conscious and

treated Mohamed differently because of his race. Europeans in Haggard's day commonly assumed that other peoples were as race and color conscious as themselves.

19. Ustane's trance in which she foretells the future in song resembles the prophecies made in trances by African seers in the areas of South Africa which Haggard knew well and which supplied the inspiration for much of his work. The same device is employed extensively in his Zulu trilogy, *Child of Storm, Marie,* and *Finished.*

VIII. THE FEAST, AND AFTER!

1. MS has "celebrity," not "character." Presumably the reference is to Joseph, who rejected the advances of Potiphar's wife only to be falsely accused by her of sexual assault and cast into Pharaoh's prison (Genesis 39:1–20).

2. Earlier in the nineteenth century many writers had distinguished between the states of "savagery" and "barbarism," the former being regarded as less civilized than the latter. Haggard uses the terms interchangeably.

3. The breech-loading revolver invented by the American Samuel Colt that was manufactured under patent in England at Enfield. The term *Colt* by the 1880s had become generic, applied to any breech-loading pistol.

4. Sorghum, or millet as the English termed it. In South Africa, Kafir corn was used to brew beer that was drunk from large pots.

5. Before embalming and wrapping, the corpse's vital organs and entrails were removed.

6. Vessels for holding wine, oil, and other liquids. The discussion that follows recalls many other Victorian debates about the relative merits of the artistic styles of ancient civilizations. In Haggard's time the Etruscans were less well regarded than the Greeks and Romans because of the "gross realism" of Etruscan art. The reference to "freedom of manner" implies explicit sexual content.

7. A lively debate was carried on in the nineteenth century concerning the color of the people who dominated ancient Egypt. An American school, associated with the slave-holding South, held that the inferior position of blacks in Egypt could be clearly discerned in tomb carvings. Others held the opposite position. The point at issue was whether black people had been capable at any time of devising or carrying on an advanced civilization. See William Stanton, *The Leopard's Spots: Scientific Attitudes toward Race in America 1815–1859* (Chicago, 1960).

8. These two species could very well have been confused because of the males' elongated spiral horns. Here again Haggard seems to have forgotten that his narrator is a classical scholar from Cambridge, not a big game hunter from southern Africa.

9. In the *Arabian Nights,* the Barmicides were a family of princes at Baghdad, one of whom once entertained a beggar by placing before him a series of imaginary dishes, pretending that each was a sumptuous dinner.

10. Hypnotized.

11. This scene, with its solo questions and choral responses, strongly resembles the process by which a Zulu witch finder "smelled out" a witch. The witch finder would make statements to which the people responded by shouts and clapping. See Henry Callaway, *The Religious System of the Amazulu* (London, 1870), 300–303, and E. J. Krige, *The Social System of the Zulus* (Pietermaritzburg, 1950), 225–27.

12. Here Haggard uses a South African term which a Cambridge academic would be most unlikely to know. A moocha is a short skirt worn in the nineteenth century by peoples in the eastern coastal districts of South Africa.

13. The passage that follows is considerably altered from MS and GS. In place of the next two sentences the MS reads: "and then, even now I can scarcely bear to write it, there was an awful heart rending shriek ending in something like a hissing sound and the next thing that I saw was the poor wretch broken loose from his captors in the despairing effort of a hideous death and rushing and rolling into the

darkness beyond the lamps the *red-hot pot jammed upon his head* completely covering it from view." The effect of the change is to soften the horror of the incident by not allowing the pot to get over Mohamed's head. To eliminate Mohamed from the plot without the horrible death, Haggard kills him with a bullet fired at the evil fat woman. However, in order to have Mohamed be hit by the same bullet Haggard has Holly shoot her in the back. Shooting in the back was regarded as cowardly. Mercy killing was controversial. When Haggard first arrived in Natal a controversy was still raging over the actions of Lieutenant Marshall Clarke, who admitted to killing dying men in the Langalibalele "rebellion." Even so, it is not clear that Haggard thought through the full implications of his changes. Why should Holly have fired at the woman rather than the assailants? He had not yet discovered her principal role in the plot. Furthermore, if Mohamed had not already been capped by the pot, he could possibly have been saved, as the subsequent fate of the other characters reveals. Haggard, no doubt, had other reasons for disposing of Mohamed.

14. The practice of inviting people to banquets for the purpose of killing them was old in myth and history by the time Haggard wrote, but the ritual question-and-answer ceremony of this scene strongly recalls the time when the Zulu king Dingane executed a party of Afrikaner settlers under the command of Piet Retief. Haggard described that event in his later novel *Marie.*

15. Cannibalism.

16. MS and GS: "As I flew over him I felt the heat from the red hot pot, strike upon my legs, and by its glow saw his hands—for he was not quite dead—still feebly beating at the hissing torment on his head."

17. The platform's probable use as an altar for religious ceremonies is revealed in chap. XV.

18. Hang in the balance. The last stand in a fight to the death in which civilized men are seized with a lust to kill is a common feature of Haggard's novels. It occurs in the climactic battle of *King Solomon's Mines*, in *Allan Quatermain* at an encounter with marauding Masai, and in *Eric Brighteyes* (1891), among others. Often these fights end like this one, in a literal loss of consciousness. The psychological theory Haggard offered for these scenes is that in primitive situations the veneer of civilized behavior is stripped away, an idea born partly of the popularity of Darwin's theories. See Etherington, *Rider Haggard*, 43–52.

19. Clutch or grip.

20. Katz points out in *Rider Haggard and the Fiction of Empire* that Haggard never missed an opportunity to score points against pacifism.

IX. A LITTLE FOOT.

1. The phrase "struggle for life" is not much different from Herbert Spencer's famous notion of "the survival of the fittest." The idea that beneath conventional appearances man was an animal who would struggle for survival like any other animal underlies all Haggard's descriptions of human battle.

2. MS and GS: "your" and "yours," not "thy" and "thine." Haggard's editor noticed his departure from the convention of rendering foreign prose as antique English.

3. MS: "wolves." "Hyaenas" is a better choice for three reasons. First, it would be odd for Billali to make the same choice of metaphor as Holly in describing the men who assailed them the previous night. Second, the hyaena, as a scavenger of dead meat, is better for suggesting cannibalism. Third, there are no wolves in Africa. Haggard was later lampooned for featuring them in his novel *Nada the Lily*.

4. A rare example of joking in a Haggard novel, if indeed the black humor is intended.

5. MS: "God," not "Providence." Two paragraphs earlier, the word *power* in the

phrase "higher power" is capitalized in MS. Haggard was a very religious person but not an orthodox Christian. He may have changed these words to fit better with the theme of reincarnation, which is introduced later in this chapter.

6. This prescient dream introduces for the first time the notion of the principal character's immense age and her reincarnation in successive ages, themes that dominate the later part of this book and its sequel *Ayesha*. "The Circle of the Spirit," which is not in MS, suggests the circular motion of the soul from life to life. The maiden who removes her veil and reveals a skeleton appears in Thomas Moore's *Epicurean*, from which Haggard was accused of lifting the basic concept of his story.

7. In MS this character is named Hompté (see chap. VI, note 19) and Job calls him Humpty Dumpty, a thought that might have been in Haggard's mind earlier, because MS sometimes calls him Dompté. This passage may recall an incident of which Haggard could have heard in Natal in the mid-1870s. An African chief, Langalibalele, was accused of rebellion. The British general Sir Garnet Wolseley, who served as governor immediately before the governorship of Haggard's first employer, Sir Henry Bulwer, referred to the chief as Long Belly, claiming he could never pronounce "his infernal Kaffir cognomen." The similarity of "Langalibalele" to "Billali" is striking.

8. Instead of "cold hands," MS has "a dagger wound in her breast." Even without this suggestion of violence, the passage is likely to startle the modern reader even more than Haggard's contemporaries because of its strong suggestion of necrophilia and fetishism. The suggestion of guilty teenage sexuality punished by a censorious mother is marked. The reference to a dagger wound might originally have been intended by Haggard to echo the ancient rivalry between Amenartas and Ayesha.

9. Oily or greasy. Many of the substances used for embalming by the ancient Egyptians were flammable: pine pitch, bitumen, asphalt, wax.

10. A large traveling bag. Its name derived from the British politician William Ewart Gladstone, who called for the Turks to be thrown out of Bulgaria "bag and baggage." The *Oxford English Dictionary* gives 1882 as the year of its first recorded use. 1st ed. included the information that Holly had purchased the bag at the Army and Navy Stores. Because *She* had been much criticized for the inclusion of this sort of mundane Victorian detail, Haggard removed that and similar passages in 1888 ed. In MS there is a footnote at this point, subsequently deleted: "This foot is still in my possession though the little toe has been broken off and lost."

X. SPECULATIONS.

1. Describing real or imagined foreign customs as a way of commenting on the mutability or absurdity of European ways of life has deep roots, stretching back through Swift's Gulliver to Montaigne's essay on cannibals. The reversal of sex roles had been explored in Bulwer-Lytton's *Coming Race*, a novel that anticipates *She* in many respects. Haggard and Bulwer-Lytton both ran into contradictions in their attempts to up-end conventional practices because neither novelist could free himself entirely—even in imagination—from patriarchal prejudices. That is illustrated in the present passage, which wreaks a masculine revenge on female insolence every second generation.

2. The reference is too vague to permit a positive identification of the "great man."

3. *Leo* is Latin for "lion."

4. The Australian scholar Peter Pierce noticed a relationship between Haggard's bird's-eye views and the aerial panoramas of cities and landscapes that were popular in the nineteenth century, as they also had been in the days of Leonardo da Vinci. See Pierce, "Rider Haggard," 13–21.

5. Smoke such as that described here was typical of the atmosphere of nineteenth

and twentieth-century London until the passage of the Clean Air Act in the early 1960s. There may also have been in Haggard's mind a subliminal association between the fens of Cambridge—marshlands along the River Cam—and "the great wen of London," a commonplace expression made famous by William Cobbett (1763–1835) to describe the undesirable aspects of city living during the Industrial Revolution.

6. A bog, marsh, or fen that quakes or shakes beneath the feet.

7. Haggard's novels set in Africa tend to treat the continent as a vast nobleman's park teeming with game, big and little, waiting to be shot. While the slaughter of wildlife in *She* is mild compared with that in *King Solomon's Mines* and *Allan Quatermain*, the eye of Haggard's imagination is ever alert for wild game—especially in this passage, where the birds are directly compared to typical game birds on an English gentleman's estate.

8. Haggard here makes the connection between bad air and fever that gave the disease malaria its French name (from *mal air*). It was not until 1894 that Sir Patrick Manson proposed a theory explaining how the disease might be transmitted by mosquitoes, a hypothesis first successfully tested in Italy in 1898. It is a curiosity of the history of medicine that the connection between the breeding grounds of mosquitoes and the prevalence of malaria was made many times, as Haggard makes it in this very paragraph, without the development of a theory postulating the insect as the agent of transmission.

9. Tincture of arsenic was another preventative agent known at this time.

10. The theme of veiled truth runs right through the book, until the concept itself is made concrete in the statue that stands at the center of the ruined city. She (Ayesha) too is veiled in all her guises, even in the foreshadowing dream recounted in the previous chapter.

11. This and the previous sentence are not in MS. It was from a peak in the Darien district of the Isthmus of Panama that the Spanish expolorer Balboa first glimpsed the Pacific Ocean. The name Darien was well known through Keats's "On First Looking into Chapman's Homer," in which the experience is ascribed to Cortez.

12. Flickering lights seen in church cemeteries and superstitiously thought to portend a funeral. Like the marsh flames referred to here, they were most likely produced by escaping gases.

13. This passage recalls Tennyson's *In Memoriam*, prologue, verse 4.

14. The widely held belief that without hope in an afterlife people would abandon conventional morality was worked out in great detail in the 1903 futuristic novel *When It Was Dark* by G. Thorne (a pseudonym for C. A. R. Gull): the world collapses into moral and physical chaos after a scientist claims to have positive proof that Christ did not rise from the dead.

15. "Mines and batterings," according to the military usage of the time, refers to the mines laid in tunnels to blow up enemy fortifications and the pulverizing effects of batteries of heavy guns or cannon.

16. See chap. I.

17. Doctors in Haggard's time were unable to distinguish between malaria and other tropical fevers by reference to the causes. They could simply describe the various symptoms, ascribing all indiscriminately to malaria.

18. See note 8 above.

19. It was a fantasy of nineteenth-century Englishmen that they alone cared about saving the lives of other people. Thus it was said that "life is cheap in the tropics."

20. Bacchus, the Greek god of wine, is conventionally depicted wearing a crown of vine leaves.

21. The wearing of the pigtail, originally imposed on the Chinese by the conquer-

ing Manchus as a mark of subservience, had by the nineteenth century become almost a cherished tradition in China. After the 1911 revolution, however, the pigtail rapidly disappeared from male fashion.

XI. THE PLAIN OF KÔR.

1. This delusion prefigures the literal division into identical parts that takes place when Leo confronts the preserved corpse of his ancestor Kallikrates in chap. XXI.

2. 1st ed.: "through which we had [not have] come." Probably a typographical error.

3. This sequence lays the groundwork for the subsequent escape of the adventurers. No explanation is given, however, for how the "savage" Billali might possess such precise information on the engineering works of a civilization that had long since perished.

4. The most admired landscape of Haggard's century was English parkland, that is, land approximating to the parks surrounding an aristocratic English country house. Such landscapes in South Africa and Australia were often remarked upon for this reason. It has frequently been suggested that such vistas were an impetus to colonization and imperialism, inasmuch as they suggested the possibility of country estates open to acquisition by adventurous spirits. The reference in this passage to oaks reinforces the point.

5. The Martini was a breech-action rifle, not to be confused with the late nineteenth-century military Martini-Henry, which combined the Martini breech action with the Henry barrel. Sporting rifles were generally double-barreled. At these close quarters the Express rifle with its flat trajectory was unnecessary. Haggard's characterization falters again here in presenting the Cambridge scholar as a practiced big-game hunter.

6. "Living rock," a phrase Haggard uses often, signifies rock native to a site, formed by geological rather than human agency.

7. "Great grass mounds" suggest further archaeological sites.

8. MS and GS: "fifty feet."

9. In Bulwer-Lytton's *Coming Race* the underground world is also lit with light reminiscent of gas lamps and the walls are lined with paintings "intended to illustrate events in the history of the race amidst which I was admitted."

XII. "SHE."

1. The adventurers had followed the usual procedure of mid-Victorian African explorers, such as Burton, Stanley, and Livingstone, who carried presents with them to provide an introduction to peoples whose languages they could not speak and whose customs they did not know.

2. A loosely fitting jacket with a waist belt, from which the twentieth-century safari jacket derives.

3. It could hardly have been discernible in an ancient sculptural relief that the fluid was hot, steaming, or aromatic. Most likely the sources for Haggard's flight of imagination in this passage are descriptions by Herodotus and other ancient writers of the techniques used in Egyptian embalming, most of which used aromatic materials such as myrrh, balsam, resin, and bitumen. It is conceivable as well that the masks worn by the embalmers suggest that the profession was despised. According to Diodorus, the person responsible for making incisions for the removal of internal organs was pursued by crowds who cursed and threw stones at him because it was regarded as despicable to do violence to a dead body. Another question is how Holly could, in the next sentence, identify the cloth covering the eyes of the embalmers

and corpse of the deceased as linen. Is he making an identification with the grave-clothes used in his own time?

4. Kowtowing, after the old Chinese way of showing respect to superiors by touching one's forehead to the ground.

5. The white hand recalls the little white embalmed foot met in an earlier chapter, thus reinforcing the predominant image in this chapter of embalmed life. In the next paragraph Ayesha makes her first appearance literally wrapped like a mummy and her hand is described as ivory.

6. Suffused with.

7. Syriac, a dead language of the Aramaic family, is related to Arabic and other Semitic languages.

XIII. AYESHA UNVEILS.

1. In MS the text of this chapter was combined with the previous one. It appeared for the first time as a separate chapter in GS.

2. The references to a font of pure water, perfumed air, and vestments are calculated to present She in a religious setting reminiscent of a Catholic church with herself presiding as priestess at the altar. Although the text of the previous chapter does not describe the small room as a raised space, E. K. Johnson, in drawing the first illustrations for GS, depicted it as elevated by two short steps, thus enhancing the impression of an altar.

3. The words after "my own dear tongue" were added after GS, as was the footnote attributed to Holly. They, like the added details of the Sherd of Amenartas in chap. III, were put in to give the narrative verisimilitude. They also help to make a more plausible version of the origin of She and the Amahagger. The footnote strengthens the hypothesis sketched above in chap. VI, note 18, that when Haggard changed the name of the people from As-kati to Amahagger he meant to suggest a descent from Abraham and Hagar's son Ishmael of an Arab people whose "blood" and language were later corrupted by intermixing with black Africans. Although there are good reasons to suspect that Haggard borrowed the name Ayesha directly from Bulwer-Lytton's *Strange Story*, the biographical details he supplies for her are his own invention. By locating Ayesha's birthplace in Yemen the Happy (after the classical usage, Arabia Felix), Haggard connects her with one region sometimes said to be the homeland of the Queen of Sheba, which in turn suggests a connection to Haggard's earlier African romance *King Solomon's Mines*. Having once assigned an Arabian origin to She, he had to find her an Arabic name. The one he chose, Ayesha, was the name of the prophet Mohammed's favorite wife, the daughter of his close friend Abu Bakr. As she too had her birthplace in southwestern Arabia, the choice was a reasonable one. This much Haggard could easily have derived from the biblical and historical scholarship of his own time. He goes beyond the conventional accounts, however, by ascribing to She notions of linguistic and racial purity that were only beginning to take hold among intellectual racists of the late-Victorian era. Thus, while the ninth edition of the *Encyclopedia Britannica* states that ancient Arab chronicles traced the origins of the first Yemenite kings to a union between Kahtan and "Himyar the dusky," a "name denoting African origin," Haggard gives his Ayesha a "pure" white skin, a "pure" Arab descent, and a "pure" Arabic dialect.

4. The Achaemenian Dynasty consolidated its hold over Persia under Cyrus I and embarked upon a celebrated series of conquests that eventually brought Egypt under its sway. In the reign of Xerxes (d. 465 B.C.) the king's brother Achaemenes was made satrap of Egypt. Thus the term *Achaemenian* used by She in this passage may signify either the line of Cyrus or that of his descendant Achaemenes. Later revolts by native Egyptians led to a period of renewed independence, which came

to an end when the Persian Artaxerxes III Ochus drove the last native pharaoh, Nekhtnebf II, into exile in Ethiopia. As this is the flight referred to on the Sherd of Amenartas in chap. III, it is quite reasonable for She to introduce the name into her conversation with Holly. His reference to Artaxerxes at the end of the next paragraph is intended to show he was sufficiently erudite to know the Persian's full title.

5. The conquests of Alexander the Great (d. 323 B.C.) led to the Hellenic dynasty of Ptolemy as ruler of Egypt. The dynasty's last queen, Cleopatra, was superseded by a Roman government. From She's ignorance of these developments Haggard implies that she last received news of the outside world in the fourth century B.C.

6. The clause after the comma in this sentence is not in MS but is quite in line with the racial generalizations and slurs that fill this chapter. Holly's reference to the Greeks being again a people is an anachronism if it is meant to imply that there was ever a united Greek nation-state in ancient times corresponding to the Greek nation established after the revolt against Turkish rule in the nineteenth century.

7. Solomon, a reference that fits well with Haggard's use of the Sheba story.

8. According to the sherd, She had already established her residence in central Africa by the time of Pharaoh Nekhtnebf II, who reigned more than three centuries before the Herod who appears in the New Testament.

9. Holly gives the Latin version of the celebrated sarcastic comment on Roman rule in classical times—"they make a desert [a solitude] and call it peace"—attributed to Calgacus, a Caledonian chieftain defeated by the Romans under Julius Agricola, c. 85 A.D..

10. The reader might well wonder how She, who did not know of Herod, knew so much of the Romans, who in the early fourth century B.C. had barely begun to conquer lands beyond the Italian peninsula.

11. Jesus Christ.

12. Holly and She here enter into a systematic and collective denigration of Jews that reflects the anti-Semitism of a fair proportion of Haggard's British contemporaries. The reference to Sense is intended to imply that the Jews were wedded to material rather than spiritual values. Subsequent references to Baal, Astoreth, and Egyptian gods reinforce the calumny by indicating that the Jews chose their religion for the wealth and connections it might bring them rather than out of any genuine commitment. The allusion to their "dark faces" adds a note of physical racism to the caricaturization. Hoariest of all the elements of European anti-Semitism brought together here are the medieval beliefs that all Jews carry a just burden of guilt for the crucifixion of Christ and that the Jewish diaspora was punishment for this crime. It is not impossible that Haggard felt personally sensitive on this point, for it was rumored that one of his grandparents was half Jewish.

13. Most likely the reference here is to the prophet Amos of the Old Testament, esp. Amos 8–9.

14. This would seem to date the disappearance of Kôr to the very earliest period of ancient Egyptian history. In twentieth-century science fiction and in books of pseudo-scientific speculation such as Erich Von Daniken's *Chariots of the Gods* (1968), this tendency to attribute the achievements of the earliest known civilizations to mysterious predecessors becomes commonplace.

15. This footnote does not appear in MS. Despite its addition, many readers fall into mispronunciations of the name. In the 1965 Hammer Studios production of *She,* Ayesha is pronounced Ayeesha. Ustane (which ought to be sounded as Oostahnee) is rendered as Ustain.

16. It is entirely appropriate to Ayesha's un-Christian philosophy of power that she should be waiting not for the Messiah expected by the Jews but for her lost lover.

17. Ayesha here evinces a thoroughly and anachronistically Victorian sense of geological time.

18. *Vegetarianism* was a word barely forty years old when *She* was written, but the ancient practice had been taken up by a wide variety of nineteenth-century groups for religious, moral, and hygienic reasons. The advanced people of Bulwer-Lytton's *Coming Race* are fruit eaters who remember with distaste the days of meat-eating and hunting. In Wells's *Time Machine* the overrefinement of the delicate Eloi is signaled by their vegetarianism. Haggard, despite his celebration of big-game hunting in his nineteenth-century novels, may have suffered inner pangs of conscience, for he turned against blood sports near the end of his life.

19. Haggard anticipated many other writers in musing on the consequences of deliberate alterations of human types to serve the ends of evil or power-crazed individuals. Wells's *Island of Dr. Moreau* (1896) explored the theme in depth. After the Nazi era made such experiments notorious, the theme was transmuted yet again in works of fantasy and science fiction.

20. A hunter in Greek myth who, because he saw Artemis bathing, was turned into a stag and killed by his own hounds. Ayesha is being deliberately titillating here, inasmuch as Actaeon was punished for gazing not at beauty per se but at nudity. The allusion underscores the chapter's teasing title.

21. The double-headed snake suggests Satan and evil. Haggard resorted to this device again in the novel he wrote with Lang, *The World's Desire.*

22. The reference is to Roman statuary, which depicted Venus in many guises, one of which was Venus Victrix, or Venus of Victory.

23. The sexual undertones of the chapter are strong from beginning to end. The last sentence is more reminiscent of a late night tryst in a lady's bedchamber than an audience with a queen.

XIV. A SOUL IN HELL.

1. Devilishness. The fascination of the abomination, as Joseph Conrad put it in *Heart of Darkness*, was a common theme in late-Victorian and Edwardian literature. It appears in another form in the vampire stories, especially Bram Stoker's *Dracula*, in which vampires succeed in first fascinating, then seducing their victims into following their diabolical way of life.

2. The enchantress in the *Odyssey* who turned the companions of Odysseus into swine.

3. Followed in MS by this passage, subsequently deleted: "And yet now I thought of it, I had heard of it, it was one of the Buddhist doctrines in fact the very nub of their faith. They believed that a man passed from earth out of this life into a state of restful beatitude called Devachan and then after the lapse of thousands of years back to another spell of earth life and so on ad infinitum." While this is hardly an accurate account of Buddhist faith, it does show how Haggard's mind, like the minds of others of his time, noticed the similarity between the Buddhist doctrine of souls evolving through numerous reincarnations and Darwinian evolution.

4. Here's to combat.

5. Despite Holly's laughter, Haggard took the idea of reincarnation very seriously and frequently expounded it in his work. While working on his autobiography in 1912, he claimed to have had visions of previous existences as a savage in stone-age England, a black African warrior, an Egyptian, and a Viking. *Days of My Life*, 2:167–71.

6. Embroidered.

7. This passage, especially the reference to "letting loose her passion on the dead," raises again the suggestion of necrophilia first made in chap. IX.

XV. AYESHA GIVES JUDGMENT.

1. A gesture of servility.

2. Polite. This word and the rendering of *corpses* as"corpseses" later in the paragraph are intended to reinforce Job's character as an uneducated product of the English working class, a figure which writers of Haggard's era believed they could make innocent fun of.

3. "Physiology" here refers not to Ayesha's physical appearance but to her resistance to the aging process. In MS Haggard wrote "physiognomy."

4. Delirious.

5. A character noted for unfailing cheerfulness in Charles Dickens's *Martin Chuzzlewit* (1843).

6. "You" at the end of this sentence was "ye" in MS. At first Haggard disregarded the nominative and objective forms of the archaic pronouns he put into the mouths of his alien characters. Between GS and 1st ed. some sharp-eyed editor intervened to correct the grammar.

7. The reference here to eating human flesh, described on the previous page as "the ancient and honourable custom of their country," invites the question of why Ayesha as absolute ruler did not abolish the barbaric custom. It is possible that Haggard deliberately ascribed to her the ruling precepts of his own mentor in the British colonial service, Sir Theophilus Shepstone of South Africa, whose practice of "indirect rule" allowed the continuation of some customs that would not have been tolerated at home in England. Like Shepstone, too, Ayesha justifies her rule in the next paragraph by saying that the people would have destroyed each other in internecine warfare had she not been there to prevent it. And like any toughminded colonial administrator She insists that her instructions can never be disobeyed, lest her prestige be diminished. The ideology of the indirect ruler of colonial Africa is aptly expressed later in this chapter when She says to Holly, "How thinkest thou that I rule this people? I have but a regiment of guards to do my bidding, therefore it is not by force. It is by terror. My empire is of the imagination."

8. MS gave a longer ending: "'My word is spoken—let my doom be done.' I turned my head but could not bear to see those poor wretches hauled off to their frightful fate. But I know that it was carried out to the last letter for on passing up the cave on the following afternoon I saw a redhanded executioner flitting down a passage and heard screams of agony even through the rocky walls."

XVI. THE TOMBS OF KÔR.

1. MS and GS: "How many men, think ye, working for how many years, did it need to hollow this cave and all its galleries." Haggard's final editing here, as in other places, strove to make Ayesha's artificially archaic language more credibly consistent with the grammar of the King James Bible.

2. MS gives the date as "seven thousand two hundred and fifty-nine."

3. MS: "seven thousand years before."

4. MS gives the date as "seven thousand eight hundred and three."

5. The passage recalls Revelation 18. For example, verse 2, "And he cried mightily with a strong voice, saying, Babylon the great is fallen, is fallen, and is become the habitation of devils . . . ," and verse 22, "And the voice of harpers, and musicians, and of pipers, and trumpeteers, shall be heard no more at all in thee; and no craftsman, of whatsoever craft he be, shall be found any more in thee; and the sound of a millstone shall be heard no more at all in thee."

6. Ecclesiastes 1:9, "there is no new thing under the sun."

7. See chap. VI, note 18.

8. In *King Solomon's Mines*, Haggard set a similar scene in the Place of the White Death, a vast limestone cavern in which the bodies of the old kings of Kukuanaland were encased in growing stalagmites.

9. In this passage Haggard again shows the influence of Shakespeare's *Hamlet*, especially the speech on Yorick's skull.

10. The next four paragraphs are interleaved as an interpolation in MS, indicating that Haggard added the dream sequence either as an afterthought or to make clearer the story that he had already imagined. His autobiography, written many years later, includes a long dream sequence purporting to summon up the memories of previous existences. This passage is similar and presents a scene related to some of the most painful memories of Haggard's youth, when the woman he expected to wed married another man. Many of his novels emphasize the evil consequences that follow such actions, almost as though they were intended to be read remorsefully by the woman who jilted him.

11. These words of prophecy conjure up one of the newly discovered terrors of nineteenth-century science. The Second Law of Thermodynamics, first enunciated by Sadi Carnot in 1824 and definitively stated by Lord Kelvin in 1851, decreed that heat cannot be transferred from a colder to a warmer body; it carried the cosmic implication that energy in the universe was dissipating in an entropic process that would inevitably end in a total coldness and deadness. This was the vision that Wells's Time Traveller glimpsed in his ultimate journey in *The Time Machine*. Haggard links a similar vision in this chapter to a great range of themes: the mortality of individuals and the vanity of their feeble efforts to cheat death through embalming or pompous funerals, the impermanence of empires, and the terror of an unstoppable progress toward nothingness in a Darwinian universe governed by chance and conflict.

XVII. THE BALANCE TURNS.

1. In the Koran, sura III, Becca is an alternative name for Mecca. MS, however, refers not to Becca but to Alexandria, which was changed to Arabia in GS. Alexandria was plainly impossible because Haggard dates the original confrontation between Ayesha, Amenartas, and Kallikrates in central Africa to about 339 B.C., before the foundation of Alexandria.

2. The Basilisk of mythology was a reptile whose breath or even look was fatal.

3. Tyrian cloth originated in the classical Phoenician city of Tyre, which was famed for the quality of its weaving and carpets.

4. Greek goddess of love.

5. An epithalamium is a classical Greek nuptial song or poem in praise of a bride and bridegroom. Several examples composed by Sappho survive.

6. This confirmation of the late-Victorian medical belief that tightly binding the waist with corseting was bad for the health comes as something of a surprise in the midst of what is nothing but a mental striptease.

7. The appearance of vegetarianism in this passage adds to Ayesha's aura of Eastern mystery.

8. Haggard here shows his awareness of the classical philosophy denying the existence of God and a life after death, as well as his acquaintance with free thinkers of his own century.

9. The section between these words and "art thou weary of me already" was added in 1st ed., as were the sentences between "Or dost thou fear" and "Faithless man!"

10. Of death.

XVIII. GO, WOMAN!

1. The reference, slightly ridiculous, to "a woman of Ayesha's age and experience" recalls the character Haggard assigned to Mildred in *Dawn*, his first novel. Mildred keeps a private museum of Egyptian antiquities at the Canary Islands and meets the main character on a ship. Another remark of Haggard's, that the passenger steamer is "Cupid's own hotbed," strongly suggests that the author, either on his way to South Africa or on his return, carried on at least a flirtation with a cynical and attractive older woman.

2. Luke 20:35: "But they that shall be accounted worthy to obtain that world, and the resurrection from the dead, neither marry, nor are given in marriage."

3. This enunciation of Ayesha's philosophy, that all means are justified by ends, echoes a general trend of thought in Haggard's era that saw the extension of colonial empires by the sword and the extermination of "lesser breeds" as harsh but necessary steps toward a better future for all mankind.

4. This passage and the vague treatment of the previous relationship between Leo and Ustane evokes the typical colonial attitude to interracial love; that it is out of bounds. The punishment meted out is also colonial, inasmuch as it falls only on the African woman. That supports the argument made by Higgins in *Rider Haggard: The Great Storyteller* that miscegenation in Haggard's fiction was inspired by his own reactions to a supposed love affair with a black woman during his period of service in South Africa.

5. MS and GS: Greek.

6. Again Job falls into Cockney speech with its misplaced and dropped *h's*.

7. A veiled reference to Ayesha's yet-to-be-revealed plan for conferring immortality upon Leo.

XIX. "GIVE ME A BLACK GOAT!"

1. Haggard takes class division to be a fact of life, as an ordinary Englishman of his period and education was likely to do. He presents class divisions without the mordant or ambiguous comments that are to be found in the futuristic novels of William Morris and Ignatius Donnelly. There is no counterpart in his novels to the relations between the Morlocks and Eloi in Wells's *Time Machine*; see Harry M. Geduld, ed., *The Definitive Time Machine* (Bloomington, Ind., 1987), 20–21.

2. A variation on the ancient *memento mori* "What you are I once was, what I am you shall be."

3. Haggard had attended séances while studying in London in his youth and had met titled ladies there who dabbled in the occult (*Days of My Life*, 1;37). This sequence, with the well of water suggesting the crystal ball of a fortuneteller, appears to recall the author's experiences and to present his own explanation for the apparently magical ability of mediums and seers to conjure up images which members of their audiences believed to be known only to themselves. Haggard's theory of memory, conventional for his time, is quite different from the hypotheses of the psychoanalysts of the twentieth-century that far more was present in memory than could be consciously recalled.

4. Still.

5. According to Tacitus's *Annals*, the emperor Nero once held a private circus in his gardens illuminated by burning crosses to which Christians had been tied.

6. Both citations come from Hamlet's graveside speech: "Imperious Caesar, dead and turned to clay / Might stop a hole to keep the wind away" and "To what base uses we may return Horatio! Why may not imagination trace the noble dust of Alexander, till he find it stopping a bung-hole" (*Hamlet*, act 5, scene 1). Finding a use for

human remains exercised the mind of the utilitarian philosopher Jeremy Bentham early in the nineteenth century. Bentham proposed that ancestral bodies be mummified and set up as statues outside the houses of their descendants; he presented his own mummified corpse to University College, London, as part of an endowment requiring its grisly presence at administrative meetings. Burning bodies to provide power is satirized by Aldous Huxley in *Brave New World* (1932). Variations on the theme abound in science fiction, including recycling for food in Richard Fleischer's film of 1973, *Soylent Green*.

7. MS: "the dust which is man's end." The change is significant, indicating the way in which Haggard vacillated between affirming and denying the immortality of the soul.

8. Haggard vacillates between horror and comedy in this scene. The reference to "a sort of infernal and fiendish cancan" suggests the *fête infernale* scene in Offenbach's comic opera *Orpheus in the Underworld* (1858), which could have been known to the author and which is the source of the music most commonly used in twentieth-century renditions of the cancan.

9. Crazed.

10. This description of spirit possession, like the scene of witch finding in chap. VIII, bears strong resemblances to scenes of possession among female Zulu prophets and seers that Haggard may have witnessed in South Africa.

11. An animal enclosure and associated homestead. The South African term is a corruption of the Portuguese word for "corral."

12. The true boa constrictors originate in South America. Another branch of the same family of snakes, the python, is found in Africa.

13. Blushed.

XX. TRIUMPH.

1. The next two sentences were added in 1st ed.

2. Zone = belt.

3. According to Hesiod's version of the birth of Venus, the goddess emerged fully grown from the sea.

4. Pseudo-classical mythology gives the name Galatea to the beautiful figure sculpted by Pygmalion that later was transformed into a real woman.

5. In *The World's Desire*, which Haggard wrote in collaboration with Lang, the theme of the woman who provokes murderous, jealous passions in all men is replayed, with Helen of Troy as the irresistible object of desire.

6. The scene recalls the funeral seduction of Ann by Richard in Shakespeare's *Richard III* (act 1, scene 2) but differs inasmuch as Richard's motives for wooing were political.

7. See Genesis 6:4.

8. Tares were used in Christ's parable (Matthew 13:24–32) to refer to an injurious weed that grows amongst corn.

9. MS first gave the song in a prose version; later Haggard interpolated this version into MS. The footnote by "Editor" first appeared in 1st ed.

10. In this poem, which Haggard took more care over than any other, there were several changes in MS. The lines that follow "the diadem of Kings" were rewritten again in 1st ed. MS version read:

The peoples of the world shall wonder and worship: blinded shall they be with our
*   might and made drunken with our beauty.*
From time to time shall our greatness roll down to victory—
Rolling like a chariot through the dust of the unending days
Onward shall we go in pomp and beauty and laughter
Laughing like the daylight as he leaps along the mountains.

Onward from triumph to triumph onward from power to power
Onward never wearying clothed with splendour as with a garment
Onward till night rushes down and our fight be accomplished.

11. The next passage, from "Nay, look not so" to "whither I shall lead you," was added in 1st ed.

12. *Hamlet*, act 3, scene 1: "sicklied o'er with a pale cast of thought." The reference is apt inasmuch as Hamlet's speech concerns the "dread of something after death, the undiscover'd country from whose bourn no traveller returns."

XXI. THE DEAD AND LIVING MEET.

1. MS: "chain of many lives."

2. MS: instead of "life," "waking which we call life."

3. Some women in ancient Greece and Rome with reputed powers of divination and prophecy were known as sibyls.

4. Eating, rather than smoking or injecting, was the commonest method of taking opium for pleasure in nineteenth-century Britain. Consuming it was legal, and it was sold in cake or powder form.

XXII. JOB HAS A PRESENTIMENT.

1. The devil.

2. The woman with reputed powers of divination who was sought out by Saul on the eve of his battle against the Philistines; she summoned up the dead (1 Samuel 28:7–25).

3. Watercress became a popular vegetable early in the nineteenth century. It could be grown indoors in a dish of water or, as Job recalls here, on a damp cloth.

4. The biblical injunctions include Exodus 22:18, "Thou shalt not suffer a witch to live," and Leviticus 19:26, "neither shall you use enchantments, nor practice augury." One reputed witch in the Bible was Lilith, demon of the wilderness; Haggard's wife used to call his lifelong passion, the woman who jilted him in his youth, "Lilith."

5. A Methodist lay preacher; Haggard evidently held no very high opinion of his kind.

6. A lame or otherwise defective animal.

7. *Cautions* is slang denoting something or someone, esp. someone eccentric who causes astonishment or alarm.

8. *Scorchers* is slang for something causing a sensation.

9. Got things done without complaining.

10. Was so idle.

11. Supercilious.

12. *Penny whip* (from penny wheep) is Scottish slang for a small measure of beer. Its use in this context is mystifying.

13. Goat hides and skins are not mentioned in this context in the Bible, but scholars of Haggard's day inferred the use of sowing bags from depictions in Egyptian tomb paintings.

14. The proverb that familiarity breeds contempt.

15. I.e., when their relationship will be sexually consummated.

16. Engrave.

17. But the end of the story tells against Ayesha's analysis and gives the triumph to Amenartas after all.

18. MS: "blasted," not "overthrown."

19. MS: "we have a tyrant only we do not call him by that name, we call him the 'grand old man' and the people whose votes hold him in power know him as their own 'William.'" The reference is to the prime minister, Gladstone, who was

called by his supporters "the people's William." There were two good reasons for changing this passage prior to publication as Lang strongly recommended. One was that openly trumpeting Haggard's Conservative politics would alienate many readers; the other was that by the time the serialization of *She* had begun in October 1886, Gladstone's government had fallen and Lord Salisbury was prime minister.

20. MS: "'and Kallikrates shall sit in the Senate in his place, and unless tyrants have really changed since I first heard speak of them, his end will much propitiate some sections of this strange people. For I have observed that tyrants ever keep their power by plundering one class of a community to enrich the others and therefore have they many enemies.'

"At this suggestion I saw a benign smile spread itself over Leo's face, for Leo I regret to say is a red hot conservative which (such is the malignancy of party feeling even amongst amiable men) prevented his treating this reprehensible suggestion with the severity it deserved. Indeed I am by no means sure but that it was only a sense of delicacy for my feelings as an advanced if somewhat theoretical liberal, for Radical theories practically applied strike me as brutal and fatal to the existence of civilised society, that prevented him from openly applauding the wicked scheme for the removal of our G.O.M. (Gladstonius Optimus Maximus as I love to render it). I however, instantly informed Ayesha. . . ."

21. MS: "'But tell me for I fain would learn more of this great Empire which we shall rule. Are there no wars, are no provinces in revolt against the Throne.'

"I explained to her in answer the exact political condition of the country when we left our native shores, and that the only province that could be said to be in revolt was Ireland. I should think that I sat for an hour or more expounding the ins and outs of this troublesome Irish problem with all the fairness to both sides of the question that I could command, while Ayesha every now and again put some shrewd question that went to the root of the whole matter. When I had at last finished my historical survey and pointed out the deductions that I drew from it she spoke.

"'Well' she said 'I understand. A turbulent people all these who declaim against your law because at heart they hate all law. So be it. I shall destroy them utterly. It is the good old Assyrian plan and the only effective one. If thou dost wish to be rid of a fruit my Holly pull up the tree by the roots and plant another kind. And now leave me, I pray thee. . . .'"

22. The passage in MS about exterminating the Irish gives more sense to this statement. MS at this point reads: "it would be at a terrible sacrifice of all the most approved democratic principles which are after all at least in the opinion of a very large section of our fellow countrymen a great deal more important than mere material prosperity which necessarily involves a certain amount of hateful Imperialism and is marked with the mark of the Beast. I mean physical force and coercive Legislation. What for instance would become of the bill for the extension of the Franchise in favour of which I, on the very day that I left London saw the people in their masses agitating with hop poles: I was convinced that Ayesha did not believe in representation on a really popular basis. On the contrary she would as soon as she came to understand our European complications, and that would not take her long, in all probability develop into a kind of glorified Bismarck! Really serious as the thing was I could hardly help laughing when I thought of the consternation her appearance on the political and social horizon would cause. And yet it was indeed no laughing matter as the Home Rulers especially were likely to find out."

XXIII. THE TEMPLE OF TRUTH.

1. Later chapters do not reveal any use of this ammunition, said in chap. XXVIII to amount to about two hundred rounds. It is possible that when Haggard wrote

this sentence he contemplated giving his adventurers a bloody escape in conflict with the Amahagger or some other hostile people.

2. *Sarcophagus* originally denoted a kind of stone reputed among the Greeks to have the power of consuming the flesh of dead bodies deposited in it.

3. In London.

4. MS: "two acres"; 1st ed.: "four acres."

5. Here is a clear indication that Haggard was aware of at least some of the possibilities of sexual symbolism.

6. Many columns in ancient Egyptian buildings had capitals resembling palm fronds. Among them were the very ornate columns of the great court in the Karnak complex, and Haggard most likely had those in mind when he wrote of ruined Kôr.

7. MS and GS: "Luxor," which lies across the Nile from Thebes.

8. MS: "sixty"; GS: "some sixty."

9. This footnote first appeared in 1st ed.

10. Know; an archaic word whose use by Walter Scott is noted in the *Oxford English Dictionary*.

11. Poetic word for temple, found for example in Tennyson's *In Memoriam*.

12. MS: "Tongues of trumpets," not "shouts of armies."

13. Haggard does not indicate here or elsewhere what might have been the inspiration for his description of this sculpture. The posture, "bending forward and poising herself upon her half-spread wings," exactly describes the *Winged Victory of Samothrace* in the Louvre. It is also possible that Haggard had in mind the allegorical figure of Justice, which he would have seen almost daily at the London Courts before he gave up the law as a profession. That figure also stands on a ball and is veiled, although in place of wings she carries the balance on which evidence is weighed. The meaning of her blindfold is, however, opposite to that of the one hiding the face of Truth; Justice deliberately blinds herself to the person who is being tried.

14. MS, GS, and 1st. ed.: "forty feet."

15. MS goes on: "Whilst I was still pondering over these things as I lay rolled up in my rug staring at the stars I fell asleep and became a victim to a most horrible nightmare. I dreamed that I saw She dressed in a modern ball dress and superintending the hot-potting of Mr. Gladstone. Mr. Chamberlain [substituted for "Lord Hartington," which has been crossed out] and Lord Randolph Churchill (unnatural alliance) were the executioners and fell to their sacriligious [sic] task right merrily. And in neat raised roman letters round the edge of the red hot vessel was engraved EXIT GLADSTONIUS OPTIMUS MAXIMUS. It was a most harrowing nightmare and the worst of it was I felt it might come true."

XXIV. WALKING THE PLANK.

1. MS: "a thousand or fifteen hundred feet."

2. These passages, which lead eventually to "the dreadful womb of the volcano" and a bottomless cleft extending perhaps to the center of the earth, resemble closely the spaces created by volcanic action in Bulwer-Lytton's *Coming Race*: "in piercing this shaft we came one day upon a chasm jagged and seemingly charred at the sides, as if burst asunder in some distant period by volcanic fires" (*The Coming Race and the Haunted and the Haunters*, Oxford, 1928, 2).

3. Recollected image.

4. A steamboat shuddering during the operation of a very powerful engine.

5. This remarkable ray of light, which pierces the darkness with the hard-edged sharpness of a laser beam, calls to mind the beam of light that opens the way for the vision of the Holy Grail in Tennyson's *Idylls of the King*. See chap. XXV, note 21.

6. An English coin.

7. MS: "Oh, how I regretted just then that rope dancing [tightrope-walking] does not form a part of our educational curriculum."

XXV. THE SPIRIT OF LIFE.

1. MS: "'Hulloa, old fellow' he sung out, 'are you there? We're having a pretty parroty time ain't we? It's really getting quite interesting.'" Throughout the book Leo's conversation, which was originally rendered in Haggard's version of upper-class slang, is recast into more formal speech.

2. 1st ed.: "my box of Bryant and May's wax matches." MS goes on: "Oh Bryant & May men of light and leading how often had we cause to bless your honoured names." The inclusion of Bryant & May matches (which are still sold in Britain) was one of those pedestrian touches for which Haggard was widely criticized. References to brand names did not possess the literary cachet in the 1880s that they acquired by the late twentieth century.

3. MS and GS: "twelve feet square."

4. Reach their maximum illumination.

5. Jules Verne's *Journey to the Center of the Earth* was available in several English translations as early as the 1870s and may well have been known to Haggard.

6. MS: "seven"; GS: "ten."

7. The introduction of the hermit Noot so near the end of the book is somewhat perplexing. He is not required to explain how the sacred fire was discovered; Ayesha could have learned the secret herself. Two reasons come to mind. First, Noot is "the old philosopher" mentioned on the Sherd of Amenartas; the discovery of his cave and tooth serves to validate that text. Second, Haggard's account of the approach to the Spirit of Life seems to be modeled on the Arthurian quest for the Holy Grail (see below, notes 8 and 21). In several versions of the Grail legend, a hermit, Naciens, raises Galahad to manhood, instructing him in morality and martial arts before presenting him to Arthur's court. In Haggard's tale also, the way to the Spirit of Life and the truth about Ayesha, which are the objects of the quest, lead through a hermit's cell. The hermit and the magician had long pedigrees in literature before Haggard's time and continue to thrive in fantasy and science fiction to this day. Lucas's hermit, Yoda, in the *Star Wars* film trilogy combines the parts of Merlin and Naciens in the Arthurian romances.

8. This incident also suggests elements of the Arthurian legend, in which a curse fell upon the Castle Carbonek because of the wounding of King Pelles with a spear in the chapel of the Holy Grail.

9. The last sentence first appeared in GS.

10. The list of Egyptian gods first appeared in GS.

11. Ayesha appears to refer here to the premonition conveyed in her dream of the previous evening.

12. Forever. Ayesha's extension of life and health acquired through bathing in the Fire of Life is strongly suggestive of the same effect produced on the subterranean Gy-ei people by "vril" in Bulwer-Lytton's *Coming Race*.

13. That which is meted out to a person by fate or Providence.

14. This clause first appeared in GS.

15. The text from this point through the words "Lord of All" at the end of the second paragraph following first appeared in GS.

16. "Now for thee I loose my virgin zone" was added in 1888 ed.

17. An antelope found in mountainous regions of Europe and Asia.

18. MS and GS: "Tartarus," also a classical term for the lower reaches of the underworld.

19. Amazement.

20. Moses' crossing of the Sinai was guided by God, who "went before them by day in a pillar of cloud, to lead them the way; and by night in a pillar of fire to give them light" (Exodus 13:21).

21. The encounter of the adventurers with the mysterious fire resembles in many respects the effects of the advent of the Holy Grail among the knights of King Arthur's Round Table after claps of thunder and a great rushing of wind in Sir Thomas Malory's *Morte d'Arthur*, ed. E. Vinaver (Oxford, 1967), 2:865: "Than entird into the hall the Holy Grayle coverde with whyght samyte, but there was none that myghte se hit nother whom that bare hit. And there was all the hall fulfylled with good odoures, and every knyght had such metis and drynkes as he best loved in thys worlde." Haggard is more likely, however, to have had in mind Tennyson's version in "The Holy Grail," a chapter of *Idylls of the King* (lines 111–20):

> . . . and the slender sound
> As from a distance beyond distance grew
> Coming upon me—O never harp nor horn,
> Nor aught we blow with breath, or touch with hand,
> Was like that music as it came; and then
> Streamed through my cell a cold and silver beam,
> And down the long beam stole the Holy Grail,
> Rose-red with beatings in it, as if alive,
> Till all the white walls of my cell were dyed
> With rosy colours leaping on the wall;
> And then the music faded, and the Grail
> Past, and the beam decayed, and from the walls
> The rosy quiverings died into the night.

Also (lines 188–92):

> And down the long beam stole the Holy Grail
> All over covered with a luminous cloud,
> And none might see who bare it, and it past.
> But every knight beheld his fellows face
> As in a glory.

22. The highest heaven. The word is derived from the ancient belief that the sphere of fire was heaven. The use of this word and the reference to the biblical pillar of fire make plain Haggard's allegorical intentions in this chapter.

23. The next two paragraphs appeared first in GS.

XXVI. WHAT WE SAW.

1. MS continues: "leaving her utterly bald." This incident was probably drawn from a scene Haggard witnessed at a spiritualist séance in London in the 1870s. See *Days of My Life*, 1:37–38.

2. This paragraph first appeared in GS.

3. Haggard put these remarks in the text of MS but later noted that they should be transferred to a footnote.

4. MS goes on: "and it is another terrifying fact that in the same way that he who kills on a large scale is called a hero while he who kills on a small one is written down as a villain and a murderer, so the individual who transgresses in a splendid wholesale fashion that appeals to the imagination, does not excite the same horror in the human heart that is called forth by the evil doing of a petty vice clamped soul. I suppose that the explanation is that though humanity has a strong law making faculty based upon the desire of self preservation it has little or no true morality.

If it had it would reprobate all offenses alike and there would be no heroes—for the heroes of the world are almost without exception the most dreadful villains for whom hanging would be far too good."

5. Female of the European red deer, which Haggard knew from his Norfolk boyhood.

XXVII. WE LEAP.

1. MS goes on: "compared to whom by the way St. Simeon Stylytes must have been a perfect fool." This suggests that the early Christian monks and hermits were the inspirations for Haggard's Noot. Simeon Stylites (390–459 A.D.), was expelled from a Syrian monastic order for excessive austerity and spent the remaining thirty-seven years of his life on a platform some three feet in diameter atop a pillar more than sixty feet tall. Haggard most likely knew of the saint through Tennyson's poem of 1842, "St. Simeon Stylytes."

2. MS: "between twelve and thirteen feet."

3. Hades, the lowest reaches of the underworld.

4. MS, GS, and 1st ed.: "and then, commending my soul to God, I ran the length . . ."

XXVIII. OVER THE MOUNTAIN.

1. MS: "The Conclusion of The Matter."

2. Haggard uses an old and mostly unscientific convention to emphasize the shock to Leo of Ayesha's death. Hair can naturally change color only from the roots, that is, gradually, not instantly. But it *can* turn white and later return to its original color; the biological mechanism responsible for that phenomenon is still unknown.

3. MS and GS: "ten."

4. A mass of hardened volcanic lava.

5. If the location of Kôr is plotted from this clue, it lies in swampy country east of Lake Malawi in the Niassa province of Mozambique. If it had been any farther west, the travelers would certainly have encountered and commented upon one or another of the great East African lakes.

6. MS: "Donald Currie boats."

7. MS ends here; the next two paragraphs appeared in slightly different form for the first time in GS.

8. MS: "Finished 18 March 86."

SELECTED BIBLIOGRAPHY

Aldiss, Brian W. *Trillion Year Spree: The History of Science Fiction*, With David Wingrove. London: Gollancz, 1986. Includes Haggard among nineteenth-century authors who enunciated themes of central importance to the development of science fiction.

Ash, Brian, *Visual Encyclopedia of Science Fiction*. London: Pan, 1977. Notes Haggard's influence on tales of lost and parallel worlds.

Atwood, Margaret. *Survival: A Thematic Guide to Canadian Literature*. Toronto: Anasi, 1972. An acute literary intelligence considers some of the vital themes of identity and wilderness which Haggard, among others, explored.

Bulwer-Lytton, Edward [first Lord Lytton]. *The Coming Race*. London: G. Routledge and Sons, 1874. A likely influence on Haggard's conception of *She*, first published in 1871.

———. *A Strange Story*. New ed., rev. London: Sampson Low, 1863. Includes a veiled character named Ayesha.

Carley, C.E. "Haggard: A Biography and a Filmography." *Classic Film Collector*, Winter 1974.

Cohen, Morton. *Rider Haggard—His Life and Works*. London: Hutchinson, 1960; 2d ed., 1968. This, the principal biographical work on Haggard, contains a good deal of literary analysis.

Dean, John. "The Uses of Wilderness in American Science Fiction." *Science Fiction Studies* 9 (1982): 68–81. Argues, as Haggard anticipated in the 1890s, that as earthly frontiers have been conquered, themes of wilderness live on in outer space.

Dumont, Hervé. "Ayesha et Antinéa: Le mythe de la reine immortelle au cinema." *L'Ecran Fantastique*, no. 57 (June 1985): 54–69, and no. 58 (July 1985): 56–69. Despite some factual errors respecting Haggard's life and work, an extremely illuminating comparison of the cinematic careers of Haggard's *She* and Pierre Benoit's *L'Atlantide*.

Ellis, Peter Berresford. *H. Rider Haggard: A Voice from the Infinite*. London: Routledge and Kegan Paul, 1978. A defense of Haggard's work and genius by an uncritical admirer.

Elwin, Malcolm. *The Old Gods Falling*. London: Macmillan, 1939. Includes an important essay on Haggard, situating him in the context of his age.

Etherington, Norman. *Rider Haggard*. Boston: G. K. Hall, 1984. A study of Haggard's fiction and politics, including some biographical details.

———. "Rider Haggard, Imperialism and the Layered Personality." *Victorian Studies* 22, no. 1 (1978): 71–88. Attempts to explain how Haggard's "imperialist" fiction exemplifies emerging concepts of late-Victorian psychology.

———. "South African Origins of Rider Haggard's Early African Romances." *Notes and Queries* N.S. 24 (October 1977): 436–38.

Fisher, Margery. *The Bright Face of Danger*. London: Hodder and Stoughton, 1986. This study of the adventure story in relation to children and adults comments on *She* as an example of the search for the unattainable.

Fodor, Nandor. *The Search for the Beloved*. New York: Hermitage Press, 1949. The psychoanalytic champion of the birth-trauma theory considers Haggard's *She* as part of the proof of his hypotheses.

Gougaud, Henri. *Demons et merveilles de la science fiction*. Paris: Julliard, 1974. The witty chapter "La Femme" considers *She* and other works.

Green, Martin. *Dreams of Adventure, Deeds of Empire*. London: Routledge and Kegan Paul, 1980. Haggard is considered along with a great many other writers in this volume, which is part of a trilogy that relates the development of modern literature to politics using concepts drawn from Gandhi and Tolstoy.

Greene, Graham. *The Lost Childhood and Other Essays*. London: Eyre and Spottiswoode, 1954. In one of these essays, this important writer analyzes Haggard's influence on his own literary development.

Haggard, H. R. "About Fiction." *Contemporary Review*, February 1887, 172–80. This ill-advised defense of romance as a literary genre provoked attacks on Haggard for alleged plagiarism and bad writing in *She*.

———. *Ayesha, the Return of She*. London: Ward Lock, 1905. Sequel to *She*, in which Leo and Holly track down Ayesha's spirit in Tibet.

———. *Cetywayo and His White Neighbours*. London: Trubner and Co., 1882. Important for an understanding of Haggard's political stance in the 1880s.

———. *The Days of My Life*. 2 vols. London: Longmans, Green and Co., 1926. Haggard's autobiography, which he finished in 1912 but withheld from publication during his lifetime.

———. *She, a History of Adventure*. London: Longmans, Green and Co., 1888. This "first illustrated edition" appeared in November 1888 and incorporated more than four hundred small changes from the first edition of 1887. Although it is by no means perfect, this New Edition is the most carefully edited text produced under Haggard's supervision.

———. *Wisdom's Daughter: The Life and Love Story of She-Who-Must-Be-Obeyed*. London: Hutchinson and Co., 1923. Haggard's last word on Ayesha, describing her early life and ancient love affair with Kallikrates.

Haggard, Lilias R. *The Cloak That I Left: A Biography of Rider Haggard*. London: Hodder and Stoughton, 1951. By Haggard's daughter.

Higgins, D. S., ed. *The Private Diaries of Sir H. Rider Haggard 1914–1925*. London: Cassell, 1980. Useful for revealing shifts in Haggard's attitudes in his last years.

———. *Rider Haggard: The Great Storyteller*. London: Cassell, 1981. With access to family papers and other sources unavailable to previous scholars, Higgins is able to shed vital light on Haggard's relationships with his wife and the cherished love of his youth, relationships that have an important bearing on all his writing about women.

Jung, Carl G. *Collected Works of C. G. Jung*, edited by H. Read, M. Fordham, and G. Adler. London: Routledge and Kegan Paul, 1954–. References to Haggard's works appear in vols. 10, 13, 15, 16–18.

Katz, Wendy. *Rider Haggard and the Fiction of Empire*. Cambridge: Cambridge University Press, 1987. A case for the prosecution, charging Haggard with racism, colonialism, and bad writing; the published version of a Ph.D. thesis for Dalhousie University, it takes no account of works published later than 1976.

Lewis, C.S. "The Mythopoeic Gift of Rider Haggard." In *Of This and Other Worlds*, ed. W. Hooper. London: Collins, 1982. A sympathetic appraisal of Haggard's work by one of the twentieth century's most sophisticated writers of science fiction, religious speculation, and fantasy.

Miller, Henry. *The Books in My Life*. London: Peter Owen, 1952. Miller's comments on Haggard reveal links to twentieth-century modernism.

Moore, Thomas. *The Epicurean*. 4th ed. London: Longman, Rees, Orme, Brown and Green, 1827. Though Haggard denied having read it, Moore's book was alleged to have been a source of ideas for *She*.

Morsberger, Robert E. "She." In Frank N. Magill, ed., *Survey of Science Fiction*, vol. 4: 1908–1911. Englewood Cliffs, N.J.: Salem Press, 1979.

Pierce, Peter F. "Rider Haggard." B.Litt. thesis, Oxford University, 1975. Especially useful for its attention to Haggard's use of space and landscape.

Rabkin, Eric S., and Scholes, Robert. *Science Fiction: History, Science, Vision*. New York: Oxford University Press, 1977. Useful in relation to *She* for its comments on the presence and absence of sex in science fiction.

Rose, Mark. *Alien Encounters: Anatomy of Science Fiction* Cambridge, Mass.: Harvard University Press, 1981. Includes some valiant attempts to distinguish nineteenth-century science fiction from fantasy.

Russ, Joana. "Amor Vincit Foeminam: The Battle of the Sexes in Science Fiction," *Science Fiction Studies* 7 (1980): 2–15. Analysis of some of the many variations on the theme of gender role reversal, a theme that followed Haggard's lead in twentieth-century science fiction.

Sandison, Alan. "Rider Haggard: 'Some Call It Evolution. . . .'" *The Wheel of Empire*. London: Macmillan and New York: St. Martin's, 1967. An important essay that attempts to dissociate Haggard from vulgar imperialism.

Street, Brian V. *The Savage in Literature*. London: Routledge and Kegan Paul, 1975. Primarily concerned with the portrayal of the primitive in modern literature, including Haggard's fiction.

Suvin, Darko. "Narrative Logic, Ideological Domination, and the Range of Science Fiction." *Science Fiction Studies* 9 (1982): 1–25. Considers some fundamental questions about the relationship between art and ideology in the mid-Victorian milieu from which Haggard emerged.

———. *Metamorphoses of Science Fiction*. New Haven, Conn.: Yale University Press, 1979. Passes judgment, in relation to science fiction, on works of "fantasy" from Poe through Haggard to Bradbury.

Whatmore, D. E. *H. Rider Haggard: A Bibliography*. London: Mansell, 1987. Supersedes earlier bibliographies compiled by G. L. McKay (1930) and J. E. Scott (1947).

NORMAN ETHERINGTON holds the appointment to the Chair of History at the University of Western Australia. His previous works include *Preachers, Peasants and Politics in Southeast Africa, Rider Haggard,* and *Theories of Imperialism: War, Conquest and Capital.*